The Golden Era of Golf

Also by Al Barkow

Dave Stockton's Putting Secrets (with Dave Stockton)

Getting Set for Golf (with Carl Lohren)

The History of the PGA Tour

Play Lower-Handicap Golf (with Phil Rodgers)

Gettin' to the Dance Floor: An Oral History of American Golf

The Master of Putting (with George Low)

The Venturi System (with Ken Venturi)

The Venturi Analysis (with Ken Venturi)

The Good Sense of Golf (with Billy Casper)

Golf's Golden Grind: The History of the Tour

The Golden Era of Golf

*How America Rose
to Dominate the Old
Scots Game*

Al Barkow

Thomas Dunne Books

St. Martin's Press ≈ New York

THOMAS DUNNE BOOKS
An imprint of St. Martin's Press

www.stmartins.com

Photo of Bill Spiller courtesy of Bill Spiller, Jr.

All other photos courtesy of AP/Wide World Photos

Book design by Michelle McMillian

Library of Congress Cataloging-in-Publication Data

Barkow, Al.
    The golden era of golf : how America rose to dominate the old Scots game / Al
Barkow.–1st ed.
        p. cm.
    "Thomas Dunne books."
    ISBN 0-312-25238-2
    1. Golf–United States–History.   I. Title.
GV981 .B39 2000
796.352'0973–dc21   00-031666

First Edition: November 2000

10 9 8 7 6 5 4 3 2 1

Contents

Introduction

No one knows for certain how golf actually came to be, and there will not be much additional speculation here on the much-belabored subject. Golf is an extension of a very ordinary human instinct. Hitting an object with a stick to propel it is as elemental as looking to see where you are going. To make a contest out of it is just as commonplace. However, these contests also could have served as religious rituals. Professor Robert W. Henderson, in his book *Ball, Bat and Bishop: The Origin of Ball Games*, reckoned that all ball-and-stick games began with polo played by Persians before the time of Christ, a game that was grounded in a fertility rite, mainly to do with agriculture. The Persians batted around an animal skull because the head was integral to their fertility symbolism. Thus, when a contemporary golfer takes a swipe at the white dimpled "head" and digs out a chunk of turf, one might say he is plowing the good earth and importuning the God of Agriculture to assure or expand the food supply. Heart can be taken from this if the divot is too deep, and the shot is a poor one.

By a circuitous route, Henderson traced all other ball-and-stick games to Persian polo—tennis, cricket, rounders, baseball, hockey, and golf, although not necessarily in that order (or in the modern-day form of those games). However, hockey, or an early version of it, seems to be the closest progenitor or relative of golf. The precise history of golf's origins has always been a mystery. Fifteenth-century paintings by the Dutch artist Van Neer depict some of his countrymen bundled up against the cold winter air and pushing or shoving an object over the ice of a frozen canal.

They are using long sticks curved at the striking end that resemble today's hockey sticks, as well as the earliest golf clubs. This game was called *het kolven* or *kolf*, Dutch for "club." There is also a depiction in a Flemish Book of Hours circa 1500 of four balls—three wooden, one of leather—said to be used for *kolf*.

There was considerable fraternization between the Scots and Dutch by way of trade across the English Channel, and it has been speculated that the Scots watched Dutchmen pass the time at *kolf*, and took it from there. The first concrete reference to golf in Scotland, circa 1350, is a section of stained glass in Gloucester Cathedral depicting a figure that is almost certainly a golfer. However, it is also known that in the early 1300s the Scots bought their golf balls from Dutch ball makers. The etymology of the name of the game is definitely Dutch. The Oxford English Dictionary says the word "golf" dates back to 1457 and is "of unknown origin." But the great British etymologist, Eric Partridge, in his *Origins*, an etymological dictionary of modern English, says the word "apparently" comes from the Middle Dutch *colf*. That's what I think, too.

The position taken here is that the Scots simply adapted the Dutch *kolven* to their own tastes, or conditions. Where the Dutch played on ice, and attempted to deposit a disk or ball into a goal atop the surface, the Scots played on turf, striking the ball so it would first fly in the air, then bounce and run. Most significantly, the Scots sought to put the ball in a hole *in the ground*. That's the big difference.

Why the Scots decided the goal would be a hole in the ground is not known, and never will be. Maybe they were acting out another version of the fertility rite—finding a release of sexual energy repressed by the well-known strict moral doctrines of their church. Men (for they were the first players) using a long stick to strike a small round white ball with the intention of depositing it in Mother Earth is not too much of a metaphoric stretch in that direction, is it? What that has to say for women playing golf we will leave to others.

The game of golf as we know it is Scots-originated. No argument. The curious thing is, the Scots didn't do much with it for some five hundred and fifty years. From the mid-fourteenth to the mid-nineteenth centuries, there were very few changes in the game in the way of the equipment that was used, the venue on which it was played, rules of play, and formal competition. Could the players have been completely satisfied with the status quo all that time? That seems to go against human nature. Maybe they didn't care enough about the game to make changes. Or perhaps there weren't enough players to cause the divisions of opinion that bring about revisions. Maybe they were dullards, without imagination. Or too frugal.

Whatever the reasons, it wasn't until the Industrial Revolution that golf began to evolve. A new energy was released in the Western world that stimulated technological innovation or was the result of it. The Earth's basic resources were mined and turned to practical use on a scale never before seen in history. New tools and machinery were concocted for the manufacture of devices large and small meant to improve people's standard of living. Modes of communications and travel were expanding, getting faster and more convenient. The economy broadened as the labor force grew and became more diversified.

The Scots were surely inspired by the vitality of the times and the manufacturing advances, and finally got off their inert golf horse. In the mid-nineteenth century the Scots began to organize their game, establish formal competitions, write the first official rules of golf, and introduce a new ball. Still, it was not until the last quarter of the nineteenth century when golf made its way to America that truly significant, golf-world-shaking innovations were made and participation grew. Scotland was the cradle of golf, but America became the game's second home and its most prolific nurturer.

The ascendance of American golf can be attributed in part to the good luck of the nation's geography. Every region of the United States is suitable for golf for at least six months out of every year. But more important, there are sections of the country in which the game can be played the entire year round. This opportunity led to the first and, in time, the most prestigious professional tournament circuits; the creation of the vacation-golf industry; and the largest body of golfers in the world—all within U.S. borders.

However, it was not only geography that allowed golf to flourish in the United States. The American economy was far more expansive and varied than Scotland's, fueled by the entrepreneurial spirit that has always signified the American character. In fact, American golf would never have achieved such preeminence if not for the democratic character of American society. In Scotland, common folk always played golf, but it was prohibitively expensive. In 1743 one handmade featherie golf ball retailed for two and a half shillings, the amount a working stiff could expect to earn in six months. What's more, because golf is a daylight game, it was far easier for those of the monied classes—the gentry and royalty—to find free time for a few hours on the links. Thus, by dint of economics and lifestyle, people of means and status in society came to control the game. There is also something about strolling along on a nicely trimmed stretch of grass that evokes a feeling of well being and bespeaks wealth. Golf became another way to exhibit preeminence in a society with a rigid class system already in place.

There was classism in American golf in the early days (and there still is, to some extent), if only because so many of the first players were émigré Britons who brought their social predilections with them. But the Old World class system didn't dominate American golf. Simultaneous with the formation of the first private golf clubs, public golf courses were being built in the United States. The first was in Van Cortlandt Park, a municipal city-owned course that opened in New York City in 1897 and is still in play. Not long after came Jackson Park, a municipal course in Chicago that quickly became so crowded, the first ever green fee—ten cents—was charged.

Although all nations, tribes and even neighborhood gangs break members into groups of different standing—from a wealthy elite to a middle class or white-collar workers to common laborers—America has always prided itself on its fluidity. Status is based primarily on one's net worth in dollars, achieved through hard work and talent. Although discrimination still exists, by and large, a Pittsburgh ironworker or Chicago butcher shop owner or a New York caddie who rises out of the ranks to become the owner of a steel factory or a packing plant or the winner of the U.S. Open, can join the private club in which his former boss is a member, send his children to Harvard or Yale, become the president of the United States Golf Association or even the United States of America. The United States is still the most successful experiment in egalitarianism the world has known, and American golf developed in that spirit.

At the turn of the twentieth century, the old Scots game was on the verge of a great eruption that would result in American dominance in golf as a business, as the paradigm of competitive excellence, and as a pastime enjoyed by millions. However, all of this didn't begin to manifest fully until the 1950s. After all, a couple of world wars got in the way and a worldwide economic depression. Still, during the first fifty years of the twentieth century, much of the groundwork and some remarkable advances were made in American golf. We will cover the main accomplishments of that period, before concentrating on the last half of the millennial century, when golf as a participatory sport and crowd-drawing professional competition grew from an arcane, inbred game for the gilded few into one that has become widely played and an integral part of the national sporting scene, and as a business expanded from a Mom-and-Pop corner store into a multimillion-dollar commercial emporium.

1 | 1900–1930: The Birth of a Golf Nation

Here Comes the Bouncing Ball; Seeding the Pro Tour;
The First American Champions

Balls!

For almost four hundred years the Scots used a leather bag filled with boiled poultry feathers as a golf ball. It was a little smaller than the modern ball, and was called a featherie (Scottish spelling). It did not have anything to recommend it, especially in wet weather, which in Scotland is as common as a heartbeat. The ball got mushy soft when wet, the cover often split, and it was easily knocked out of round. Even when in its best condition, fresh off the workbench, a featherie flew only 150 to 175 yards and hardly rolled at all. Yet, the Scots used this obstinate orb for some four centuries! Talk about complacency.

At last, in the mid-1840s, this golf ball torpor was breached. The story revolves around the Reverend Doctor Robert Adams Paterson, of St. Andrews, Scotland, and his son, Rob, and although the advance came by accident, or as an afterthought, progress was made. A little. The new golf ball was called, generically, a guttie, short for the material from which it was made—gutta-percha, a rubberlike material derived from the latex or sap of several types of sappy Malaysian trees.

The times were hard in 1846. The economy was in a downturn and money was in short supply. Given this state of affairs and Scotland's climate, a top priority in everyday life was a pair of shoes that didn't leak. This must have been on Rob Paterson's mind when his father received a marble statue of the Hindu god Vishnu from the Orient—protected against breakage by slabs of gutta-percha. The packing material was put aside until the day Rob Paterson got the notion that it could be heated, reshaped, and used to resole shoes. He did just that, and it worked.

A few weeks later, Rob perceived yet another use for gutta-percha—a golf ball. He again softened the material, but this time molded it into a small sphere, then went out on the links to hit it. The ball's flight was satisfactory, but after a few strokes it broke into pieces. Rob gave some thought to how the ball might be made to stay in one piece: Curing it for a week was the answer. The Patersons got a patent on the creation, and went into the guttie golf ball business.

The guttie very quickly took the place of the featherie. For one thing, it was much cheaper to produce and therefore buy, which appealed to the Scots' legendary parsimony and the poor economy of the moment. Leather was far more expensive than gutta-percha, and producing just one featherie was a lengthy and laborious process. Many more gutties could be made in a day's time and demanded little skill. Although a guttie didn't go much farther than a featherie, its greater durability and resistance to wet weather also made it more practical.

The first gutties flew erratically, diving like a duck or just darting one way then another in the air. However, it was soon noted that the flight became less and less erratic the more the ball was used. Someone put two and two together and realized that the nicks and gouges made from hitting the ball produced more stable flight. The science of this would be worked out some years later, but until then ball makers took hammer and chisel and purposely made nicks and gouges in the surface of gutties. Eventually, the molds in which the balls were formed were designed to produce an orderly pattern of these "irregularities" on the surface of the balls. Gutties were an advance, but they didn't last very long and no one minded except their manufacturers. The solid and rocklike piece of goods stung the hands miserably when mishit, especially hands chilled by brisk, damp Scottish air. The featherie was used for four hundred years, but the guttie lasted only fifty. Its replacement, an American invention, truly revolutionized the game.

The Bounding Billie Rules the Waves

In 1898 Coburn Haskell, with the considerable help of his friend Bertram Work, an executive with the Goodrich Rubber Company, in Akron, Ohio, invented the three-piece golf ball. Actually, two-piece at first. Some hard-nosed traditionalists would continue to play the guttie for a few years after Haskell's ball came into play, but that stony orb was effectively rendered a thing of the past in a matter of minutes. Haskell's ball was to mercury what the guttie was to lead. It sped off the clubface like a zephyr, and danced a happy jig when it landed. It went farther in the air and on the ground with much less effort, and no pain.

Haskell was an American rendition of the English gentleman. He dabbled in business, but having married well (i.e., into money), he mostly indulged in pastimes—horses, shooting, book collecting, light opera, and golf. A poor golfer, he was anxious to at least increase the distance he hit the ball as compared to his more skilled friends. Something of an aesthete, he was not fond of how the guttie felt when he struck it poorly, as he often did. There are a number of versions of how Haskell came up with his idea, all different in minor details but basically amounting to the same thing.

One day, while browsing about the Goodrich plant waiting for Work to join him for a round of golf, Haskell noticed some thin bands of waste rubber lying about. He realized they could be wound into a golf ball that would be as lively as a tennis ball, which was made of the same material. He suggested to Work that a ball of very tightly wound rubber thread or bands covered with a thin sheet of gutta-percha would make a terrific golf ball. Work saw the possibilities, added his manufacturing and rubber expertise, and called on shop foreman Emmet Junkins and master mechanic John Gammeter to assist with execution. Gammeter would prove the most important figure.

At first Haskell tried winding the rubber himself by hand but he kept losing control of it and the bands would fly all over the place. Junkins's contribution was to have nimble-fingered women in his shop wind the balls, also by hand. The first ones were covered with gutta-percha, until Work found that balata, another rubberlike substance made from the milky juice of a tropical bully tree, was a better material for the job. It would be used in its natural form for the next sixty years, and then after in a synthetic formula.

Junkins's women did a good enough job winding the balls, but it was labor-intensive and not at all cost-effective (to use modern-day terminology; Junkins et al. probably just said it cost too much). Work asked Gammeter, described as a mechanical wizard, if he could devise a machine to wind balls. Gammeter, the homely story goes, shifted the wad of tobacco in his mouth and said he could. His ball-winding machine used a relatively nonelastic core on which to wind the rubber strands. Then the two elements were covered, creating golf's first three-piece ball. This was the standard construction for the next sixty years. The machine made it possible to turn out a thousand golf balls in the time it took to produce one featherie or five gutties, and it also made a more reliable product. Gammeter, who was not himself a golfer, received a patent on his ball-winding machine, which had an enormous impact on the growth of the game.

To test the first modern golf ball, Haskell enlisted Joe Mitchell, the pro at his club in Akron. Mitchell didn't know what was in store, because the ball had been pressed in the same mold as gutties and therefore didn't look any different. But when he hit it, ahhh. Golf writer O. B. Keeler wrote an account of the moment.

> Out across the fairway of the first hole was a bunker which never had been carried by anybody. It was so far from the tee that only an occasional tremendous poke with the old guttie would send the ball rolling into it, in dry weather. And it was right over the middle of that bunker that Joe's drive with the new ball sailed, high in the air, landing yards beyond.
>
> Joe Mitchell stood watching the ball with eyes and mouth wide open. Then he let out a yell and began a sort of dance and began to implore Mr. Haskell to tell him if he was dreaming, and if not what was in that ball. So that's the way it started.

Some adjustments would be necessary. The nicks and gouges that helped the guttie fly more true did not work all that well on the cover of the Haskell ball. Jim Foulis, winner of the second U.S. Open and at the time the professional at the Chicago Golf Club (where Haskell was also a member) accidentally made a contribution. A Haskell ball got into a batch of gutties Foulis was remolding one day in his shop. He couldn't tell the difference, because it had the same cover markings. Foulis's mold had a bramble pattern—raised bumps—which went onto the Haskell ball's cover. When Foulis hit it, right after sending off a couple of gutties, he was astonished. It flew much farther and true.

Foulis cut open the ball to see what he had and discovered it was Mr. Haskell's invention. Haskell quickly had all his balls brambled, but there was another important alteration still to come. William Taylor, whose firm in Leicester, England, was the world's largest golf ball mold manufacturer, discovered that the brambles on the golf ball cover were flattened from constant hitting. When that happened, the ball would exhibit the same erratic flight characteristics of the smooth-surfaced gutties. Taylor reasoned that if he turned the pimplelike brambles inside out and made them dimples, the golf club would strike the larger radius of the ball instead of the smaller radius formed by the brambles. This prolonged the life of the ball and provided a more predictable flight pattern. Taylor's son, William Taylor, Jr., who made his career in Cincinnati, Ohio, recalled in an article in *Golf Illustrated* magazine that his father had used the scoop end of a blackhead remover to carve the first experimental dimples out of a beeswax coating applied to a ball. The birth of the dimple. How prosaic the tools of invention can be.

Taylor patented his round dimple in 1908, and sold the Spalding Company, of Massachusetts, an exclusive twelve-year license to produce and market golf balls with dimples of that configuration. This did not stop other manufacturers from horning in on the concept. They simply made square dimples and other variations on the theme that worked just as well, but didn't infringe on Taylor's patent.

It is fascinating to consider that when Taylor later became interested in the aerodynamics of the dimpled golf ball, he devised a dimple pattern that could keep the ball from hooking or slicing—or at least modify these flight patterns. However, when his son told him this "would take all the fun out of the game, and no golfing association would tolerate it," Taylor, Sr., gave up the idea. (What an innocent time, such high ideals.) Today, golf ball manufacturers produce balls with dimple patterns that do in fact reduce, if not entirely eliminate, slices and hooks. However, the golf association that governs such things, the United States Golf Association (USGA), has only barely tolerated this development and, in recent years, has threatened to modify the technology.

Haskell's ball was nicknamed the Bounding Billie, not in all cases a term of endearment. Traditionalists decried it for how much it bounced and rolled after landing, and for the greater (read, "excessive") distance it achieved. Here was the birth of one of golf's longest-running conflicts, one that persisted through the end of the twentieth century (and will surely go beyond). That is, the ball goes too far and therefore takes a measure of the skill out of the game. Another anti-distance argument is that a longer ball also requires lengthier courses, which means more costly real estate on which to build them, increasing the cost of playing the game. In fact, the longer ball (and it got much longer as the century progressed, but not entirely by virtue of its construction) has only affected the scoring ability of the highest level of players—tour pros, mainly. It has had little to no effect on the scoring ability of the average golfer in Haskell's day or ninety years later. Instead the Haskell ball made the game more enjoyable for the average golfer, who could mishit it without getting a "guttified" electric shock in his fingers. He also got a little something for his effort. A half-topped Haskell might bound nearly as far as a full-struck guttie. These features made golf more fun than it had ever been before, or at least somewhat less discouraging, and brought thousands and eventually millions of new players to the game.

A New Way to Work Wood

There was another innovation in equipment that occurred around the same time as the introduction of the Haskell ball. It was not as flashy as the Bounding Billie, but it would have a significant impact on the growth of golf. That is, the copying lathe as it was used in the making of wooden club heads.

For centuries the wooden heads of golf clubs were made entirely by hand. Craftsmen, including most golf professionals, shaped thick blocks of wood called flitches into a club head using saws, files, chisels, and sandpaper. It took days to finish just one head. That slow, toilsome process went the way of the quill pen when a woodworker from a shoe manufacturing plant in Lynn, Massachusetts, happened to see Scots-born golf professional Robert White crafting a club head the old-fashioned way. The story was reported by Herb Graffis in his magazine, *Golfing*. One day in May, 1897, a carpenter named Gardner was watching White chip away at a new club head in his shop at the Myopia Hunt Club, between Lynn and Boston. Said Gardner to White, "I always thought the Scots were smart, but they must be damn fools. There's a shoe factory at Lynn that could do that wood job of yours in two or three minutes." White gave the carpenter a chance to match deed to word and later said, "The fellow turned out some beautiful heads."

Gardner fashioned the club heads on a copying lathe that was used to produce lasts at the shoe manufacturing plant. A copying lathe in its simplest manifestation is what is used by your local hardware store to duplicate house keys. A stylus traces the model, while a cutting edge replicates the model on a piece of raw material. The adaptation of the copying lathe to golf was soon picked up by all golf equipment manufacturers, who were able to produce hundreds of identically shaped heads in one day. This led to the mass production of woods, which in turn made them less expensive, which of course helped widen participation in the game. One of the first such lathes, used by the MacGregor Golf Company, is now in a museum, literally and figuratively, for it was rendered obsolete with the coming of metal "woods."

Competition Arises, Rules Follow, and Eighteen Holes Become a Round of Golf

Golfers wagered against each other from the moment the game came to be. But official competition in the form of tournaments took almost as long to get on the boards as did a replacement for the featherie. It wasn't until 1744 that the Honorable Company of Edinburgh Golfers staged the first competition intended for a large field of players, with a trophy going to the winner. The city of Edinburgh provided the trophy, a silver cup, with the stipulation that the competition be open to noblemen and gentlemen, or commoners from any part of Great Britain and Ireland. However, only ten men, all from Edinburgh, played. (This lack of interest seems odd until you remember that these were the same people who had been playing golf for three centuries with a leather bag full of feathers.) The event was held again the following year, again to a sparse entry, then it faded from the scene. The Edinburgh tournament did engender the first written rules of golf, though. Compiled by the Company of Edinburgh Golfers, these rules, except for one inconsequential clause, are the very same that the Society of St. Andrews, which would become the Royal and Ancient Society of St. Andrews (R&A), issued ten years later. (It has long been thought, or claimed, that the R&A wrote the first rules.) The original rules of golf drafted in 1744 contained thirteen items, none over a sentence long—although some of the sentences are fairly long. Many traditionalists decry the enormous expansion of the rules over the years and claim the first rules are still good enough. However, the original rules are not all that clear in themselves, and they don't address many of the changes that have taken place in the game, including innovations in equipment and course conditions, and man's penchant for drawing fine lines in the sands of regulations. For instance, original Rule Thirteen reads: "Neither trench, ditch, or dyke made for the preservation of the links, or the Scholars' holes, or the Soldiers' lines, shall be accounted a hazard, but the ball is to be taken out, teed, and played with any iron club." Go apply that to today's game.

In time the R&A became the official ruling body of golf throughout most of the world. The ascendance of the St. Andrews group also led to eighteen becoming the accepted, official number of holes in a full round of golf. Until 1754 the number of holes on any given golf course was based on whatever the plot of land allowed and how long the members decided the holes should be. Some had five holes, some twelve. St. Andrews had twenty-two holes until 1754, when the club's powers-that-be decided to lengthen their course. Most of St. Andrew's greens serve two holes. For instance, the second hole and sixteenth occupy the same stretch of putting surface, albeit the expanse is big enough that the actual holes are separated by some fifty or more yards. In the process, the club eliminated the two double greens closest to the clubhouse, which reduced the course by four holes and left eighteen holes total. As St. Andrews became the dominant golf club in Scotland, and its eighteen-hole course dictated the official number of holes for a round of play. No mythological or symbolic association determined the number eighteen, nor was any practical convenience served. Eighteen holes make a round of golf by chance, or whim.

Over a century after the Edinburgh golfers put on their unsuccessful "open" tournaments, the R&A inaugurated a national championship: the first British Open, played in 1860. No one can say why it took so long to get formal golf competition started, and even when it began it didn't go much further than that one championship. The first British Amateur was not played until 1885.

Although formal, national-level competition was not a compelling item on the agenda of eighteenth- and early-nineteenth-century Scots and English, they did bring the game to foreign lands through overseas exploration, domination, and emigration. Golf was being played in India by the early nineteenth century. The first golf club in Canada was founded in 1873.

America Tees It Up

As the nineteenth century melded into the twentieth, golf's most fertile new soil was the United States. The generally acknowledged birthplace and birthdate of American golf is New York, 1888. However, there are numerous traces that suggest golf was being played elsewhere in the country prior to 1888. In the early nineteenth century, a golf club was formed in Charleston, South Carolina—the game played on the city common—but it disappeared prior to the Civil War. Golf also was played in White Sulphur Springs, West Virginia, in the 1870s. Long buried under fields of hay, this course, Oakhurst Links, was restored in the early 1990s and opened for play in the grand old tradition—using gutta-percha balls, wooden shafted clubs, knickers, and other golf relics. Golf was played in Foxboro, Pennsylvania, in the mid-nineteenth century, too. The club, Foxboro Country Club, is still in existence.

The official father of American golf was John Reid, an American born in Scotland, who lived in Yonkers, New York, just north of New York City. Reid knew about golf from his youth in Dumfermline, Scotland, of course, but he hadn't play it then. Because his ironworks business had made him comfortably well-off he now had time to indulge in sport. Reid asked a friend and fellow Scots émigré, John Lockhart, to bring back some golf clubs and balls when he visited their homeland. Lockhart did as requested and in February, 1888, he, Reid, and a few other cronies played for the first time on a makeshift three-hole course set up in a three-acre pasture Reid owned. Everyone was enthralled, of course. More equipment was ordered, and in November of that year, the group formed the St. Andrews Golf Club in homage to the "cradle" of golf. It also changed venues, moving first to a thirty-acre piece of farmland, then to an old apple orchard, which led to their nickname, the Apple Tree Gang. When the membership grew to nearly twenty and the newcomers wanted more room for their money, the club moved again and nine holes were built. Three years later the club move to a site with room for eighteen holes.

St. Andrews was very soon followed by the formation of other golf clubs. In 1891 the Shinnecock Hills Golf Club was founded on the far end of Long Island, New York. It boasted the first American course designed by a golf architect, the Scots professional Willie Dunn, who put together a twelve-hole layout. The course was soon extended to eighteen holes, to accommodate the heavy play. Shinnecock also led the way in golf clubhouse styles, with its simple but elegant wooden-frame building designed by the famed American architect Stanford White. It stands to this day.

Then came the Newport Golf Club in Rhode Island; the Chicago Golf Club; and The Country Club in Boston. In December, 1894, these five clubs joined to form the United States Golf Association, which immediately became the game's ruling body in the country. No vote was taken, and the association was not then and has never been officially invested with that power. Its claim to hegemony over American golf came by virtue of being the first of its kind, the tacit agreement of the golfing public, and perhaps by taking the name it did. How could any organization top the *United States* Golf Association? Only one group, the Western Golf Association, founded in 1899, ever tried to seriously challenge the USGA's dominion. But that attempt was early on, and it did not succeed.

The founding fathers of the USGA were all men of some means through business or the professions, almost all were college educated, and all accustomed to leadership. It followed that the association took on an elitist attitude. Membership in the USGA was open only to private golf clubs. Any amateur player who wanted to compete for the national amateur championships, men's or women's, and be eligible to play on the Walker Cup and Curtis Cup teams needed to belong to a private club. Only then would he or she have the proper credentials—mainly a USGA-approved handicap, which was issued only through member clubs.

In 1922 the USGA sought to diffuse its reputation for snobbery by inaugurating the U.S. Public Links Championship. The Committee on Public and Municipal Golf Courses was formed to conduct it. Other than establishing that tournament, the USGA did almost nothing concrete until the 1960s to enhance the golfing lives of the great majority of American golfers—that is, golfers who do not belong to private clubs. On the other hand and to its everlasting credit, the USGA did not overlook or ignore the game's professionals. Even though in the early years its attitude toward professionalism was still permeated with Victorian and Edwardian antipathy, by staging the U.S. National Open championship at its inception, the USGA recognized the golf professional. By comparison, in American tennis, another "minor" sport with an elitist history, the U.S. Lawn Tennis Association (the equivalent of the USGA and founded about the same time), did all it could to keep professionals in second- or even third-class status. It did not put on a national open championship until 1968, and until then actively discouraged the development of a professional tournament circuit.

Because games grow as spectator and participatory attractions on the strength of *nationally* recognized competitions, the USGA served the American game well by immediately sponsoring national championships. The first U.S. Amateur and U.S. Open championships were played in 1895, both at the Newport Golf Club. By open it is meant, of course, that both professionals and amateurs are eligible to enter, although professionals, who devote their lives to the game, are almost invariably the winners. Amateurs have won the U.S. Open (eight times out of ninety-nine so far, the last in 1933) but since its inception it has effectively been a professional competition and the foremost national championship in American golf. And as the game has developed, the competition has become the most comprehensive, definitive championship in international golf as well.

The USGA's position as the leading authority in the game at the outset of American golf was also justified because it gave order to potential chaos. It served as a ruling body everyone accepted for settling rules disputes. Many USGA policies on matters other than the rules of play would be questioned over the years, particularly in regard to equipment regulations, but the association has managed to solidify its authority and maintain itself as one of the most potent unelected powers in sports.

It is interesting to consider that American golf was established in large part by men of Scottish heritage, many of them émigrés from the game's birthplace. Yet, while it took the Scots of Scotland all those centuries to write a set of rules and establish an authority to sustain them, put on a national championship and come up with a decent ball with which to play, all of this was accomplished in the United States within a decade after the game took root. Was there something in the North American air to stimulate such energy that was missing in Great Britain? Certainly, the tenor of American society had something to do with it—a free-enterprise system in which ability, audacity, ingenuity were not repressed by social ranking.

The Beginning of Golf's First Professional Tournament Circuit

America's vaunted free-enterprise system was at the heart of the development of golf's first professional tournament circuit. It started on a very small scale, and almost certainly not with the intent of founding the extensive and hugely lucrative tournament circuit that has grown up since. But as we know, from small acorns come great oak trees.

On January 1 and 2, 1898, at the Ocean County Hunt and Country Club (now the Lakewood Golf Club), in Lakewood, New Jersey, a thirty-six-hole stroke-play tournament was held for professionals. Ten men competed on a frigid weekend—the temperature was in the thirties and the ground was frozen solid—for a total purse of $150. Val Fitzjohn defeated his brother, Ed, on the first play-off hole to take the $75 first prize. The *New York Times* journalist covering the event wrote: "The meeting was one of golfing giants, to each of whom was granted an unknown degree of skill and each of whom had their particular partisans." Golfing giants would hardly be an accurate description by current standards—the Fitzjohn brothers shot 92–88 to gain the play-off spots—or even those set a few years later, but the tournament in Lakewood set a precedent. It was, as far as most in-depth research reveals, the first tournament of its kind—an event open to any professional who wanted to enter, not an exhibition but a real competition for prize money, *put on for commercial reasons*.

At the time Lakewood was a resort area, midway between New York City and Philadelphia. The golf tournament for the best of players was staged by the hoteliers as a way to entertain their current patrons and, by word of mouth and newspaper reports, attract new customers. That was, and remains, the foundation of professional golf tours: they are a way to drum up business, and not just golf business.

Before the turn of the century, resorts in more southern locations also featured golf. These included hotels in Hot Springs, Virginia; Asheville, North Carolina; Augusta, Georgia; and Ormond and Jacksonville, Florida. The innkeepers at these sites had been staging amateur tournaments for their guests to play in or watch, and it wasn't a big jump to bring in professionals to heighten interest. Eventually, chambers of commerce around the country began putting on tournaments for pros as a way to get publicity for their towns and cities and attract people to live, work, and play there.

At first most of this activity was in the American South and Southwest. Although golf can be played in inclement weather, it is generally associated with a warm sun and light breezes. A report in a Minnesota newspaper of a golf tournament being played in Miami, in mid-December, gets ice-bound Minnesotans thinking of warming their bones for a week in Florida. Or maybe for the rest of their lives. Professional golf tournaments in resort areas were an American innovation not picked up in Great Britain or elsewhere until a good bit later. If there had been a subtropical region in Great Britain, such as Miami Beach, golf tourism might have developed there. But there wasn't, and it didn't. Americans saw a unique opportunity, and they took advantage of it.

The Straws That Stirred the Interest

Some small-scale exhibitions by well-known professionals had been played in the United States in the last years of the nineteenth century, but it was an exhibition series at the turn of the twentieth century that encouraged America's first significant golf growth spurt. In January, 1900, Great Britain's Harry Vardon, touted as the "greatest golfer in the world," began an American exhibition tour that would take him to almost every state east of the Mississippi River. The trip was sponsored by the Spalding Sporting Goods Company, the first American sporting goods manufacturer. It was organized to promote Spalding's newest gutta-percha ball, the Vardon Flyer, but also to promote interest in the still new game. In another respect, Vardon's trip was a farewell tour to an old way of golf. At the same time Spalding brought Vardon to the United States to sell its guttie, Coburn Haskell's livelier three-piece golf ball was being marketed and sold to American golfers. How many Vardon Flyers were sold as a result of Vardon's tour is not known, but the other purpose of the trip, to expand Spalding's customer base, was quite successful. Vardon drew an average of 1,500 people to each of his eighty-three exhibitions, a fine turnout in a country with no more than 100,000 golfers.

Vardon capped off his trip by winning the U.S. Open. He was best known for his accuracy, and the story goes that when he played two rounds on the same course in the same day, he played in the afternoon from the divots he had made in the morning. (It could be said that if he was that good, he would have avoided the divots. But never mind.) In his memoirs, he wrote an assessment of the American sporting temperament that resonates even today: "At that period the Americans were not sufficiently advanced to appreciate some of the finer points of the game. They did, however, appear to thoroughly enjoy the type of ball I drove. I hit it high for carry, which resembled a home run."

What Vardon also left behind was an image of excellent golfing form. He was long considered the father of the modern golf swing. His sobriquet, The Greyhound, was a reference to the exceptional symmetry of his movements back and through when hitting the ball.

Walter Travis, America's First World-Beater

Because Americans have been no less fervent nationalists than the peoples of other sovereign states, in the earliest years of American golf, great emphasis was placed on a native-born American winning his own national championship and that of Great Britain. But the fact remains that the United States was founded by immigrants, so it is appropriate that the country's first international champion was a naturalized American citizen— Walter Travis, Jr., who was born in Australia and emigrated to the United States as a young boy. Travis was a middle-aged golf prodigy, belying the notion that a golfer must begin playing golf as a youth to reach a high level of competence. He didn't take up golf until he was in his thirties, but once he did, he became a major force in the amateur game. Small physically, Travis compensated for his lack of power by learning excellent control of his long shots and becoming a brilliant, almost unerring, chipper and putter.

Travis was not a hail-fellow-well-met type. He had an aloof manner, and could be short and irritable with people. Still, at the 1904 British Amateur, he had good reason to feel he was ill-treated by the hosts. After winning the U.S. Amateur Championship three times (in 1900, 1901, and 1903), this jockey-sized American was a definite threat who might take Britain's most cherished golf trophy back to what was not all that long ago one of its colonies. However, Travis was not assigned a locker in the Royal St. George's Golf Club. Nor did he get accommodations in the hotel where the British players stayed, and which was the best one in town— Sandwich. Furthermore, he was assigned an incompetent cross-eyed caddie who Travis thought was also mentally retarded. Yet, when another caddie became available, Travis's request for him was ignored. Early in his first-round match, played in heavy rain, Travis called a violation on his opponent—for grounding his club in a bunker—which for some reason set a nasty tone for the rest of the championship. Was it the tone of voice in which he called the infraction? Or was a gentleman supposed to over-look it? In any case, after Travis won the match he was not given extra time before his next one to change into dry clothes.

On the other hand, the British thought Travis was a rude guest because he refused various invitations to attend dinner parties. Travis's reason was he was intent on winning and did not want these distractions. Be all that as it may, Travis won the championship—largely on the strength of his putting ability—and the British were aghast. He was at the heart of a ridiculous hassle over the legality of golf equipment that highlighted the golf rivalry developing between Great Britain and the United States. He used a new type of putter, called a Schenectady, after the city in upstate New York where the inventor, A. W. Knight, lived. The central feature of the putter was that its shaft emanated from the center of the mallet-type club head—it was a center-shafted putter. The British were so peeved with Travis and his victory that five years later, the R&A ruled all center-shafted putters illegal in its events. At least the British had the polish to wait until Travis was no longer competing to get even. However, the ban on center-shafted putters held into the early 1950s; it was one of the reasons American legend Ben Hogan always gave for not entering the British Open. He used a center-shafted putter. Although the R&A never admitted it, it was widely believed that they lifted the ban in order to get Hogan to play in their Open, in 1953.

After Travis quit the competitive circuit, he went on to make a number of significant contributions to American golf. He founded and was editor of *The American Golfer*, not the first American golf periodical but for many years the best of the genre. The Old Man, as Travis was often called, also became a golf course architect. He designed some seventeen courses, which in the lingo of the profession are considered representative of the penal school of design. One of Travis's layouts, the west course of the Westchester Country Club, in New York state, has for years been the site of a PGA (Professional Golf Association) Tour event. It remains almost entirely as Travis designed it, and all these years later, it is still considered an excellent course on which to tune up for the U.S. Open.

America's First "First Golfer"

Just as America was beginning to make its weight felt in golf (pun coming is intended), the nation's first golfing president, William Howard Taft, who weighed over three hundred pounds, arrived on the scene. He led the nation from 1909 through 1913 and was often pictured on golf courses. Theodore Roosevelt, whom Taft had succeeded, told the "First Golfer" that he should not play the game because it was undemocratic, which at the time might have had some validity. But Roosevelt also said that golf was a "sissy" game and for that reason should be ignored. The Rough Rider preferred the more manly sport of hunting with powerful guns stags and other grand but essentially helpless creatures.

TR was not the only one who thought golf was a game for pantywaists. This strange and totally unfounded notion would persist for some time. Even into the 1960s, sports editors of major newspapers looked down on golf, which they viewed as "unathletic." Theodore Roosevelt's poorly conceived attitude toward golf did not catch on among American presidents, however.

Taft's successor in the office, Woodrow Wilson, was an unabashedly avid golfer. So was his successor, Warren Harding, who has gone down in history as one the of more casual leaders of the nation and overseer of one of its most corrupt administrations. It might be assumed that there were a lot of gimmes in a Harding foursome. Photographs and old movie footage of Franklin D. Roosevelt playing golf as a young man reveal a well-formed swing; he came close to making his college golf team. FDR was very fond of the game, and he deeply missed playing after he was stricken with polio. During World War II, when the PGA of America considered canceling its professional tour for the duration, President Roosevelt advised the association to continue the tour as best it could, to entertain and keep up the morale of war workers. Although President Truman was well-known for his brisk morning walks, swinging a stick as he strode along, he was never seen with a golf club. John F. Kennedy may have been the best golfing president ever. Movie footage shows him performing a quite graceful and technically sound golf swing, although he was never seen at golf while in office, perhaps because of his back problems. Or perhaps he did not flaunt his hobby because he came to the presidency on the heels of Dwight Eisenhower, whose considerable and much recorded involvement with golf (he even had a putting green constructed on the lawn of the White House) met with more than a little derision, almost all of it from his political opponents.

All Republican presidents since Eisenhower, however, must have thought Ike's celebrated interest in golf was not such a political liability. And why shouldn't they? Golf has always been associated with the Republican Party, the party of business and money, and a relatively conservative approach to the world that the game itself demands to play consistently well. Thus, President Nixon, who was not very adept at athletics, took a stab at golf to create a photo opportunity. Although he played only occasionally during his short term in office, President Gerald Ford was a solid golfer while in the White House. Afterward he became a regular on the celebrity pro-am circuit. Ronald Reagan didn't play golf, but George Bush most certainly did (and does). In fact, Bush has an impressive family golf resume. His grandfather on his mother's side, George Walker, donated the cup after which the long-standing competition between the best American and British amateurs is named—the Walker Cup. President Clinton was also a fervent golfer while in office, and probably because of his other well-known trespasses was often written up as a master mulligan man, who repeated shots until they came out right and only then recorded the score.

Whether American golf drew more adherents or less when the nation's president played the game is hard to measure. One way or the other, it got or kept the game in the news, and as a good publicist will tell you, any mention is worth something.

The First Homebred American Champion

Except for Harry Vardon, the winners of the first sixteen U.S. Opens, from 1895 through 1910, were immigrant Britons who shipped out to America to fill the need for men with golf experience. Some were professionals back home or at least competent players. More than a few, though, were deemed qualified golf professionals simply because they had a Scottish accent. Private clubs were just about the only ones hiring golf professionals, and many members felt only a Scot could handle the work because his forebears invented the game. Native-born Americans entertaining a professional career didn't like this situation, but couldn't do much about it. (This was the motivation for the Ryder Cup Match, as will be outlined further on.)

American-born professionals became more optimistic about the future when the first American-born professional, John McDermott, won the U.S. Open in 1911. McDermott was unmistakably homebred, sometimes exhibiting the brash, cocky manner stereotypical of the young and upcoming American. It was apparently a superficial image, though, an effort by McDermott to compensate for his true nature. Until McDermott began winning tournaments, he was characterized as quiet, mannerly, and religious, a nondrinker and nonsmoker. He was, in fact, a shy man from a difficult family background, whose role-playing caused him an abbreviated career and a long, sad life.

McDermott was born in west Philadelphia in 1891, the son of a mailman who was a heavy drinker and, later documentation would suggest, a physically abusive father. His two sisters became nuns and McDermott himself never married. His father and mother took no interest in their son's golf career, which began when he was a nine-year-old caddie. McDermott immediately revealed a gift for golf, which was noticed by the club's pro, who became his mentor.

In 1909 the one-hundred-and-thirty-five-pound, five-foot-eight-inch McDermott finished fourth in his first U.S. Open. In the 1910 national championship, McDermott shot his way into a three-way play-off with the legendary Smith brothers, Alex and MacDonald, who had emigrated from Carnoustie, Scotland, to make excellent careers in American golf. Alex Smith won the play-off, but McDermott, to everyone's amazement, beat Mac Smith by two shots to take second place. McDermott's sister, Gertrude, recalled that their father was "surprised to see his son's name in the headlines, because he didn't even know Johnny was in the tournament."

McDermott was good in play-off situations. In his first U.S. Open victory, McDermott, described as a "self-assured, determined alumnus of the Philadelphia caddie sheds who feared no one on a golf course," defeated Mike Brady and George Simpson in the play-off for the title. He won his second consecutive U.S. Open outright, by two strokes, on the strength of a pressure-packed closing 71 that held off Tom McNamara, who finished with a fast 69.

McDermott's second open victory came in Buffalo, New York. In the gallery was twenty-year-old Walter Hagen, from nearby Rochester, who was still contemplating whether to become a baseball player or golfer.

Hagen opted for golf after watching McDermott, although not for the expected reason. Some years into his own fabulous career, Hagen would say with typical bravado that because he wasn't all that impressed with the play he saw in Buffalo in 1912, including McDermott's performance, he decided he could do all right in that line of work.

It was early in 1913 when McDermott ran into the media buzz saw that sent him down the road to Griefdom. Just prior to that year's U.S. Open, McDermott won a tournament at Shawnee-on-the-Delaware—by eight strokes over Alex Smith and thirteen strokes over Harry Vardon. With a score of 292, he was the only player to break 300. Afterward he made a quick victory speech that was reported in the papers as "We hope our foreign visitors had a good time, but we don't think they did, and we are sure they won't win the National Open." McDermott got slammed for rudeness. He claimed that he didn't say anything as contemptuous as was reported, and said he was broken-hearted over the affair "and the way the papers used my speech."

To no avail. There was good copy here, and the incident was taken beyond the sports pages of U.S. and British newspapers. The editorial pages took their shots at McDermott, who was castigated for his uncivil deportment. An international cause célèbre was roiled up. McDermott fought back, saying, "I have been horribly misquoted and people not cognizant of the true facts are censuring me right and left. The correspondents as well as some of the golfers at Shawnee took up my words in the wrong light, and this caused all the trouble." Again for naught. Although the 1913 U.S. Open was a historic, upbeat event in American golf, for McDermott it was when his career and life began their tragic downward spiral. The fact that he finished eighth in the championship was only a minor part of his eventual demise.

Next McDermott entered the 1914 British Open, but missed his travel connections and arrived too late. He booked passage back to the United States on the *Kaiser Wilhelm II*, which collided with an English ship in mid-voyage and sank. No one died in the accident, and McDermott was not injured, but he never shook the experience off. McDermott drifted in a lifeboat for almost a day before being rescued. It was the final straw in what had been a devastating period in his life. There was the Shawnee incident, his performance in the '13 U.S. Open, and the British Open debacle. He had also lost money in the stock market. In late 1914 he quit his job as a professional at the Atlantic City Country Club and announced he was retiring. He was twenty-three. He then entered the Norristown Hospital in Pennsylvania, where he remained for the rest of his life. The fine art of euphemism was not yet in place, so he was committed as a "lunatic." Later he would be described as manic-depressive (now known as bipolar disorder). Over the years he played an occasional round of golf on a six-hole course built on the hospital grounds with McDermott's (and the doctors') recreation in mind.

McDermott's last day in the golfing sun began as another ignominious moment in his life, but was saved by none other than Arnold Palmer. At age seventy-nine, McDermott went to the nearby Merion Golf Club, north of Philadelphia, to watch some of the 1971 U.S. Open. Because he was dressed poorly, a young assistant pro thought McDermott was some sort of vagrant and told him to get out of the golf shop. Outside McDermott was recognized by Palmer, who put an arm around him and asked after his game. "I'm hitting the ball good," the old champion replied, "but my putting is not what it should be." Palmer told him he knew exactly how he felt, and that the only thing to do was "keep practicing." About two months later, eleven days short of his eightieth birthday, McDermott died in his sleep at a home in Yeadon, Pennsylvania. The August 2nd *Philadelphia Inquirer* reported his death with a brief notice, the headline of which read: "Yeadon Man Dies; Won Open."

The Boston Miracle

The 1913 U.S. Open was poor John McDermott's last hurrah, but it was one of the most historically consequential competitive events in American golf history in every other respect. The championship ended in a three-way tie between Harry Vardon, Ted Ray, and Francis Ouimet. Vardon and Ray were the Sam Snead and Ben Hogan or Arnold Palmer and Jack Nicklaus of their day—the two dominant professional golfers of their time. Ouimet, on the other hand, was the darkest of dark horses, a twenty-year-old amateur from the Boston area with no national reputation and a only minor regional one. He lived across the street from the site of the championship, The Country Club in Brookline, Massachusetts, and had been a caddie at the club. He had not intended to play in the 1913 Open, but when someone had to drop out at the last minute, the USGA offered him a spot in the field. He took it and made history.

Ouimet (pronounced *WeeMet* in the U.S.) shot rounds of 77, 74, 74, 79 to tie Vardon and Ray. In an eighteen-hole play-off the next day, during a steady drizzle, Ouimet was remarkably poised for someone so young and with no experience in golf at this level facing the two most accomplished golfers in the world. He shot a one-over-par 72 to defeat Vardon by five shots, and Ray by six. It was an astonishing turn of events that thrilled the nation. Even Americans who cared not a whit about golf were deeply pleased. Ouimet's victory represented another manifestation of the nation's growing strength in all things. Sport has always been a platform for flaunting national pride, and Ouimet gave the nation a splendid opportunity to puff itself up. It was all the more gratifying that Ouimet demolished the British near Boston, the epicenter of the American Revolution.

Ouimet, like McDermott before him, had his country's pride in mind during his remarks at the trophy presentation. However, with the advantage of a higher education (McDermott quit school after the sixth grade), Ouimet was more circumspect and tactful than McDermott presumably had been. Said Ouimet before the assembly, "Naturally it always was my hope to win out. I simply tried my best to keep this cup from going to our friends across the water. I am very glad to have been the agency for keeping the cup in America."

Ouimet's victory was no fluke. He had a fine, measured swing and an excellent mind for golf. Although he remained an amateur, a few years after his success at Brookline, he came into sharp conflict with the USGA over his amateur standing. He and a partner opened a sporting goods store in downtown Boston, and because golf equipment was sold in it along with baseball bats and more, the USGA classified Ouimet as a golf professional. There was such a public outcry over this ruling that the USGA quickly backed down from its position. Subsequent to this foolishness, Ouimet won the U.S. Amateur Championship twice (in 1914 and 1931), played on eight U.S. Walker Cup teams, and captained them six times.

Although Ouimet's monumental 1913 victory naturally got big headlines in the Boston newspapers the following day, it didn't elicit the media frenzy we have come to expect today. There were no follow-up stories in the papers and only one national golf periodical to keep the story alive. The first commercial radio station wasn't established until 1920. Nonetheless, it is safe to say that Ouimet's achievement definitely helped grow the game.

We know for certain that Ouimet galvanized the golfing ambitions of some young men who would become the best golfers in the country and even the world. At various times during their lifetimes, Walter Hagen and Gene Sarazen commented that Ouimet's victory at Brookline had stirred them to keep working at their game. Bobby Jones also said as much. But even more important, Ouimet, who came from modest means, helped diminish golf's for-rich-men-only image. He deported himself without even a hint of a strut, helping golf expand its base of interest into the social and economic middle class.

Here Comes Walter, an American Original

The next major figure in American golf came immediately on the heels of Ouimet, and comported himself in the opposite manner. His name was Walter Hagen, and he became golf's first and foremost show-business personality. Because Ouimet's tour de force at The Country Club was so astounding, Hagen's emergence was lost in the delirium. During the 1913 Open, Hagen was tied for the lead with five holes to go, and he eventually finished tied for fourth with the second lowest seventy-two-hole total. Ouimet, Vardon, and Ray had 304; Hagen, Jim Barnes, Mac Smith, and Louis Tellier had 307.

However, during the week leading up to Ouimet's unexpected heroics, Hagen did not go unnoticed. Certainly no one could miss his sartorial display. He wore white flannel slacks, colorful striped shirts, a bright red bandanna around his neck, a checkered cap, and red-rubber-soled white shoes tied with wide and colorful laces. He played his golf with similar panache, employing a wide stance and using a long and loose-jointed swing that brought predictable results. Hagen was a wild driver. But he had a marvelous gift for recovery shots from difficult positions, and he was a brilliant putter, especially under pressure. Hagen was a flamboyant dandy next to Ouimet's gentle knight, and for that reason, and also because he decided to make golf his profession, he became an instrumental figure in the rise of American golf.

Hagen was a character, defined here as someone who stands out from the crowd either purposely or by dint of innate personality traits, or a bit of both. He had a flair for the grand gesture. Because of his wildness with the driver, he had many opportunities to play tough shots, and it was his shtick to make them seem even tougher. He would take a lot of time considering all the problems, checking angles like a pool shooter, grimacing as if in psychic pain, then play a brilliant recovery at which the crowd raved. Many didn't know much about golf and didn't realize they were getting a bit of a con job; but even those who were in on it enjoyed the act.

Born in 1892 in Rochester, New York, Hagen was the son of a blacksmith. But there was never in Hagen's posture or bearing any hint of his proletarian background. He carried himself with the erect, self-assured posture of the inherently gifted athlete and of a gentleman or nobleman. With his head held high and back-tilted, he peered down at the world through half-hooded eyes like the king of the realm. This demeanor led to the sobriquet by which he was best known, Sir Walter. Hagen had a high-pitched voice, and from accounts of friends who knew him well, was not nearly as witty as he seemed. But never mind, he was a superb actor and a great golfer.

Hagen was the first professional golfer, as opposed to golf professional. That is, he made his living exclusively by *playing* golf. He did not follow the conventional professional track of holding a job at a club and going off to play tournaments only when it was closed for the winter or the members allowed him some time off. The one club pro job he did take was at the now famous Oakland Hills Country Club in Detroit, and it did not last long. They were building the course and clubhouse when Hagen signed on as head pro, but the day the club opened he resigned and recommended his friend Mike Brady for the post. Walter Hagen was not about to stand on a lesson tee four or five hours a day explaining to some 90 shooter how to put his hands on the club. He probably couldn't have explained it even if he had tried.

His old friend and rival Gene Sarazen said Hagen didn't a know a thing about the golf swing and didn't care. He was a natural. And a free spirit. Evincing the classic American image of the lone gunslinger riding into the sunset, Hagen took a chance that he could earn enough money in tournaments and exhibitions to pay his way in the world. It was quite a risk at the time, given that golf was such a new game in America and the few tournaments available offered very small purses. However, Hagen based his prospects on being able to establish himself not only as an outstanding golfer and a winner of important titles, but as a personality who could attract large crowds. He did both.

Although Hagen toned down his wardrobe after his peacock display in the '13 Open, he always looked spiffy and was an obviously expensive dresser all his life. He wore two-tone shoes, silk shirts, tailored knickers. He became a champion before the Roaring Twenties were officially aroar, but he would become one of the best-known athletes to personify that giddy time. He was golf's Great Gatsby.

The Hagen style wasn't all caprice; he had some method up his sleeve. For example, he did everything slowly, from reaching for a saltshaker to taking his time to line up a putt. It appeared he was acting cool, even indifferent to everything. But the slowing down had a very practical purpose. In golf, speed kills. Golfers do everything they can to slow their metabolism so they don't rush their swing. Ben Hogan, a fast swinger, tried to play as many practice rounds as he could with players who had smooth rhythmic swings—George Fazio was a favorite—so he might inhale, as it were, that tempo and slow himself down. By the same token, when paired with Hogan, Sam Snead never watched his swing for fear he would inhale some of its speed. When Hagen walked like a ship plowing against a heavy sea or brought a drink to his lips with the deliberation of a hung jury, he was slowing himself down.

Hagen liked his whiskey and gin, and after retiring liked it too much for his own good, but during his playing days he cultivated a reputation for heavy drinking that fed his nightlife-loving playboy image. It made good copy, and it also might have rendered an opponent overconfident. Believing Hagen had just come to the tee after a long night of babes and booze, the competition might think he wouldn't need his best golf stuff to emerge victorious. But as Gene Sarazen once pointed out, Hagen was doing a number on everyone. At parties he would order a drink and nurse it, then surreptitiously dump most of it in a vase or toilet and return to the crowd asking loudly if a body could get a drink around here. He was famous for showing up late for his tee time still wearing his evening clothes, which were wrinkled as if he had slept in them. In fact, he went to bed early when he had important golf to play. But he would rise early, roll his tuxedo into a ball, and throw it against the wall of his hotel room to wrinkle it. Then he'd put it on and head off to the golf course. His long-time caddie, chauffeur, and foil Spec Hammond would wear Hagen's golf shoes until after the master showman had hit his opening drive wearing patent leather pumps. Then, he got spiked up.

Whether the public knew that Hagen was playing with them—and it probably did—was immaterial. Hagen was fun, he fit the tenor of the times, and he was a winner. A major winner.

In his late teens Hagen had a tryout with the Philadelphia Phillies and was offered a contract. Even after his excellent performance in the 1913 U.S. Open, he considered a baseball career. But after winning the 1914 U.S. Open, he cast his star once and for all on golf. For the next nineteen years hardly a season went by without Hagen winning at least one major championship. These included two U.S. Opens, four British Opens, five Western Opens, an unprecedented five PGA Championships (four of them in a row), as well as three North & South Opens. He won forty-five tournaments in all. A splendid career record.

However, there was more to Hagen's career than the essentially ephemeral entertainment of winning tournaments. He made a major contribution to the sport by playing a bustling and wide-ranging exhibition schedule. This exposure was for his own welfare, of course, but by not limiting his exhibitions to already established golf centers, he spread the story of the game. He appeared in such out-of-the-way places as the Dakotas, Wyoming, and Utah, striding regally along dusty fairways and putting on sand greens, but always giving the crowds a show. Many of the spectators may not have known a thing about golf and were just there to catch a glimpse of a celebrity, but because Hagen didn't seem to take golf too seriously, he made the game all the more appealing to the tyro golfer as well as those not yet baptized but thinking about it. How many new golfers were enticed to the game after a Hagen visit is impossible to say, but even if it was just a few at each stop, this interest was what golf needed in its American infancy. Hagen was the Johnny Appleseed of American golf, a big planter of the game in the soil of the nation.

By 1920 Hagen was the undisputed king of American golf, but he had yet to prove himself in Great Britain. Final judgment on a player's position in the game still depended on his record in golf's birthplace. The drive to beat England was also fed by increased national pride among Americans because of the decisive role the United States played in Germany's defeat in World War I. The gist was, if we can go over there and win *their* (Great Britain's) war, we should be able to beat them at golf. Although Walter Travis, Jr., won the British Amateur, that was a long time ago, and it was only the amateur championship. The Open, as the British refer to their championship, as though it were the only one of its kind, was a far more telling achievement. Victory didn't come easily for Hagen, at first.

After winning his first U.S. Open, Hagen did not travel to the British Open of 1914, because the start of World War I was looming. After the war began, the championship was suspended—from 1915 through 1919—so it wasn't until 1920 that Hagen played in the oldest of all golf championships. He had just won his second U.S. Open, in 1919, and much was expected of him. But he deeply disappointed everyone with surprisingly high scores—he averaged just over 82 for the four rounds. The next year, Hagen finished a respectable sixth, but it was first place that he, and the American public, was after. Although he was considered the only American with a realistic chance in this quest, some became concerned that maybe his rapid rise to stardom was an accident and that his loose and gregarious golf swing—and personality—was not up to winning in the Scottish wind.

Although Hagen never gained complete control of all his shots, his swing had become less rambunctious. He never did have a problem putting, and his will to win was far more intense than his manner suggested. It all came together in 1922, when The Haig, another of his nicknames, won his first British Open by a single shot. He was runner-up the following year, won again in 1924, and to allay any lingering doubts about his aptitude for links golf, he won the British Open twice more, in 1928 and 1929.

Even while Hagen was drubbing the British at their own game, he didn't make enemies of them, as did Walter Travis. He had a genius for playing well to both the boxes and the cheap seats upstairs. He was at ease among both the peerage and the steerage, never flaunting his relationship with the gentry, or condescending to the hoi polloi. It was in this regard that Hagen extended his influence and furthered the Americanization of the game. A favorite anecdote from the Hagen canon is that he once kept Edward, Prince of Wales, who was a golf addict, waiting on the first tee. It was also rumored that he called the Prince Eddie. The lateness was a fact, the familiarity was probably not. Witnesses suggested that

Hagen was really calling his caddie, who was standing near the Prince. Whatever the facts, the "Eddie story" was the one the American man on the street wanted to hear. It accented the quintessential American side of Hagen's persona, the average American's disdain for class distinctions and, of course, British royalty.

Another example of Hagen's egalitarian side came at the 1923 British Open at Troon. Hagen and all the other pros were banned from the clubhouse because they were professionals. This was a reflection of the British landed gentry's fanciful disdain for anyone "in trade," and the related attitude about the purity of amateurism in sports as opposed to the crass money-grubbing of professionals. A miffed Hagen had his hired Rolls Royce parked where all the snoots of the club could see it and him, and the fancy picnic he had spread out on the lawn. He still wasn't allowed in, but he made his point.

Hagen was so reputed for his help in the the democratization (or Americanization) of golf that he was sometimes given credit for advances in this direction he might not really have deserved. For instance, he was often credited for the opening of American clubhouses and their facilities to golf professionals. After the 1920 U.S. Open at the Inverness Club in Toledo, Ohio, the pros who played, including Hagen, gave the club a clock inscribed with a poem thanking the club for its hospitality—to wit, full use of its clubhouse facilities. This incident was widely accepted as the precedent setter. However, Herb Graffis, the pioneer American golf writer and publisher, told a different story about the pros' emancipation and Hagen's role in it. In the days leading up to the 1914 U.S. Open at the Midlothian Country Club outside Chicago, the members of the club wondered where the pros were going to hang their coats. They had always used nails on a wall in the back of the pro shop, but there were not enough for such a large gathering. A member suggested room for the pros be made in the clubhouse. When other members claimed the pros were not gentlemen, the maverick member replied that the club's own professional, George Turnbull, was one of the finest gentlemen in the world. Everyone agreed to that, and the pros were allowed in the clubhouse. Apparently, because Hagen was the first professional to walk in and use the locker room, he received credit for the breakthrough, but he also got the credit because he won the championship, Graffis concluded.

Sarazen, "The Melting Pot Pro"

It wasn't too long after Hagen rose to eminence that he was challenged by another typically American personality, Gene Sarazen. Sarazen was the second American golfer to make a career out of just playing the game— the second professional golfer. He took club professional positions because they meant a guaranteed income, while the less provident Hagen didn't bother. However, Sarazen didn't spend any more time than Hagen in the shop selling clubs and balls. In the 1920s the money was in exhibitions, and like Hagen, that's how Sarazen made most of his income. None of that would have been possible, though, without a reputation as a top-drawer player.

Sarazen was born Eugenio Saraceni in 1912, in Harrison, New York, a suburb north of New York City. His Italian immigrant father was a carpenter who struggled to make a living in the New World. To help with family finances, Eugenio dropped out of elementary school and began to caddie at a private club in the area, Apawamis Country Club. He quickly showed an aptitude for golf and just as quickly decided that that was where his future lay. His father thought golf a poor choice and recommended carpentry instead, but Eugenio marched to his own drummer. Interestingly, he took something from his father's trade into his golf style. He would say the keynote of his golf swing was that he hit the ball like you hit a nail with a hammer, a crisp, wristy blow.

In his late teens Eugenio Saraceni changed his name to Gene Sarazen. He often said it was because "Saraceni sounded like it belonged on a violin." But the change may have been an effort at assimilation, too. Many a Jew and Italian and Pole made their names over after immigrating to the United States, usually Anglicizing their names or just making them sound less "ethnic." Sarazen also remarked once that after coming up with his name, he researched telephone books to see if there were any others. He found none and went with it because it would help make him stand out even more from the crowd. It was important to get your name noticed if you were going to go anywhere in the increasingly crowded and competitive American social and sporting scene. Sarazen would prove a master at self-promotion.

Short in height, olive-skinned, pugnacious in temperament, Sarazen moved swiftly up the game's competitive ladder. In his second-round match in the 1921 PGA Championship—nineteen years old and virtually an unknown in the game—he trounced Jock Hutchison, the legendary Scottish émigré professional who earlier in the same year won the British Open. Sarazen lost his next match, but the victory over Hutchison gave everyone notice of his presence. He opened eyes forever when he won the 1922 New Orleans (or Southern) Open early in the year, then became the youngest winner ever of the U.S. Open. And just to make sure no one thought he was a flash-in-the-pan, Sarazen also won the 1922 PGA Championship. A new major player had arrived upon the scene.

Sarazen's impact on golf began with his competitive record, but he was a force in extending golf's franchise to the American middle class, as Hagen did, but also to the swelling numbers of eastern and southern European immigrants to the United States. Sarazen may have changed his name to something that seemed less Italian, but he never forgot his ethnic background, if only because he was not allowed to forget. When he was coming up in American golf during the first quarter of the twentieth century, the game was dominated by men of Scots and British heritage who brought their ancestral racial prejudices with them. Many young Italian-Americans from poor economic backgrounds got into golf by caddying like Sarazen, but didn't get many opportunities to rise above that rank because they were not "WASPs." The best they could expect was to become an assistant professional working in the back room of the shop, cleaning clubs and doing other menial tasks, or giving the odd lesson the head pro couldn't fit into his schedule.

Sarazen helped break that mold by his championship play, and also by his aggressive response to ethnic typecasting. A defining incident was an experience he related involving Jim Barnes, the British-born winner of the first U.S. PGA Championship and a U.S. Open: "Yes, it was tough for a little Italian," Sarazen recalled:

The Scots and English pros didn't like us very much. I remember in 1922, at Skokie Country Club [where Sarazen won his first U.S. Open], Francis Ouimet asked me to join him, Chick Evans, and Jim Barnes for a practice round. Barnes said he didn't want to play with me—that little guy, as he put it. Well, after I won that Open there was a special match arranged to be played in New Jersey between the current Open champion, me, and the previous one, Barnes. The night before the match Barnes asked me if I wanted to split the purse, and I told him no, it's winner take all. I beat him six and five.

After Sarazen made his mark in golf, many other Italian-Americans became outstanding players, teachers, club designers, and golf course architects. There was Tony Manero, winner of the 1936 U.S. Open; Toney Penna, a brilliant, innovative golf club designer (who put an "e" in his first name to be different and gain notice); the seven Turnesa brothers, among them pro champions Joe and Jim, and amateur champion Willie; Henry Ciuci, Al and Abe Espinosa, Olin and Morty Dutra, Doug Ford (né Fortinaci), and George Fazio, among many others. Other ethnic minorities began to excel as well, such as Billy Burke (born Burkauskas of Lithuanian extraction) who won the 1931 U.S. Open. This expanded and enriched America's store of golfing talent, and except for the omission of black Americans, gave the game an archetypal American character. Then again, leaving the blacks out of the club was part of the American way at the time.

Sarazen's flair for keeping his name in the news took some clever turns. He once complained that the golf hole should be bigger than its 4.25-inch diameter—he was having a bad stretch with the blade. An 8-inch hole was tried during a 1930s tournament in Florida, and as expected the best putters just made more putts than the less skilled ones. Sarazen had no better success on that green than he had been having with the regulation hole, but the idea drew attention. Sarazen once insured his hands for $100,000, which got him a notice as the Heifetz of the fairway.

He also had a talent for dramatic golf, although this entailed a bit of luck, of which Sarazen had plenty. The most famous example was the four-wood second shot he holed for a double eagle on the par-five fifteenth hole in the last round of the 1935 Masters tournament. It led him into a play-off for the title against Craig Wood, which Sarazen won. The shot had something to do with establishing the Masters' stature as a major event in golf.

Many years later during the first round of an honorary appearance in the 1973 British Open, the 71-year-old Sarazen aced the famed par-three Postage Stamp hole at Troon. The next day, with the television cameras now focused on him, he holed from a bunker on the same hole for a two.

But the most significant and long-lasting contribution Sarazen made to the game was the sandwedge—the first *legal* one. In the late 1920s a Texan named McLain designed a sandwedge with a massive rounded sole stretching from the top line to the bottom line of the club face, which was concave. Bobby Jones used a McLain wedge once, and to good purpose, hitting a crucial bunker shot in the final round of the 1930 British Open, the third leg in his Grand Slam. (The term may have derived from bridge, a popular card game among golfers and sportswriters at the time.) But the McLain wedge was declared illegal in 1932, because of the concave face, which caused the ball to be struck twice with one swing.

In that same year Sarazen brought out his wedge. It had a conventional straight face, which made it legal. But what made it really unique and effective was a wide-soled flange that was angled so the rear part of the club made contact with the sand before the leading edge—what has come to be called "bounce." Until McLain's wedge and then Sarazen's, greenside sand-bunker shots were being played with a niblick—a nine-iron—which had an overall thin head and, most troublesome of all, a knife-blade-thin leading edge. The leading edge was the big problem: It was apt to dig too deeply into the sand. Golfers learned to pick the ball out cleanly with the club, but this took exceptional skill and, under pressure, a lot of nerve. Few had enough of either, even the best players. As Sarazen would say later, "We were all terrible bunker players before the wedge, even Jones and Hagen."

Sarazen had a few versions of the inspiration behind his wedge. The one he gave most often was that one day, when he was flying in a small plane with Howard Hughes, the famous oil industry multimillionaire, he noticed that in pulling back the control stick the rear of the plane dipped down and the nose rose up. This essentially is what the angled flange did for the sandwedge. Another inspiration Sarazen once suggested was the time he watched geese land in a pond and noticed their rear end hitting the water first, with their head raised. This observation seems more in line with the principle action of Sarazen's wedge.

To get the effect he was looking for, Sarazen built up a wide flange on the back of the niblicks he was using to experiment and develop his idea. He would say that in so doing he also introduced the first flanged irons, but that is not accurate. Flanged irons were already in existence. It was the angle, or bounce, that made Sarazen's club so effective, but for some reason he said very little about it. In any case, the back end of the flange makes first contact with the sand. The club head then drives down into the sand and moves under the ball, creating an explosion of sand. The leading edge is less apt to dig in, and the club face never actually touches the ball. The moving sand is what propels the ball up and forward.

Sarazen put his wedge into play for the first time during the 1932 British Open. How he kept it from the scrutiny of the rules committee is telling, given that the R&A and USGA were—and still are—both inclined to slow down, if not altogether stamp out, innovation in equipment technology. During his practice rounds Sarazen was getting down in two from the bunkers with such regularity that the gallery began to wonder what kind of weapon he was using. Shrewdly aware of how the conservative rule makers would react to his new club, Sarazen kept it upside down in his golf bag so no one could see it, and took it with him to his hotel every evening hidden under his overcoat. As he explained many years later, "If the British had seen it before the tournament, they would have barred it. Oh, yes. In the tournament I went down in two from most of the bunkers." He also won his first and only British Open. It has been estimated that Sarazen's wedge took two strokes off the handicap of every golfer in the game after he introduced it, and it still does.

The Amateur Attitude as Expressed by "Chick" Evans; The Club Pros Join Hands; The Pro Tour's Mom-and-Pop Days; The Origination of the Ryder Cup as a Job Action; The Steel Shaft Further Changes he Game; The American Woman Golfer Arises; Bobby Jones, the Greatest Amateur of All

"Chick" Evans's Long and Good Ride

Champion golfers, internationally celebrated men of the world, and successful businessmen, Walter Hagen and Gene Sarazen were welcomed into the homes, offices, and clubs of America's monied class. However, golf professionals in general were still considered second-class citizens in American golf's country club milieu, which in effect controlled the pros' lives because it provided the jobs. As late as the 1960s, members of the Rumson Golf Club in Rumson, New Jersey, would not let their own professionals take a meal in the clubhouse or even use the facilities. One of the club's head pros was Dave Marr, who finally quit because of this treatment; he went on to win a PGA Championship and enjoy a long career as a golf announcer-commentator on television. The attitude was certainly un-American, but typical of people of wealth and position the world over, golfers and otherwise.

Thus, during the first quarter of the twentieth century in American golf, the amateur golfer, or simon-pure (a name derived from Simon's attempts to bribe St. Peter and St. Paul, who rejected the offers and were thus simon-pure) was still considered the highest order of golfer—and perhaps of human being, too. American private club golfers justified their emulation of this British upper-class attitude as maintaining precious golf tradition, and there were a number of fine American amateur golfers during this period to keep the snobs happy. These included Walter Travis, Jr., Jerry Travers, Ouimet, and Charles "Chick" Evans, Jr. Evans's stance on amateurism was about as pure as it could get. However, it did not at all ring of social class distinctions. Evans made one of the broadest ranging and most valuable contributions any golfer has ever made to society at large.

A tall, slender man with a friendly manner, Evans was born in Indiana, but from the age of three, lived the rest of his life in Chicago. Born in 1890 into a solid middle-class family background, he took to caddying at eight, became a brilliant player early on, and gained a national reputation by the time he was in his late teens. He was so determined to remain an amateur that he quit caddying when he turned sixteen, because the rules of the time said caddies above that age were deemed professionals.

At one point Evans was considered as good as any professional playing the game, even when he failed time after time to win the U.S. Amateur or the U.S. Open. He had a number of near misses in both championships, then finally broke through. In 1916, at age twenty-six, he won them both and became the first golfer to hold both of these titles simultaneously.

During World War I Evans was one of a number of golf notables who played exhibitions to raise money for the Red Cross. This was the first golf played for charity, which later would become a cornerstone of the PGA Tour. Evans's participation was also an expression of his benevolent nature, which flowered fully when he established the eponymous caddie scholarship program. After his breakthrough year as a national champion, Evans received offers to write a golf-instruction book, play a lucrative exhibition schedule, endorse products—in short, turn pro. He refused, not because he thought it a lowly trade, but because he liked being an amateur. However, when Evans was offered the opportunity to make some instructional recordings, he did so only after notifying the USGA that the money he earned would be used to create a college scholarship fund for caddies who could not otherwise afford a higher education. It was his librarian mother's idea. Candidates for the scholarship did not have to be good golfers, or golfers at all, but they did have to demonstrate the need for financial help and have good high-school grades.

The first two Evans Scholars entered Northwestern University in 1930. By the end of the twentieth century, more than seven thousand men and women had graduated from some eighteen different colleges and universities as Evans Scholars. Many more young people have been given similar opportunities because the Evans Scholars idea generated numerous other programs of its kind operated by various regional golf associations and private golf clubs. Evans got a lot out of his game, but gave even more back in the name of amateurism and, if you please, the American dream.

Professionals Organize

In 1916 the Professional Golfers Association of America (PGA) was founded. The association didn't stump for a minimum wage or better working conditions or job security—it was not a union, per se—but it helped legitimize the professionals' profession in the minds of the club members for whom the pros all worked. A constitution with bylaws and an emblem give an air of respectability, as well as authority. The professional needed some of that. While he was not actually indentured, it sometimes felt that way. An item in a 1910 *Golf* magazine told of the day a member of a club who didn't have a game that morning asked the professional to join him for a round. The pro cited duties around the shop, including club repairs by which he earned extra money, and told the member it would cost him $1.50 for his time on the course. The member replied that he never paid a pro to play with him. The pro billed the member, anyway, and the member threatened to have him fired. The pro backed off, and for a number of years played with the member for free. The PGA of America helped do away with that sort of exploitation.

Playing the Tour

Most people who become golf professionals do so because they love the game and are better than average players. They also discover early on that when they get into the business, they don't get to play nearly as much as they thought they would and want to. In this era before there was enough money in tournament play, the professionals competed in local or regional tournaments on their day off—Monday—and slipped in nine holes in the late afternoon or very early morning, and were satisfied with that. If they managed to qualify for the U.S. Open, played in June, the middle of their work year, the members would allow the trip out of pride—*their pro* was good enough to play in the national championship.

Some professionals of a more adventurous type gave the budding tournament circuit a whirl. It was a winter tour at the start. Most of the club professional jobs were in the northern states, and only after these clubs closed for the winter—usually from November through the end of March—were the pros able to get away for any length of time without risking the loss of their jobs. Even the free-spirited Jimmy Demaret, on a roll winning three tournaments in a row, didn't try for a fourth. Instead he hurried back to his club for fear he was away too long and might get canned. The regular paycheck kept him and his family in food and shelter.

In the early days, the winter circuit was played mainly in the South, but by the mid-1920s a string of tournaments was being staged regularly in California, Texas, and Arizona. Most of the pros who made the circuit had to pay their own way. A few obtained financial support from members, who formed a kind of syndicate that raised a couple of thousand dollars or so for their pro to make the tournament swing. Some syndicates wanted a return on their money and a percentage of any profit, although that was rare in the earliest days of the tour. Other sponsors were philanthropic, as Paul Runyan, who had just finished his first full year as head professional of the Metropolis Country Club in White Plains, New York, recalled:

Gerald Rosenberger had seventy of the members put up $50 each—a pot of $3,500—to send me and my wife on the winter tour. They drew up an agreement that I was to send any checks I won back to them and if there were any profits we would split them fifty-fifty. This was the tour of 1931–32, which began in November. It was my first full tour . . . The $3,500 was a little more than enough to pay for our whole expense, because you got a train ticket from New York to Florida to southern California to northern California, back down to southern California, then through Arizona, Texas, and Louisiana back to Florida and up to New York for $202. There was berthage, of course, that was extra. You paid about $8 a night for a berth, but it was overall a very reasonable rate.

Well, I won about $4,700. I figured, pretty nice, made my winter expenses and lived quite well, didn't have to spend any of the pennies I saved during the summer, and got fifty percent of the purse money I won—another $2,200 or so. When I got back home nothing was said by the members, and they had a dinner party for me; the whole membership was there and me and my wife were wined and dined, and they didn't take their share of the profits. They gave me my share, plus a nice big check which I've still got, canceled, for $1,500.

Not all the pros had such an agreeable arrangement. The pros who couldn't work out such a deal or were simply not brave enough to try it on their own (as most did), took a factory job for the winter or any other employment they could find that kept a paycheck coming in.

There was also a practical side to the tour pro's adventure. If he played well and made a reputation as a top player, it could lead to a better club job. Out on tour, he heard about better jobs opening up. He also benefited from talking with colleagues about the golf swing, for the edification of his own game, but also to find better or newer ways to teach it that would help fill his lesson book at home. The tour was a combination workshop, business conference, networking party, and chance to compete. It took some nerve to try it and a bit of cunning to make a go. "Wild" Bill Mehlhorn described what it was like to play winter tournament golf in the very early, unofficial years, a decade before Paul Runyan's experience, in my book *Gettin' to the Dance Floor: An Oral History of American Golf.* In November, 1919, at age twenty-one, Mehlhorn took a train south to Miami, Florida, making stops along the way.

I paid my way to Florida giving golf clinics and selling subscriptions to *Golf Illustrated* magazine. I stopped in towns on the way, set down my golf bag and a big trophy in the lobby of the main hotel, and got the word out that I was a golf pro giving lessons at two dollars an hour, and would also give a clinic or an exhibition if they could raise the money. I also tried to get people to sell subscriptions to *Golf Illustrated,* at four dollars each. If they sold fifty of them, they got a trophy like the one I was carrying, which they could use in a tournament. It was a beautiful-looking trophy, three feet high. I wasn't out to sell it, I used it as a sample, but I'd take an order if someone wanted to buy one. I left Chicago with seventy dollars in my pocket, and when I got to Miami I had seven hundred.

In Miami I'd stay at the Martinique Hotel for three dollars a day, a special rate they gave golf professionals. There was a tournament at the Miami Country Club, about two miles from the hotel, one up in Palm Beach, some others up north on the east coast, and there was one over on the west coast just outside of Fort Myers. Nowadays you can drive straight across [from Miami to Fort Myers] in an hour and a half, but back then I had to take a train up to Jacksonville, another across to Tampa, then one down to Fort Myers. It took about three days, at three cents a rail mile.

Ben Hogan once said Mehlhorn was the best shot-maker he'd ever seen. After his playing days ended, Mehlhorn enjoyed a long life as a brilliant theorist and teacher of the golf swing. He ended his days teaching players on the Florida International University golf team. He died in his nineties, not far from the Martinique Hotel where he stayed in 1919.

Mehlhorn was in the vanguard of tour pros who were more or less spawned in Lakewood, New Jersey, in January 1898. Beginning in the early twentieth century, the golf resort business began expanding to the southern and southeastern states—in particular North and South Carolina, and especially Florida, where Henry Flagler, who made his first fortune as a partner of John D. Rockefeller in the oil business, concentrated his efforts. Flagler bought and consolidated a number of railroads and length-ened their lines all the way to Key West. He then built hotels and golf courses near them. It was the start of the Florida land boom and the state's winter resort business.

Getting publicity for the hotels that led to paying guests was what the golf tournaments were about. The events were reported in the newspapers of the North, where the customers came from. The success of these no-tices depended in part on having as many well-known players as possible competing. If Hagen and Sarazen, national and international champions respectively, played in the Miami Open, it got the attention of the editors of the Chicago *Tribune*, the Cleveland *Plain-Dealer*, and the Boston *Herald*. The trouble was, Hagen and Sarazen did not play in every tournament, because the purses were usually too small. They could make a lot more doing exhibition tours and without nearly as much work. Sarazen would often say in later years that he never considered himself a tour player.

Getting the stars to enter the events was then and would remain a problem for those running tours. The players were always and still are independent agents, a status they guard jealously. They have always been determined to play wherever and whenever they wanted. In Europe and the Far East, when pro tours developed there, sponsors assured a name player or two with an appearance fee—money over and above what he might win out of the announced purse. The American system, though, has never *officially* allowed this pre-paying system; in America merit is the code of honor, that in this great capitalist system there should be no guarantees. At least not in an open competition.

As the circuit began to grow, though, other golfers developed who became regular winners or high finishers—such as Paul Runyan, Leo Diegel, Bobby Cruickshank, Johnny Farrell, Harry Cooper—and built name-recognition so the tours were less dependent on Hagen and Sarazen. Eventually, you became a "name" pro simply by being a tour player. From 1919 into the early 1930s, the pro tour was run in a catch-as-catch-can way. It was in the truest sense a Mom-and-Pop shop. Some of the players' wives, namely Estelle Armour, Nellie Cruickshank, and Josephine Espinosa, did a lot of leg and phone work finding sponsors, sweet-talking them into increasing the purse money, thanking sponsors who had put on tournaments, and making travel and accommodation arrangements for the players. It became a little more corporate, but not much, when Tommy Armour, Bobby Cruickshank, and Craig Wood cajoled a sportswriter for the *Newark* (New Jersey) *News* to get involved. The writer, Hal Sharkey, took a trip to the West Coast in late autumn of 1925 to set up a tournament schedule for the pros the following January and February.

Sharkey was the first tour manager, although not officially; there was nothing official about the tour in those days. To make that point even clearer, Sharkey didn't get paid for his work, which is why he arranged the tour just that one time, as a friend of the pros. He dickered a pro rate for hotel rooms and rail fares, got sponsors for a couple of tournaments, and also identified some problems that others would have to deal with. The tour would have to get a lot more professional if it was going to grow, and the opportunity for growth was there. The economy was strong in the

1920s, and resort hotels were proliferating in the South and Southwest. Furthermore, junior chambers of commerce were also getting involved, using the sponsorship of a pro tournament named after their city or town to publicize it as a resort, a place to vacation, settle down, or do business.

The first notable example of this marketing scheme in action was the Texas Open, held in San Antonio in 1923. The total purse was $5,000, the most money ever offered for a pro tournament; it was put up by the city's business community. There were seventeen money places, bonus money for lowest daily round, and course-record scores. All of this was not in keeping with the stoical tradition of golf as practiced by the eastern golf establishment, especially the attitude toward money. But this was Texas, and the sense of largesse always associated with Texans expanded golf's personality, giving it a broader, deeper aspect more fully reflective of the American character.

Jack O'Brien, a San Antonio sportswriter who helped promote the event, captured this new dimension when he called the Texas Open of 1923 a "gladsome giggle." He added, in his vernacular way, that the "prizes won't be cups, they're useless nowadays, but will be those silver discs produced at Mister Uncle Sam's factory. The king will be crowned with 1,500 cool iron men, place putting 750 smackerinos in his kick, the show entry bulging his wallet with 500 bucks." The old Scots game had never heard such language before, let alone understood it.

In 1926 the Los Angeles Junior Chamber of Commerce made an even grander splash by putting up a $10,000 purse for the first Los Angeles Open. This amount was so eye-catching it caught the fancy of nationally syndicated journalists such as Damon Runyon, who left his Times Square–Broadway beat and took the long train ride to the West Coast to see the pros play for what he would call "the moolah."

Through his pieces about the guys and dolls on New York's Great White Way, Runyon gave American popular culture such theatrical characters as Nathan Detroit, Sky Masterson, and Nicely-Nicely. In keeping with his style, Runyon also gave golf one of its earliest player handles. Harry Cooper won the 1926 L.A. Open (and a $3,500 check), and because he played so quickly, Runyon dubbed him "Lighthorse" Harry. The epithet stuck to Cooper for the rest of his long life in golf. In this small way, Runyon helped cut the ancient game a bit farther away from its conservative European mooring, giving it more of an American slant. There was

"Lighthorse" Harry, then "Slammin' " Sammy Snead, "Lord" Byron Nelson, "Bantam" Ben Hogan, and Ed "Porky" Oliver, among others.

Besides a big purse, the Los Angeles Open also gave the tour its first association with the burgeoning motion picture business, which had settled in Hollywood. A lot of movie stars were taking up golf themselves and they glittered up the gallery. Their presence on the scene increased newspaper coverage of the tournament. Richard Arlen, Harold Lloyd, and especially Bing Crosby became friendly with the pros. And when things got tough during the Great Depression, some of them helped raise purse money so their pals had something to play for. Crosby even founded a full-scale tournament that exists to this day. Golf's show business connection made in the 1920s has never gone away. It has just gotten stronger.

On the way to becoming a more organized operation, the pro tour took a significant leap forward when the PGA of America took control of the circuit in 1929. However, the association didn't pay all that much attention to the tour. Its main purpose was the well-being of club professionals, and the administrators of the association resented the greater public attention the tournament players received. There was a strained relationship between the two categories almost from the beginning of the PGA's involvement, and it grew more and more acrimonious over the years until the final break, in 1968.

However, when the PGA of America assumed responsibility for the tour, it gave the circuit the same sort of increase in status the association had gained for the club pros. The tour began to be seen as a legitimate sporting enterprise. But to really grow it would need smart promotion and more precise organization. It got both when Bob Harlow came on as the first official PGA tournament bureau manager, in 1929.

Harlow was a newspaperman by profession who in the early 1920s became Walter Hagen's business manager. Through his association with the celebrated Sir Walter, Harlow was well known in the golf world. To this was added his own considerable talent. Harlow, who was well educated and a sophisticated man of the world, made numerous good friends and connections that served him and the pro tour well as the Great Depression sank in and times got hard.

Harlow, the son of a Congregational pastor, was educated at Phillips Exeter and the University of Pennsylvania. He was well organized, articulate, a gourmet and gourmand who had an abiding interest in the theater—musical theater, in particular. Through his experience with the flamboyant Hagen, plus his own predilections, Harlow developed and expounded the notion that tournament golf was a form of show business. This was a new direction in a game played by men who generally were dour by nature or made so by the uncompromising game they played. The Ziegfeld of the Pro Tour, as Harlow was sometimes called, once remarked that "golfers cannot do their best playing to empty fairways any better than actors can give a fine performance to empty chairs."

When Harlow took on the tour manager's job, the circuit was in need of geographic organization, for starters. Until then, there would be a tourney in Los Angeles one week, the next week up in Sacramento, the next week back south in San Diego. Harlow fixed this, and other organizational aspects of the tournament circuit. He was particularly adroit in the production of events. He pre-set official starting times and pairings (players had been showing up when they felt like it and made up their own games—especially the star players) and got them published in the local newspapers so fans could plan their day at the course. Harlow used his newspaper background to persuade sports editors to list the standings in the tournament in order of merit starting with the leader. He had banners strung across the main streets of the tournament town plugging the event and had window-display cards placed in local stores and on the bulletin boards of every golf club within a hundred-mile radius. Slide photos of top players were shown in local movie houses and radio interviews were set up for the players. Harlow was responsible for instituting nuts and bolts that sound simple and obvious now, but were advances in his time.

Although he was correctly dubbed the Father of the PGA Tour, because of political and personal differences Harlow had a hot-and-cold relationship with the PGA of America. Mostly cold. He was on the side of the players—his "performers"—and that did not sit well with the resentful stay-at-home club pros and their leadership. The club pros detested the fact that equipment sold in their shops carried the names of headliner tour pros. Didn't they, who toiled every day in the shop and on the lesson tee, deserve as much or more recognition? Harlow could not reconcile with that point of view. (Neither could the tour pros, although they didn't say much at the time because for all of them, save Hagen and Sarazen, their club job was their main source of income.) Harlow was fired, rehired, and finally "retired" from the job. He went on to found *Golf World* magazine, the first weekly golf periodical, and would die in 1954 at sixty-five, after a severe head injury. (He walked into a beam while developing photographs for the magazine in a makeshift darkroom.)

When Harlow first came on as the manager of the PGA Tour, the total purse money for the year was approximately $70,000. In a year's time, Harlow got it up to $130,000, and the total would surely have continued to increase if not for the advent of the depression, in 1929. One way or another, the pro tour was beginning to catch on as a sports enterprise.

The Steel Shaft Further Grows the Game

Another equipment advance in the highly formative 1920s in American golf had as much impact on the game as Sarazen's wedge. That is, the steel shaft. For centuries golf clubs were fitted with wooden shafts, usually made of hickory. Like the first golf balls and wooden heads, the shafts were handmade. They required a degree of artisanship to make and a lot of grunt work. Each shaft had to be trimmed down from a long, thickish hunk of wood, then sanded to its final form and varnished. No matter how adept the craftsman, it was difficult to find two shafts with the same degree of flex and feel. It took Bobby Jones some ten years before he put together the set of clubs (meaning shafts, really) that he used to win most of his championships, including his celebrated Grand Slam of 1930.

The first known steel shaft was made in Scotland in 1893 by Thomas Horsburgh, a blacksmith. It was a solid steel rod only slightly more flexible than the average hickory shaft. Horsburgh received a patent for his shaft, but allowed it to expire because he could not get anyone interested in it. Probably because the shaft was too heavy.

After Horsburgh's shaft there were other efforts, one in 1910 by A. F. Knight, the same gentleman who gave us the center-shafted Schenectady putter. Knight's shaft was a tube of steel, which was getting closer to the final solution. In 1915 Allan Lard of Washington, D.C., was issued a patent on a perforated steel shaft. The perforations in the tube were meant to eliminate rotary motion or torque during the swing, not, as it would seem, to increase swing speed. Neither of these shafts got very far as the USGA and the R&A, which were beginning to get involved in the approval of equipment, resisted steel. No reason was given, because there wasn't one. It was new, and different, and was rejected. At first.

In the early 1920s a British fishing rod manufacturer called Apollo began making a viable, quality steel golf shaft. But of course, the R&A wouldn't approve it and golfers had to wait for events to unfold in America. And indeed, in the United States an individual's vitality, wits, and self-interest had an impact on history and led to the acceptance of steel shafts. In 1920 the Bristol Steel Company in Connecticut, also a fishing rod manufacturer (in the earliest days golf shafts were most often, and rather logically, products developed by the fishing rod manufacturers), devised a way to make a seamless steel golf shaft. This was a marked improvement over all the steel shafts preceding it, which were closed with a welded overlap. The Bristol closure gave the shaft more consistency in its playing characteristics and a sleeker and more attractive appearance.

Bristol put its new product under the direction of Harry Lagerblade, a one-time club professional who was wise to the politics of the American golf scene. Lagerblade knew that the Western Golf Association, based in Chicago, was at sharp odds with the USGA. The WGA was founded only four years after the USGA and ran a number of preeminent championships; the Western Open, inaugurated in 1899, was long considered a major national title, although it was never so noted. The WGA had always resented the USGA's dominant position in the game and considered it a "closed corporation," an elitist clique. It was especially put off by the way the USGA followed in seeming lockstep everything the R&A did. This attitude reflected a traditional midwestern American spitefulness toward the East Coast "establishment," but was also an expression of the region's isolationism in the aftermath of World War I.

In any case, Lagerblade perceived that the WGA might welcome his company's steel shaft as a way to tweak the USGA. He was right. Lagerblade arranged a test of the Bristol shaft in Chicago and invited WGA president Albert Gates to attend. On a cold, windy day in April, 1922 Chick Evans and Jock Hutchinson, who was a club pro in the Chicago area, hit balls with the shaft. They claimed there was no difference in respect to accuracy, distance, or steel's "ability to overcome a bad swing." However, the steel shaft would change the way the golf club was swung and for the better. That was down the road a bit. At the time of the test in Chicago, the main selling points for steel were of an economic nature; it was cheaper by far to produce than hickory, far more durable, made for a more consistent product—you could get dozens or hundreds with the exact same flexibility—and, last but not least, there was an increasing shortage of good hickory that would only get worse as the game's popularity grew.

WGA president Albert Gates put off final judgment on the Bristol shaft, citing the poor weather conditions. But after another test on a nicer day a month later, the WGA announced it would permit steel shafts in all its competitions. The USGA declared it was holding fast to its ban, but did allow steel shafts to be used in a few tournaments to assess them. The USGA appraisal took a couple of years, but in 1924 the organization approved the steel shaft for all its competitions, too.

Bobby Jones won all his championships with hickory, but was progressive enough to endorse steel when it came about. In fact, after retiring from competition, Jones became a consultant with the Spalding Company and designed a set of irons sold under his name that had steel shafts. However, to salve the feelings of traditionalists, these shafts were painted a bamboo color so they *appeared* to be made of wood. One way or another, the steel shaft became standard for golf clubs played in the U.S.

The R&A did not approve the steel shaft until 1929. When the Ryder Cup Match was played that year in England, the American players, all of whom had been playing with steel for at least four years, were required to go back to hickory. This was surely a factor in the U.S. loss of that match. Later that year, the R&A also finally gave in to modern times and approved steel shafts.

The Founding of the Ryder Cup

The Ryder Cup competition has always been heralded as a convocation of comrades in arms, a hands-across-the-sea celebration of the brotherhood of golf professionals. In fact, it began as kind of job action, like a union seeking to improve its workplace situation. There was also a bit of straightforward business implicated. According to Herb Graffis in *The PGA*, the official history of the PGA of America, the Ryder Cup was conceived by American-born professionals in an effort to gain more head professional jobs. The idea that a British-bred pro was better qualified for the post simply because he came from the cradle of the game still prevailed among many American club members. A British or Scots accent also lent a certain panache to the club, giving the impression that the club was steeped in the game's ancient culture.

Leaders of the PGA of America thought that if American-born pros could compete favorably against their British counterparts, their employers or potential employers might look more favorably upon them. As George Sargent, an influential U.S. club professional at the time, explained, "Too often, when American clubs need professionals they get lads from the old country, and we have been training very good American boys as pros. So, to show a strong offense as the best defense we . . . began the Ryder Cup Matches [which] stopped the idea that British golfers were easy superiors of American professionals."

The scheme didn't quite work, at first. The competition was initiated, informally, when a group of top American and émigré American pros traveled to Great Britain two weeks in advance of the 1921 British Open to play against a group of the best British pros. It was considered a warm-up for the Americans, a chance to get back their sea legs and stomachs in preparation for The Open. Most of the Americans' expenses were picked up by *Golf Illustrated* magazine, then published out of Chicago, as a way to increase circulation. One member of the American squad was Jock Hutchinson, who was Scots-born but by this time a permanent resident of the U.S. He was twice a runner-up in the U.S. Open, and when in 1921 he won the British Open it was the first time the prized trophy— the claret jug—traveled to the United States.

However, in the intercountry matches that year, the Americans "got slaughtered at Gleneagles," as Bill Mehlhorn, one of the American players, described the 9 to 3 loss. In a 1926 renewal of the still informal competition, once more in Great Britain, the U.S. was again slaughtered, 13½ to 1½. In the gallery for this competition was Samuel Ryder, an English seed merchant who was taking golf lessons from Abe Mitchell, the well-known British professional. Through Mitchell, Ryder was introduced to the British professional golf establishment, including George Duncan, who suggested that Ryder put up a trophy to encourage the continuation of the international competition. Ryder readily agreed. He commissioned and paid for the gold cup that bears his name and the golfing figure atop modeled after Abe Mitchell. It should be noted that Samuel Ryder was already selling some of his grass seed to golf courses in America, and after the match his firm began doing even more business in that direction.

It was not until the Ryder Cup became an official biennial competition that the American plan to enhance the prestige of its homebred pros began to bear fruit. In the first official Ryder Cup Match, played in Worcester, Massachusetts, in 1927, the U.S. defeated the British handily, 9½ to 2½ . The next time out in the home-and-home competition, the U.S. lost in Britain. The Yanks won at home in 1931, lost in Britain in 1933, then won nineteen of the next twenty-one matches. American-born golf professionals no longer had trouble getting the head pro jobs.

Because the Ryder Cup was meant to show off the competence of American pros, it was decreed that to be eligible for the American team, a player had to be born in the United States. (The British went along with the proviso and made it so that only those Britons born on the sceptered isle were eligible for their team.) This eligibility issue was mainly an American concern at the onset of the competition, and because of these rules, outstanding foreign-born players such as Tommy Armour (Scotland) and Harry Cooper (England) never represented the country in which they became citizens and made their golf careers. The rule was contrary to the immigrant history of the United States, and it was finally modified in the year 2000. Now anyone born abroad of American parents, or who becomes an American citizen before his eighteenth birthday, is eligible for the American team.

The Women's Way

It is peculiar that although women were often featured on the covers of the American golf magazines of the 1920s and earlier, not many American women actually played golf during the first quarter of the twentieth century. Those that did were given short shrift by the golf (read, male) establishment. Were the editors seeking to stimulate more interest in women's golf? Or was it a sop to women, so men would feel less guilty about spending many hours at the game while their wives waited for them at home? In almost every instance the representations of women on these covers were illustrations rather than photographs—drawings and paintings—and were generic women wearing billowy skirts down to their toes, flounced-sleeved blouses, and huge hats. Photographs of the best women players would have been available by the 1920s; most of these women were rather slim and attractive, and by this time wore casual clothes comfortable for golf. Instead the editors opted for idealized, romanticized, premodern depictions of women. Perhaps the editors and their readers were struggling with the problem of women athletes of any kind. It wasn't their place as *women*, was it? The question would dog women's golf through much of the century.

Despite these attitudes, some excellent women players arose in the early days of American golf. There was Alexa Stirling from Atlanta, who grew up learning and playing the game with Bobby Jones. But the best of the women during the early twentieth century was Glenna Collett, who was born into high society—as virtually all women golfers were at the time. Collett grew up in Providence, Rhode Island, was an excellent baseball player, took up tennis only because her mother felt it was more feminine than baseball, but finally settled on the game she wanted to play, which was golf.

Collett was a groundbreaker for women's golf; she made a full, very athletic and at the same time graceful swing at the ball. Women golfers until then were more conservative, to suit the mores of the day. A proper woman did not play athletics at full stretch any more than she let loose when dancing at a cotillion. Collett hit the ball with considerable power, however, and remarkable consistency. In 1924 she lost only one of her sixty matches—there was very little stroke-play competition, except for qualifying rounds. Finally, she was good-looking without being erotic, intelligent without being too brainy, and courteous to a fault. She had the makings of a much admired national champion, and that's exactly what Glenna Collett became—within a prescribed domain. She won six U.S. Women's Amateur Championships, the last in 1935, when she played as Glenna Collett Vare, the mother of two. During the final match of her last hurrah, Glenna defeated a teenage Patty Berg, who later became one of the great pioneers of women's professional golf.

One other woman golfer from the 1920s, Marion Hollins, must be mentioned. Hollins won the U.S. Women's Amateur in 1921, establishing herself as a competitive force in the game. But Hollins was the first "feminist" golfer long before the term was popularized. Her ideas about women in golf may have taken a toll on her tournament showings, but they also would reverberate much deeper into the fabric of the American game and the country's social structure.

Hollins was born into a wealthy Long Island, New York, family, and was involved in athletics very early—she was a tomboy. A fine horsewoman, she was one of the very few women to play polo at the time. Hollins had an eye for good form, physical and topographical. She conceived and designed one of the most famous and often photographed holes in golf, the sixteenth hole at Cypress Point Golf Club on the Monterey Peninsula on California's coast. The hole plays across an inlet of the Pacific Ocean, its green set on a kind of plateau just above a steep cliff that's pounded by the sea.

Hollins also founded the Pasatiempo Golf Club in Santa Cruz, California, widely considered one of the finest courses in the game. Although Alister MacKenzie was the official architect, Hollins had considerable input. In fact MacKenzie, who with Bobby Jones designed the Augusta National Golf Club course, home of the Masters tournament, was so confident in Hollins's eye for design that he sent her to Georgia to do some work on Jones's course when it was in its early stages of development.

But before her California days, Hollins made far more significant contributions to golf history. In 1924, three years after winning the United States Women's Amateur Championship, Hollins formed the Women's National Golf and Tennis Club, on Long Island, New York. It was the first, and to date the only, golf club organized by and for women. The club provided a place for a woman to join in her own name and play golf whenever she chose. This in a day when women were members of a private club only in their husband's name and had even more limited access to the facilities than they did at the end of the nineteenth century. An unmarried woman member was unheard of. These constraints on women golfers would persist through much of the twentieth century, although women did begin bringing suits to the courts of law against country clubs to achieve more equitable arrangements.

Hollins also hired the Englishman Ernest Jones to be the teaching professional at her club, thus introducing to American golf one of the most interesting, intelligent, and eloquent golf teachers ever.

Alas, just as Ernest Jones's teaching concept, "Swing the club head," never gained wide acceptance (as one grizzled club professional once put it, "It's too easy, it'll put us all out of business"), Hollins's golf club on Long Island was eventually, and shamefully, disbanded. Women's National operated independently for almost twenty years, until the onset of World War II, when it ran into financial difficulties and was merged with the exclusive men-only Creek Golf Club. At first, the gentlemen of the Creek, some of whom had wives who belonged to Women's National, followed through on a promise to the women that the two clubs would continue to operate independently. However, it wasn't long before that promise was broken. The president of the Creek was also president of Manufacturer's Trust, the bank that held the mortgage on all of the Creek's property, including Women's National. To get out of financial distress, he decided to pay off the mortgage by selling Women's National. End of story.

Marion Hollins had by this time moved to California, where she had created Pasatiempo and the sixteenth hole at Cypress. She would fall on hard times following a serious auto accident, and die in 1944 financially broke and mentally imbalanced as a result of the accident. Hollins was largely forgotten by the golf world in which she had been a progressive force, until David Outerbridge told her story in his 1998 book *Champion in a Man's World*.

Bobby and the Slam

For all the progress the pro tour had made up to 1930, the game's powerful elite—the country club set—still considered amateur golf to be the best expression of golf's essence. Competitive professional golf was not yet a totally respectable undertaking. Golf's baronial stroll along a manorial expanse of lawn didn't fit with making a living at it. Golf was for those who had already made it. Hagen's and Sarazen's gifts for the game were surely appreciated, but shouldn't this wonderful walk in the park be made for the love of it?

This was another reason why the feats of Bobby Jones were so exalted by the game's establishment. After "Chick" Evans and Francis Ouimet, no other golfer better exemplified the spirit of amateurism than Robert Tyre Jones, Jr., known universally as Bobby. Throughout his competitive career, right up to the completion of his Grand Slam in 1930, Jones adhered almost religiously to the amateur code. Except for 1926, when he felt beholden to defend his British Open title and paid his own expenses, he played in the British Open and Amateur only in the years when he was a member of the United States Walker Cup team. Then, his transportation to and from Great Britain and accommodations during the week of the competition were picked up by the USGA. Jones's father, an attorney, was a member of the East Lake Country Club in Atlanta, but not so wealthy that he could support his son's golf in the style of Jack Nicklaus, for example. (An executive with the MacGregor Golf Company who scouted Nicklaus all through his high school days said that Jack's father, Charlie, spent as much as $25,000 a year on his boy's golf; a lot of money in the 1950s, but obviously worth it.) Thus Bobby's entry into the 1930 British Amateur was especially important to him. He had not won the championship and had already made up his mind before the year began that this would be his last competitive campaign. He had a wife and children, and a law practice to develop to support them. Also, he was weary of the tension of competition and adulation.

Normally, anyone who is as hugely successful as Jones playing at the highest competitive level spends hours upon days upon weeks and months at a time practicing and playing. Thus, it is all the more a measure of Jones's enormous talent that he was not a ball-beating practice range "rat," and he did not play all that much competitive golf when he was in his prime—from 1923 to 1930. He played in only twenty-four full-fledged tournaments, excluding the Walker Cup matches, and perhaps ten exhibition matches. He won fifteen of those tournaments, thirteen of which were national championships (four U.S. Opens, five U.S. Amateurs, three British Opens, and one British Amateur). In 1928, the year he finished second in the U.S. Open and won the U.S. Amateur, Jones also passed the Georgia bar exam after only two years of law school. Even before 1923, he only played in the Southern and Georgia Amateur tournaments a few times, in one Canadian Open, and only twice in the Western Amateur, a very prestigious event. Jones never played in the North and South Amateur, another distinguished championship. Except for a few appearances at pro tour events, Jones only played against the pros in the U.S. Open. Yet, in his last eight U.S. Open appearances, he won four times and was runner-up three times. He also won three British Opens. This impressive record is why the pros of Bobby's time had such tremendous respect for him. They also liked him as a person.

Jones was the perfect combination of superior golf ability and unpretentious gentility. Walter Hagen, a son of the laboring class, reinvented himself as a stagy depiction of nobility. Gene Sarazen, who had the same economic and social background, dressed in finely styled clothes, and through his wife and the educated friends he made after he became a celebrity golfer, developed a certain sophistication. But Sarazen still unmistakably exuded the tough little street fighter, just as closer observers knew Hagen was a kind of social hustler.

Jones, though, was true to his genteel Old South background. He spoke in a slow, soft drawl, in long and well-crafted sentences, and he was modest about his accomplishments and always complimentary of his opponents. His golf swing mirrored his public personality. It was a sweeping, rhythmic motion that made the sport look easy, as is so often the case with superlative athletes. Beneath the exterior, of course, Jones was as anxious as anyone who tries to play golf well, especially those who play at the highest competitive level and in front of big audiences. He would lose as much as eighteen pounds during the week of a tournament because of tension, lack of appetite, and inability to keep food down. He countered the emotional tension with his innate ability to play outstanding golf. Jones also survived the pressure via the more prosaic comforts of whiskey—or "corn," as it was called in southern patois. During a tournament, Jones would have at least one hearty whiskey every day while taking a warm predinner bath. Then another after dinner. Perhaps two. He grew up in an alcohol-oriented culture and took part in it without compunction.

Jones came onto the national golfing scene as a fourteen-year-old entrant in the 1916 U.S. Amateur Championship. He arrived with a reputation as a phenomenon, but left better known as a kid with a petulant temper. He did not shake that reputation until after he had picked up his ball and quit playing in the middle of his third round in the 1921 British Open. He had gone out in 47, then double-bogeyed the tenth hole. Jones was so embarrassed at having quit a competition in such an uncivil way that he vowed to control his emotions. That's when he hit the high road to greatness.

Jones's greatest season, of course, was his last, in 1930, when he won the Grand Slam. The Grand Slam championships at the time were the British and U.S. Opens and Amateur championships. To win all four in one season was a prodigious achievement not only because Jones topped the pros in the Opens, but because the two Amateurs were won at match-play. This format gives a mediocre player the chance to knock out a superior player if he's having the day of his life and the latter is a bit off. (Arnold Palmer said the toughest victory in his career was the U.S. Amateur, for that reason—anything can happen in an eighteen-hole match.)

Moreover, Jones had to screw his mind to the task over a period of approximately three months, with at least a three-week break between each segment of the Slam. Then again, the time between each championship could well have been fortunate, giving Jones time to recharge for the next foray. One way or the other, Jones's multiple victories were a stunning feat.

It is conventional to say that Jones's Grand Slam was just the right thing to ease the pain of the Great Depression, which began with the stock market crash of October, 1929. However, economics historians have said that the crash of 1929 didn't register as a widespread problem until about twelve months after it happened. Despite the few who reportedly dived from skyscraper windows to land on the pavement of Wall Street, the crash was thought to be just another one of those downturns that happen periodically in a free market. Still, this Bobby fellow (he never liked the diminutive, preferring Bob) with the supple swing and cool manners winning four championships in one season was a refreshing fillip for the general public. He was rewarded with a ticker-tape parade up Broadway, in New York City, after the third leg of the Slam.

Jones also benefited financially from the distinction he acquired through his golf game. In 1932 the Spalding Sporting Goods Company brought out a line of Bobby Jones Signature golf clubs—both irons and woods. Jones had considerable input in their design and received a royalty for each club sold. Even in the depths of the depression they sold well. Jones also was well compensated for a series of instructional movies about golf technique that were filmed in Hollywood, and he wrote at least one best-selling instructional book. In other words, Bobby Jones became a golf professional the moment he quit playing amateur tournament golf. The only competition Jones entered after 1930 was his own tournament, the Masters, in which he competed as an amateur—an anomaly that will be addressed later.

The period from 1900 through 1929 in American golf was remarkably rich in inventive energy and infinite creativity. So many foundation blocks were set in place upon which the game would grow—or *could* grow, actually. Just as the nation as a whole was defining its New World character, so was the game of golf. A combination of industrial or mechanical or engineering ingenuity and a willingness to gamble on talent and nerve won out against the Old World constraints. To use a theatrical analogy that Bob Harlow would have appreciated, American golf had a knockout first act. It kept everybody in their seats, interested in how the play would come out.

2 | 1931–1949: The American Character at Golf

The PGA Tour Survives; Snead, Nelson, and Hogan Emerge as the First Great American Triumvirate; The Masters and the First Women's Pro Tour Are Born; Lord Byron's Phenomenal Streak

When Wall Street crashed in 1929, purses on the pro tour naturally plummeted with it. The Los Angeles Open cut its once biggest-ever purse by half, to $5,000. A number of tournaments shut down altogether, and many of those that stuck with it dropped their purses from the standard $5,000 to only $2,500. Or less. Joe Turnesa won the Miami Open but earned only $400 out of a purse gathered together from players' entry fees ($5 apiece), gate receipts, and a $500 contribution by a local hotel group. For the 1932 Los Angeles Open, the $5,000 total purse was guaranteed by the actor Richard Arlen. It was a wonder there was any tour at all. That there was is a testament to the lure of the game. It is also a measure of how important the resourceful, dogged Bob Harlow was to the tour, as was the man who replaced him as manager of the tour, the imaginative publicist and promoter Fred Corcoran.

It is very often the case that the most creative and effective achievements come out of a situation in which there is little money to work with. This is true in the arts and in business. In the struggle to survive on limited resources, either out of desperation or mad hunger, some of the best ideas are generated, along with the verve to push them through. So it was with the PGA Tour and its clever manager, Bob Harlow. An example: In 1932, as the breadlines got longer and longer, Harlow saw an opportunity. Henry Doherty, head of Cities Service Utilities and owner of the huge Miami-Biltmore Hotel, was having serious federal tax problems. One of his aides, Garry Hammond, along with Harlow and Carl Byoir, a publicity and public relations trailblazer, made a connection with the Warm Springs, Georgia, town fathers. Warm Springs, a small resort town noted for its reputedly healing waters, had become President Franklin D. Roosevelt's getaway. He went there often, hoping to cure the polio that had crippled him. The owners of the Warm Springs Spa were in need of money to modernize and expand; after all, the most famous man in the country was their regular guest. Hammond and Harlow got the idea that if Doherty put on a big golf tournament with a healthy purse, perhaps $10,000, and turned the profits over to the Warm Springs folks, some nice things might come out of it. Such as an easing of Doherty's tax problems.

Everything went according to plan. But the outcome went far beyond easing a rich man's tax troubles. The Miami-Biltmore Open helped kick off the March of Dimes campaign, which Roosevelt founded to raise funds for researching a cure for polio—which was eventually achieved. What's more, most of the people who helped make the tournament possible were women who volunteered their services in the fight against a dread disease. In this, a foundation stone of the tournament circuit was hammered into position. Two stones, actually. Tournament sponsors learned that they could put on their events without having to pay taxes on the profits, *if the profits were donated to a charity*. They also realized that through the use of volunteer labor, the profits were going to be greater.

A PGA tournament is a hard dollar if it is run like an ordinary business; that is, paying for all the help, and paying taxes on the profits. By avoiding those two prime cost factors, the PGA Tour grew into a multimillion-dollar enterprise by the end of the twentieth century. And it all started with a deal to get a rich man out of his tax bill. A fair trade-off, don't you think?

However, Harlow was fired from his job as manager of the tour before the Miami-Biltmore Open took place. He just couldn't get along with George Jacobus, a gruff, unsophisticated, and willful man who was president of the PGA of America at the time. Fred Corcoran came on in Harlow's place, but the circuit didn't suffer from the switch. Not at all. Corcoran was not as imperious in style as Harlow. He came from a tough Irish section of Boston—his roots were "Shanty Irish"—and he knew how to do politics. He had a long and quite successful run in the job.

Corcoran was often mistaken for an ex-newspaperman. He did have the temperament of an ink-stained wretch that the real ones warmed to and a knack for coming up with the angles and stories that he knew the newsies were always looking for. Corcoran also displayed a gift for promotional stunts. One publicity-gathering scheme was an exhibition round of golf featuring Gene Sarazen and Jimmy Demaret; the quondam heavyweight boxing champs and rivals, Jack Dempsey and Gene Tunney; and Fred Waring's big orchestra and chorus. The four sports stars golfed while Waring's group played and sang popular music. A kind of rhapsody in the rough. The idea was to prove that golf didn't have to be a hush-hush game—all quiet on the fairways while the players contemplated and hit their shots. Some five thousand spectators showed up for the Music Match, in Norwalk, Connecticut, which garnered a lot of newspaper coverage. (By the way, Demaret and Sarazen shot 70 and 71 respectively while the band played on.)

Another time, Corcoran booked Sam Snead into Wrigley Field, where the Slammer hit a golf ball over the scoreboard high atop the back of the bleachers in dead center field. The distance was easy to cover in golf terms, but most people didn't know that and were amazed. Interestingly, in the 1990s the super-long ball hitter John Daly made a television commercial in which he hit a golf ball out of a ballpark. Freddie Corcoran was well in the vanguard on that one.

The American pro tour was the first of its kind in golf, in which tournaments were held in every region of the country and the golfers paid their own way, surviving on their competitive ability and the paychecks that their play brought in. No professional athletes had ever gone so naked into competition, without the security blanket of a contract guaranteeing some income. The tour evoked a favorite and not altogether inaccurate perception of the all-American hero. The touring pro was a hardy, intrepid individualist, the solitary gunfighter taking on the world with naught but his own nerve and talent. A pure capitalist entrepreneur.

The invention of the automobile helped support this image. By the 1930s Henry Ford's revolutionary production line method made the car accessible to all but the poorest Americans, and it became one of our most passionate symbols of personal independence. A man could get in his Ford or Dodge or LaSalle and drive off whenever and to wherever he pleased. In real life, most people weren't that free; their cars just gave them the sense that such liberty was possible. As the tour grew, and it was possible to make a living solely at playing tournament golf, the tour pro became an even more quixotic figure on the American social landscape. He was on the road in his horse of steel, chasing at once the windmill of golf—the impossible-to-conquer game—and a living.

A rich tapestry of golf lore came from these Dust Bowl days—tales about droll characters and travel on the pocky two-lane highways of the American South and Southwest. Sam Parks, Jr., dark horse winner of the 1935 U.S. Open, remembered driving from one tournament site to the next one through dead-flat west Texas at night and turning off his headlights for a moment or two to look into the distance for the glare of a town where he might get a cup of joe and a sandwich, gas up, rest his eyes. Ky Laffoon, one of the lustier golf personalities of the era, recalled having breakfast one morning in Los Angeles with Byron Nelson, who was making his first West Coast tournament swing—in a Model-T Ford. "Byron wanted some potatoes like I had on my plate. When he found out they cost an extra quarter, he decided to go without." Nelson netted a grand total of $12.50 on that 1932 run. Not even small potatoes.

And yet, although the nation was diving into its deepest economic abyss, the 1932 PGA Tour was worth an all-time annual high: $130,000 in total purse money. Bob Harlow even talked about the tour becoming a full-time, year-round circuit. Such optimism was remarkable given the country's economic circumstances; again, a tribute to golf's pull. The game has always seemed to find someone of influence, and funds, to keep it alive and help it grow. That someone was inevitably a person who had been seized by the captivating nature of the game.

For example, President Roosevelt had tremendous personal influence on golf in America, as has been remarked on. During the Great Depression, the Works Progress Administration (WPA), one of Roosevelt's most popular and effective New Deal programs to get citizens on a payroll, planned to spend some $10.5 million on new public golf courses and the improvement of existing ones. Approximately six hundred new courses were planned. Although not nearly that many were built, a good number were completed, and many of these courses are still in operation as state- or county-operated facilities.

The Birth of the Masters

Bobby Jones wasn't a missionary out to win the Grand Slam in order to recharge a national psyche that had fallen on hard times. The achievement brought Jones a level of acclaim and veneration that made possible the creation of two eventual icons of American—indeed world—golf, the Augusta National Golf Club, and the Masters tournament which is played there.

The story of how the Augusta National Golf Club was formed is definitely germane to the tale of the Masters tournament, but not critical enough for us to get overly involved with the machinations and intrigues of its inner workings. It is the Masters tournament that is our primary interest here, for it has had a deep impact on the game of golf and everyone who plays it, even the average golfer who has never seen the inside of such an exclusive golf club and probably never will.

The story begins with Jones's desire, after he retired from competition in 1930, to create a first-rate golf course on which important competitions would be played. He especially had his eye on the U.S. Open and the U.S. Amateur Championships, neither of which had ever been played in the South. Jones's partner in the project was Clifford Roberts, a Wall Street stockbroker. They decided to build the club in Augusta, Georgia, a small city on the South Carolina border, about 135 miles due east of Atlanta. Atlanta seemed the more likely site: It was Jones's hometown and a bigger city with a considerably larger number of potential members to solicit. But Roberts had in mind a national membership, or at least one composed of New Yorkers and Bostonians, who would use the club as a springtime getaway. The cost of the property was a consideration, too; the club was being formed in the midst of the Great Depression. The price was right for a one-time nursery in Augusta, and Jones agreed on it.

Land costs aside, Augusta possessed other features attractive to Jones. One, its relative seclusion. Jones was anxious to stay clear of the madding crowd after his highly celebrated competitive career. He never really enjoyed the fawning and pawing he experienced as a star. He lived and worked in Atlanta, therefore Augusta could be a quiet and accessible getaway for him. Then, too, Jones's wife was from Augusta.

The property itself was difficult to resist. Jones remarked upon first sight of the rolling terrain that it was already a golf course; it only needed to be mowed and have the holes cut. To the great disappointment of Donald Ross, the acknowledged master golf architect of the day, Alister MacKenzie was chosen to design the course. (Jones would be a very close collaborator.) MacKenzie's gorgeous Cypress Point layout, right by the

Pacific Ocean on the Monterey Peninsula, completed in 1928, was what sold Jones.

Jones meant for his course to be inspired by the links of Scotland, specifically the Old Course at St. Andrews, which he revered. Inspired by, but not physically replicated. The terrain on which Augusta National is built is exceptionally hilly, while true links are almost by definition dead flat. Augusta's greens are extremely undulated, while the putting surfaces on true links are lumpy at most. Augusta had no rough (until 1999, and then only a smidgen), while true links have vast swaths of tangled gorse, whins, and heather. And of course, Augusta has many imposing trees whereas links courses have nary a one. The St. Andrews aspect, it would seem, had to come simply from Jones saying so. That would become the abiding disposition at Augusta National and the Masters, which the tempestuous Tommy Bolt once said "made up its own rules."

Although the golf course drew almost unanimous rave reviews when it opened, no doubt inspired by the great respect everyone felt for Bobby, Gene Sarazen, as bluntly honest as always even into his ninety-seventh and last year, remembered that the original course "was a terrible layout." Jones never said as much publicly, but if anyone had dared to press him, he might have conceded that his course became the Chartres Cathedral of golf only after many changes, alterations, and modifications over the many years. For instance, the original sixteenth hole was a 145-yard par-three with a small, humpy green set just behind a narrow ditch—a far cry from the photogenic hole it became after being redesigned by Jones and Robert Trent Jones, Sr., in the 1940s.

Jones's hope of staging a U.S. Open or Amateur at Augusta National Golf Club proved impossible. They were played in June and August or September, respectively, when golfers had had enough play in the year to get their games to peak. The course would not have been in good enough condition for such championships owing to the heat at that time of year and its effect on the grass.

Cliff Roberts would have liked those two championships to be played at Augusta National, but he badly wanted any tournament with top players for the same reason chambers of commerce and resort hotels wanted them—as a selling tool. The publicity would hopefully generate sales of memberships to the club. Roberts was having trouble in this department in 1931, because the depression was affecting even the well-to-do businessmen he was courting as members. (It is interesting, in light of how self-contained and exclusive the club became eventually, that the original plan was for a membership of 1,800, with two golf courses, tennis courts, and residential homes along the fairways; that is, the upscale gated golf and residential community that became prevalent beginning in the 1970s.)

Once the course was in place, Roberts took over the administration of the club and the tournament. Jones would always have more than just a hand in changes to the course, and was involved in the basic competitive workings of the tournament, but he seemed by temperament unwilling or uninterested in the day-to-day details that make any organization or enterprise function. Besides, he had a law practice and children to raise. Then, as the illness—syringomyelia, a spinal disease—developed that would make the last twenty or so years of life a misery for him, Jones became even less involved.

Roberts was not married when the club was organized, and although he eventually had three wives, none of the marriages produced children and were, by all accounts, cold affairs. The Augusta National Golf Club and the Masters tournament were his bride and progeny. He was not merely a doting husband and father, however, he was an obsessed and exceptionally autocratic lord and master.

Jones and Roberts made an odd, antithetical pairing. Jones was a son of the antebellum South, with a soft drawl and a gentlemanly manner couched in, or perhaps coached to, dispense selfless modesty. He had a taste for ribaldry, but only when among friends and in private. He was an excellent writer, as his autobiography and golf instruction books reveal, and he had a deep interest in literature and opera.

Roberts was a hard-nosed man from a far less sophisticated background. His father was a restive small-time capitalist who was, at various times, a farmer, shopkeeper, restaurant owner, and land speculator. He moved his family with disconcerting regularity between Iowa, Kansas, Texas, and Oklahoma. Although he was sometimes in the money, most often he was not. Roberts's mother was a suicide—possibly because she could no longer take the helter-skelter lifestyle her husband provided. Clifford, who was the second of five children, quit school at sixteen after finishing the ninth grade in order to help with the family finances. He scraped his way up in the world as a traveling salesman, oil-lease speculator, and eventually a stockbroker. He had a haunting capacity for work and for giving his undivided attention to business and all the related minutiae. He could be as obliging as any fawning salesman trying to close a deal, which surely helped him cultivate the men of wealth and influence he was after to join Augusta National.

However, after Roberts worked himself into a position of power and his club became successful, he was a tyrannical and humorless autocrat. In the beginning Roberts depended heavily on the city of Augusta, which gave him a tax advantage, helped promote the Masters, and provided some members. But after the club became successful, he referred to Augusta as a hick town and had little to nothing to do with it, or for it. Roberts was also a celebrity hound. He worshiped his partner, Emperor Jones, and at least in the earliest days of their relationship was proud that he had established a personal and business relationship with one of the greatest sports figures of all time. Getting President Eisenhower to join Augusta National was *the* coup of all Roberts's personal coups.

In order to shape the Masters into what has become a kind of liturgical observance as much as a mere golf tournament, Roberts played the Jones card completely. It was all he had to work with. No one was going to join a golf club tucked away in a small southern town because of Roberts's name. Those who joined, or helped financially, did so because of Bobby, which was also why the pros were enticed to play in the tournament. Only for Bobby would they make the trip to this out-of-the-way town to play for a small purse—the total purse for the inaugural Masters was only $7,125—with only twelve money places (sixteen places had become the norm by 1934). From the first year through the 1942 tournament, by which time the depression was easing off and a number of tour events had gotten up to an average $7,500 total purse, the Masters paid out only $5,000.

Roberts made some smart moves to curry the favor of the pros, Jones's lure aside. He called the event an invitational, even though every player of note, and some half-notes, got an invite. Still, getting an actual invitation gave the event a special cachet. Roberts also saw that the pros were treated well, with a kind of deference not accorded them at ordinary stops on the tour or even at their own clubs. For a week the pros were made to feel like members of Augusta National Golf Club. It felt good.

Roberts also took a note from Bob Harlow's book and cared for the press as carefully as the players. The journalists were fed free lunch and drinks and given access to the clubhouse, this fine garden of a golf course, and Bobby Jones himself. Flowery copy flowed after such hospitality.

Finally, Roberts implored Jones to compete in the Masters. Jones was not interested at first, feeling he had been away from competition too long and would be unable to perform at anything near his old standards. Roberts convinced him it would help generate much-needed press coverage, which would help the tournament and, even more important, the club. He was right, of course. Jones complied with Roberts, and his return to the list of competitors was big news. In time Jones came to more or less enjoy playing at the Masters, although his best performance was his first time out, in 1934, when he tied with Walter Hagen and Denny Shute for thirteenth with a 6-over par 294. During that competition, his best single round was a 72, which would be the best round he'd shoot over the total of twelve Masters tournaments in which he played. Although Jones was unquestionably the major factor in establishing the Masters, the event didn't really take hold until television cast its eye upon it, starting in the 1950s.

Women Professionals? Why Not?

In the excitement of the Roaring Twenties, women were freed of some of the old Victorian social strictures—dresses got shorter, cigarettes were smoked, and liquor drunk openly and even lasciviously. And in that era arose the first women golf professionals. They included Bessie Fenn, May Dunn, and Helen MacDonald, who turned pro in 1924 and taught golf in an indoor studio in Chicago. Women were not permitted to join the PGA of America then, and none of the pioneering women pros ever had jobs in the pro shops of private clubs, but they persevered.

MacDonald was the first woman to sign on with a major equipment manufacturer, Hillerich & Bradsby. The first woman professional to go on the road promoting a manufacturer's equipment and giving golf clinics was Helen Hicks, in the late 1930s. She worked for the Wilson Sporting Goods Company, which would become the most supportive of the equipment companies in women's golf. Then came Opal Hill, Helen Dettweiler, and Patty Berg; the last became the most prolific and dynamic espouser of women's golf.

Women's professional golf got a tremendous boost when Mildred

"Babe" Didrikson, considered the greatest woman athlete at the time, decided to take up the game. Her decision was made only a day or two after she had earned world-wide acclaim for her performance in the 1932 Olympic Games in Los Angeles. Didrikson set new women's records in the javelin throw and the high hurdles, and if she hadn't been restricted to participating in no more than three sports, she might well have set records in other categories. In the National Amateur Athletic Union track-and-field championships, two weeks before the Olympic Games, Didrikson won the javelin and baseball throws, the shot put, broad jump, and eighty-meter hurdles. She tied for first in the high jump, and came in fourth place in the discus event. Elsewhere, the lean young woman from Port Arthur, Texas, had shown herself to be an excellent basketball and baseball player, as well as an accomplished swimmer and diver, bowler, and tennis player.

Didrikson, legend has it, played her first round of golf the day after the Olympics ended. She said she had hit some golf balls before at a driving range, but had never played a hole. Perhaps, although Babe was known for self-aggrandizing exaggeration. In any case, Grantland Rice, the doyen of American sportswriters in the first third of the century, told all his press box pals that this Didrikson girl could really hit a golf ball.

The next day, in the company of Rice, Paul Gallico, and Braven Dyer, all well-seasoned and nationally known sportswriters, Babe proved Rice right. She showed considerable power off the tee, which surprised no one, and while her ability to score was not there yet, it was clear to one and all that in hardly any time she would be carding sub-par rounds.

The Wilson Sporting Goods Company was making a big push to get women involved in golf, and in 1934 Didrikson signed a contract with the firm, which then set up an extensive exhibition tour for her and Gene Sarazen, the star of Wilson's professional advisory staff. The tour was a great success, if only because everyone wanted to see the sensation of the Olympic Games, and Didrikson gave a show. She was quite a ham, loved a crowd, and had an earthy sense of humor. Once, after hitting a powerful drive that drew raves from the crowd, Babe rubbed her chest and said that if she didn't have "these," she could have hit it twenty yards farther. Nonsense, of course, but good show biz.

Didrikson was popular, and her exhibitions with Sarazen drew sizable crowds. Nonetheless, women's professional golf didn't take much of a hold on the sporting public in the 1930s. There were very few tournaments for them to play, and those that were staged offered little, and often no, prize money. Helen Dettweiler won the 1939 Western Open playing as a pro, and she got only a silver bowl for her trouble. When Patty Berg won the same title, in 1941, she took home a check for $100, the first prize money ever given to a woman golfer by the Western Golf Association.

In the face of this slim compensation, Berg and Didrikson—who became Didrikson Zaharias in 1938, when she married professional wrestler George Zaharias—led the way to the 1949 formation of the Ladies' Professional Golf Association. The LPGA superseded the Women's Professional Golf Association, formed by Hope Seignious, Betty Hicks, and Ellen Griffin in 1944. The WPGA initiated a winter tournament circuit in 1945 and created a teaching division, but the organization foundered because of poor management. Seignious, Hicks, and Griffin ran the WPGA's day-to-day affairs and tried to play competitive golf at the same time. It didn't work.

Berg and Zaharias took a better approach by enlisting the financial backing of L. B. Icely, president of Wilson Sporting Goods. Icely hired Fred Corcoran, who had departed from the PGA Tour, as the LPGA's executive director. It was Corcoran's idea to change the term "women" to "ladies," which feminists fifty years later would claim pandered to nineteenth-century attitudes toward women. In fact, Corcoran changed it to avoid a lawsuit with the WPGA.

The Wilson Sporting Goods Company and the Golf Manufacturers Association put thousands of dollars into a prize fund for which the women could play. The tournament schedule gradually grew, but the money compared to the men's tour was minuscule. LPGA historian Liz Kahn once reckoned the ratio in purse money between women and men professionals in the 1940s was $1 to $28. It was a start, though, and in time the LPGA, the first enduring organization of women golf professionals, would be playing for millions.

Slammin' Sam Captures Our Fancy

In January, 1937, the men's pro tour and American golf had another super-talented player and uncommon personality who would propel the game further into the public's consciousness. He was Samuel Jackson

Snead, out of Hot Springs, Virginia. A remarkably gifted athlete who swung the club with balletic elegance, Snead also hit the ball with imposing power. He instantly became one of the longest hitters on the circuit—the Tiger Woods or John Daly of his time. The combination of power and rhythm of motion was irresistible. This, in turn, was coupled with a personality that charmed the crowd. Snead was seen as a guileless country boy, an innocent abroad. This perception—which was not entirely authentic—was set loose by Fred Corcoran, who cleverly picked up on an incident at the very outset of Snead's career that may not have happened as Corcoran retailed it, but worked for promotional purposes.

Snead won his second event on the 1937 winter circuit, the Oakland (California) Open. When he was told that his picture had appeared the next day in the *New York Times*, Snead wondered aloud how that could be since he had never been to New York City. That was how Corcoran told the tale to everyone drawing breath. Snead was immediately and for all time pigeonholed as a kind of colorful, simple-minded bumpkin.

Snead was anything but simple-minded and bumpkin wasn't right, either. He was suspicious of strangers as is customary of people who grow up in mountain enclaves, and he was a shrewd investor of his money. When reminded many years later about the picture-in-the-*Times* story, Snead said with a sly grin that he wasn't that dumb, but let it go out because it made a good story. The story did reflect Snead's real-life sense of humor, and his way with a tale or joke. He was always a superb storyteller in the mountain man tradition.

Snead also became known as a tightwad who kept his money in tomato cans buried in his backyard. He also let those fables go on, again because they made good copy. In fact, George Low, the putting wizard who sometimes traveled with Snead, recalled that Snead more than once signed a blank check for Ed "Porky" Oliver, a rotund tour pro from the forties and fifties who had a gambling and drinking habit. As Low put it, "Every once in awhile when Porky got into trouble, Sam would sign a check without any numbers filled in. He'd tell Porky to try and keep it under five. Meaning five thou."

Snead the personality would have been only an interesting amusement if he wasn't such an outstanding golfer. After winning in Oakland in 1937, his first official PGA Tour victory, Snead played the next week in the inaugural of a tournament sponsored by Bing Crosby, who was himself an ardent and good golfer. Snead won the tournament, which was further proof of his ability, but the victory also had wider implications.

Hollywood actors and producers had helped the tour with donations of purse money before Crosby's involvement, but the crooner's commitment was of more substance. His Crosby Pro-Am was intended to be an annual affair, and indeed it has been on the schedule every year since its inception (except during World War II). It moved from the San Diego area up to Pebble Beach, California, in 1947, and since 1986 has been called the AT&T Pebble Beach National Pro-Am, but old-timers still call it the Crosby.

Again, American golf was fertilized by an individual's passion for the game. Crosby deeply loved golf (coincidentally, he died on a Spanish golf course in the 1970s). His tournament featured many show business personalities at the beginning, as it does to this day, who gave the tournament a more popular cachet than any chamber of commerce or resort hotel could possibly match. The timing of the Crosby and his movie stars with the coming of Slammin' Sammy Snead was most judicious. With his Virginia drawl and the stories Corcoran was passing along about him, Snead was a character professional entertainers appreciated. And there was the fluid power of his game. Sam Snead hitting a golf ball was a mesmerizing combination of Fred Astaire's glissando dancing and John Wayne's overhand right to the jaw. He was good box office.

In 1938 Snead won eight tournaments and was the leading money winner on the tour, earning a total of $19,534. This was considered a phenomenal amount of money, and many of his fellow pros predicted such a large amount would never be reached again. When you're in the trenches you can lose sight of the war's big picture. Purses would continue to climb, of course, and Sam Snead had a lot to do with that escalation.

The history of sports in the United States has shown that a single outstanding player can raise a game high in the consciousness of the public. American golf during this time was triply lucky in this regard. In the mid-1930s it had Snead and Byron Nelson. Then Ben Hogan in the early 1940s, when he got his game together. All three were born in the same year, 1912.

"Lord" Byron, the Streak King

Nelson's appeal did not include a sparkling or unusual personality. Byron was simply a great player, amazingly accurate, incredibly consistent.

Also, at six feet, Nelson was tall for his time in golf, and this too was a distinguishing component.

Byron (actually, John Byron) Nelson was born and raised in Fort Worth, Texas. His family had a small grain business, and although Nelson was certainly not a rich kid, he did have an economic advantage as a youth over Ben Hogan, also from Fort Worth, whose family struggled from day to day. The two were caddies together at the Glen Garden Country Club in Fort Worth. Nelson's quicker ascent up the golf ladder may have been because he was an open, chatty, and courteous youngster, whereas Hogan was quiet, if not sullen. The fact that Hogan's father was a suicide must surely have contributed to his social reticence.

When Nelson was a teenage golfing phenom, he was welcomed and helped along by the local gentry, whereas Hogan had to fend for himself. But all that aside, the main reason Nelson matured as a player early on was that he simply had a natural gift for the game. Nelson, like Hogan and many others from their milieu, was not of sufficient means to make any sort of campaign as an amateur golfer. He turned pro when the depression was close to its nadir. He recounted how it happened in *Gettin' to the Dance Floor*:

Ted Longworth [the Glen Garden head pro who helped Nelson begin his golf career] started a tournament in Texarkana, where he was head pro. The total prize money was $500, and there's people playing in it like Dick Metz and Ky Laffoon. I rode a bus over there from Fort Worth, carrying my little Sunday bag and a suitcase, paid my $5 entry fee, and played in my first tournament as a pro. That was November 22, 1932. In that day and time all you had to do was go pay your entry and say you were playing as a pro, and you were a pro.

Well, I finished third and won $75. Boy, did that encourage me. The next spring...I got a telephone call from Ted Longworth. He said, "Byron, I know you don't have much experience, and it's not much of a job over here, but I think I can get it for you." Head pro at Texarkana Country Club....So I went over there. I made about $60 a month at the start. That's not salary, it's what I made from my lessons and so on...Very seldom did anybody come to the club before noon on any day, so I had an excellent practice field and I'd hit balls. I'd hit 'em down there and go down and hit 'em back. I didn't need anybody to shag for me, although there wasn't anybody to shag anyway. So I got better and better.

Yes. The final element in the mix that made Nelson a great player was the remaking of his swing to adapt to the steel shaft. He is credited with creating the steel-shaft golf swing. Nelson grew up playing hickory shafts, like everyone else of his generation, and he had a swing to suit the material. A hickory shaft in the moment before impact with a driver bowed close to a U-shape. Therefore, the club was swung on a longer arc or path and around the body. The hands had to be very active in order to square the club face to the target at impact, and there was considerable pronation and supination during the swing. That is, in the backswing the hands rotated so the palm of the right hand faced up in the backswing (supination), and downward in the forward swing (pronation). The flexibility of the hickory shaft also required a very smooth, deliberate turn of the body. It was very much like what is required today when swinging the lighter (compared to steel) graphite shaft.

Consistency was hard to come by when swinging a hickory shaft, even for the finest of players. The margin for error was huge. Nelson realized that with steel, he didn't have to supinate and pronate. A less "handsy" swing produced greater consistency. The club could also be swung on a more upright path or plane, which made for more precise ball-first contact with the irons. Indeed, Nelson became the archetype for precision iron play. The most dramatic example of this came in a play-off for the 1939 U.S. Open against Craig Wood and Denny Shute. Nelson holed a one-iron second shot on the par-four fourth hole for an eagle. The shot propelled him to his one U.S. Open title and secured his reputation for accuracy.

Nelson's ultimate achievement in golf came in 1945, when he had a winning streak that may never be broken, or even equaled. He won eleven straight tournaments. The length of the streak can be quibbled about. In the first one, the Miami International Four-Ball, Nelson had a partner, Harold "Jug" McSpaden, a fine golfer who certainly helped in the victory. Also, many top players, such as Ben Hogan and Jimmy Demaret, were serving in the military and only entered two of the events in Nelson's fabulous skein. Other excellent players who might have shortened Nelson's streak if not for their military service included Lew Worsham and Lloyd Mangrum, both of whom would become U.S. Open champions soon after World War II ended. Jim Turnesa, Vic Ghezzi, and E. J. "Dutch" Harrison were excellent players who also were missing because they were in military action. On the other hand, Sam Snead played in all but three of the events Nelson won.

Another cavil is that winter rules were in effect in most of the events, because of the war-induced shortage of machinery, fertilizer, and manpower necessary to properly maintain a golf course. Nelson got to improve his lies. But so did everyone else.

For all the quibbling, Nelson's golf was unsurpassed. He still had to hit the shots, good lies or bad, full field of stars or not, and in the nine stroke-play events of the run (he also won the PGA Championship, then played at match-play), Nelson was 113 under par for 38 rounds. That's an average per round of 67.92 strokes. He had only four over-par rounds. In the PGA Championship he was 37 under par for the 204 holes he played. In short, he played out-of-this-world golf. He earned $62,437 in 1945, which was paid in U.S. War Bonds. He cashed them in for around $45,000 and bought outright a ranch in Roanoake, Texas, just outside Fort Worth, that he long had his eye on. He has lived there the rest of his life.

Nelson announced his retirement from competitive golf after the Streak, but it was not quite final. In 1946 he won six tournaments, including the Los Angeles Open, and he was in a play-off for the U.S. Open, which he (and Vic Ghezzi) lost to Lloyd Mangrum. He also usually appeared for the Tam O'Shanter All-American and the World Championships, in Chicago, the richest events in the game in that era. Still, Nelson cut back enough for people to feel he left competitive golf too soon. He was only thirty-four, not old for a golfer, and he was in good condition. Then again, he was a somewhat nervous man and the tension had taken its toll. He was known to have trouble keeping his breakfast down when he was in the lead.

Nelson's historic impact on golf rests in large part on his winning streak. It is the equivalent in golf to Joe Dimaggio's fifty-six-game hitting streak. It is a good talking point, a frame of reference that will come down through many years. But Nelson made other contributions after he did indeed retire. His presence as an analyst and color commentator on television in the early years of the medium's coverage of golf gave the broadcasts credibility. Nelson also became an instruction guru. He was instrumental in helping Ken Venturi and Tom Watson hone their championship games. Nelson was also an outgoing ambassador of golf who always made himself available for an interview, even going so far as to return the phone calls of obscure journalists. He had excellent recall of how it was when he came up in golf, and his telling of those tales enriched the game's lore. He left behind a taste of the early days of American golf, and life, in an account of his experience as a young pro at the Texarkana Country Club, again, in *Gettin' to the Dance Floor*:

> I played a lot of golf with a man at the club named Arthur Temple. Par at the Texarkana Country Club was 73, and when I played with Mister Temple he would bet me a dollar I couldn't break par. If I broke par I got a dollar; if I didn't, why he got a dollar. So any time I won I could have a date with Louise [whom he would marry soon after]. We could go to a show and have a Stuttgart, which is ice cream and a very thick chocolate. There's a place up in Arkansas called Stuttgart where they made the chocolate, which is like a fudge. We could go to the show and get a Stuttgart after for a dollar—if I broke par. If I didn't, we stayed at home and swung on the front porch swing. Anyway, I got to where I did it pretty regularly—break par. It was almost as though he was just giving me a dollar.

"Bantam" Ben Hogan, the Comeback Kid

When Ben Hogan died in 1998, Byron Nelson was rather ignored, if not altogether shunned, at the funeral services. He was not asked to take part in them in any way, despite the fact that he and Hogan had grown up together and, with Sam Snead, shared the golf spotlight as their generation's great triumvirate of champions. For some reason, Hogan seemed to hold a grudge against Nelson. Being famously private, he never said why. The most common guess is, he resented Nelson from the time they were kids, when Byron's middle-class family could give him some basics of daily living that Hogan's could not. When Hogan's father took his own life, he left the family nothing but a struggle to survive.

While Hogan grappled for years to find the golf swing that would catapult him to the top of the game, Nelson was winning a U.S. Open, a Masters, a PGA Championship, and many other tour events. Furthermore, when Hogan finally did find his game, he was called to serve in the U.S.

Air Force during World War II, while the exempt Nelson continued to play the circuit and compile his great record. Nelson had a form of hemophilia.

None of this was Nelson's fault, of course. He didn't go out of his way to diminish Hogan or make him suffer. Nelson was very competitive, to be sure, but he was simply looking out for himself, as do all who reach for the stars. But it was in Hogan's nature to resent and get revenge when the chance arose.

His opportunity came first near the end of 1945, after Nelson had just about completed his Streak. After Hogan's discharge, in late summer, he won five tournaments on the tour. Clearly, he had been practicing more than a little in the Air Force. In one of those five victories, the Portland Open, he set a new 72-hole record score of 261, two below the mark set by Nelson, and beat Nelson by 14 shots. Two weeks later, Nelson beat Hogan's record when he won the Seattle Open with a 259. Hogan could claim that his 261 was the better golf at 27 under par, where Nelson's 259 was *only* 21 under. He made the claim, but privately.

Hogan said very little about his personal life. He came close once, in the mid-1980s, when he encouraged this writer to seek a publisher for his autobiography. It took but two days to get four offers, all with six-figure advances. When informed of the offers, Hogan said he thought the book had to be written first, then you get the money. When reminded of who he was in golf, and how intrigued people had always been with his life, he nodded and said he'd think about it. That was the end of it. He never did the book, and it's possible he might not have revealed much anyway. For example, when asked how it was that his brother and sister were christened with rather unusual and grandiloquent names, Royal and Princess, and he was given just plain old William Benjamin, Hogan was aware of the anomaly, but said he had never asked his parents or siblings about it.

Hogan projected one American image, Nelson another, Snead yet another. They represented in their diverse personalities the overriding patchwork-quilt of American character. Nelson was the outgoing chamber of commerce type, looking at the bright side, a glass half full. Hogan was the silent American, the singled-minded obsessive striver willing to work as hard as necessary to succeed. Snead was pure jock, proud most of all of his physical achievements. Nelson and Hogan led quiet private lives;

Snead liked to play the field and tell some of the raunchiest jokes ever heard, even to black-tie audiences.

Hogan was the more intriguing personality. Silent types usually are, because they are silent. Then again, compared to Nelson's and Snead's lives, or those of most anybody, Hogan's life was one of exceptionally dramatic, monumental overcoming. His accomplishments were impressive by themselves, but even more so given the context in which they were achieved. The trauma of a parent's suicide, especially when a child is young—Hogan was nine—can never be fully measured. But all studies show it deeply influences the survivor's personality. Hogan never discussed the episode, even after it became public knowledge late in his life. Nor did Hogan ever quite forget the hard economic times of his youth, when he had to take jobs he felt were demeaning, like dealing cards at an illegal gambling house. When he became a success, he wore the finest clothes money could buy. He was not a natural athlete, with Snead's gift of rhythm and form or Nelson's size and innate talent. And then, there was the accident.

At 8:30 on the evening of February 2, 1949, Ben Hogan and his wife, Valerie, were driving east out of Van Horn, Texas, in a heavy fog. Hogan was at the wheel, driving slowly. A Greyhound bus coming the other way at a much faster clip moved into the left lane of the two-lane highway to pass a vehicle. It smashed head-on into Hogan's car. When Hogan saw the collision coming, he instinctively leaned to his right to cover Valerie. He saved her from serious injury, and his own life. The steering wheel of Hogan's Cadillac was driven like a cannon shot into the back seat. It would have impaled and killed him in an instant. As it was, Hogan suffered severe injuries—a fractured collarbone, a broken left ankle and crushed left leg, a broken pelvis, and a fractured rib.

About ten days later, a blood clot was discovered to have moved up from Hogan's left leg to his right lung. In fact, there were many clots developing, and the prognosis was definitely life-threatening. Brilliant vascular surgery pulled Hogan through, but the requirements of the blood-clot work were such that his legs would never again be at full strength, especially the left leg.

Even before the blood-clot problem developed, people who saw Hogan immediately after the collision were certain that even if he did live, and many doubted that, he would never play golf again. A pity. Hogan had finally broken through after a long and torturous struggle to find his game. He had reached the championship level, having won his first two majors— the 1946 and 1948 PGA championships. He was also the leading money winner on the tour for those years. However, he was the only one who thought, and said, otherwise about his future in golf after the accident. Of course, he was right. He did return to play, and play exceptionally well. In doing so, Hogan showed a level of determination, courage, willpower, and capacity for adaptation that go down as one of the greatest comebacks in sports history.

As a second act, the story of American golf had what might seem to be troubles. Second acts often do, but sometimes only by comparison to a stirring Act One. The period from the 1930s to 1949 was about consolidation of golf's own institutions—the PGA Tour became a permanent entity on the national sporting scene; women's professional golf got on its legs; and on the wider international level, it was clear that the American game was the best being played on both the amateur and professional sides. An air of confidence emanating from the accomplishments of the nation's best players flowed down to inspire the general public to take up the game. Ben Hogan's dramatic return to action kicked off the last half of the twentieth century and personified the final American thrust to dominance in world golf.

3 | The 1950s: American Golf's Great Leap Forward

Hogan's Remarkable Return; Television Turns the Game On; The Demise of Amateur Golf; The LPGA Grows Up; The Race Issue Addressed at Last; College Golf, The Game's New Farm System

Incredibly, eleven months after his collision with the Greyhound bus, Ben Hogan competed in the 1950 Los Angeles Open. Everyone thought it would be nothing more than a token appearance. How could he possibly contend? But Sam Snead had to birdie the last hole at the Riviera Country Club *to tie Hogan for the title.* Snead won the play-off, which was delayed a week for reasons of weather, but the real victory, the one over severe physical distress and the gods of bad luck, was clearly Hogan's.

Five months later Hogan topped that astounding effort a hundredfold when he won the U.S. Open at the Merion Golf Club, on Philadelphia's Mainline. It was not only the higher pressure compared to the L.A. Open that made Hogan's victory in the 1950 U.S. Open so tremendous—there was never any sign during his career that he lost his nerve or "choked" from the urgency of competition—it was the sheer physical effort of it. The championship's format still called for the last two rounds to be played on the same day. Thus, Hogan had to walk some eight miles on Saturday to play the last thirty-six holes on legs that for a normal human being could not have made a mile. All the while he had to hit powerful and precise golf shots. Then he had to walk another four miles and hit more powerful and precise golf shots the following day in the eighteen-hole play-off, which he won handily with a 69 to Lloyd Mangrum's 73 and George Fazio's 75.

Hogan was close to collapsing at least once during regulation play in the 1950 Open. He came to the seventy-second hole needing a par-four to tie Mangrum and Fazio, and although by now extremely leg weary, he managed to drill a fine one-iron second shot onto the green. Hogan hit his first putt with none of his usual deliberation, and the three-foot second putt for the par and the tie was played with even more dispatch. He told writer Charles Price later that he felt he was going to vomit and just wanted to get off the course.

Years later, when asked if there was one shot that was the most important in his career, he said it was the one-iron at Merion. The *Life* magazine photograph of Hogan in his follow-through, looking at the green after hitting that shot, has become one of golf's most universal icons. Even the divot he took was preserved. In 1987 a subscriber to *Golf Illustrated* magazine sent the bit of grass and soil to the editor in a glassine bag with a note swearing he had run out into the fairway and snatched it up after Hogan played. Nobody would make that up, would they?

A further manifestation of Hogan's tenacity and his talent for golf was that after the accident he won six of his career total of nine major championships. To accommodate the condition of his legs, especially the left one, he had to revamp his swing. After working so hard for so long to develop the action that eliminated the dreaded career-delaying (or ending?) hook, he now he had to change it again. Furthermore, every day he played golf, from the time he left the hospital to the end of his competitive days, he arose very early in the morning to bathe his legs in warm water, apply balms, and encase them in elastic bandages. He once remarked to Carol Mann, the LPGA Hall of Famer, that not a day went by since the accident that he didn't feel some physical pain somewhere in his body. He also once suggested that the vision in his left eye began to fail in the early 1950s, and that it may have provided him only limited vision from then on. That is to say he won two U.S. Opens, a British Open, two Masters, and five other high-quality tournaments (the Tam O'Shanter World, and three Colonial Invitationals among them), with limited vision. And they called him the Hawk for the intense glare he gave to the public!

In 1953 Hogan had his best ever season of major championship play. He won three majors—the Masters, the U.S. Open, and the British Open in his only try for it. He was the first to achieve that single-season triad, known as the Triple Slam, and to date is the only one. (Hogan did not try for the fourth leg of the modern Grand Slam that year, the PGA Championship, because it was played too close in time after the British Open.) Hogan also won the only two regular tour events he entered that year, the Pan-American Open, in Mexico, and the Colonial Invitational, in his hometown. In sum he entered five tournaments, won them all, and there wasn't a squeaker in the lot. He took the Pan American by three strokes, the Colonial by five, the Masters by five, the U.S. Open by six, and the British Open by four.

After the accident Hogan never again played in the PGA Championship. The match-play format by which it was played then (it went to stroke-play in 1958) could mean two full rounds a day, and a one-day thirty-six-hole final. It would be too much for his legs. For the rest of his competitive career he played a very limited tournament schedule, concentrating mainly on the Masters and the U.S. Open, and a few other tournaments where he liked the courses. In a historical sense, and despite the ongoing brilliance of Sam Snead, the 1950s must be designated the Hogan Decade.

Golf Gets Out There and On the Tube

Ben Hogan received hundreds of letters expressing sympathy and good wishes while he convalesced from his death-defying highway accident. He was surprised by the outpouring. He didn't think he was that popular. Actually, he wasn't in the usual sense. He was of such grim demeanor on the course, gave off such a chilly aura, that while the gallery could not help but appreciate his ability and was mesmerized by the eerie, machine-like consistency of his game, it could not warm much to him as a person. The accident changed that, to some extent. He would be deeply respected from then on, but his unmitigated pursuit of perfection still had a chilling effect on the gallery. It was only after he was long retired from competition that the generosity of nostalgia turned Hogan into a cult figure.

While the response of the golfing public immediately after Hogan's accident clearly showed a regard for him personally, it also reflected the growing interest in golf in the United States. American society changed dramatically almost the moment World War II ended in 1945. Despite the enormous cost of the war in dollars, the money spent to produce the armaments, warplanes, ships, and all the other materiel brought the nation well out of the deprivations of the depression. Jobs were plentiful, salaries were good, and there was peace at last. Home builders and real estate developers jumped into this felicitous atmosphere and enhanced it by putting up and selling thousands upon thousands of relatively inexpensive single-family homes on the outskirts of the bigger cities. The move to suburbia by the American middle class was under way.

The majority of those who moved out to the suburbs had survived the dread days of the depression, and they remembered them only too well. In having their own home and a bit of lawn, they were getting a nice taste of well-being. The sense of largesse included an inclination for assuming the ways of the monied class. Golf was a symbol of that category and of upward social mobility. Most golf courses were in the suburbs (what was once the boondocks) anyway, and more were being built. Golf was on the verge of an explosion in participation.

The proliferation of the automobile was an attendant factor in the growth of golf, for obvious reasons. Golf courses are not like baseball fields or tennis courts, just around the corner or a few blocks away in a nearby park. Even if there was public transportation going past a golf course, schlepping a set of clubs and a pair of spiked shoes on a bus was hardly in keeping with the new feeling of prosperity. Besides, a family car came with the move to the suburbs as naturally, and necessarily, as the mortgage, lawn mower, and barbecue grill. The car made access to golf easier and led to more people playing more often.

Although the family car was a factor in the growth of golf in America, it was the emergence of the television set as a household appliance as common as the kitchen sink that would become the most potent element in the expansion of the game. For one thing, it made the sports world's worst live-spectator tickets obsolete or a kind of indulgence. Unlike any other popular spectator sport, in which the game is played out in its entirety on a contained field with the fans in surrounding seats able to see it all from start to finish, a golf tournament is scattered over a four-mile expanse. It is impossible for spectators to see all the players all the time, and they must be lucky or clever, and tall, to get into a position to see crucial shots or the conclusion of play. They will never see the entire tournament as a whole piece of work. Television changed that, although not immediately.

By the 1980s, with the development of hand-held cameras and greater expertise in producing a live telecast of a golf tournament overall, a golf fan could effectively see the whole tournament (at least the action of the leading contenders) from start to finish of every round. Some golf journalists, and many thousands of fans still trek out onto the course to get a more palpable feel of the competition's energy, the wind, the humidity, the nature of the turf, the voice of the crowd, but eventually they (at least most of the reporters) end up in front of a television set to see the competition played out. It would take a bit of time before the advances in technology came to make all that possible, but it had to start somewhere at some time.

In the late 1920s British engineers were experimenting with television, a new invention, and in the process did some televising of sporting events. Golf was included, on a very small scale—a tournament outside London, one time. The onset of World War II put all that research and development off, and after the war, the physical and economic devastation Great Britain faced would not allow a resumption of such a comparatively trivial pursuit. It was much easier for Americans to develop the new medium. No bombs had fallen on the United States, no battles had been fought on its land, and its economic recovery was vibrant. Once again, the geography of America was a factor in its steady assumption of dominance over the old Scots game. But so was its resourceful, commercially oriented New World dynamism.

Golf first appeared on American television in the mid-1940s, not all that long after the first sets were sold to consumers. It took the form of a half-hour program called "Pars, Birdies and Eagles" that was developed by two Chicago public-fee golf course owners, Joe Jemsek and Charles Nash. It was shown only on a local Chicago station, and consisted of instruction delivered by area pros Johnny Revolta, a former PGA champion, and Jimmy Hines. In another segment of each show, Jemsek explained the rules of golf based on questions sent in by area golfers. Jemsek also conducted interviews with current notable tour players—Cary Middlecoff, Sam Snead, and Jimmy Demaret, among others.

Putting golf tournaments on television would seem to be a natural. The venue has an attractive visual quality—landscaped terrain, treelined fairways, water hazards. (In fact, viewer surveys in the eighties and nineties have shown that nearly half the television audience doesn't play golf, but watch because they like the ambiance.) At the same time, golf is a very slow-moving game, even slower than baseball. Its pace is not compatible with the nervous nature of television and the people who produce it, which may explain to some extent why the networks didn't rush to put golf tournaments onto the newest miracle medium. Another being the still relatively small following of golf compared to baseball and football.

Those in golf's important administrative posts also failed to make a push to get the game telecast. Those in power were older people, settled comfortably in a game that breeds conservatism and resists innovation. Horton Smith, winner of the first and third Masters and a powerful president of the PGA of America during this period, thought the combination of television and golf would be but a passing fancy, not here to stay. The USGA, though, however stodgy it was in many ways, took a dip into the new medium when it allowed the 1947 U.S. Open in St. Louis, Missouri, to be telecast. It was the first live telecast of a golf tournament, although it was only broadcast locally. Afterward, Joe Dey, the executive secretary of the USGA at the time, included a clause in its contract with host clubs for future U.S. Opens that covered USGA television rights. But the association did not renew telecasting the Open until 1954, after a more daring individual was offered the opportunity and took it, despite the price of the privilege.

This momentous live telecast took place in 1953. Again, a Chicagoan supplied the energy—the imaginative entrepreneur George S. May. May headed a business engineering firm, George S. May International, and also owned and operated the Tam O'Shanter Country Club in Niles, on a northern border of Chicago. Beginning in the early 1940s, May began sponsoring a tournament for the pros at the Tam O'Shanter club. He offered a substantial purse that gradually escalated into a sum no one dreamed would ever be offered.

May had a flair for the flamboyant—he wore colorful Hawaiian-print shirts with vanilla white slacks, gold-framed glasses and a gold watch chain, and liked to make a big splash—more of everything, especially money. He started out with one tournament and soon began sponsoring four in one week and four more the next—one each for men and women professionals and men and women amateurs. The first week was the Tam O'Shanter All-American, the next week it was the Tam O'Shanter World Championships, which had a smaller and more elite field of players.

May was accused of hyperbole for calling the second of his two events the "World" championship, but he did in fact invite many international players. It was the first time Americans got to see the likes of Australians Peter Thomson and Norman Von Nida, the great Argentinean Robert DeVicenzo, Belgium's Flory Van Donck, South Africa's Bobby Locke, and an Egyptian whose name has been lost to memory but is recalled as playing in a fez. May's World Championships were well ahead of the Masters in this respect. May was also one of the very few sponsors in his day to allow African-Americans to enter his tournaments and play against whites. More on that subject, later.

All the Tam O'Shanter tournaments were seventy-two-hole stroke-play events, and the money for the men pros gradually increased so that, by 1953, they were playing the "World" for the richest total purse in golf history—$50,000, including an astounding $25,000 first prize. The dazzling winner's share alone constituted at least twice as much as the total purse for most other tour events of the time. No pro golfer had ever played a tournament for that much money.

May's prize money got a lot of attention, which was what he was looking for. He wasn't making much money, if any, from the tournaments themselves. Most years he sold daily gallery tickets for only $1 a person, which bulked up the crowd and, by the way, also introduced many more average Americans to the game. May personally enjoyed the limelight his tournaments put him in, but his main aim was to gain publicity for George S. May International, a firm that righted the mistakes and poor judgment of failing businesses. May was essentially an efficiency expert, which is why his tournaments were run so well—four tournaments at once, all players beginning their rounds on the first tee, and everyone finished before dark.

Golf traditionalists ridiculed May's tournaments as overblown extravaganzas that made a mockery of the grand old game of golf, but in fact May introduced a number of innovations that in one form or another would become standard operating procedures at all tour events. May was the first to erect grandstands around the course and position scoreboards at various locations displaying the running scores of the leaders. He also put numbers on the backs (actually, the rear waists) of the golfers, so the gallery could more easily identify them. Some players didn't like this numbering business and refused to wear identification, so May paid those who did wear a number additional prize money. Most complied. In time, May simply put the numbers on the backs of the caddies, which in turn led to the actual names replacing the numbers.

But it was the amount of prize money May put on offer that was most impressive. It led to the first live *national* telecast of a golf tournament. How this came to pass is an interesting study in personal perspicacity. About ten days before the 1953 Tam O'Shanter World Championship was to be played, Harry Wismer, America's premier sports announcer, phoned May to tell him the American Broadcasting Company wanted to televise his tournament. Wismer worked for ABC, which had only recently been established in television (February 1953). If May was interested it would only cost him $32,000. May was not available to take the call, and one of his aides, Chet Posson, did. Wismer gave Posson a rush act, telling him he needed an immediate decision because it would take time to get the production set up. Posson tried to put off a decision until he could talk to his boss, but Wismer insisted on an answer then and there. Posson said it was a deal, and no sooner did he give the nod then he worried he would lose his job for spending so much of his boss's money without authorization. However, when he told May about it, the promoter responded with the heart and soul of a John T. Barnum. "You mean they want to put us on television? I don't care if it costs a million. Do it."

On Sunday, August 23, 1953, just one camera with a wide-angle lens was propped atop the grandstand behind the eighteenth green at Tam O'Shanter Country Club for a one-hour live telecast of the last day of play. The historical consequences of the moment were well served, to both May's and golf's good luck, for televiewers were treated to one of the most wondrous shots ever played. With only some ten minutes of airtime left in the telecast, Lew Worsham came to the last hole of the tournament needing a birdie to tie Chandler Harper and get into a play-off for the $25,000 first prize. On the par-four hole, Worsham hit a good drive and had a second shot of 109 yards to a green slightly raised above and just beyond a fairly wide creek. He decided to use a wedge, and after his tough-egg caddie wisecracked a reminder that the creek wasn't frozen, Worsham hit the ball. It had a low trajectory for the loft of the club he used—for years Worsham would be joshed that he didn't really hit the ball well, that he caught it "thin"—and it was dead on line. It landed on the front of the green and ran some 40 to 45 feet smack into the hole.

An eagle two, and the outright victory! Some who saw the shot at home on their television sets reported falling out of their chairs when the ball went in. Jimmy Demaret was doing the radio broadcast, and his call of The Shot has become a part of broadcast lore and a peek at the social circumspection of the day. As the ball raced up the green after landing, Demaret said, "The ball's running toward the hole. Oh, I'll be damned, it went in." It was golf's version of Clark Gable's "damn" line in *Gone With the Wind*, and it received a similar tsk-tsk.

Years later A. C. Nielsen, the television ratings firm, checked back and reported that approximately 646,000 television sets were tuned in to the broadcast, which was seen in some fifteen states around the country. That brought the estimated number of individuals to around one million who saw the show and The Shot. Needless to say, never before had so many people watched a golf tournament or any part of one at the same time. Worsham's timing was exquisite, in more ways than one.

Moments after Worsham's shot went dashing into the hole, George May came striding out onto the eighteenth green joyously twirling his walking stick. He announced then and there that the following year the winner of his championship would receive $50,000, an even more astonishing sum. Actually, victory would be worth $100,000 if the winner took up May's bonus offer—play fifty one-day exhibitions around the world, at $1,000 per, all expenses paid. Most winners did this deal, and some lost their game because of it from the rigors of travel and being too much away from real competition. Bob Toski was the first winner of the $50,000, took the trip for the other $50,000, and never did much afterward on the tour. Ted Kroll was another. But the money was hard to turn down.

May set a precedent by raising the ante on the tour in respect to purse money, but he didn't immediately usher in the big-money era. He only hinted at the possibilities. Other tour sponsors did not have May's deep pockets, or if they did, they were not willing to dig as deep as he did. In time they would, largely because of the outgrowth of that initial one-hour national telecast he paid for. Of course, ABC was able to sell advertising for its golf telecasts after The Shot show, and May did not have to pay the network a fee after 1953. (His tournament was televised every year until 1958, when he canceled the event.) Indeed, with the millions in fees television networks now pay for the right to broadcast golf tournaments, it seems unimaginable that a tournament sponsor would have to pay a network to do so. But that is the way it was in those innocent days of yore.

Such was the marvel of Worsham's Shot and the exposure it received that the following year, the USGA began its annual national telecasts of the U.S. Open. Three years later the Masters first telecast was aired. Then came the PGA Championship in 1958, which was in conjunction with the switch to the more television-friendly stroke-play format. The first PGA telecast was a fifty-five-minute program with no commercials. The following year, the event was shown on both Saturday and Sunday, with one-and-a-half hours devoted to the events of each day.

Golf and television married because Harry Wismer needed an attraction for his then infant network, because George S. May had the astuteness and mettle to pay for putting his event on the air, and because he had an aide who was wired into his boss's vision and propensity for publicity. But as progressive and daring as they were, May and ABC only tilled the television field. Seed planting was now in order if the rich harvest of money that television promised was to be reaped. It wouldn't be until the 1960s that telecasts would bring regular tour events to the air. That will be detailed in the next chapter. In the meantime, in the 1950s, aside from the continuing telecasting of the Tam O'Shanter Tournament and then the major championships, made-for-television golf competition turned the television earth.

Once again, Joe Jemsek was a pioneer. Inspired by the ABC broadcast of Worsham's wonderful wedge shot, Jemsek and a friend, Pete DeMet, put together a program called *All-Star Golf*. DeMet was a Chicago automobile dealer who also dabbled in television by producing a popular show called *All-Star Bowling*. The golf show was a spin-off of that concept. Jemsek and DeMet had been toying with the golf idea for about three years, on their own learning how to move and place cameras, pick up and follow the ball in the air, and so forth. "We were amateurs making home movies," Jemsek recalled.

The *All-Star Golf* pilot aired in 1954 and featured a match between Cary Middlecoff and Sam Snead. It was an eighteen-hole contest played at Jemsek's Cog Hill Golf Course, in a western suburb of Chicago that became the home of the Western Open in the last quarter of the twentieth century. Snead won by a stroke. It was the first of 153 shows at 26 a year that Jemsek and DeMet produced. The winner of each match got $1,000, the loser $500. It was an elimination series, and Snead once won thirteen matches in a row. However, no one tired of watching his silky swing. The announcer for most of the series was Jimmy Demaret.

Eventually *All-Star Golf* matches were filmed in Arizona, and on such famed courses as Winged Foot and Oakland Hills. The last match of the series, which ended in 1961, was between the winners of the year's major championships—in this instance, Arnold Palmer (the Masters and British Open), Jack Nicklaus (the U.S. Open), and Jerry Barber (the PGA Championship). This matchup inspired another television spin-off, the *World Series of Golf*, which was produced by *All-Star Golf's* ad salesman, Walter Schwimmer. The *World Series* program was the first live broadcast of a made-for-television golf competition, and it was broadcast nationally. It was a thirty-six-hole stroke-play tournament held at the Firestone Golf Course, in Akron, Ohio, with no more than a four-man field. The *World Series* held to its original format from 1962 through 1975, then reverted to a conventional full-field tour event until 1998, when it was discontinued.

The coming of television to golf would have a number of lasting consequences on the growth of the game, and certainly on its events and personalities. Television would be the conduit through which Arnold Palmer became one of golf's all-time popular figures. This would redound on the general popularity of the game itself. Television was the motor that in time revved the purse money up into the many millions. This, in turn, set the stage for the final battle between the PGA of America and the tour pros over control of the tour.

The Masters Becomes *the Masters*

It was through the medium of television that the Masters tournament became an evocation of golf as a kind of secular religion. By the late 1940s the tournament had unquestionably become a special event highly regarded by the players and golf's cognoscenti. But it had not made that much of an impression on the average fan. He heard it was played on a pretty good course, and Nelson and Hogan and Snead had won it, and that one year way back this old guy Sarazen made a double-eagle to win the tournament. Also, Bobby Jones had something to do with it. Sounded good.

Then, the average golf fan got to *see* the Masters courtesy of television, beginning in 1956. It was a revelation. One of the most striking things about it was how the ball looked flying against those close stands of very tall pine trees. What a beautiful backdrop for following the ball in the air. It made the flight seemed so majestic. And there was Bobby Jones, sure enough, in that room talking to the winner at the end of the tournament. With a southern accent. How about that! And President Eisenhower was a member of the club. Ike! Gee! And the announcers speaking in a nice easy tone of voice—slowly and properly. A classy operation, name and all—the Masters.

All that, and the time of year in which the tournament was played, early April, were in perfect juxtaposition. With its scenery—all those big trees—and what everyone now could see for themselves was a pretty good layout, the Masters was just the ticket to send a signal that spring was here. It reminded everyone in the midwest and northeast, where the majority of golfers still resided, that dread winter had staggered to a close and a new golf season was upon them. And all of that was when the telecast was still in black-and-white. When it went to color, in the mid-1960s, the Masters became a rite of spring.

The Masters and its venue have always been associated with Bobby Jones, as though he were the creator, founder, organizer, guiding light, and spirit. That is only partly right. The course was Jones's work and his golf spirit infuses the tournament, but the whole production is to a very large extent the creation of Cliff Roberts, who must go down as one of the cleverest promoters to ever come down the sports pike. Jones's persona was the tone of the tournament Roberts wanted, and he knew how to get it: understatement, no pomp, ostentation, glitz, and no mention of money. Money at the Masters was made to seem irrelevant, an afterthought. When television came in, Roberts made it clear to the network producing the programs that the purse money must never be mentioned on the air. To assure that, and also to keep the print journalists from running the exact amount, it was not announced until the tournament ended.

But of course, the Masters has always been about money. Certainly it was for Roberts in the early years. Jones was earning well over $100,000 a year during the depression from his instructional books and films and the sale of Bobby Jones Signature golf clubs through the Spalding Company. It was a huge sum at the time. Jones also had a developing law practice. He could live nicely without the club or the tournament. But that was at the outset. When his health began to deteriorate in the late 1950s, and the cost of his care rose and his law practice diminished, he would need the income from the club and tournament.

But Roberts was in it for the money right from the start. He was only a casual golfer and took up the game some years earlier mainly to make contacts with potential stockmarket investors. He was not doing especially well as a broker (with Reynolds & Company, in New York City) at the time the club was being formed. He did not see the stockmarket crash of 1929 coming any more than anyone else, and he took a bath with all the other losers. He was in serious personal financial straits; at one point he took a $35 commission for every member he signed up. He must also have thought he would acquire some investment accounts from members of the club. In time, he did.

Also, as the Masters tournament grew more and more popular and fetched higher television fees and bigger galleries, money came to Roberts as a partner in the tournament and Augusta National Golf Club. Many people didn't realize it for a long time, but Augusta National was a business venture. It was not an equity golf club, each member owning a piece of it. It was owned by Roberts and Jones and their underwriters. By the 1950s Roberts had become at least a minor millionaire through profits from the club and the brokerage customers he gained through the club. Maybe a major millionaire. He was as private about his personal finances as he was about those of his club, but it is safe to say he made much of his pile directly and indirectly through Augusta National Golf Club.

Well after Roberts died in 1977, a suicide (he was eighty-three and very ill with no hope of recovery), the club became much more aggressive in the way of money making. It boasts, in its understated way, that the cost of a sandwich and soft drink on the grounds is very modest compared to any other tournament on the calendar. (True, but so are the sandwiches very modest. Very.) For years golf shirts, sweaters, umbrellas, golf balls, golf gloves, et cetera, all with the emblem of the club on them, were sold only out of the club's pro shop. The co-professionals made the profit. Or some of it. It was something of a show to stand around and watch a customer come into the shop during Masters week—in the high-flying 1980s he was often Japanese—go to the shelves and empty them, getting his hands and arms around each stack of sweaters and shirts—the size or color didn't matter—and carry them to the trunk of his Cadillac parked in the driveway at the front of the clubhouse. He would make four or five trips, and pay for the goods in cash, peeling the hundred dollar bills off a choke-a-horse wad. He was not buying souvenirs for friends. He was going to resell the goods at a goodly profit.

In 1990 the club took over this business and grew it from a neighborhood family store to a mini-Macy's—or Saks Fifth Avenue. A permanent, canvas-topped pavilion was erected just inside the main public entrance to the course; there, every conceivable item on which a Masters logo can be fitted, from cashmere sweaters to souvenir ballmarkers, is on sale. The lines to get into the shop are long and deep and persist for the entire week of the tournament. Of course, the Masters does not reveal how much it does in business that week, but fair estimates by those in retail put it around $3 million. Maybe more. The club also announced in 1999, that it will be bringing out its own line of clothing, just as Jack Nicklaus, Greg Norman, and others do.

The Masters tournament's impact on golf is a phenomenon in that the event is staged by an independent, private golf club that in no official or even semi-official way represents golf at large. The United States Golf Association, and the Royal and Ancient Golf Club of St. Andrews, see after the rules of golf, formulate and administer a handicapping system, regulate the amateur code, keep a check on equipment technology, do research on grasses and the construction of greens, and are committed to sustaining interest in the game and generating more appeal. That the two most representative or significant national championships in golf, the U.S. and British Opens, are staged by these two organizations is a natural outgrowth of their place in the game.

The Augusta National Golf Club does none of the above, and in no way represents professional golfers, as does the PGA of America (sponsor of the PGA Championship), and the PGA and European tours. Whereas the USGA and R&A spend the money derived from memberships and television on its operations, and the profits from PGA Tour events go to charity, the Augusta National Golf Club for many years put most of the revenue it acquired from its tournament in a bank. One supposes. The club doesn't say and doesn't have to. In 1997 it did reveal, for the first time, that the club provides some funds for various charities and foundations. It was not a great amount. In 2000, however, perhaps feeling a need to further alter its ungenerous image, the club announced it had donated $3 million to national and local charities.

Yet, the Masters is perceived by much of the golf world as carrying the most weight, power, and influence in and on the game. The highest placed officers of golf's official organizations speak of the Masters in the hushed tones of pilgrims in the presence of their Holy Father. Criticism is entirely out of place, practically unheard of. One criticizes the Masters at great risk. Of what, no one can say. Life and limb? The loss of their tickets or credentials to attend the event?

In a strange way, the Masters' effort to retain its unostentatious atmosphere has become so obvious over the years as to be itself ostentatious. But so what? What does the pretense about money being of no matter and the projection of a benevolent image by a membership that is deeply rooted in a classic capitalist ethos have to do with the golf? Nothing to do with the golf itself. The Masters tournament has produced some of the most exciting, dramatic, and excellent golf the game has ever had. One can argue that the greens of Augusta National are far too undulated for the speed at which they are for the tournament. One can quibble that the course has gotten much too short for a major championship, even with the lengthening in 1999, which didn't make all that much difference; even players of average length off the tee were playing nine-iron and wedge approaches to almost all the holes. One can quibble that the field is not deep enough in professionals to be a true major championship. All good quibbles. But the Masters is still good sport and superb sporting theater.

It is for the sake of clarity that I point out the Masters is not exactly the benign entity that so many take it to be. If the club didn't make money running its tournament or was forced to conform to someone else's rules and regulations of entry by competitors, or otherwise, it would stop running it. It is worth remembering that Cliff Roberts had nothing like the deep, ingrained-from-birth devotion to golf that Bobby Jones did. If Jones had been his equivalent in tennis or horseshoes, and the same kind of opportunity arose to build a private club and put on a nationally regarded tournament of those games, then tennis or horseshoes would have been Roberts's game. Hord Hardin, the third chairman of the club and tournament after Roberts, who was in fact a fine golfer, said before he died in 1989 that it was conceivable the Masters could someday be canceled.

It's not anything I'd want to do, and it wouldn't happen overnight. But I'm not enough of a Solomon to know where we're going to be five years from now. Let's say prize money gets to $5 million. Maybe the membership will say, "Oh, what the hell, we've got to go with it." We wouldn't be the same, and I'm not sure that this membership, made up of the heads of big businesses and who take pride in what we are today wouldn't say, "Let's quit." Or do we go down with everybody else? I think I know what Bob Jones would do; he'd say, "No, we don't go down."

Hardin was reminded that the Masters had become something of a national institution, and that being the case, as caretakers of a such a treasure, could the members of the club arbitrarily cancel the event? Said Hardin: "That suggests what we've done for the most part has been good, and that it's appreciated and wanted by the golfing public. It's hard to be objective, but I don't feel we're the caretakers you speak about, and I think we can cancel it if we want to."

In other words, it is dodgy to put all your eggs, emotional and otherwise, in the Masters basket. The U.S. Open will never go away, because it effectively belongs to the people. The Masters very definitely does not, even if "the people" like to think so.

The LPGA Casts Off

The Ladies Professional Golf Association didn't exactly break out of the gate on top when it began its first season, in 1950. Fred Corcoran said, "It touched off a national storm of indifference." There were only about seventeen to twenty players who competed, and although Babe Zaharias was a big draw and worked hard to promote the circuit, nothing came easy. When Zaharias was diagnosed with cancer in 1953, panic reigned. The tour had other fine players—Patty Berg, Betsy Rawls, Louise Suggs, Betty Jameson, Peggy Kirk Bell, Kathy Whitworth, Betty Dodd, and the teenage Bauer sisters were interesting to watch with their superlong backswings—but the Babe was the one everybody wanted to see. She had a colostomy in 1953 and a year later was back in action, making a comeback that rivaled Hogan's. Clearly not the powerful athlete she had always been, Zaharias gritted it out to win the 1954 U.S. Women's Open.

It was a heartwarming, dramatic moment. However, a year later the cancer returned and she died in 1956 at age forty-five.

In 1953 the three equipment manufacturers supporting the LPGA Tour, Wilson, MacGregor, and Spalding, dropped out and Fred Corcoran left for another brief stint with the PGA Tour, so the tour's organization was all up to the players themselves. They were the cooks and bottle-washers, doing the legwork, the paperwork, cutting the holes, playing the golf. The group was lucky in that it had Betty Hicks to help run the shop. She was a bright woman with a lot of energy, and a good writer who put out the group's publicity. There was always Patty Berg, a tireless and effective promoter. And Betsy Rawls, a Phi Beta Kappa at the University of Texas, where she was a physics major. Rawls was also an outstanding player (fifty-five career wins). Rawls described those early days of the LPGA in *Gettin' to the Dance Floor*:

> Fred Corcoran booked the tournaments, but that's all he really did; none of the promotional stunts he was known for when he ran the men's tour. We handled the day-to-day operation of our tour, did it all, and it was a kind of interesting situation. One of us kept the books and wrote out the checks, someone else did all the correspondence. I look back and can remember making rulings on other players in a tournament I was competing in. Good gracious!

A few angels arose to pick up the slack left by the departed equipment manufacturers. Alvin Handmacher, who made a line of women's clothing, put up $17,000 for a series of four Weathervane Opens played in Califor-nia, Chicago, Cleveland, and New York. George S. May, who had a hand in launching the original women's tour organization, the WPGA, held his Tam O'Shanter tournaments in Chicago. They offered the most prize money the women ever played for, and gave them considerable exposure as part of his four-tournaments-at-once show.

Things also began to pick up in 1956 when an Indiana sportswriter named Bob Renner was hired (at $15,000 a year, a huge sum for the LPGA) as the tournament director. However, he would say that with only twenty-five players to field it was a struggle: "Many newsmen do not regard women's sports as important." But one of those players, beginning in 1956, was Mickey Wright. That augured well for the LPGA, for Wright would become one of the best woman golfers of all time. She won her first U.S. Women's Open in 1958 and another one in 1959, but it wasn't until the 1960s when she became the dominant player on the LPGA circuit. Things got better then.

They Too Came to Play

Bobby Jones was the last amateur able to compete successfully against the pros. There would a be few simon-pures after Jones who occasionally beat the professionals in open competition, but no sooner did they show their stuff than they themselves turned pro. The age of professional golf dawned in the 1930s in the United States. This development was just another articulation of the nation's way in all things. Whereas the British were notorious (by American standards) for a lackadaisical (amateur) way of doing business and playing games, Americans prized efficiency and an almost scientific approach to the manufacture of products, providing services, and playing games. This way of being and doing are largely responsible for the nation's success as an economic power and military force, and the most prolific sporting nation the world has ever known.

Golf is especially responsive to a systematic routine; it attracts, even demands, the mindset of an engineer. People interested in or fascinated by how mechanical things work are drawn to golf—American professional golfers included. Beginning in the 1930s, they became the first golfers to take practice seriously, beating out hundreds of balls and with each shot dissecting their swing and finding ways to improve on it. They had a difficult time finding a place to practice in the 1930s. Golf course architects in the first half of the century rarely included a practice range in their plans. That includes the builders of such temples as the Winged Foot and Merion Golf clubs. It wasn't because land was dear or in short supply. It was that no one practiced. Not like they began to, in the thirties.

Ben Hogan is conventionally considered the paradigm of practice, the all-time ball-beating range rat. Johnny Bulla, another pioneer of the PGA Tour, and a deep-thinking student of the game, always snickered at that image: "Ky Laffoon used to hit balls by the thousands, and Bill Mehlhorn, and Sam Snead. And me. We all were leveling the practice tees, when we found a good one."

Indeed, because of Hogan's unique intensity and his success in the U.S. Open, he became the prototype of the professional golfer. However, there was an imposing cadre of others who distinguished themselves at the game after World War II. What made the group especially interesting was how it reflected the diversity of the nation itself—America in all its variegated ethnicity and provincial idiosyncrasies.

Texans were a large contingent, and they suffused (poisoned?) the air with the regional chauvinism peculiar to the state. Among them was Lloyd Mangrum, a lean, hard-eyed pro with a thin mustache emblematic of his nickname, the River Boat Gambler. He was one of the few top-of-the-line pros to experience combat action during World War II; he earned two Purple Hearts. Mangrum often wore knickers at play even in the 1950s, and he had an exceptionally deliberate backswing, which didn't speed up when the pressure was on. He was a tough competitor, a money player, and winner of thirty-six tournaments, including the 1946 U.S. Open.

Jimmy Demaret, a contemporary of Hogan by age and Texas upbringing, became the first three-time winner of the Masters when he last took the title in 1950. His others victories came in 1940 and 1947. Demaret was a far more accomplished golfer than he was ever given credit for—he had enormous hands and was a brilliant player in the wind—because, for one thing, unlike most of his compatriots, he preferred the nightlife over the drudgery of the practice tee. In private conversation, when Hogan's name was brought up and there was mention of his so-called mystique, Demaret would chuckle. He was never overtaken by the Hawk, whom he often beat like a drum in private games. Demaret was one hell of a player.

Demaret could dazzle with his game at times, but he preferred to shake everybody up with his sartorial splendor and witty repartee. In show business terms, Demaret played vaudeville to Hogan's Hamlet. Demaret single-handedly changed the dress code in golf, giving it a distinctly American look. He remarked once that his fashion inspiration was the locker rooms he knew as a young man, which "stank" of sweaty wool; he also complained that "golfers all looked like they were going to a funeral." On a visit to New York City's garment district during the 1940s, Demaret noticed rolls of vividly colored, decoratively patterned material and asked if he could get golf shirts made up from it. Told it was for ladies' dresses, he said he didn't care. A dozen bright and silky shirts were made, and while few of his fellow pros would follow Demaret's glowing color scheme, the drab, bulky British style of dress that had come with the territory was on its way out.

There was a practical value to Demaret's sartorial contributions, as well. The shirts he introduced were looser fitting and made swinging a golf club easier. Demaret combined form with function and made it fun to dress for golf.

Jack Burke, Jr., whose father was Demaret's early mentor, won a Masters and PGA Championship and in 1952 won four straight tour events, the third longest winning streak in tour history. Burke's golf lineage is pure American. His father was a Philadelphia working-class Irishman—his grandfather was a hod carrier. Burke, Sr., did a little of that labor, but after working as a caddie, he became a good enough player to challenge for the U.S. Open. He then had a long and influential career as a club pro and teacher, mainly in Texas.

Jackie grew up eating dinner regularly with legends of early American golf—Hogan, Nelson, Picard, Demaret, and so on—who talked golf long into the night. After his tour days (seventeen career wins), Burke went into partnership with Demaret and founded one of the best golf clubs in the country, the Champions in Houston, where a U.S. Open, a Ryder Cup Match, a U.S. Amateur Championship, and the PGA Tour Championship have been played.

Burke in his later years has become America's grand golfing sage, dispensing insightful comments on everything from swing technique to the state of the American novel with a humor and edge all his own. In the 1990s he remarried and tutored his young wife into a finalist for the U.S. Women's Amateur Championship. But he also has been "discovered" by Phil Mickelson and other stars of his generation. Mickelson was asked once what it was like to take a lesson from Burke, who is famously impious in the presence of anyone but his personal God, and Mickelson said, "No one ever talked to me like that." Mickelson went back, though.

The Slavic contingent in American golf began with Billy Burke, né Burkauskas, but in the 1950s Eastern Europe was especially well represented. There was Bobby Toski, Ed Furgol, Ted Kroll, and Julius Boros, who was of Hungarian lineage. Boros grew up in a working-class town in Connecticut and learned bookkeeping just in case he couldn't make it as a pro. He had a beguiling and wholly disarming style of play. His long and loopy swing and seemingly indifferent manner hid the fact of a shrewd, self-controlled, and fiery competitor. Boros had a knack for winning the bigger money tournaments, and he had an outstanding U.S. Open record that included two victories and many top-ten finishes. He also won the PGA Championship at age forty-eight—the oldest player to ever take this major title. Boros liked to say Arnold Palmer was his "pigeon," and indeed he seemed to have a way with Arnie. Boros beat him in a play-off (along with Jacky Cupit) for the 1963 U.S. Open, and he dashed Palmer's hopes of winning a PGA Championship in 1968, when he hit a long chip tight on the last hole to beat out Palmer by a shot.

Olin Dutra was the first golfer of Spanish heritage to win a major tournament, the 1934 U.S. Open. Doug Ford, né Fortinaci, fed the growing Italian presence in American golf. He was a New York City type—fast talker and player, a gambler with a short and homely swing that he could repeat time after time. He also had the cojones of a safecracker. He won a Masters (1957), and PGA Championship (1955) at match-play, a format at which he was born to thrive.

Younger readers may think it is irrelevant or immaterial and oldfangled to distinguish one ethnic group from another. But it was something the people who came of age in the forties and fifties grew up with. America was composed of a lot of ethnic neighborhoods—the Irish lived over there, the Poles on one side of town, the Italians on another—and each group found strength in having a particular tribal heritage. It was a point of honor, a matter of pride for an Italian kid if he knocked off a Swede or a German in a contest. The difference was one of the driving forces in his effort. That sort of thing seems to have diminished in today's McDonaldized, Disney-fied popular culture, but these distinctions were drawn in the period under discussion and they affected performance.

In most cases the pros of the 1950s had bypassed amateur golf, mainly because they came of age in the years of the depression and couldn't afford to play for free. Besides, the pros were where the game was, where the best players were. Lawson Little turned pro after winning both the U.S. and British amateur championships two years in succession. The day after Dr. Cary Middlecoff, a practicing dentist, beat the pros to win the highly regarded North and South Open, he turned professional and made a fine career of it. A tall man who cultivated a distinctive pause at the top of his backswing—not easy, if only because he was a high-strung individual—Middlecoff won two U.S. Opens and a Masters, among his thirty-nine total victories. Like many others of his era, his competence was somewhat overlooked because of Hogan's compelling presence. After his playing career, Middlecoff was one of the first pros to do television golf commentary. Frank Stranahan, a scion of the Champion spark plugs fortune, enjoyed an exemplary amateur career during the 1940s and early 1950s, then turned professional because it was more competitive.

Further proof that professional golf had taken over the game was in the redefinition of the Grand Slam. The U.S. and British Amateurs were dropped, replaced by the Masters and PGA Championship, which effectively meant that no amateur could ever pull off such a quad. Amateur golf didn't quite become a backwater, though. It became instead a stepping-stone to the pros, a training ground, and in the process created a new category of high-rise golfer, the "professional amateur." This contradictory term marked one of the less savory episodes in American golf.

Harvie Ward and the Amateur Code

By the 1950s American golf was going the way of the nation as a whole, becoming increasingly mercenary. However, despite some advances in the USGA's Amateur Code—you could now caddie beyond the age of sixteen and not be considered a professional—it was still rooted in nineteenth-century social laws or moral mythology. The effect was not unlike that of Prohibition. Amateur golf took on speakeasy traits. The time of the gentleman amateur had passed. Most serious amateur golfers, those who played the main tournament circuit, were from the middle- to middle-lower class, and used their golf as either a stepping-stone to the pro game or to improve their business prospects. It was expensive to play the circuit—the North and South Amateur, the Trans-Miss, the Western Amateur—but often the costs of travel and equipment were taken care of through "quiet arrangements" with employers or "supportive friends."

There was nothing new in this, but the incidence was far greater during this period. The secrecy was an outgrowth of a clause in the Amateur Code that was and remains impossible to police and shouldn't even be on the books. The rules say that amateur status is forfeited by "accepting golf balls, clubs or other golf merchandise from anyone dealing in golf merchandise without payment of current market price." Amateur status is also compromised by "receiving or contracting to receive compensation or personal benefit, directly or indirectly, for allowing one's name or like-ness as a golfer to be used in any way for the advertisement or sale of anything, whether or not used in or appertaining to golf."

The latter stipulation was (and remains) especially vexatious and un-realistic. If a high-level amateur golfer who plays the national circuit is in a line of work by which he is able to use to advantage his reputation as a golfer—insurance salesman, stockbroker, and the like—he effectively uses his reputation as a golfer to support his golf. A U.S. Amateur cham-pion, or state amateur champion, or even a club champion has a better chance of completing a business deal—or at least getting easier entree to a customer—than a fellow with a 25 handicap, if the customer is into golf. That is the way things are, and every quality amateur golfer in the world knows this and plays on it.

All of this came to a dispiriting head in the case of E. Harvie Ward, whose amateur status was suspended in 1957 for having accepted ex-penses from his employer to play in golf tournaments that included the Masters. This was not a minor incident, because it effectively destroyed the career of a man who at the time was considered one of the ten best golfers in the world, professional or amateur.

Ward was raised in Tarboro, North Carolina, and won his first amateur tournament, the Carolinas Junior Championship in 1940, at the age of fifteen. He served two years in the U.S. Army during World War II, and upon his discharge because of an inner ear problem, he went home. After five months of hard practice, he had put his golf game in shape for the major leagues. Said Bill Campbell, a former U.S. Amateur champion and president of the USGA, "Harvie had outstanding instincts for golf. A sim-ple swing, with no mechanical problems. He was a very straight hitter, with adequate length, and could read greens wonderfully." A writer on golf at the time waxed a bit more poetic, calling Ward's game "a flawless expression of the art."

In 1948 Ward hit the big time by winning the North and South Amateur at Pinehurst, North Carolina. The field included such future pro stars as Julius Boros, Doug Ford, Dick Mayer, and nineteen-year old Arnold Pal-mer. Ward defeated Palmer, five and four, in a semi-final match, and Frank Stranahan in the final. Stranahan was then one of the best amateur golfers in the world. The next year Ward won the NCAA individual champion-ship, representing the University of North Carolina. Before he won his first U.S. Amateur Championship, Ward won the British Amateur, in 1952, again defeating Stranahan in the final, seven and five. He won his singles and doubles matches playing for the 1953 U.S. Walker Cup team, and in 1954 Ward won the Canadian Amateur.

Ward won his first U.S. Amateur in 1955, when he crushed William Hyndman, Jr., nine and eight, in the final. Earlier that year, during the U.S. Open, Ward was tied for the lead with Tommy Bolt after two rounds and eventually finished seventh. Ward successfully defended his U.S. Amateur title in 1956, and in the 1957 Masters, his sixth appearance in the tournament, Ward, along with Palmer and Canadian pro Stan Leonard, was one shot off the lead with a round to play. Ward shot a 73 to finish fourth. (Palmer had 76; Doug Ford won.) Ward was at the top of his game, at the top of *the game*, which is when he was cut down.

As he stepped from the plane that brought him home to San Francisco from the 1957 Masters, Ward was shown a headline on the front page of the San Francisco *News* that said, "Harvie Ward's Amateur Status Questioned!" It was the first Ward had heard of it. He was cited by the USGA for accepting expense money over the past five years to compete in golf tournaments. The money was from his boss, Ed Lowery, a San Francisco automobile dealer. Ironically, Lowery was the ten-year-old caddie for Francis Ouimet when Ouimet became the improbable and first amateur to win the U.S. Open (1913). Lowery stayed involved in golf and worked his way up the USGA executive ladder. From 1953 through 1956, he was a member of the USGA's prestigious executive committee. This was a critical element in the Ward affair.

Lowery was undoubtedly helping Ward's golf career when he let him off during working hours to play and practice and to travel to tournaments. No rules violations there. Lowery also knew Ward's reputation would attract customers. Ward could count on that, as well, which is where the issue becomes shaded. It would have been a blatant violation of the Amateur Code, under the "Lending Name or Likeness" clause, if Lowery had sent out brochures saying Harvie Ward the golf champion was one of his salesmen, or put Ward's name and picture playing golf up on a billboard. But people who knew golf knew this by word-of-mouth, including Lowery's and Ward's. Is word-of-mouth a form of advertising? Of course. Lowery may have liked Ward personally and considered him a terrific

salesman, but he also hired him because Harvie was going to attract customers who played and knew golf. In San Francisco, that demographic
was potent.

This sort of business practice did not originate with Lowery and Ward.
Dale Morey, who had a fine amateur career in American golf from the late
1940s through the 1960s that included playing U.S. Walker Cup golf, tried
the pro tour as a young man. Deciding he couldn't make good, he resolved
to get into selling something, anything, by which, as he put it, "I could
use my golf." He went into furniture. Bobby Jones himself advised Jack
Nicklaus, when he was considering his future, to remain an amateur. Said
Jones to Nicklaus: "The right amateur in the right boardrooms could make
tons more [money] than any tour pros, and still bring a pure glory to golf."

It is certain that Jones himself, as pure an amateur as he was according
to the rules, acquired a client or two for his law practice because he was
Bobby Jones the famous golfer. Even Chick Evans, who was by all accounts not a very astute businessman, had good-paying jobs in the dairy
business around Chicago because he was a golf champion. As Bill Campbell, an attorney who was dubbed Mister Amateur, but probably got more
than a few clients from his championship reputation, said of the Ward
matter: "Much of the rule about taking expenses was honored in the
breach."

Ward was in violation of Rule 2, Paragraph 1 (now Rule 1, Paragraph
10) of the Amateur Code, titled "Expenses." It was only because Lowery
was brought up on a federal tax-evasion charge and his finances were made
public that it came out that he paid Ward's expenses to play in tournaments. Various individuals remarked at the time that all Lowery would
have had to do was raise Ward's salary or commission rate to cover the
expenses and the exchange wouldn't have appeared on his books.

In other words, this portion of the code was easily sloughed or circumvented and was done so regularly that Lowery didn't even think to raise
Ward's salary. In recalling the affair in 1997, Ward said, "If I wasn't the
amateur champion at the time it would have gone right by the boards.
Nobody would have cared, and nothing would have been done." Ken
Venturi also sold cars for Lowery at the same time, but did not get involved in this matter, perhaps because he wasn't the U.S. Amateur champion at the time. Or, Ward speculated, years later, Lowery might have

warned Venturi of the coming trouble—"He treated Kenny like a son, I was just one of the guys"—which may be why Venturi turned pro before Lowery's books were opened to the public.

Apparently because Lowery was a USGA executive and Ward one of the best players in golf, the USGA felt it had to do something. "I don't know it for a fact," Ward said, "but Lowery told me that a number of people on the USGA board at the time resigned after it all happened. So there must have been a lot of dissension or disagreement in that group. An attorney friend of mine called me right after it happened and asked if I wanted a lawyer. He said I had them dead to rights, a sure win, they couldn't lay a glove on me. I said no, because I thought it would look bad."

Ward's amateur status was suspended for one year, not two as the infraction called for in the book. The abridged term was invoked because, USGA executive secretary Joe Dey explained, "There were mitigating circumstances." That is, Lowery was a former USGA executive committee member and assured Ward that the expenses were permissible.

Nonetheless, Ward was crushed emotionally. And deeply disillusioned. He remembered that when he tied for twenty-fourth in his second Masters in 1952, he was approached by John Danforth, a USGA bigwig out of Boston, a member of Augusta National, and a friend of Lowery's, who told Ward that there was a spot open for the British Amateur that year and asked if he would he be interested in playing. A spot open? "It meant my expenses would be paid," Ward explained. "It happened a lot. You didn't know who paid them. An airplane ticket just came in the mail, and the hotel bill was picked up." Ward repaid the "gift" by winning that British Amateur.

Ward's punishment in the Lowery affair was confusing, and it compounded Ward's disenchantment with the system and the USGA. It was as if the USGA wanted to appear virtuous, but also lenient and merciful. As Ward commented,

If I was guilty, then give me the whole penalty, or give me none at all. You can't be a little pregnant. Why not go the whole hog or just forget about it? Also, there were so many others who were taking equipment. Everyone knew about it. After the suspension, one of my friends asked me why I didn't blow the whistle on the others who were taking. I said I didn't want to do that.

Ward immediately applied for reinstatement of his amateur status, and again following the strange logic the USGA applied to his case, he was allowed to compete in the 1957 U.S. Open as "an applicant for reinstatement." He tied for twenty-sixth and was selected to the 1959 U.S. Walker Cup team. And yet, during his suspension period, Ward was invited to play in every prestigious non-USGA amateur tournament in the country, but the USGA warned the other competitors that if Ward played, their amateur status would be jeopardized. "I guess they thought I'd contaminate everybody," Ward said.

The USGA's fence-straddling contributed to Ward's response to the entire episode. Immediately after the suspension period ended, he did get back into competition. But with little fire for it. He got to the fourth round of the 1959 and 1960 U.S. Amateurs and to the third and fourth rounds in 1961 and 1962, respectively. Those were mediocre showings next to his pre-suspension play. After 1962 Ward quit altogether.

"I was very hurt and bitter," Ward remarked. "The assumption was that I wasn't earning the money by work. But we were promoting cars." Ward may not have made long, involved personal calls on auto dealers where he traveled to play tournaments, but he did make the calls. So did Frank Stranahan justify the expense money he received from the Champion's company to play amateur golf, by noting that he visited automobile dealers and repair shops wherever he went. Stranahan had a very heavy tournament schedule that included playing pro tour events, but his amateur status was never questioned.

Why didn't Ward turn pro, as Venturi did? "There wasn't enough money in it," he responded. "I couldn't foresee the money that was coming in tour golf anymore than anyone else. It started in 1960, with Arnie [Palmer], but even then not right away. I could make more working for Lowery."

Then why not come roaring back as an amateur, after the suspension? "Basically, I said to hell with it," Ward recalled, some forty years later. "I sort of said I'd show those guys by not playing anymore. Silly, I guess. I took up tennis, played some social golf, went about making a living."

It wasn't quite that serene. Ward had always been a partying type—some say, and Harvie agreed, that he might not have had the discipline for the pro tour—but when he quit golf he began drinking more heavily. His first marriage, the one that friends say gave him the stability that made him a star golfer, ended. He would marry four more times. Eventually, Ward did turn pro. In the early 1970s he tried an Arizona mini-tour, but it was too late. "I couldn't beat those kids," he said. He became a club pro, first in North Carolina, then Florida. Finally, with his fifth wife, he moved to Pinehurst, North Carolina, where he has settled in for the duration. He gives the occasional lesson, plays casual golf, and generally lives the life of a country gentleman. (His wife brought great wealth to the marriage; she even gave Harvie a Rolls Royce for one of his birthdays.)

Harvie Ward was always a charming gentleman with a warm smile, and he was one hell of a golfer. When asked if he would have done well as a tour pro had he taken that next logical step, he nodded, chuckled and said, "Oh, I think I'd have done pretty well." All those who knew Ward back then said he would have done *very* well. "But we'll never know, will we?" said Ward in conclusion.

American golf lost a player of great talent to the hazy and inherently hypocritical doctrine concerning amateur status, which should read, very simply, "Any person who makes his living playing and teaching golf is a professional; everyone else is an amateur." Period.

College Golf with Expenses Paid—the New Training Ground for the Stars

By the time of the Ward suspension, amateur golf had lost much of its former consequence. The Ward affair may well have been the final blow that rendered it a relic no longer worthy of the serious attention of the golf-watching public. The irony was that the new amateur field of battle became college golf, which was fueled by the college golf scholarship. In other words, a young man could trade in on his golf talent for a college education, worth some $25,000 or more in the 1950s, but couldn't take money for playing on the regular amateur circuit. It could only happen in America.

Many countries around the world put considerable emphasis on a particular sport, soccer in many cases. But only in America is there so much emphasis on so many sports. And no where else in the world can a young person get a college education by virtue of his or her ability to play a game, any game. The original clause in the USGA's Amateur Status Code read that amateur status was forfeited if, "Because of golf skill or golf reputation, accepting any consideration as an inducement to be a student in an educational institution. However, a student may accept a scholarship granted and approved by the institution's regular central authority awarding all scholarships."

Here again, with the conditional "however," the USGA was fence-straddling, leaving room for infringement of a rule. The above reading means a student who happens to be a good golfer and makes the team can accept a scholarship, but only if its not offered by the athletic department. But what is to stop the athletic director from making a gentleman's agreement with the admissions dean to give a scholarship to a young fellow who can play first-class golf and not say it is for golf? Nothing. The USGA caught itself out on this, eventually, because it later amended the scholarship clause to read that forfeiture of amateur status can occur only if the scholarship is not under the regulatory control of the National Collegiate Athletic Association, the National Association for Intercollegiate Athletics, or the National Junior College Athletic Association. All athletic scholarships are controlled by those groups, so the USGA had its out. And young men had an in. College golf took off and became a leading factor, perhaps *the* leading factor in how America came to dominate world golf.

Most college athletic scholarships are for football and basketball, which fill stadiums and television screens with paying customers. The scholarships are paid off many times over by the amount of money raised from the packed stadiums and arenas in which these sports are played. Golf, though, doesn't earn a school a dime in hard cash. It's all outlay. Then why golf scholarships? Or for that matter tennis, baseball, track and other sports that earn little or no money? For the same reason chambers of commerce sponsored pro golf tournaments in the old days of the tour, to get the school's name in the newspaper, hopefully as a winner, and thereby attract *paying* students.

College golf in the United States goes back to when the game got its first foothold in the country. Yale University and Harvard College had golf teams in 1897, and Princeton began competing a year or so later. This is not surprising, given the upper-economic class milieu in which golf mainly flourished. From 1897 through 1933 the NCAA team golf champion was either Yale, Harvard, Princeton, or Dartmouth, which only won once. It was considered a major breakthrough for the common golfing college man when the University of Michigan broke the Ivy League stranglehold by winning the NCAA team title in 1934. Michigan was the first state-funded university to accomplish that in golf.

None of those Ivy League golfers were on scholarships, as far as anyone knows. Elsewhere in the country, though, there was some movement in golf scholarships beginning in the mid-1930s. Significantly, it was in the midst of the depression and was prompted, at least in part, by Huey "Kingfish" Long, a famous Louisiana politician who served as both Governor of Louisiana and Senator from Louisiana. Long made his reputation by increasing the taxes on business firms and creating a "Share the Wealth" program to help people on the lower rungs of the economic ladder.

Fred Haas, Jr., told about Long's influence on college golf from his own experience. Haas played in the first Masters, and when he won the 1945 Memphis Open, as an amateur, he stopped Byron Nelson's winning streak. Haas was born and raised in Arkansas, where he became a junior golf phenom under his father's tutoring and encouragement. At the age of twelve he played in the 1930 Southeastern Open, which Bobby Jones won by twelve shots in a warm-up for his run at the Grand Slam. In his junior year in high school, Haas was told that the only way he could get a scholarship to the University of Arkansas was if he won the state high school championship. "I needed that scholarship if I was going to go to college," Haas recalled, "because there was just no money around." He won it twice in a row. But just before heading off to the university, his father took a job as golf pro at a course in Louisiana. The family moved there, and young Fred began playing some tournaments around New Orleans and Baton Rouge and making a name for himself. In the Louisiana State Championship he lost in the final round, but Huey Long was in the gallery, and after the match he told Haas he ought to be playing golf for Louisiana State University. When Haas told Senator Long that he was planning on going to Arkansas, Long talked him out of it; he told him he wanted him at LSU and instructed him to recruit some players and make it the best college team in the country.

"I remember telling Long that we needed to have a golf course for the team," said Haas, "and when he asked where it would go, I pointed to a pasture near the football stadium where a lot of cows were grazing. Long said he couldn't do that, because LSU was a mechanical and agricultural school and he'd lose a lot of votes if he turned that pasture into a golf course." Thirty years later, a nine-hole course was built on that pasture. Haas dedicated it.

Haas played for LSU on a scholarship, and over the years he recruited a number of excellent golfers to play for his alma mater, many of whom became fine professionals. They included Earl Stewart, who would win the NCAA individual, and Gardner Dickinson, who became a disciple of Ben Hogan. Haas himself won the NCAA individual championship in 1935. After getting his degree in journalism, and before taking a newspaper job offered by the *Chicago Tribune*, Haas decided first to try playing more top-level golf. After stopping Nelson's streak in Memphis, he turned pro and played the tour for a number of years with moderate success. He made the bulk of his living selling insurance, a lot of it to his fellow tour pros, and retained his license to sell insurance all his life. Haas may not have been the very first recipient of a college golf scholarship, but he was close, and Senator Huey Long played no small part in the development of the system.

The last time an Ivy League school won the NCAA team championship was in 1943, when Yale took the title for the twenty-first time. In 1943 Notre Dame won the national collegiate championship and the Ivy League domination was over for all time. The first post–World War II college golf powerhouse was North Texas State, which won four NCAA championships in a row between 1949 and 1952. From this team came such players as Don January, winner of over thirty PGA and Senior PGA Tour events, including the 1967 PGA Championship. On the team with January was Billy Maxwell, who had a solid career on the PGA Tour, and Stan Mosel, who became an outstanding teaching pro.

But it was the University of Houston, under coach Dave Williams, a master recruiter of young talent, that made everyone sit up and take notice of college golf. Between 1957 and 1970, the school's team won twelve NCAA championships and had seven individual champions. The roster of Houston players who went on to pro careers is most impressive: Phil Rodgers, Fuzzy Zoeller, Fred Couples, and Bruce Lietzke, among many others. At the same time, Oklahoma State was becoming a college golf power, as were Florida and Florida State, Stanford, and the University of Texas, where Tom Kite and Ben Crenshaw played. Wake Forest became

another perennially strong college golf school, beginning with Arnold Palmer and going from there to Lanny Wadkins, Curtis Strange, Jay Haas,
and many others who would have excellent careers on the pro tour.

College golf became, and remains, the amateur minor leagues of professional golf, just as college football and basketball and baseball have
been the funnel into their professional leagues. It has become such a
valuable workshop that even young foreign golfers have come to play for
American universities. Steve Elkington came from his native Australia to
play for the University of Houston with the express purpose of sharpening
his game for the pros. Englishman Luke Donald played golf for Northwestern University and won an NCAA championship. It is hard to find
one golfer playing the PGA Tour who has not played in college and almost
invariably on scholarship.

The golf scholarship became available to women after the institution
of the federal government's Title IX program, which required equal funding for women's sports. The outcome has been excellent programs at
schools such as Tulsa University, the University of New Mexico, Rollins
College, and Arizona State University. They have been pipelines to the
LPGA Tour for Nancy Lopez, Julie Inkster, Hollis Stacey, Beth Daniel,
and many other prominent women golfers, including more than a few
women from foreign countries—Sweden's Annika Sorenstam (University
of Arizona) and Helen Alfredsson (U.S. International University), and
Spain's Martas Figueras-Dotti (University of Southern California).

The college golf scholarship program has expanded to include many
hundreds of small colleges and universities. Some superb players have
come out of these conferences of smaller schools, which constitute a kind
of Class A ball to the triple-A of bigger universities. Bruce Fleisher was
a National Junior College champion. Paul Azinger attended Brevard Junior
College in Florida before moving up to Florida State.

The ratio of college scholarship golfers who graduate school is about
what it has been for football and basketball players, which is not very
high. Jack Nicklaus played three years of golf at Ohio State University,
but didn't graduate. Arnold Palmer played for Wake Forest, but after joining the Coast Guard in grief over the accidental death of his best friend
and teammate, Buddy Worsham, he did not return to college. Tiger Woods
spent two years at Stanford, but couldn't keep his head in the books when

there were millions of dollars being offered in endorsement money alone. He turned pro after his sophomore year. Still, even if these scholarship golfers didn't receive a degree, they did get a taste of higher education, which is better than nothing. A few of them, Palmer for one, sponsor golf scholarship funds for their alma mater, or almost alma mater. The next generation, however, seems to be on a different track. Nine members of the Georgia Tech men's golf team, the nation's number one team in 2000, made the Dean's List.

The Black American Joins the Game

The conventional historical judgment on the 1950s is that it was the Silent Generation, a period of spiritless conformity in which nothing of social significance happened. No one cared. Which of course is nonsense. For one thing, the war against racial discrimination was seriously heating up in the fifties. Mainstream American professional golf was more than a little touched by this movement, and an important bridgehead was established.

The story of black American participation in American golf is, like all black American history, convoluted, intricate, disturbing, and occasionally reasonably gratifying. It begins at the very beginning of American golf. The second U.S. Open championship was played in 1896 at the Shinnecock Hills Golf Club in Southampton, New York. Among the entrants was John Shippen and Oscar Bunn, both of whom lived on the nearby Shinnecock Indian Reservation and worked on the building of the Shinnecock Hills course. Bunn was a full-blooded Shinnecock. Shippen's father, who taught elementary school in Washington, D.C., before becoming a Presbyterian minister, was a West Indian Negro. Shippen's mother was a full-blooded Shinnecock Indian.

Shippen and Bunn entered the 1896 Open, and at that the rest of the competitors, almost all émigré Scots and Englishmen, notified the USGA officials that they would not play if Shippen and Bunn did. The reason being, of course, that they were dark skinned. Shippen was their main target, as he had definite Negro facial features. Theodore Havemeyer, a department store magnate and at the time president of the USGA, told the boycotters that the USGA had no entry restrictions based on race, and if they didn't want to play that was their business—the championship would go on without them. The boycott ended the instant after his declaration. Everyone played, and Shippen finished tied for fifth after sharing the first-round lead. He had rounds of 78–81 in the thirty-six-hole contest, and took home a check for $10.

Shippen played in four more U.S. Opens, getting another fifth, his highest ever finish, in 1902. He then worked as a professional at golf clubs in the New York City metropolitan area and elsewhere in the east, but didn't make much news. According to Calvin Sinnette in his book tracing the history of black American golf, *Forbidden Fairways*, Shippen took to heavy drinking, left his family, and died poor and obscure in New Jersey, in 1968.

Shippen, of course, was the first African-American to play in the U.S. Open or any other tournament in the United States in which whites also played. And for some time afterward, he was the only one. The majority of African-Americans who got into golf at all during the first half of the twentieth century were from the South, but they worked only as caddies or club cleaners. Some would play in the early morning at the courses where they worked and occasionally sneak on a public course where they were not allowed. Walter "Chink" Stewart, an African-American from Virginia who became one of the first of his race to hold a professional's job— at a public course in Baltimore with mainly Afro-American patronage— recalled times when he and his pals were shot at by whites passing the course in a car. "We'd get down on our stomachs and when they went away we'd get up and finish the hole. These guys were hired to shoot at us. This was on all the golf courses down around Virginia. Of course it was our fault, because we were told not to play. So we took our chances."

African-Americans were always able to enter the U.S. Open, but until 1948, when Ted Rhodes made the cut, very few did. The main reason was that few blacks had been able to develop games for that level of competition. They had at best limited access to public courses in the North or South. In some cities blacks could play the city-owned course one day a week, usually on Monday. Often private clubs were used for qualifiers, and upon learning that a black man was entered, some would tell the USGA to find another venue. If the black man was allowed on, he was hardly made to feel welcome. Often he would have to play practice rounds alone, because whites would not play with him. Bob Sommers, former editor of the USGA's *Golf Journal*, remembered that when Chink Stewart tried to qualify one year for the Open, at the Congressional Country Club, in Washington, D.C., he wasn't allowed to eat lunch in the clubhouse. "They gave him lunch on the verandah, outside. With a lot of people around him," Sommers recalled.

Eventually, enough African-Americans took up golf that in 1928 an association was formed, the United Golf Association, with twenty-six member clubs (organized groups that played at public courses). The headquarters was in Stowe, Massachusetts. The UGA put on a National Open and other tournaments. Other African-American golf organizations formed, such as the Eastern Golf Association, and a black pro tour developed. The purse money was sometimes put up by heavyweight champion Joe Louis and middleweight champion "Sugar" Ray Robinson. The tournaments were played on municipal courses, and for very small purses—usually $300—and there were times when the money wasn't available at the end of the tournament. Or ever after.

Interestingly, the blacks didn't keep white pros from playing in their tournament, and some did, often after missing the cut for a PGA Tour event. With the advantage of having played more high-level competitive golf, the white "cherry pickers" often took the first-prize check. They would collect their money, then head back to the whites-only circuit.

In the early 1940s African-American entries were accepted for a few PGA Tour events—the St. Paul Open, the Los Angeles Open, the Canadian Open, and George May's Tam O'Shanter All-American and World tournaments. The sponsors of these events were brave enough to go counter to the prevailing attitude, which kept blacks in their own backyard. These progressive groups were going up against the notorious "Caucasians Only" clause in the constitution of the PGA of America.

Membership in the PGA was limited to whites only. How the term Caucasian was selected is a mystery, a euphemism that perhaps had a less offensive ring than "Whites Only." In any case, the clause was written into the association's constitution in 1943 and may well have been a response to the stirrings of racial equality in the air. President Truman had desegregated the United States military around this time, and there were other intimations that widespread desegregation was coming. When Herb Graffis, author of *The PGA*, was asked why the "Caucasians Only" clause was inserted, the normally gregarious and articulate (if sometimes quite obscene) Graffis mumbled something about job opportunities for its members.

If African-Americans could have joined the PGA, they might have had some chance of being hired by a private club, but it was hardly likely. For the record, before 1943, only one African-American ever was a professional at a white private club. And it was an accident. In 1928 the application for membership in the PGA of America submitted by Dewey Martin was accepted. Martin was a light-skinned Negro without the facial features stereotypical of black Africans; he had passed as white. He worked at various private clubs in New Jersey as an assistant pro, club maker, and teacher. A talented club maker, he once made a set of clubs for Chick Evans, as well as sets for members of Baltusrol Golf Club, Morris County Golf Club, the Knoll Country Club, and Shawnee-on-the Delaware. But in 1934 Martin's membership in the PGA of America was revoked. No reason was ever given, but it was almost certainly because the PGA discovered Martin's racial ancestry.

The PGA of America was administering the PGA Tour (which wasn't its official title at the time, but we'll use it for convenience sake), and only members of the association were allowed to play events it co-sponsored, which was almost all of them. Most of the sponsors of tour events and the PGA Tour didn't want African-American participation in their game any more than major league baseball, football, and basketball did at that time. The sponsors noted earlier who did let blacks play were able to thwart the PGA by offering such good purses (as did George S. May's Tam O'Shanter events), or had so much prestige (like the Los Angeles Open) that the white pros couldn't pass them up.

This determination to let blacks play by tournament sponsors helped kick off the protracted, but eventually successful fight against discrimination in American golf. In January, 1948, two African-American pros, Ted Rhodes and Bill Spiller, finished in the money in the Los Angeles Open. Spiller shot a 68 in the first round, to tie for second with the eventual winner, Ben Hogan. He got a lot of notice from that one round, although he eventually finished thirty-fourth. (Rhodes finished twenty-first. The PGA Tour's system at the time had it that any golfer who finished in the money in a tournament automatically qualified to play in the next event on the schedule.

Thus, after the Los Angeles Open, Rhodes and Spiller traveled upstate to play in the Richmond Open. After their second practice round they were notified by George Schneiter, a tour pro and at the time the chief of the PGA's tournament bureau, that Spiller, Rhodes, and Madison Gunter, an African-American who got into the field as a local qualifier, would not be allowed to play. Schneiter pointed out that the provision allowing in-the-money players entree to the next event was superseded by the "Caucasians Only" clause.

Inspired by Jackie Robinson, who had recently broken the color barrier in major league baseball, and also out of his own wrath, Spiller took action. He was the first of his race to challenge the PGA's system. Spiller was born in 1913, in Tishomongo, Oklahoma. He lived there until he was nine, then moved to Tulsa to be with his father and attend elementary and high school. He then went on to Wiley College, a small all-black school in Marshall, Texas, where he got a degree in education and sociology. He was certified to teach in Texas, but the only job that came through was in a rural school at $60 a month. Seeing no future there, Spiller moved to Los Angeles, where he got a job as a redcap at the central railroad station.

In his spare time Spiller took up golf. A good athlete who ran track in college, Spiller quickly picked up the knack for golf and became a good player. Only a few years after getting into the game, he was one of the best players on the African-American tournament circuit. But more significantly, Spiller was one of the few African-Americans in golf at the time with a higher education, and he was intelligent, articulate, and angry. After being told he couldn't play in the Richmond Open, Spiller connected with a lawyer in Oakland, John Rowell, who had some experience with discrimination cases. Spiller, along with Rhodes and Gunter, announced they were going to sue the PGA of America for $250,000 for denying them employment in their chosen profession.

The three did not play in Richmond, but when E. J. "Dutch" Harrison won the tournament, he was handed a blank check because the lawsuit froze all funds. Spiller and Rhodes returned to Los Angeles and left Rowell in charge of the lawsuit. However, on the train to Los Angeles, where the suit was to be tried, the PGA's attorney met with Rowell and struck a bargain. If the suit was dropped, the PGA would not discriminate against blacks in tournaments designated opens, as most were. Rowell convinced Spiller that the PGA would follow through, and the suit was dropped.

Howell, Spiller, Rhodes, and Gunter were snookered, however. The PGA began to designate most if not all its tournaments as invitationals or open invitationals, which meant everyone who played was invited by the sponsors. Needless to say, no blacks got invitations. Spiller and Rhodes went back to playing on their circuit, hauling luggage at the railroad station, caddying, hustling. Ted Rhodes became Joe Louis's personal pro and traveled with the heavyweight champ, who loved his golf. Singer Billy Eckstine took a young up-and-comer named Charlie Sifford under tow and helped him financially to play the game. There was no movement in regard to playing the PGA Tour, though. Only Tam O'Shanter, Los Angeles, St. Paul, and Canada could be counted on.

Spiller recalled that one year when qualifying for the U.S. Open, at the Bel-Air Country Club in Los Angeles, Fred Astaire noticed him in the locker room changing shoes. "Astaire stared at me as if to say, 'What the hell are you doing here?' If eyes could kill, I would have died right there. But I looked right back at him, didn't bat an eye. Astaire finally said, 'Well, I guess maybe you're supposed to be here.'

"Then there was a time at the L.A. Open," Spiller continued, "when they paired Ted Rhodes, myself, and another black pro. When I came out on the first tee I told the starter, 'You know, something puzzles me. How come we all three got paired together, all blacks?' He said, 'You know how it is, we got some Texas guys to deal with.' I said I thought this was the L.A. Open, not the Texas Open. If they don't want to play with us, tell 'em to go to hell back to Texas. Well, the starter's microphone was on all the time and boy, the crowd heard all that and went wild, clapping, and whistling. They didn't do those kind of pairings anymore.

"Even at Tam O'Shanter, they put us in the basement locker room at first, so I asked Mister May why that was so and he said we just had to go slowly or we wouldn't have it at all. But we were put upstairs after that."

Then, at the 1952 San Diego Open, there was an episode that moved things well forward. It was, effectively, the seminal event in the new order for African-Americans in American golf. The tournament was billed as an open and a charity money-raising event, and Joe Louis was playing as an amateur and drawing card. It was presumed to be an event not under PGA Tour jurisdiction, and Spiller and Rhodes were encouraged by some local white professionals to try qualifying. Both tried, and did. But this time Horton Smith, the president of the PGA of America, stepped in. A Missourian of ordinary means who married into great wealth (Singer sewing machines), Smith took on the manner of an arrogant overlord when it came to African-Americans. He told Rhodes and Spiller that they would not be allowed to play in San Diego. Neither could Joe Louis, said Smith.

Spiller remembered that when Louis heard this news, he remarked that Smith was another Hitler, and added, "If you think I can't play, listen to Walter Winchell on Sunday night." Winchell was a nationally syndicated newspaper gossip columnist who also had a popular Sunday evening radio program. "Hello, Mister and Missus America, and all the ships at sea," was how Winchell opened his radio show, with a news ticker in the background echoing his own staccato speaking style. Winchell commented on the San Diego Open matter, saying that if Joe Louis could carry a gun in the U.S. Army he could certainly carry a golf club in San Diego.

Because Louis was involved, the issue was now very much in the public eye. Horton Smith allowed Louis to play, but not Spiller and Rhodes. In protest Spiller delayed the start of the tournament by standing on the first tee in the direct line the players had to hit on. His action led Horton Smith to call a meeting that included Louis, his friend Leonard Reed, and Euell Clark, an African-American amateur golfer. Spiller was conspicuously not invited. When Jimmy Demaret spotted him standing in a hallway outside the meeting room, he told Spiller he should be in on it. Spiller confronted Smith, and later related what happened:

So I go into the room and Horton Smith says, "You're Bill Spiller, aren't you?" I said I was and he asked if there was something I wanted to say. I said, "I know and you know that we're going to play in the tournaments. We all know it's coming. So if you love golf like you say you do, and like I do, I think we should make an agreement so we can play without all this adverse publicity. And take this Caucasians-only clause out so we can have opportunities to get jobs as pros at clubs." I went on about how the PGA has a job-placement service and only PGA members are appointed to jobs and I would like to get one of those jobs. So Horton Smith says, "Yeah, we've got a job-placement service, but golf is social and semi-social and we have to be careful who we put on the job." So I said, "Mister Smith, I heard that you made a statement that if you were as big as Joe Louis you would knock me down. Well, if I hated someone that much I wouldn't let size bother me."

So someone said let's not turn this into personalities, and I said he should talk to me like a man, not a kid who doesn't know what he's talking about. Then I said I wanted to know why I wasn't entered in the pairings for the tournament after I qualified. Smith said it was because I didn't have a PGA player's card. I said that wasn't good enough for me, and Smith says, "If you don't want to take my word for it, I'll just let the chips fall where they may." I said okay, I'll see you in court. Leland Gibson and Jackie Burke, two white pros, stopped me at the door and asked me to give them a chance to work it out, and I said I would but if they don't I'll see them in court. I told them they ran over me the last time, but they aren't going to do that this time. I promised them I wouldn't bring the suit right away, and I never did.

The result of this confrontation was an amendment to the PGA's constitution whereby players who were not members could play in tour events as approved entries, if they were invited by the sponsors. The "Caucasians Only" clause remained on the books, but was being more or less circumvented in respect to playing the tour. As part of the bargain, Horton Smith went on the record to say the PGA ought to revise its rule barring Negroes from tournaments.

Joe Louis was allowed to play in San Diego, but Spiller and Rhodes were not. However, Spiller and Rhodes did play the following two events, in Tucson and Phoenix. A rent was made in the white sheet that had been covering mainstream American golf. Spiller, Rhodes, Charlie Sifford, and a few other African-Americans began to play portions of the PGA Tour, beginning in the early 1950s. They were advised not to go into the South by sympathetic but realistic white tour pros, such as Jimmy Demaret, and they didn't until Sifford played in the Greensboro Open in 1959.

Both Spiller and Rhodes were in their forties by this time, and being a bit past their prime as golfers they did not play much of the tour once it opened up for them. Rhodes might have done very well, if he had gotten an earlier start. A slender man who smoked heavily, his health began to deteriorate about this time. He died of a heart attack in 1969. Rhodes was the best African-American golfer of his day. He had a fine golf swing, the result in part of being one of the few blacks of his time to get quality instruction—from Ray Mangrum, brother of Lloyd. The best Spiller did on the PGA Tour was fourteenth place in the Labatt Open in Canada, which was good for a small check.

It would fall to Charlie Sifford to pioneer the African-American presence as a player on the PGA Tour. In some respects he may not have
been the right man for the job. Sifford, who came up in Charlotte, North
Carolina, was anything but a smooth public-relations type. Then again,
he needed a hard-shell finish to withstand the vicious treatment he sometimes received. When he became the first African-American to play against
whites in the South, he was taunted with racial slurs from the gallery. He
once received a phone call in which his life was threatened if he showed
up on the first tee in the 1959 Greensboro Open.

"I had a good chance to get in the Masters if I finished good," Sifford
recalled of that event, "and I was going good. Suddenly, I was intercepted
by five white men who started following me around the course. They
threw beer cans at me and called me nigger and other names. This went
on for several holes. The men were finally arrested, but after that I lost
a lot of strokes and finished far down the money list."

Strangely, the National Association for the Advancement of Colored
People wouldn't take part in Sifford's efforts. In the early 1950s he asked
the NAACP to step in and support his entry in the Houston Open, but
the association refused, saying that he was not facing racial discrimination.
For all that, Sifford held his game together with a compact, nicely formed
golf swing and picked up checks with some regularity. In 1957, when he
won the Long Beach (California) Open, he became the first African-
American to win a tournament on the PGA Tour. It was an "unofficial"
event, because the total purse was below the minimum, but the victory
was over more than a few white players who were regulars on the tour. It
counted as official as far he and golf were concerned.

Sifford's victory in Long Beach aside, there were other bright lights for
blacks as they went through their ordeal. Bob Rickey was president of
MacGregor Golf Company during the 1950s, and he provided equipment
for Sifford, Spiller, and other black pros. Suitably, Rickey was a nephew
of Branch Rickey, the Brooklyn Dodger general manager who brought
Jackie Robinson into major league baseball.

Spiller related how this happened:

When I was in Cincinnati once, I went to the MacGregor factory to
get some woods made up. Bob Rickey was in the front office at the
time and he asked me if anybody was giving me any clubs. I said no,

so he told someone to fit me up with what I wanted—irons, woods, bag, balls, shoes. Everything. He said, "You don't ever have to buy clubs anymore. Just send a letter and tell us what you want." Then the Wilson company started giving Teddy [Rhodes] his equipment.

Sifford never complained that he was treated badly by the white tour pros, and in his autobiography, published in 1998, he lauded Jimmy Demaret, Sam Snead, Porky Oliver, Dave Hill, Jack Nicklaus, and Bob Rosburg for their support and encouragement. Spiller also remarked that Sam Snead, to his surprise—"He being a hillbilly"—was friendly.

Bill Spiller was the Martin Luther King, Jr., of African-American golf in the United States, with a touch of Malcolm X's radical pugnacity. However, he went largely unrecognized for his contributions, including the last one, which led to the termination of the "Caucasians Only" clause. In this struggle, there was very important input from the California Attorney General.

For the sake of continuity, I will forgo the chronological organization of this history and skip into the next decade. The 1962 PGA Championship was originally scheduled to be played at the Hillcrest Country Club in Los Angeles. At this time Spiller was caddying in the L.A. area to make ends meet. (He was also doing some golf teaching at local driving ranges, and he operated a doughnut shop in east Los Angeles.) One day he was caddying for Harry Braverman, who knew of Spiller's golf ability and asked why he wasn't out playing the tournament circuit or working at a club. Spiller explained the situation for blacks, and that while some progress had been made there was the "Caucasians Only" clause that stood in the way of job opportunities at private clubs. Braverman suggested Spiller write a letter outlining the situation to his friend Stanley Mosk, the California State Attorney General.

Spiller wrote to Mosk and the attorney general, who had also heard from Sifford on the issue, responded by telling the PGA of America it would not be allowed to play any of its regular tour events on public courses in California if African-Americans were barred from entry; never mind the sponsor invitations and all the rest. Many of the tour events were played on public courses in California at the time, and the edict was a problem for the PGA. Nevertheless, its initial response was to say that it would schedule its tournament at private clubs. This included the up-coming PGA Championship.

Mosk, who later became a judge on the California Appellate Court bench, told the PGA that he would find a way to legally bar them from that diversion. What's more, Mosk informed State Attorneys General around the country of his action, which put the tour in jeopardy elsewhere. By now, the Hillcrest Country Club, which had a predominantly Jewish membership, was not inclined to host the PGA Championship. The PGA relocated its 1962 championship to the Aronimink Country Club, near Philadelphia. History includes some amazing ironies. African-American John Shippen represented Aronimink when he played in the 1899 U.S. Open. And the 1962 PGA Championship that was shifted to the club was won by Gary Player, the white South African whose country in those years practiced its system of apartheid. When Charlie Sifford won his most pres-tigious PGA Tour event, the 1959 Los Angeles Open, he defeated Harold Henning, another white South African, in a play-off. Be all that as it may, after Mosk's moves and threats, the PGA of America rescinded its infa-mous "Caucasians Only" clause in 1961.

Spiller's work was done, although he never drew any personal benefits from it. He didn't even get a lot of succor from his own people during the early struggles. Although Joe Louis made significant contributions to the cause of African-American golf, in the heavy going in San Diego in 1952, he told Spiller that he talked too much. And, when Spiller said he was going to use the bathroom in the clubhouse at the Tucson tournament in 1952, Rhodes told him he should just go in the refreshment stand near the 10th tee and don't rile things up any more than need be.

Spiller became increasingly bitter as he aged. His eyesight failed badly, he suffered two strokes, and contracted Parkinson's disease. Because of his illnesses and continuing anger over his personal fate in golf, his family placed him in a convalescent home, where he died in 1988 at age seventy-five. At one point his son, William, Jr., castigated his father for letting his passion for golf and the fight he fought get in the way of properly sup-porting his family. But in time William, Jr., who became an attorney, learned to appreciate what his father stood for and what he accomplished. When Spiller died, the event went unrecognized in the general golf press. "The man died with a broken heart," said Maggie Hathaway, the black activist who was a backroom factor in the fight for African-American golf equality.

The 1950s was the decade when the tree of American golf began to bear fruit. Television's fateful eye was unveiled, African-Americans got closer to the game's mainstream, the men's and women's pro tours were growing in numbers of events and purse money. And, a new cadre of young players, led by Arnold Palmer, began to dominate the game. The 1960s was when the ripening process began.

4 | The 1960s: The American Game

First Comes Arnie, Then Comes Jack; Golf and TV Consummate the Marriage; The Agent Arrives; Mickey Wright, the Magnificent; An Even Newer Ball Spawns the Metal "Wood"; The Dance Floor Changes Owners; The New Immigrants

The 1960 U.S. Open had all the elements of a classic Hollywood western. A fresh young fastest-gun hits town and wins a shoot-out against the reigning fastest-gun, who has seen his best days. The old-timer is hurt bad, but manages to mount his horse and ride slowly into the sunset. Not far out, he passes another young buck with a hungry look in his eye heading for town to lock horns with the newest fastest-gun on the block.

The 1960 open was all that metaphorically and rather close in reality. It had an all-encompassing dynamic. The competition itself—the shot-making and scoring were dramatically exciting and of high quality—but there was also considerable historical consequence and symbolism.

To begin at the beginning, in the final round, at the Cherry Hills Country Club in Denver, Colorado, thirty-year-old Arnold Palmer fired a six-under par 65 to come from seven shots off the lead to take the title. No one had ever come from so far behind in the last round to win the national championship, no one had ever shot that low a final-round score, win or lose, and no one had ever shown the emotion Palmer did upon concluding his play; he flipped his visor high in the air, which sounds tame from a 1990s viewpoint but at the time was unconventional and, in the long run, a gesture in which the sum effect was much greater than the ordinary part.

Some fifteen minutes before that expression of joy, forty-eight-year-old Ben Hogan concluded his last serious attempt to win the championship he prized above all others and for which he was supremely suited by nature and technique. On the par-five seventeenth hole (the seventy-first of the tournament), Hogan had a short wedge third shot to a pin cut very close to the front of the green, which is situated just behind a creek. A sucker pin, as the saying goes. Hogan would never have been suckered in the past—he was a conservative golfer who took few risky shots. But he knew that Palmer, playing a hole behind him, was on a roll making a lot of birdies and shooting a low score. Hogan also sensed, perhaps knew, that this would be his last serious crack at his fifth U.S. Open title. No one had won that many, and he wanted it badly. He determined he needed a birdie on the seventeenth and he took a chance. He shot for the pin, not behind it. His ball carried to the front edge of the green, but spun back into the water. He made a six and slumped visibly. It was over. The triple-bogey seven he made on the last hole for a ninth place finish was immaterial.

As it turned out, if Hogan parred the last two holes with a five and four he would have tied Palmer. Then again, had he made those two pars it might have changed Palmer's strategy, made him more aggressive and perhaps not as effective. But Palmer might have risen to the challenge and made the birdie he would have needed to win. As it was, when Palmer came to the seventy-first hole he knew about Hogan's score on the hole, laid up short of the creek with his second shot, and played safely in.

At the very same time Hogan was going through his last-ditch travails, twenty-year-old amateur Jack Nicklaus, who was paired with Hogan on that last day of play, finished in second place two strokes behind Palmer. It was the highest finish by an amateur since Johnny Goodman won the Open in 1933. Also, at two under par 282, it was the lowest total score ever registered by an amateur in the U.S. Open. Nicklaus was not an unknown at the time. He won the U.S. Amateur Championship in 1959 and other high-level amateur events. But as history would prove, his 1960 Open performance had a special significance. Two years later he would vanquish Palmer in a U.S. Open play-off and begin his own not unexpected rise to supreme eminence in the game.

That day at Cherry Hills, the last two competitive hours of that day marked the end of one distinctive era in American golf and the beginning of a very new and different one. It also solidified the United States's position as the ascendant leader of world golf. This changing of the guard in Denver was not between Americans and Britons or British-born immigrants, as it was when John McDermott won his two U.S. Opens to become the first native-born American national champion; when Francis Ouimet defeated Harry Vardon and Ted Ray at the Country Club in 1913; or when Walter Hagen became the first native-born American to win the British Open. At Denver in 1960 American golfers who had proven they were the best in the world were replacing Americans who had held that same status on the game's totem pole.

It's Show Time!

Again, it is not really fair to Sam Snead to designate the 1950s the Hogan Era, but Hogan was the sharpest reflection of an approach to playing the game professionally, and behaving at center stage, that prevailed up to then. Hogan was asked once, late in his life, whether as a tournament golfer he ever considered himself an entertainer. Ordinarily, he responded to such questions only after long pauses during which he gathered his thoughts and considered the language he would use. In this case his response was immediate, but characteristically succinct. "No," he said. He never thought of himself as putting on a show for the gallery. Hogan regarded himself as a professional golfer in the same way an auto mechanic regarded himself as an auto mechanic. He took pleasure and pride at being able to take a car apart and put it together again, but he did not romanticize it. Hogan often said he enjoyed the challenge that golf presented and that he liked to practice and improve, but he was not inclined to rhapsodize about the grand sweep of a dew-fresh course on an early summer morning with robins atwitter in the trees or the untrammeled bunkers awaiting the errant interloper, the shades of the game's Scottish sires hovering over his shoulder. The golf course was Hogan's office, and he went there because playing golf was what he happened to know and do best, and at which he could make a living. More than a few later stars of the game would carry on about how they played golf not for the money but simply to excel and to win championships. Easily said when you grew up in suburban comfort and had millions to play for. Did you play golf for money, Mister Hogan?

"Yes," he said, "you have to eat."

Hogan, like all his contemporaries, was a product of the Great Depression. They played tournaments for a pittance in prize money compared to what the purses would become, but even that trifle was more than nothing and they meant to have it. To play such a difficult game so well was a source of pride to be sure, but there were a lot of people out there with talent, and to survive, Hogan and all the tour pros of this era took the game very seriously. To not was to die, figuratively. Maybe even literally. Even those who projected a lighter demeanor, who acted as though it was only a game, were often throwing up a facade. Jimmy Demaret could be flip and smiley when his game was not going well. It was his saving grace. But when he was on his game and had a sniff at victory, he showed his determination in much the same way as Hogan and Nelson and Snead, and all the others. Cocoons fell over them with the force of a bear trap. Eyes hardened behind a crafty, resolute squint, all movements were made with a purpose. A kill was at hand, it was time to stalk.

Hogan was the point man, the most visible mirror of this unvarnished attitude toward the work of the tour pro. Hogan was the paradigm in part because of his accident and astonishing recovery, but also because of the way he looked even before the accident as he went about his business—the body language, the set of his jaw, and the uncommon control he had over his golf ball. He obviously devoted his whole being to golf, defining his life through it.

By comparison Jimmy Demaret had a nice tenor voice and liked to sing to an audience—as a young man he sang in a nightclub in Galveston, Texas. He enjoyed cavorting with show business people, hunting, and fishing. He raised a family, invested his money, had a few "pops" at the bar most days, and just about every night. Sam Snead played a cornet, hunted and fished, produced children, and was a master story- and joke-teller.

Hogan decided not to have children because, he said, he would not have been an attentive father; that is, children would interfere with his golf. Apparently, his wife Valerie had no say in the decision. Hogan had no close friends, didn't go to the movies, didn't read books or fish or hunt or womanize. He did play cards at one time, but gave it up. Mainly, Hogan hit golf balls and played golf while he was an active competitor. After that, he didn't teach golf except for offering an occasional tip to a very select one or two people. He went into business making golf equipment and spent most of his time in the factory. Otherwise, he hit practice balls and drank gin, usually by himself because it appeared by the cast of his presence that he didn't want company. He did, but you couldn't tell.

But Hogan was also part of an attitude about being an athlete that exemplified society's value system and the competitive behavior of his era. One did not show any passion if a shot went well or a tournament was won, because, after all, as a professional you are supposed to hit good shots and win tournaments. That's what you are paid for. But if a round or even a single shot goes poorly, the response is the same. There is no show of emotion, because that would not be manly. And, too, wouldn't a display of frustration indicate weakness and perhaps give the opponent a psychological edge? To get down on yourself and express it could bring more poor shots.

This restrained behavior was a hallmark of the culture of the period. One did not boast or showboat. Joe DiMaggio once touched the brim of his cap for an instant in response to cheers after a great catch and it made headlines in the next day's paper. Perhaps this, too, was a product of the depression. Don't get too optimistic, because the roof could come down on your head any second and probably will. Modesty, at best a cautious enthusiasm, was the way to be. Ben Hogan would smile in victory, and it was a fine smile, but only at the trophy presentation ceremony.

Which explains, to a large extent, the enormous popularity of Arnold Palmer when he came upon the scene. He broke a mold, one that apparently needed breaking, because everyone loved his exuberant response to his victories and his defeats. When a putt slid by the hole, Palmer's body writhed and his face contorted in the agony of it. When he clinched his victory on the last green at Cherry Hill in 1960, and with a stiff-legged hop onto his toes whipped his visor off his brow and tossed it high in the air toward the gallery, it was refreshing. How human after the laconic, phlegmatic, stoic, impassive self-possession of "the wee ice mon," as the Scots dubbed Hogan; and all those other breadline types. The depression was long gone, the war, too. Palmer unleashed the raging hormones of melodrama, the buried urge to effervesce. And how effective it was when it came over that small and terrifically intimate television screen.

It is sometimes forgotten that before his histrionics at Cherry Hill, Arnold Palmer had already won eighteen tournaments on the pro tour. He won his first Masters in 1958; his second earlier in 1960. In many of those wins he had made similar birdie-filled charges from behind the leaders. And he had displayed the agony and the ecstasy for all to see. The 1960 U.S. Open was really just another link in a behavioral chain that was already fairly long. But in another sense, it was a first because it was for the national championship. Arnold Palmer did not become Arnie, "the King," until the camera caught him at his best as a player and actor in his game's most important theater.

Palmer's very style of play spoke of unchained energy, of having a fling, of letting it all hang out, an expression that became current vernacular after Palmer's rise, and—who knows?—could have had its root in Palmer's famous flying shirttails. The solemn existential mien of the 1950s and before was blissfully buried by the rambunctious young Palmer fellow from Pennsylvania. His swing was not at all graceful like Sam Snead's, and it was not at all the consciously controlled, perfectly balanced mechanism that was Hogan's. Arnie took a hard whack at the ball, really tore into it, and had this follow-through in which the club flailed around like a swizzle stick in a blender on high. He watched the flight of the ball with his head bent low and to the side, like a young guy in a crowd trying to get a peek at the long legs of a beauty queen. The average guy who played once a week at the local muni and never took a lesson in his life could identify with *that* swing, as well as the emotions. And he did.

Palmer was a hit, a big hit. A large and loyal following formed called Arnie's Army, and the enlistees would remain in service long after Palmer had stopped winning tournaments. Palmer would transcend identification with only his game. He became more than a famous golfer, he became a folk hero recognized even by churchly old ladies in the far reaches of Iowa who didn't know a golf club any more than they did a Gulf credit card. Bob Harlow told the tournament pros back in the 1930s that they were in "the show business," but they couldn't or wouldn't comprehend his wisdom. Palmer did. So did his clever manager, Mark McCormack.

Palmer's arrival as a golf champion was perfectly timed. He was in the vanguard of a new and uniquely American zeitgeist that was prodded into being by the miracle of television. The world was entering the Visual Age, in which image became reality. Insights to people were not based on what they said or even how they said it. Products were no longer sold on the strength of the written word and the persuasiveness of those words. Perceptions would be made on the basis of how something or someone looked. The face of things can be manipulated so much easier than language in print, which takes time and thought to discern. The exterior was becoming the measure of content and value, and as the modern world became increasingly visual, judgments were necessarily speeded up. One picture began to speak more than a thousand words or ten thousand. America led the video revolution, and being almost exclusively business directed, arose as the world's most adroit and persistent advertiser of goods, services, and personalities. The advertising agency was an American institution, as was its first cousin, the public relations firm. Arnold Palmer fit the new cast like a glove.

This is not to suggest that Arnold Palmer's remarkable popularity was a contrived scheme he and his agent cooked up or that it was based on creating false images. He and Mark McCormack recognized the essence of his appeal and knew how to take advantage of it. At the height of his preeminence some of Palmer's fellow pros, Jack Nicklaus included, commented that Arnie was always aware when the television camera was pointing his way and that was when he'd start hitching up his pants, one of his most celebrated nervous tics, and sulk or smile as the situation dictated. Another time, this writer was a firsthand witness to Palmer's consciousness of his image. In a match filmed for the television series *Shell's Wonderful World of Golf* in 1966, Palmer was playing Julius Boros. It was on the island of Eleuthera in the Bahamas. The R&A's rules were in effect, because the island was a British protectorate, and if they chose, the golfers could use the smaller British ball that was still extant. Boros did, feeling it would give him a bit more distance in the windy conditions. Arnie stayed with the bigger American ball, and Boros was outhitting him with the driver. This was contrary to what people expected. Palmer was Mr. Power. (In fact, he wasn't as long a hitter as his swing would suggest. Jack Nicklaus proved that decisively in his 1963 U.S. Open play-off with Palmer.) Midway through the match on Eleuthera, after once again being out hit from the tee, Palmer sidled up to announcer George Rogers and off-camera suggested that he remind the audience that Boros was playing the smaller ball. Rogers did. Palmer's image was preserved or protected.

Palmer's common-man manner, his nervous energy, his willingness to take chances in his golf were a genuine part of his being. He was in fact the working-class sort of guy he projected. Palmer grew up in a small town near Pittsburgh—Latrobe, Pennsylvania, the only son of the greenskeeper, and later the professional, at the Latrobe Country Club. Deacon, or Deke, Palmer was a man with an Old-World concept of social place. He didn't allow his son to use the golf course to play and practice except on Monday morning, the conventional caddie day, or to use the club's pool any time, even when no members were around. Deke himself would never take a meal in the clubhouse. He knew his place as a golf professional. Obviously, Arnold found ways to play and practice. And many years later, he bought the Latrobe Country Club.

Palmer may not have enjoyed the restrictive atmosphere his father enforced, and he rebelled as any young man would. His father was a tough egg, and the relationship between him and his son was often stormy. Palmer's wife, Winnie, who died of cancer in 1999, told the writer of times when Arnold and Deke sometimes got physical in their disagreements, especially when they had been drinking, and Deke only once in all the years ever gave his son a pat on the back and a word of encouragement. Perhaps Arnold's desire to reach the crowd and make it love him was a way of filling the void his father's reticence had left within him.

During a tournament round Palmer could be as sternly, firmly, and quietly competitive as Ben Hogan and his ilk. And like all super achievers in sports, he had few really close friends among his competitors on the circuit. But somehow or other it didn't come off that way. He cultivated the image makers or image sustainers—the journalists who covered golf. They liked him because he responded to the press easily and, more to the point, willingly. Getting a worthwhile quote out of Hogan was root-canal work. Snead's quippy country-boy comportment was a veneer—Sam was a hard case especially when things went badly. Arnie was not very witty and certainly not profound, but he remembered the first names of the writers and addressed them that way. On occasion he bellied up to the bar with them. He didn't really reveal much about himself. There was a lot of hold-back in him, a well of privacy for reasons that would only become apparent in the years ahead. But when the writers learned that Arnie, a married man, had a roving eye, the journalists buried it. Arnie was lucky in this. He came on the scene just before sportswriters and their editors began revealing the off-course behavior of famous athletes. Arnie was the boy-next-door; not too complicated, an okay guy, an easy write for the print journalists, and a perfect fit for the quick-cut, no-time-for-depth nature of television. And best of all, he was a winner. He could really play and in an exciting way.

Jack Nicklaus may have snickered a bit when he thought Arnold Palmer was playing to the camera, but he too came to understand the power and value of image in the world of televised sports. Nicklaus came out on tour a stout young man wearing baggy, nondescript clothes, a military style crew-cut, and a kind of self-assurance that was taken, to some extent for good reason, as arrogance. When you are very good, you are allowed a certain amount. And if you don't have a certain amount, you aren't going to be very good.

Nicklaus was not well liked, image-wise, by the golf fans, especially after he defeated Palmer in a play-off for the 1962 U.S. Open. Where does this spoiled kid, brought up a member of a country club, get off raking our guy from the caddie yard over the coals? Fat Jack, they called him, and Nick-*louse* not Nick-*luss*.

Nicklaus wouldn't say as much publicly, but he was stung by that first response to him as a celebrity. He thought just being excellent at what he did was enough to win the good graces of the public. It didn't work that way, not anymore, and so Nicklaus had a makeover. He grew his hair long and lost a good bit of weight. His hair came out with some shape and in an attractive yellow-blond. The weight loss got him a clothing contract with Hart Schaffner & Marx, which smartened up his wardrobe. He looked good, and the arrogance began to be seen as self-confidence. The reception toward him grew warmer. Nicklaus would never achieve the kind of adoration that Arnie did, but in time, as his record reached a monumental level and Palmer's game declined, he gathered a solid and appreciative following. And when he won so dramatically in the 1986 Masters, and he and his son, who was caddying for him, embraced at the end, Nicklaus became a more sympathetic figure than he had ever been in the public's mind. Or eye.

Golf and Television Consummate the Wedding

Like so much history in general, the evolution and development of golf has more often than not been the result of a single individual's effort to satisfy his own personal needs or agenda. Arnold Palmer didn't set out to save golf from the austere bearing Ben Hogan gave it; he wasn't thinking about helping the tour grow so those who came after him could play for millions. Arnie was looking out for himself, trying to rise up out of an ordinary economic background and make a good living for himself and his family. That he did de-Hoganize the tour and otherwise become a major force in golf's growth was a bonus for the rest of us. And him.

By the same token, television's connection with golf, which has been such an immensely important component—you could say *the most important*—in the game's rise to prominence in the last half of the twentieth century was not the result of a grand plan devised by an all-knowing, all-powerful committee of geniuses. An individual here, George S. May, an individual there, Harry Wismer, out to sell something, used television to their own ends. That a greater good came of it was okay, but incidental.

Monroe Spaeght, the chairman of the Shell Oil Company in the 1960s, was another such individual. Spaeght liked golf, to be sure. He had played it all his life and had a good sense of its history and a respect for its traditions. But Spaeght was also a man of his time and place, an American who headed up a very large international business concern and thought that he could probably peddle a lot of Shell oil and gasoline through golf. He was right.

One Sunday afternoon in the summer of 1960, after playing a round of golf at his club in Westchester County, New York, Spaeght watched an *All-Star Golf* show on television. He didn't like what he saw, thought it was not up to the high standards the old game deserved. He remarked to two of his executives that maybe the Shell company could do something better along that line. The executives misread Spaeght's informality, and when he asked them a month later what they were doing about his golf program, they looked quickly into the matter. The upshot was *Shell's Wonderful World of Golf*, a made-for-television series that had a weighty impact on American and world golf, world tourism to boot, and Shell Oil's ledger.

The original Shell show was produced by Filmways Productions in New York City, which was headed up by Martin Ransohoff. He assigned Fred Raphael, a New York City advertising man with no background at all in golf, to the project, which, to use the actual introduction to every show, was "A series of international golf matches played on the world's most famous courses."

Raphael didn't know anything about golf when he started, but he knew how to find the right people for the job and let them do it. His first hire was Herbert Warren Wind, who gave the program considerable golf expertise and immediate credibility in golf circles. He was golf writer for *Sports Illustrated* when the magazine was introduced, and he would later become the golf correspondent for *The New Yorker* magazine for many years. Wind also authored a comprehensive history of American golf, helped Gene Sarazen and Jack Nicklaus write their biographies, and collaborated with Ben Hogan on Hogan's hugely successful instruction book *Five Lessons: The Modern Fundamentals of Golf.*

Wind was instrumental in shaping the basic format of the Shell show, an eighteen-hole stroke-play competition between a well-known American professional and, whenever possible, the best golfer, pro, or amateur in the country where the match was played. He also recommended many of the courses on which to stage the matches and suggested that Gene Sarazen host the program. Sarazen by this time had become but a dim name in the game's history books, but golf buff Monroe Spaeght knew it well and took up Wind's idea without hesitation. In his dressy knickers and Panama hat, Sarazen gave the program the impression of golf history and tradition Spaeght sought. For Sarazen the program was a resurrection of his career.

Aside from fulfilling Spaeght's vision and reviving Gene Sarazen's public (and private) life, the program also floated the idea that Americans could play golf overseas in places other than Scotland and Ireland. It was not well known in the 1960s that golf was played in Greece, Denmark, Luxembourg, Malaysia, Monaco, and Thailand. To be sure, it wasn't all that prolific. Greece, for example, had only one course. And still does. The concept of the Shell show changed that; it also fed directly into the advent of the jet airliner as the newest mode of transportation. Filmed during the summer months for broadcast the following winter, one thirteen-show season series began in Houston, Texas, then went to Nova Scotia, Japan, the Philippines, Malaysia, Greece, Spain, Denmark, and Great Britain, all in approximately three months. A production crew of some thirty people made that and all the other world-wide trips. Seven cameras were used, and each one filmed every shot played. Some matches drew only a few hundred actual spectators—there were about as many golf buffs in Greece as there were golf courses—so local citizens were picked up off the street and movie and theater extras were hired to create a crowd. Being employees, these people were also positioned to hide the cameras—Spaeght didn't want anyone to see the production workings. The matches were filmed in color and the editing and other preparations for airing them took some six months. In all, it required close to ten months to put together a thirteen-match season series. The cost was in the $3 to $5 million range at the outset, around $10 million at the end.

Red Smith, a premier American sportswriter in the sixties and seventies, was asked once how he liked the Shell show. He remarked that he didn't care much whether Germany's Friedel Schmaderer or Louisiana's Jay Hebert won a match that didn't mean anything on a golf course in Hamburg, but he did enjoy the travelogues. Smith wasn't alone. Almost half the audience for the program—which was between ten and twelve million—did not play golf (although many would be stimulated to take it up), but enjoyed the three-minute travelogue that was part of every show. This segment, known in-house as the Postcard (because the producer-director got his material by checking the postcard stands in local stores), did more than a little to generate world tourism.

Except in a few instances, however, most notably the match between Sam Snead and Ben Hogan, the Shell show did not light any competitive fires. But that wasn't really the point. It was an entertainment and rather exotic for the time because of the locations. And of course, it sold the Shell Oil Company. The money for producing the program came out of Shell's public relations budget, and the advertising segments never mentioned a specific Shell product or a price. It is what is called institutional advertising, which projects the company's image. This does not mean hard sales aren't expected. At the end of the Shell show's ten-year stint on television, the oil company's net sales had increased by some forty percent. It was widely conceded that the Shell show had a lot to do with that rise.

The Shell show aired from 1961 through 1970, a long run for a television program. The prize money at the beginning was $2,000 to the winner of the match, $1,000 to the loser. It eventually went to $7,000 and $5,000, plus expenses, which wasn't a bad payday for the time. But it wasn't the cash that made it important for the players: it was the chance to appear on the program. Being seen by a few million people on the tube was worth many times over the prize money in endorsements, or the potential for them, plus lucrative corporate outings and exhibitions. Just being on television confers celebrity and bestows an air of importance.

The most memorable match of the series, which has become an heir-loom of its kind, was Snead versus Hogan. The career-long arch rivals, the two best golfers of their generation (after Byron Nelson retired), played at the Houston Country Club in Houston, Texas, in 1964. Every-one was surprised Hogan agreed to do the show. He had been saying he would not show his game in public anymore, because it was not up to his standards. It was also common knowledge that his putting had become an agonizing affair. He would stand over a putt for what seemed like an hour, obviously struggling just to get his club in motion. Years later it was revealed that Hogan didn't play on the Shell show for the love of the game, or to test himself one more time against Snead, and certainly not for the entertainment value. He did it to promote his company, the Ben Hogan Golf Company, which was still a fairly new enterprise. Hogan may not have been in show business, personally, but he was not above using it to his advantage. He also knew how to take advantage of his peculiar mystique. He was paid a hefty appearance fee, which no one else who played the matches received.

Hogan gave a good show, though, and in the one way he could. He was magnificent from tee to green. Just about perfect. Although he and Snead had to wait as much as twenty minutes for the cameras to be moved and set up before each shot, and there was a two-hour delay for a violent thunder and lightning storm that passed over, Hogan did not miss any of the fourteen fairways from the tee, and he hit every green in regulation. It was an enthralling display of precise ball control, and he defeated Snead 69–71.

While he was alive, Hogan would not allow the Houston match to be rerun on television or sold in video form when videos became a popular commodity. But after he died in 1998, the show went into release and has been the best-selling video in the Shell show series. Every golf teacher who is at all serious about his profession has a copy of the show so they can study Hogan's swing, and hear him, however briefly, talk technique. Hogan filmed a one-minute piece of instruction for the program that re-vealed how concise and insightful he could be when talking golf me-chanics. It is one of the few motion-picture records of his swing and discussion of his methods. It should also be mentioned that the video offers the opportunity to watch Snead's swing when he was still in his prime. It was a wonder of physical motion.

The Shell show inspired other made-for-television golf programs in the 1960s. There was *Big-Three Golf*, featuring Arnold Palmer, Jack Nicklaus, and Gary Player playing against each other on various courses around the world. This prompted a spin-off called *Challenge Golf*, which included a fourth player—a different one every week—who paired up with either Palmer, Player, or Nicklaus in a best-ball competition. The two shows were little more than showcases for the three stars and were not especially well produced. Each of the stars took turns doing play-by-play announcing, which came off as rather odd. But an audience was drawn. The shows brought the Big Three a lot of exposure, good money, and by the way, also promoted golf.

Another made-for-TV golf show in the sixties was *Match-Play Classic*, which was produced by the Columbia Broadcasting System. This had a far better competitive atmosphere than the Shell or Big-Three shows. All the matches were played at the Firestone Country Club's South Course, an excellent championship layout, and were between the best current PGA Tour players, excluding the Big Three. Sixty-four pros started out each "season" in an elimination series, with all the matches played in less than two weeks. The program was well produced by Frank Chirkinian, a pioneer golf television producer and director who had much to do with the successful television presentation of the Masters for over thirty years.

Also in 1960, a watershed year in American golf, live broadcasts of real golf tournaments—PGA Tour events—began. American free enterprise was on the go, although the major networks didn't take the first risks. Again, one man with no particular interest in golf, but plenty of nerve and a willingness to take a chance, got live PGA Tour telecasts off the ground. His name was Dick Bailey, a New Yorker who owned and operated Sports Network. He got into golf more or less accidentally. In 1959 ABC canceled its telecast of that year's Bing Crosby National Pro-Am tournament in order to broadcast the first championship game of the new American Football League. Crosby had only thirty days to find another outlet for his tournament. He was recommended to Bailey, who had a good reputation from his telecasts of college basketball, Cleveland Browns football games, and other sports. Bailey had to pay $25,000 for the rights to the Crosby tournament, which was considered a bargain and got some of his money back by taping the show and selling it to Japan and other foreign countries. "It was a delayed broadcast," said Bailey, "but it may have been the first time golf was on international television."

Bailey recognized that PGA Tour golf was going to be a hard sell in terms of advertising, but nevertheless thought there was a future in it. That year after the Crosby tournament, which was played in January, Bailey produced live telecasts of the Los Angeles, Phoenix, Tucson, Western, and Cleveland Opens, and a tournament in Las Vegas sponsored by casino operator Del Webb, called the Desert Inn Invitational, offering a total purse of $777,777.77. Hey, it was Vegas!

Bailey's Sports Network golf productions gradually increased in number. In 1966 he did twelve events. Bailey then sold his company to the Hughes Network, which was owned by the reclusive, eccentric billionaire Howard Hughes, who had once been a low-handicap golfer. The Hughes Network telecast as many as twenty tour events in some years, but by 1967 the major networks were beginning to see the possibility of a decent bottom line telecasting golf and formed their own production teams to cover tour events. In 1967 the three major networks bid a total of $1 million for the rights to cover the PGA Tour. Each got a few tournaments.

The Dancers Take the Floor

With so much money now involved in the tour, the problems that cropped up were inevitable. Who was going to control the getting of it, and who was going to keep it? The solution to these questions was a major factor in the enormous growth of the PGA Tour and in the Americanization of the game. Indeed, the rebellion within the ranks, as it were, was in the best American wild west tradition. The independent operator, the freelancer, the nonconformist intent on living apart from the ordinary mainstream battles the establishment to get his way. And gets it.

As far back as the late 1920s, the men who played the pro tour sought to run the circuit themselves. In the beginning, they actually did, with the help of their wives and a friendly sportswriter. But by 1934 the tour had grown enough that the PGA of America took over its administration. The relationship between the tour players and the PGA was never amicable, but the tour pros didn't object to PGA control at this time because Bob Harlow was running the tour and they liked him. Also, they made their main living as club pros and didn't have the time to both run a nationwide tournament circuit and play it or, at least, play well on it. High-level golf is a very demanding mistress. Since it was now possible to play the tour full-time, and because television had raised the ante, the issue of who was going to run the tour came to a final boil.

There were a number of elements involved in this power struggle. Pride, for one. Generally, the pros who went out around the country playing tournaments were better players than those who stayed home and gave lessons and sold balls and clubs in their shops. If they weren't better when they started out, they were after being out there for awhile. Most club pros could hit the ball as far as if not farther than many a tour pro, and could hit fine irons, and putt well, but they didn't do it as often. Consistency is the operative word. It takes a lot of hard work to get it and getting it is a result of will. Sometimes you have to force yourself to stay on the practice tee. There is a huge expenditure of physical energy and about the same on the mental side. Golf is a brain drainer; tournament golf turns the gray matter white. There is no rest for the weary, either. Once you get it, you have to work like hell to keep it.

Then too, it takes a lot of courage to test yourself against others who have worked just as hard. There is also the financial risk. The win-to-loss ratio for even the best players in the game is on the loss side. Losing is harder to take, because the entire onus is on the golfer. A team-game player can rationalize a loss when it's a teammate who causes it. A golfer who fails can only look inward. The look is invariably painful, full of self-blame, even guilt.

By the same token, the successful golfer also looks inward and takes full credit. He thinks of himself as all-powerful, all-knowing, the sole and only possible arbiter of his life and fate. Jack Nicklaus was known among his contemporaries as Karnak, a character devised by late-night talk show host Johnny Carson who knew everything about everything, including a lot of things he didn't know anything about. What tour pros really know is how tenuous their hold on the game is and that today's finely timed swing can dissolve overnight into a clumsy swat. To deal with the intransigence of golf, they put up an illusion in the form of absolutely positive wisdom, knowledge, and insight.

There is also the celebrity factor. The tour pro is much admired by those who come to watch him. The folks in the gallery, golfers themselves, are confounded by the inextricable mystery of golf and are overawed by the facility of these pros; how easy they make it look, how far they can hit the ball with such ease, how amazing that they can roll a ball at just the right speed and on just the right line so it curves perfectly into the hole from six feet, fifteen feet, forty feet. That these fellows are special pulsates in the gallery, and the pros feel the throb. It lights up their stars.

All of the above was at the core of the conflict between the tour pros and the PGA of America. The argument from the club pros' side was, they were doing as much for the game, if not more, by helping the average golfer improve and keep up his interest in it. That in turn kept him paying to watch the tour pros play. The club pro saw himself as the true foundation of the game, because he was in the trenches day after day working with the game's customers. The tour pro just flitted about playing tournaments, looking out for himself only. That the tour pros stimulated interest in the game by virtue of their fine play, which sent golfers to the club pros to buy equipment and lessons, seemed to have escaped the club pros.

On the practical side, because the PGA of America administered the tour and the great bulk of its membership was club professionals, the tour pros felt not enough attention and resources were paid them. They had a good argument. A very small and poorly paid field staff handled the day-to-day operation of the tour. Joe Black became the tour manager in 1958 for $1,000 a month and a car and had to pay his own expenses. His four assistants were paid less, and they also had to cover their own expenses. For all forty-five tournaments around the country, this small group set up the courses and the starting times, made rules decisions, kept the scores, saw after the press. The tour pros were not pleased at being given such short shrift.

The PGA of America's resentful attitude toward the tour pros was expressed by a system in which Arnold Palmer, for example, could not collect prize money for the first six months he was on the tour in 1955. In this way a fellow who didn't serve any time in a pro shop and just went out on the circuit put in his time as an apprentice. But Palmer and his contemporary tour players had no intention of becoming club pros. They were professional golfers, like Hagen and Sarazen were, not golf professionals.

The argument would soon be settled, and television was the mover. The PGA of America was negotiating the television contracts and by all accounts not doing a very good job of it. Rights to tournaments were in some cases sold for as little as a few thousands dollars. What's more, and this was terrifically galling to the tour players, whatever money that came in from television was put into the association's general fund to be used to pay its bills and salaries, which were rising, and to support various programs to aid club professionals. The PGA said it had a right to do this, because it had supported the tour out of the fund during the hard times in the thirties and forties. The tour pros said the money should go into increasing the purses and to upgrading the field staff.

The PGA of America balked at these demands. Unable to move the PGA, in 1969 a maverick group of tour pros led by Gardner Dickinson, Dan Sikes, Tommy Jacobs, and Doug Ford organized the Association of Professional Golfers and hired ex-FBI agent and quality golfer Jack Tuthill to run it out of a New York City office. Tuthill was assigned the task of rounding up sponsors for a new tournament circuit. Almost all the tour pros were for the APG, including Nicklaus and Palmer, the kingpins, and Tuthill had no trouble finding sponsors. In two days just working the phones, he lined up thirty-five tournaments for the 1969 season. A qualifying tournament was arranged, in which those not otherwise eligible to play the circuit could qualify.

It was a fight the PGA of America couldn't win, and its president at the time, Leo Fraser, a wise and amenable man who had been in the golf business all his life, got the matter settled the only way it could be. The tour pros were given their way. The runaway APG never played a tournament in its name. In 1969 the Tournament Players Division of the PGA was formed. (A few years later it would be given its current title, the PGA Tour.) It had a ten-man policy board comprising three businessmen who were also serious golfers, three PGA of America officers, and four TPD players. The inclusion of PGA of America officers was a sop to ease the transition, the businessmen were to provide their financial expertise and, perhaps, get entree to corporate sponsorship of tournaments. The tour pros, who had the majority on the board, controlled "the show."

The first thing the new TPD did was to hire a commissioner. This was designed to give the tour the same kind of status that the office afforded major league baseball, football, and basketball. The man hired as the first commissioner was chosen to add even more distinction. He was Joseph

P. Dey, Jr., who for some thirty-five years had been the executive secretary of the USGA.

On the one hand, Dey was an odd choice. Although he had never graduated from college and had been a second-line sportswriter in Philadelphia before taking the USGA position, he exuded an aura of austere propriety, not at all the sort of attitude one would associate with tough-nut professional golfers and such sordid stuff as money. Dey remarked more than once how as a youth he considered making a life in the church. He stood very erect, head held high with chin up, and was almost always seen wearing a coat and tie and starched shirt. During his long career with the USGA he came to be known as Mister Rules, and otherwise he stood as the prototypical advocate of amateurism. For all that, one good reason Dey took the job was because the pay was much higher than what he had been making at the USGA.

Dey's stature in the game was the main reason he was brought on to be the commissioner of the pro tour. The players wanted to upgrade their image in the eye of the public and give the circuit an air of exemplary virtue and integrity. Older pros such as Jimmy Demaret and Cary Middlecoff had a sardonic chuckle at this—at Dey's expense. They remembered a U.S. Open back in the forties when Henry Cotton, the British champion, was invited to play. Cotton was found to be playing the smaller British ball, and when it was brought to the attention of Dey he did not disqualify Cotton, because he didn't want to cause an incident.

But Dey gave the pros good service. His appointment to the commissioner's job did indeed gave the tour a positive aura. On the ground, in real life, Dey raised the pay of the field staff and took over their expenses. He saw to it that the pros were paid the $100,000 purse for the 1969 Michigan Classic that the sponsors could not come up with when the tournament ended. This payout came some months after the fact, but it gave the tour pros a feeling of confidence in their new commissioner and where the circuit was going.

Some projects Dey tried to develop didn't work under his watch, but came to pass under another. He wanted to form a second tour as a kind of high minor-league circuit for players with a game not quite up to big league standards. A few events were played, thirty-six-hole tournaments held in conjunction with the bigger event and with the same sponsor. A mini-Kemper Open, for example, during the week of the Kemper Open. However, the sponsors decided they couldn't handle the additional purse money. Dey was ahead of the game by some fifteen years, when the Hogan Tour was initiated (which became the Nike Tour and currently is the Buy.com Tour).

Dey also initiated the Tournament Players Championship, which was originally meant to be played in October as an all-star, major-level wrap-up of the season. It became the Players Championship, played every March at the PGA Tour's home course in Ponte Vedra Beach, Florida, and is a major championship, although not designated as such.

Another Dey initiative was an effort to guarantee sponsors the best possible field and as many marquee players as possible in order to generate a good gate. This was a conflict that had existed from the very beginning of the tour. The pros had always jealously guarded their freedom to play wherever and whenever they chose and still do.

Dey retired as commissioner in 1974, and he was replaced by Deane Beman. Beman, as we shall see in the next chapter, was a stronger cup of tea than Dey and took the tour to its present status as a full-scale major-league professional sport.

The Agent Comes to Golf

There is no aspect of modern popular culture more American than the agent—the representative of a star performer who makes the deals for appearances and endorsements. The agent is another of Arnold Palmer's contributions to golf and, in fact, to the world of sports. There had been a few agents or business managers in other sports before Palmer joined with Mark McCormack, or vice versa, but none had taken it so far. McCormack's success effectively spawned a very lucrative and influential calling that in real ways controls the economics of professional sports.

The very first athlete agent or manager, at least of note, was Charles C. "Cash and Carry" Pyle, whose nickname referred to his business method. He took no checks, signed no long-term payout contracts. It was cash on the barrel head, or there was no deal. Pyle got his start representing Harold "Red" Grange, when the great University of Illinois runningback, nicknamed the Galloping Ghost, was ready to go into pro football. Pyle had the brass to get George Halas, the notoriously cheap owner of the Chicago Bears, to pay Grange a percentage of the gate for every game. Grange earned over $100,000 for eight games from an owner who paid his other players $50 for one. Grange was worth it. His enormous popularity at the time helped establish the then infant National Football League.

Bob Harlow was the first in golf to represent a player, although he wasn't so much of an agent for Walter Hagen as he was the person who kept track of the bookings and tried to keep some of the money for a rainy day. Hagen was an easy spender.

Harlow's successor as manager of the PGA Tour, Fred Corcoran, was more of an agent in the modern sense, although he got into the business by default. He took the job as tour manager at the same time Sam Snead began his career on the circuit. When Snead won his first tournaments on the West Coast, in 1937, he was swamped with offers to play exhibitions that would have kept him from playing the weekly tournaments. George Jacobus, the president of the PGA of America at the time, told Corcoran to become Snead's manager so he could keep the new star in line—playing the tour. The connection between Corcoran and Snead lasted from that winter of 1937 until Corcoran died in 1972. There was never a written contract between them, only a handshake.

There wasn't all that much product endorsement business available before Arnold Palmer made his mark. But with the advent of television and Palmer's ability to light up the tube with his persona, many more opportunities opened up for making off-course money, as it came to be called to differentiate it from tournament prize money. By 1959 Palmer's celebrity was bringing him so many offers to endorse products and play exhibitions that it became too much for him and his wife, Winnie, to handle on their own. Mark McCormack was asked to take over that part of his life. Palmer got to know McCormack when he lived in the Cleveland area, first while serving in the U.S. Coast Guard and then as an amateur golfer and paint salesman. McCormack was a lawyer in Cleveland and about Arnold's age. He was a good golfer, who had played on the team at William and Mary University and qualified for a couple of U.S. Amateur Championships and a U.S. Open.

In 1958 McCormack and a partner had formed National Sports Management to arrange exhibition dates for golf pros. But it was when he took over Palmer's business affairs in late 1959 that his career as an agent really took off and the profession developed. It was also when Palmer got on the path to impressive financial wealth. However, it wasn't long after the relationship took shape that observers began to believe Palmer paid a high price for his riches. The feeling was that, because he was kept so busy doing off-course work—a heavy schedule of exhibitions, evening appearances for business clients, time out to make commercials and made-for-television golf shows, such as *Big Three Golf*—the quality of his game ran down. Was McCormack running his popular and salable client into the ground? Perhaps. McCormack's energy and imagination were boundless. Early on he got Palmer's name associated with a chain of cleaning stores, laundries, and a maid service, miniature putting courses, and a host of commercial products. Then there were the exhibitions, which were the main time and energy drain because many of them required long trips to distant places—such as Australia and the Far East.

When Palmer began to win less and not make as many or any of his patented winning charges, it was blamed on his being too tired and preoccupied with business. But between 1960 and 1964, Palmer won thirty-one times, including two Masters and two British Opens. That record would suggest that McCormack's rationale for taking over the financial reins and leaving Palmer free to concentrate on his golf was working. When Palmer's game did begin to fade—in 1965 he only won once—it may well have been that he was simply running out of game. After all, he had been playing the tour for ten years, entering many events in each year, and his style of play alone was surely taking its toll. Palmer was a slugger—the ground shook with his iron shots and a lot of shock was running up those shafts into his hands and body. And too, as Jimmy Demaret remarked at the time with a knowing smile when asked what he thought was wrong with Arnie's game, "He's discovering that those forty-foot putts don't go in forever."

Despite all that, the claim persisted that McCormack and his International Management Company (IMG) staff were overworking their clients for the sake of their own good fortunes. Nonetheless, his list of clients grew impressively in quantity and quality. He signed Jack Nicklaus and Gary Player soon after Palmer came on. Both would leave, eventually, unhappy with the twenty to twenty-five percent McCormack took out of their purse money. McCormack's riposte to that has always been that they wouldn't earn as much in tournament play if they had to handle all the business affairs he had taken over for them. A circular argument.

McCormack also had a response to the criticism that he was wearing out his players' meal tickets: all a player had to do was say no. Don't take the exhibition for $10,000. Don't do the corporate outing for $15,000. But it can be very difficult to turn down such relatively easy money when you've struggled long and hard to become a quality golfer, in the process going through a lot of your own money, maybe some of your family's, and that of a sponsor or two. Almost all the tour pros at this time came from modest financial backgrounds and were inclined to grab at any money that came their way.

One way or another, McCormack spawned an industry. In golf alone, agents began appearing from everywhere. Not all were qualified by training to deal in contracts, and a few lacked in the way of ethics. Lee Trevino had at least two financially depleting experiences with managers who appeared to benefit more than he did from the arrangement. That is something each individual has to work out on his own, and it doesn't affect the game as a whole. However, there are some aspects of the player-manager relationship that do affect the tournament circuits and golf in general. Agents can entice their star players to play a highly lucrative exhibition and pass up a PGA Tour stop or even a major championship. Curtis Strange was accused of this when he bypassed a British Open to play a tournament in Holland that gave him a huge appearance fee. This denies the game the value of a top player's presence in the way of competitive quality and prestige, not to mention gate receipts. Strange was well-known as being "into money," but it was certainly the case that his agent at IMG, a friendly goad to his proclivity, arranged the appearance (for which IMG got a percentage of the "action.")

An exceptionally aggressive agent, McCormack became a major factor on the European PGA Tour by contracting to operate tournaments for a substantial fee. His carrot was that he could fill the field with some of the best players in the game, who were his clients. He also stacked the television tower with client-announcers. And himself. McCormack installed himself in the TV booth doing color commentating of many European PGA Tour events, invariably the ones in which he had a financial or business interest. Because McCormack controlled who played in tournaments to some extent and what was said about them, he could manipulate their image to his own ends. Truth, if you will, or authenticity took a backseat to business interests.

In the late 1980s, IMG devised a world-ranking system for golf under the name of one of its clients, the Sony Corporation. Golf never had this sort of system, although it is common in big-time tennis. A high ranking provides a selling tool for higher exhibition and endorsement fees, and it has been deemed not necessarily coincidental that many of the top-ranked players according to the Sony system were (are) represented by IMG. In other words, a game's credibility comes into question and the fans begin to doubt its legitimacy. Nonetheless, athlete agents and managers have become a permanent part of the sporting landscape. They are here to stay, for better and for worse.

Women Try to Get It (W)Right

Although men's golf in the United States, as measured by the growth of the pro tours, was beginning to boom, the women's side was struggling. In 1960 the PGA Tour had a forty-one tournament schedule with a total purse of $1,335,242. The LPGA had twenty-five events on its calendar that year, and a $186,000 prize fund. This during a period when one of the best woman golfers of all time, Mickey Wright, was establishing herself.

Wright began her pro career in 1956, and by 1960 she had won thirteen tournaments, including two U.S. Women's Opens and an LPGA Championship. But there was much more to come. In 1961 she won ten events, including a U.S. Open, an LPGA Championship, and another women's major, the Titleholders Championship. In 1963 Wright broke the bank, winning thirteen tournaments, an all-time season victory record. It was not as if Wright had no one to beat out there. Patty Berg could still put up a game. Kathy Whitworth was a fine player who won fifty-three times in the 1960s, and would become the winner of more tournaments than any other golfer man or woman—88. Carol Mann made her Hall-of-Fame career in the sixties, winning 28 times. Betsy Rawls won 14 events, Marilynn Smith 13, in the sixties. In that same time frame, Wright won 65 tournaments. An amazing accomplishment, and done with one of the finest golf swings, man or woman, the game has ever seen. What's more, Wright defied the typical detraction of women's golf, that it was devoid of what the American sports fan loved more than anything else, power.

A bit over six feet tall, with a deceptively slender figure, Wright was quite strong and quite long off the tee. Her swing was a model of perfect golf form. Born in 1935, she grew up around San Diego and at eleven took her first lessons from John Bellante, a storied teacher in the area. Bellante spearheaded a city junior golf program that became a chrysalis for a generation of outstanding golfers such as Gene Littler, Phil Rodgers, Phil Mickelson, and Wright. Wright's game was also influenced by Harry Pressler, another noted California teacher. Later, she would get advice from the legendary Harvey Penick. Wright by personality had a penchant for perfection and took as much pleasure out of hitting pure shots as she did winning tournaments. Which may have had something to do with why she did not stir the hearts of America's golf fans. Wright's approach to golf and life was in the Ben Hogan mode. She was internally motivated and externally shy. She had a profound distaste for being a public figure, and that she became reclusive after she retired from golf surprised no one.

Perhaps because Wright did not have a particularly feminine presence, or a masculine one, she did not have a perceived impact on the persistent dilemma of the LPGA, and indeed that of all women athletes during this period in the United States; the tomboy image, or, to be brutally honest, the idea that all women athletes and especially those who could hit a ball hardest, run fastest, and generally excel were lesbians.

In 1961 Lenny Wirtz, a promoter and part-time professional basketball referee, became the LPGA's new manager. He tried to combat the tomboy stereotype. He insisted the women wear lipstick and short pants that were not too short or tight. They were also asked to not wear sweat socks. The LPGA golfers complied, but it didn't seem to help. Wirtz himself said the "lesbian image was tough to shake." Women athletes, as a group, in all sports carried this burden. To be sure, there were (and are) some homosexuals among LPGA players, just as there were (and are) in men's sports, including the National Football League. A player's sexual orientation should have nothing whatsoever to do with how he or she is received as an athlete (or as a human being), but as unreasonable and unfortunate as it may be, it did then and to some extent still does. The LPGA has always resisted acknowledging there are lesbians in the group. Carol Mann blanched when asked why the LPGA just didn't come out and admit it, in order to get free of all the innuendo. She said it would "kill the tour." When tennis champions Billie Jean King and Martina Navratilova "came out" it did in fact hurt them financially, but women's tennis did not collapse. Quite the contrary. One LPGA player did—Muffin Spencer-Devlin—to little notice; however, she was not a star player.

One way or the other, in the 1960s the LPGA was making some progress and was still the only place in the world where women golfers could try to make a living playing competitive golf. And the quality of the golf kept improving.

Plastic + Steel = High-Tech Golf

There was another innovation in golf ball manufacturing in the 1960s that would take the game to another dimension in its economics, growth, and eventually how it was played. Taking the advice offered the Dustin Hoffman character in *The Graduate,* a hugely popular movie from the sixties, golf got into plastics.

The second most desirable feature of a golf ball, after distance, is durability. A ball with a cover that doesn't cut, even when the club comes down on it with the force and sharpness of a lumberjack's ax was long one of the pots of gold at the end of the game's rainbow. Near the end of the 1960s, the dream was realized. The so-called fourth revolution in golf ball manufacture took place with the invention of the uncuttable surlyn-covered ball. James Bartsch, a chemical engineer for the DuPont Chemical Company, developed it. And not because he was cutting so many balls of his own. Bartsch didn't even play golf. He got into the business simply because he wanted to get into business on his own, any business. Once again, history is the product of one person's personal objective.

In March, 1959, Bartsch responded to an ad in the *Wall Street Journal* offering a golf ball business for sale. Bartsch knew golf was a game on the rise, and it didn't take him much research to discover that golf balls were the biggest turnover product in the game. They got lost regularly, but more often the cover was cut and the ball had to be taken out of play. Bartsch thought he might be able to do something about the latter, and he bought the golf company that was for sale.

At the time all golf balls were covered with the imminently cuttable/ nickable/gougeable balata. Bartsch began experimenting with ways to harden the balata so it would be less impressionable. He didn't find a way to save balata, but one thing led to another and in his laboratory he came up with a synthetic derived from crude oil that had possibilities. It was a form of very hard plastic that combined various elastomers. Bartsch didn't give the material any sort of trade or commercial name at the time. Out of it he molded a one-piece golf ball and tested it for durability by bouncing cold chisels on it and getting his wife to hit hundreds of them in the desert of New Mexico. No marks were made. Eureka! The Faultless Company, a manufacturer of golf equipment, took a license to become the major distributor of Bartsch's uncuttable one-piece golf ball it called the White Streak. Bartsch marketed another one, separately, called the PCR/Bartsch.

However, neither of the balls met with a warm and wild reception. This was because the first part of the acceptable-ball equation was missing—they didn't go far enough. Also, although they didn't cut, the paint chipped easily. They also didn't feel good; they gave up something like the guttie's uncomfortable shock. At fifty cents a ball, it was acceptable to beginner golfers not consumed (yet) with trajectory or feel, but that did not represent a big enough market. Bartsch's one-piece uncuttable ball went the way of the guttie.

The idea of a hard plastic cover for a golf ball was spreading, though. The Spalding Company, which had been experimenting since the 1950s to find a suitable hard-plastic cover, took Bartsch's idea and added to it. Spalding used Bartsch's material as the core of the ball and covered it with a polybutadiene material. It was the first two-piece ball since the featherie, only much much better. In 1967 Spalding brought out the Executive. It was better by far than Bartsch's ball, but not entirely satisfactory.

In 1961 Dr. Richard W. Rees, a DuPont scientist who had been experimenting with polymers, devised a plastic-based material similar to that which Bartsch had come up with. It was given the name surlyn. In 1966 Rees and DuPont obtained a patent on it. Surlyn was meant originally to be used for soda pop bottles, auto parts, sneaker soles, lacrosse sticks, and ski boots. But when Terry Pocklington, a Canadian chemical engineer working for the Campbell [golf] Ball Company, learned of Rees's surlyn he thought it would be the answer to a two-piece uncuttable ball attractive to golfers for its feel and distance, as well as it durability. Pocklington couldn't sell the Campbell Company on investing in this project, so he took a job with the Sportsman Golf Company based in a suburb of Chicago, which soon after changed its name to Ram Golf.

The Hansberger family, which owned and operated Ram, decided to make the investment in Pocklington's idea. However, to achieve the full range of values, they devised a three-piece unit—a solid core wound with rubber thread and covered with surlyn. It was called the Golden Ram. It didn't go quite far enough to satisfy the better players and still had a harder feel than balata, but it was a big improvement over any of the plastic balls that came before it. Other manufacturers quickly got into the act with their own versions. Ram's surlyn cover was quite thick, which retarded the distance it could give, but Spalding, which had more financial resources and facilities for research and development, found a way to make a thinner cover. Spalding also discovered a way to produce a viable two-piece ball, which eliminated one step in the manufacturing process and made it less expensive to produce.

Spalding marketed the first commercially successful surlyn-covered golf ball, called the Top-Flite. It had the durability, and it also gave good distance. It changed the face of golf for all time, literally and figuratively, and not only the ball end of the game. The surlyn-covered golf ball engendered the metal wood, or the woodlike club made of metal. Or the metal. Whatever.

The "Invention" of the Metal Wood

For the sake of maintaining a continuous flow of related events, we will again depart from the decade-by-decade chronology of this history and outline the consequence of the surlyn-covered golf ball.

In 1978, while monitoring a long-drive contest at the Firestone Country Club, in Akron, Ohio, Gary Adams put one and one together. At the time, Spalding was touting its surlyn-covered, two-piece Top-Flite ball as the longest in the game. But in the driving contest, Adams noticed that Spalding's ball was about seven yards shorter than the two balata-covered balls also being used, a Titleist and a PGA. Curious, Adams took a closer look at the Spalding ads and noticed the small print that explained its claim as longest ball was computed from a combination of two shots, one with the driver, the other with a five-iron. The proverbial light bulb lit up. All the drivers in the contest Adams was monitoring were made of wood.

This led him to think that perhaps the combination of the metal of an iron against the hard surlyn cover would create more distance. A good golfer, Adams hit test shots with a five-iron using the same three brands of balls as in the driving contest. Sure enough, the Top-Flite outdistanced the two balata balls, and by enough to make good the claim that it was the longest ball of all.

Adams decided he would make a metal driver. This was not exactly new. Driving ranges had for many years been providing customers, usually beginners, with metal-headed drivers because of their durability. Adams himself sold them when he worked for the Wittek Company, the country's biggest supplier of driving range equipment. The metal drivers at the ranges were not very well made in terms of balance and appearance, but Adams would take care of that. There was already a metal driver on the market, called the Leroi, that was meant for use on the golf course. But it was hardly known, and few were sold because, Adams believed, it had an ungainly chunky look. Also, golfers were accustomed to playing wood woods and habits are hard to break.

Adams was a firm believer in the well-established business practice that getting top-name players to use a certain brand of equipment will entice the average golfer to buy that same brand. Accordingly, Adams went about making a club the tour pros would like the look of, and of course one that played well. But it would first have to look good. Adams and Terry McCabe, an accomplished club designer, worked up a driver head they thought would be appealing to tour pros. It was not unlike a classic MacGregor or Wilson persimmon head. Adams found someone with the technology to cast the club—Bob McClellan, owner of Alfacast in California—and he brought in John Zebullion, who had been involved with the Leroi metal driver, to provide tooling expertise. Adams would do the marketing and promotion, at which he would prove to be superb.

In 1979 Gary Adams founded the Taylor-Made Company. It was an obvious play on words, but one he backed up by having an employee named Taylor—Harry Taylor, a tour-quality golfer who would take the club out on the PGA Tour to get the pros to try it. The club was called the Tour Burner. It was also referred to as a metalwood, an oxymoron that the industry has not been able to shake. Adams had some fun with it when he said his clubs were made of "Pittsburgh persimmon."

Harry Taylor coaxed Jim Simons, Ron Streck, and Mike Sullivan to use the Tour Burner in 1979. It wasn't all that hard to get the pros to at least try it. It did look good, it did produce very impressive distance, and what may have sold it more than anything else, it could be played off the fairway just like a three-wood. Because the head was basically hollow (it contained only a thin coat or sheet of foam lining), weight could be distributed at will. To create the Tour Burner, more weight was put in the bottom portion, which gave it a lower center of gravity. This helped get the ball airborne even when not teed up. The Tour Burner used from the fairway into the wind on a long par-five was worth ten to fifteen more yards. The pros loved that.

Jim Simons got the first victory using the Tour Burner—the 1982 Bing Crosby National Pro-Am. But the real breakthrough came when Lee Trevino used the club when he won the 1984 PGA Championship. That did it. According to Adams, and the National Golf Foundation, the association representing the golf industry from 1979 through 1989 Taylor-Made alone sold close to eight million metalwoods. By 1994, some fifteen million of the clubs by a variety of manufacturers were in golfers' hands around the world. By the end of the century the total number of metals in play were as many golfers as were playing the game, multiplied by at least two. After the driver there came the three-metal, and even more lofted ones.

Because a metal is so much less expensive to produce, and the material is more consistent and will never be in short supply, the wood has become a relic of the past, a curiosity to the newest generation of golfers, a nostalgia item for older ones. The combination of a hard plastic ball and a metal eliminated a lovely golfing aesthetic, the sweet tick of persimmon striking a softish piece of rubber. The metal drove out the very source of that sound and an even more delightful visual aesthetic, the persimmon wood, a piece of nature refined into an elegantly contoured, polished reminder of the artisan's craft. Going from wood to metal was like trading in Audrey Hepburn for Madonna. But that's the way the world was going.

New Blood Enriches PGA Tour's Life

In the 1960s the PGA Tour began to thrive as never before because of the strength of Arnold Palmer's allure. Even if his best championship days were clearly on the ebb, Palmer still was an important draw. But the tour was not entirely dependent on this one super-celebrity player. Jack Nicklaus may not have been as dear to the heart of golf fans, but by the mid-1960s he was clearly the man to beat whenever he entered a regular tour event, and even more so when he competed in a major championship. What's more, he drew gasps at the length he could hit his driver, and especially the height he got with his two-iron. With that small-headed, low-lofted club, the toughest to hit well, he got the ball higher than anyone had ever seen before. And of course, because the ball descended on a more vertical line, it held the green better. A Nicklaus two-iron was not unlike a seven-iron hit by any other golfer. Well, make it a five-iron.

Nicklaus was drawing crowds, but others were giving good golf and were interesting to watch, too. There was a lot more character among the players than most of the journalists would lead you to believe. Journalists are no less subject to image perception than anyone else, and they also look for the easiest way to get good copy in and on time. Palmer made it easy. Others took a little digging, because most golfers are not very demonstrative at play. Everyone who wants to do well boils inside, but that steam has to be held in check. The game demands composure, which does not always make for good theater.

Billy Casper came on strong in the sixties with twenty-nine victories, including his second U.S. Open. This victory had a very dramatic conclusion, and pointed to the power that charisma has over substance. Casper won the 1966 U.S. Open, but it will always be the Open that Arnie lost. Too bad for Billy. In that championship, at the Olympic Club in San Francisco, Palmer had a seven-shot lead over Casper going into the final nine holes of regulation play. They were playing together. Arnie then shot a 39 on the back nine, four over par. This was not a very good nine holes of play, but it wasn't a total blowup. The trouble for Palmer was that at the same time Casper shot a 32. Three under par on the last nine of the U.S. Open, when in contention, is a very good score. It made up the difference, and Palmer and Casper were tied after seventy-two holes. In the play-off the next day, again Palmer had a lead after nine holes, although in this case it was only by two strokes. Then on the back nine he shot a 40, while Casper shot a solid one-under par 34 to win.

It was an excellent victory for Casper. He held his game together for the length of the tournament, which is why the stroke-play format is a more conclusive test than match-play. Palmer would say that during the final round of regulation play, he got caught up with trying to break the U.S. Open scoring record and played too boldly. That leads to the conclusion that he was not the consummate U.S. Open player. He won but one. This championship, more than any other, is determined almost always by conservative strategy and consistently accurate shot-making. These characteristics are why Jack Nicklaus and Ben Hogan won four U.S. Opens, Hale Irwin three, and Billy Casper and Julius Boros two.

Casper never got enough credit for his 1966 Open victory, or for that matter what he accomplished over his entire career—fifty-one victories on the PGA Tour, including a Masters. He won on the golf course, but lost in the house of public appeal. It was his own fault, in a way. He remarked once in retrospect that when he first came out on the PGA Tour in 1955, he chose Ben Hogan as a role model for how to comport himself on the course. He said he wished he hadn't, and that if he had been himself, he might have gotten a more favorable read from the public.

Those who knew the private Casper knew a witty, wise-cracking pool shark. He did a bit of pool hustling as a kid growing up around San Diego and also drank a lot of beer. And fooled around. But somewhere in his middle twenties he decided the dissolute life was not for him. He married a Mormon woman and took up that religion, which served also to tamp his natural ebullience. Casper also had a weight problem, which didn't help his image. It was a genetic inheritance. His father, who died of a heart attack, weighed over three hundred pounds. Billy fought his weight constantly, often with diets and supplements that made him seem more bizarre than anything else. Food containing desiccated ox blood, for example. When it was discovered that he ate buffalo meat, he was immediately dubbed "Buffalo Bill." Naturally. His weight and the figure it produced cost him a valuable clothing-endorsement contract.

Lee Trevino translated more easily into sound and picture bites although there was a lot more to him than the wisecracking stand-up comic that met the eye. A short, stocky man of Mexican-American heritage, Trevino grew up in Dallas, Texas, quite poor and without his father. His home during his early years was a simple wooden structure set in a vacant field that had no indoor plumbing. Its location, however, turned out to be his savior. It was hard by a golf course. Trevino earned his first money selling golf balls that were hit out of bounds and into his putative backyard. He took to caddying, then playing at a local public course, and began to play in earnest while working at a Dallas driving range. His main job was picking up balls, but he probably hit more than he picked up. He hustled at golf playing money matches, sometimes with his own cash but more often backed by gamblers. He won bets hitting a ball with a Dr. Pepper bottle for distance.

Trevino was a reminder of the depression era pros, but without the grim exterior. He had wit—a quick mind for repartee and the tongue to go with it—and a terrific golf game. Once again the ubiquitous Ben Hogan had an influence, although he didn't know it. When Trevino came to the national golf scene, he had the swing that made his career, an odd-looking action in which the club is taken back to the outside, then slung back in toward his body. His own description was that he didn't hit the ball so much as he kind of "shoved it out there." The swing looked ungainly, and it was long assumed it came out that way because he was a kid from the wrong side of the Texas tracks who couldn't afford lessons. In fact, at the start and well into his teens, Trevino had a "classic" golf swing, such as any good teacher would have taught him—long, low takeaway to the inside, back to the ball from inside to out with a high and pretty follow-through. Trouble was, it produced a wild hook. Just as Hogan's original swing did.

One day Trevino watched Hogan practicing at a course in Fort Worth, and upon seeing the flight of Hogan's ball—the slight fade to the right—he decided that was what he needed if he was going to go anywhere in the game. He never approached Hogan to ask how to do it, knowing or perceiving that it wouldn't do any good. Hogan was notoriously unapproachable, especially when it came to talking golf swing with strangers. Trevino figured it out himself and came up with the peculiar form that everyone saw. "It took me seven years to get that sonofabitchen swing," Trevino said, but when he got it, he was off and running to a long and exceptional career.

After a four-year stint in the Marine Corps, Trevino turned pro and had some success in small Texas tournaments. In 1967 his wife persuaded him to enter that year's U.S. Open, played at the Baltusrol Golf Club in New

Jersey. He finished fifth, behind Nicklaus, the winner, and Palmer, Don January, and Billy Casper. Some people thought Trevino's showing was a fluke, others thought there was something to say for this chatty little Tex-Mex with the funny swing.

The next year, all questions were settled. After the 1967 Open, Trevino went on the PGA Tour and had some good showings. Then, at the Oak Hill Country Club in Rochester, New York, he won the 1968 U.S. Open. He beat Nicklaus by four shots, with the same score—275—Nicklaus had made to win the previous year's Open. From then on, Trevino was a major factor in the game. He would win another U.S. Open, in a play-off against Nicklaus at the Merion Golf Club (1971), a PGA Championship (1974), and two British Opens in a row (1971 and 1972). He won twenty-seven times, in all, on the PGA Tour, and then he had a splendid record on the Senior PGA Tour.

Trevino won three of the four modern majors or Grand Slam events. The only gap in his resume is the Masters tournament. Trevino didn't play well at Augusta National Golf Club—his best finish was a tie for tenth in 1975, his best single round an opening 67 in 1989 that led the field. However, the omission of a victory at the Masters revealed more about Trevino's personality and socio-economic background than his ability to play the course. He often said the hilly Augusta National layout didn't suit his low-flying left-to-right shot, but he could have adjusted if he wanted to. He became one of the best shot-makers to ever play the game, right up there with Hogan, and when he needed a high hook he could hit one with no trouble at all. The fact is, he didn't like the Old South plantation ambiance of the club. He made that very clear when he turned down invitations to the 1970 and 1971 Masters, an almost unheard of act. When he did go back to play, he never used the clubhouse. He changed shoes in his car, went straight to the course, and reversed the procedure when his round was over. The Masters atmosphere was too close to his childhood memory bone.

One year he recalled an incident that reflected that past. He had become a successful, famous golfer and had his eye on buying a piece of land in the Dallas area. It was owned by a wealthy Anglo for whom he shagged balls and caddied as a kid. A call was made, the landowner said he'd see Trevino, and told him to meet him for lunch at his home in

Florida. Trevino put on a suit and tie for the occasion, hired a private plane to fly him to the remote location, and was prepared for a fine lunch and business talk in the clubhouse. When the landowner was introduced to Trevino he looked at him asquint, as if trying to remember if he'd seen him before, and then realized he had: "Why, you're the little Mexican boy who shagged balls for me," he said. He then took Trevino down to the snack bar near the tenth tee for a stand-up hotdog lunch.

Even though Trevino was genuinely funny, with the capacity to ad lib one humorous crack after another while inside the gallery ropes, and although he was unquestionably a superb championship golfer, Trevino was never warmly embraced by the golfing public. Image is a strange and precarious phenomenon. Trevino was as representative of the American dream as Arnold Palmer. He pulled himself up out of the lower economic stratum by his own pluck, audacity, and hard work; he was part of an ethnic minority in America, who served his country in the military. But not far beneath his Merry-Mex front lay another facet of his personality. Trevino could be downright surly to autograph hounds. He came to despise that bane of all celebrities—being discourteously interrupted while at dinner in a restaurant. Perhaps he took it as another show of disrespect for his poor Mexican-American background. He finally decided to take all his meals in his hotel room when on the road. This side of Trevino's makeup was usually masked by his jocularity when he was in a good mood, however. In any case, Trevino is truly an emblem of the American experience who represents why and how golf became the American game.

Trevino represented just one cross-section of the American population that made up the PGA Tour. (The women are not being ignored in this; there just wasn't the same kind of diversity among them yet.) In the sixties there was the tall, slender Tony Lema, out of the Oakland, California, area. He brought to the tour a refined caddie swing, his body in the downswing forming a supple sway that was beautiful to watch. It was a swing refined by the black driving-range pro Lucius Bateman, and Lema never forgot Bateman for his help. Bateman turned a few other white fellows from the area into tour players, the Lotz brothers among them.

Lema had an elfin quality, a glint in his eye that reflected the pleasure he was having seeing the world, being a well-known person, making good money, and enjoying it with others. Champagne Tony he was called forever after he served up some bubbly to the press following a particularly satisfying victory. Lema died in the crash of a small plane in 1965, a year after he won the British Open. A tragedy for him and for the game. He had a lot more to give and get.

As a young man Ken Venturi was tallish and slender—the son of the starter at Harding Park, San Francisco's best-known and most heavily played city-owned public course. Shy of society because of his heavy stutter as a boy, Venturi hung out by himself at a far reach of Harding Park hitting balls, forming a classic golf swing that Byron Nelson would make even better, and practicing victory speeches to overcome his speech impediment. Venturi almost won the Masters as an amateur—he took a four-shot lead over Cary Middlecoff into the final round in 1956, but shot an 80 to lose by a stroke to Jackie Burke. Venturi turned pro in 1957, and got off to a good start with two victories that year, four in 1958, and two in 1959. In 1960 he had another chance to win the Masters. Only one shot behind Arnold Palmer going into the final round, he caught Arnie at one point and took the lead. But then he was felled, psychologically as much as anything else, when Palmer got a favorable ruling at the par-three twelfth that Venturi thought should have gone the other way. Palmer won over Venturi by a stroke.

Venturi's game afterward fell into decline. It was the result, he said, of a neurological problem that took the feel from his hands. Always an edgy, high-strung personality, he struggled on tour, almost fell completely out of the game, but made a dramatic comeback to win the 1964 U.S. Open, which took place in torrid heat at the Congressional Country Club in Washington, D.C. He nearly collapsed during the last day of play, which required two rounds, but although playing in a daze, he managed to make the shots and win by four over Tommy Jacobs.

That final day at Congressional prompted the USGA to alter its format and drop the thirty-six-hole final day of regulation play, although it was widely held that the television networks had some influence on the decision. Two days of U.S. Open golf on a weekend sell more advertising and are easier to produce than thirty-six holes in one day. Venturi won two more times in 1964, both regular tour events, won another one in 1966, then quit tournament golf to become a television commentator—a nice result for a one-time stutterer.

Doug Sanders came along in the 1960s with a swing short enough to complete in a closet, but for a few years was very effective. He took over and exaggerated Jimmy Demaret's role as the tour's neon clotheshorse. Sanders wore complete outfits in Day-Glo purple and fuschia, including matching patent leather shoes. Demaret, it must be said, had more class. In Sanders's one real chance to win a major, the 1970 British Open, he missed a three-footer on the seventy-second hole that would have given him the title. In a play-off the next day against Jack Nicklaus, Sanders lost by a stroke.

Gene Littler came out on the tour about the same time as Arnold Palmer, and many thought he would be the star player of the two. With his smooth and well-formed swing, Littler came to be known as Gene the Machine, but while he had a long and accomplished career that included winning one U.S. Open championship (he also won the U.S. Amateur, in 1953 and the San Diego Open as an amateur), Littler never blazed as many expected. A placid personality who grew up in tranquil San Diego, he may not have had the so-called fire in the belly that makes for great champions. Nonetheless, he graced the stage with his serene presence and fine technique.

The Foreign Presence Emerges

A further indication of how powerful the American game had become: In the 1960s foreign players began to join the circuit as full-time participants. The American pro tour was the ultimate measure. It had the best competition in the world, was the best publicized, and was paying out the most attractive purse money by a long shot. The European tour was mainly a series of small, low-paying tournaments in Great Britain, plus a few national championships on the continent—the French, German, Italian Opens. Australia was developing some excellent players, but had a limited tour. Japan was not yet as heavily into golf as it would become when its high-flying economic times came in the 1970s. If a foreign golfer wanted to play against the best, and for the most, American was where he or she came.

The Australian invasion began in the sixties when Bruce Devlin and Bruce Crampton arrived, and because of their success, stayed. But the most notable foreign arrival on the American golf scene in that decade was Gary Player, who came from South Africa. A small man not much bigger than a jockey, Player clocked millions of miles traveling the international tournament circuit from his homeland over many years. He kept himself in the best physical condition possible by eating carefully, but in particular through a rigorous exercise program that he followed so intensely, and talked about so much, it was seen as a fetish. Part of his fitness program was lifting weights, which in the sixties was considered not good for golf. The conventional wisdom was that weight lifting bulked up the chest and shoulders, which needed to be loose and flexible for golf.

Player took his weight-lifting lead from Frank Stranahan, the outstanding amateur champion (and later a tour pro) in the fifties, who was even further ahead of the time in this regard. (Despite Player's success, it wasn't until the nineties that tour pros began to realize weight-lifting was not destructive to golf, but in fact helped achieve more power. It was one factor in the greater distance the pros began to hit the ball, toward the end of the century.)

Player had other singular mannerisms that made him stand out from the crowd. For a number of years he wore all black clothing on the course because, he said, black held heat and kept him warm and loose for golf. Sometimes he broke the monotony of black by wearing a pair of pants with one black leg, the other white. A born diplomat, he cultivated a remark that allowed him to never say anything derogatory about anything. He might play an exhibition on a golf course with no character whatsoever and in poor condition to boot, and Player would say afterward that it was the finest course "of its kind" he had ever seen. The modifier has never been used so judiciously as it has by Gary Player.

But first and foremost, Player was an outstanding golfer. Second, he always displayed the fierce drive to excel in athletics often found among undersized people—the Napoleon complex, ball and stick division. Player was a good athlete in many sports as a youth growing up in and around Johannesburg. He got interested in golf through his father, and he was locked in for all time when he met a young girl whose father was the professional at the local golf course. Player went to work for the pro, Jock Verwey, married his daughter, and began to make his career in the game.

He had won only one small tournament in South Africa when he traveled to Great Britain for the first time in 1955, at age nineteen. The following year he won his first South African Open, for which he failed to qualify the previous year, and a tourney on the British circuit when he returned for the second time. He also finished fourth in the British Open. A hint of Player's dedication to succeed was implicit in his recall of his first visit to Great Britain and the Scottish links courses. He remembered taking his bag of practice balls onto a stretch of perfectly flat and tightly packed beach alongside St. Andrews, where he hit the balls off the sand with his irons to learn how important it is to hit the ball first. "You can't hit behind it off that sand, you know. Dreadful shots come of it, and it hurts your hands like hell," Player explained.

Player made his first foray onto the American tour in 1957. His best showing was a third in the Greensboro (North Carolina) Open. The next year was better, despite missing the cut in his first Masters. Two weeks later he won the Kentucky Derby Open by three strokes. He lost a play-off to Sam Snead in the Greenbrier Invitational, a pretty good performance against the great master in his own backyard. Player lost another play-off to Snead (as did Julius Boros and John McMullin) in the Dallas Open. But it was in the 1958 U.S. Open that he made his biggest imprint. In the heat of Tulsa, Oklahoma, in June, Player finished second to Tommy Bolt. He was clearly going to be a factor from then on.

In the time frame above, Player had made some remarkable changes in his swing, and like so many others before him and after, Ben Hogan was the inspiration and paradigm. He began in the game with an unorthodox grip, the right hand well under the handle, and an ungainly out of balance swing that reflected a small person's urge to hit the ball as far as he could. After watching Hogan practice for hours at a time, and of course without speaking a word to the great man, Player narrowed his stance, took a more athletic butt-jutting sit-down position at address, and kept his body much stiller throughout the swing. Ironically, some years later when he was having some difficulty with his game, Player called Hogan from Asia to ask for some advice. Hogan, who was getting his equipment company going at the time, asked Player what brand of equipment he played. Player said Dunlop, and Hogan told him to go ask Mr. Dunlop for some help. End of conversation. A gem from the Hogan canon.

In 1959 Player won the British Open and established himself as a world-class player on the rise, and in two years he was once and for the rest of his career at that level. In 1961 he won his first of three Masters (the others came in 1974 and 1978); the following year he won the first of two PGA Championships (the other in 1972). He also won two more

British Opens (1968 and 1974). Player won the U.S. Open in 1965 and became one of only four golfers, so far, to win all four major championships during his career. The others are Ben Hogan, Jack Nicklaus, and Gene Sarazen.

Player's career has been unique. The enormous mileage he racked up to compete is phenomenal even among men who make their living on the road, and all the more so for maintaining the highest standard of play for twenty years. At the same time, he had an unpleasant social issue to deal with as a native of a country that maintained a vicious official policy of racial apartheid. In the late sixties and early seventies, when racial discrimination was being protested strongly in the United States, Player was subjected to demonstrations that struck him directly. There were times when people in the gallery would yell loudly just as he began his swing, throw drinks at him, send life-threatening letters and phone calls. He did not accept South Africa's racial policies, and did what he could to counter them. He made a point of having a black caddie when he played the U.S. tour, often played practice rounds with Lee Elder and other black pros on the American circuit, and one year invited Elder to South Africa to play some events on the 1972 South African tour.

While it is certainly true that Gary Player learned much from his experiences in many foreign lands about playing golf, and of course in his homeland, it is also safe to say it was in the United States where he made himself into a world champion. It was in the hot furnace of American golf where Player, like all the others, forged his talent. Many others would follow in his footsteps as American golf moved into the 1970s.

5 | The 1970s: Following the Leader

Nicklaus Rules; So Does the Commissioner; Nancy and Her Smiling Face; The American Golf Course; The American Golf Swing; The Australian Connection; Color Barrier at Masters Falls; Another Equipment R(e)volution

A striking example of how American golf had become the game's bell-wether world-wide: In 1968 the British professionals decided to play only the American-size ball in their tournaments. The reasoning is instructive. The British pros felt that because the bigger American ball (1.68 inches in diameter compared to 1.62 inches—both weighed the same, 1.62 ounces) was harder to play in the windy conditions they regularly encountered, learning to manipulate it under those conditions would make them overall more adept players. They would then have a better chance at competing against the Americans, at home *and* away.

Tony Jacklin, one of the best British players at the time, took the concept a step further. In 1968 he traveled to the United States to play full-time on the American PGA Tour. He believed this would raise the level of his game in all respects, because the European circuit was not nearly as deep in talent. In America week after week he would go up against a field in which at least fifteen players were capable of winning the tournament. Also in the U.S. he would get the experience of a wider variety of courses and climatic conditions. And of course, he would play exclusively with the bigger ball.

Going to play the American tour to broaden your experience was not a new idea. Henry Cotton, a British champion, did it just prior to World War II and he encouraged other Britons, including Jacklin, to take the plunge. Jacklin's experiment paid almost immediate dividends. In his first full season on the U.S. tour in 1968, he won the Jacksonville Open and had a number of high finishes in other events. But it was in the 1970 U.S. Open, at the Hazeltine Country Club in Minneapolis, Minnesota, where his cross-breeding experiment came to full flower. On the first day of play the wind blew hard, at times up to forty miles per hour, and an already difficult course became a world-class brute. Jacklin slugged out a brilliant one-under-par 71. The closest anyone else came to that score was the wily veteran, Julius Boros, with a 73. Arnold Palmer, Gary Player, and Jack Nicklaus shot rounds of 79, 80, and 81 respectively.

The fifty-year-old Boros, now past his prime, faded out of contention as the championship progressed, and although the winds calmed considerably over the next three days none of the more likely contenders could recover from their slow starts. Jacklin stayed firmly in the lead with three fine rounds of 70, and won the championship by seven strokes over Dave Hill. Jacklin was the first Briton to win the U.S. Open since Ted Ray in 1920. At the risk of sounding a bit jingoistic, Jacklin's monumental victory in Minnesota was in good part the result of his learning to play American-style golf with the American-sized ball.

Needless to say, the R&A did not pick up immediately on the switch to the bigger ball by the British professionals, and being no fool, Jacklin used the smaller ball to win the 1969 British Open at windy Royal Lytham. But in 1972 the R&A did finally make the bigger ball mandatory in the British Open. With that, the American ball became universal, and the smaller one a museum piece. Only Peter Thomson, the cerebral Australian champion, carped about the change. He won five British Opens with the small ball, so he was naturally convinced it was the only ball to play.

Nicklaus Rules

Tony Jacklin's successful excursion into American golf was a nice item of interest, but it didn't take Americans by storm. Jacklin's game was not all that imposing in any of its details. He didn't hit the ball especially far, the flight was ordinary, his iron-play was just solid, and he was a worthy putter. But no particular aspect of his game stood out. He dressed neatly, but conventionally. A very good player on a bit of a roll and nothing more. A few years later, though, as the vibrant captain of the European Ryder Cup team, Jacklin would become a great pain in the American golfing heart. But in the 1970s nothing Jacklin or anyone else did could stand in the way of Jack Nicklaus, to whom the decade belonged.

Nicklaus had already become a giant in the game, with twenty-nine victories in the sixties, which included seven major titles. But in the seventies he won thirty-eight times and added seven more major titles. An all-conquering voyage. With Arnold Palmer nearing the end of his own magical passage through the game (he won his last PGA Tour event in 1973, the Bob Hope Desert Classic), there was no choice but to accept Nicklaus for all he was worth. He wasn't idolized as Palmer was, because he just didn't give off an air of accessibility. And, he was not one to make dramatic late in the day charges to victory. But the power of Nicklaus's game and his consistency were awesome.

Nicklaus was the proverbial bastard who grinds you down. More often than not he let the others beat themselves, while he just kept making par after par after par in between the birdies and the now-and-then bogey. Double-bogeys were almost unheard of. He was also one of the best day-to-day putters the game has ever had, and under pressure no one, in this writer's mind, has ever been better. Or can be. When a short putt (and as we shall point out, even some longer ones) had to be made, Nicklaus made it. You could make book on it. He was also an imaginative and exceptionally deft trouble-shot golfer, but that skill got lost in the flow of his power and steadiness.

Nicklaus's golf technique was very sound, but as is often the case with special players who rise above the standard, he had a quirk. His right elbow came away from his right side in the backswing rather than staying tucked in close, which was the more common way. His elbow "flew," and as a result Nicklaus's swing was more vertical in its path than the players from the generations preceding him, including Arnold Palmer. This piece of technique is one reason why he hit the ball so much higher than anyone had before, especially with the long irons. From wizened observers of the game to the newest conscripts, the one thing above all else that everyone marveled about when Nicklaus first arrived was how high he hit his two-iron. In his hands, the hardest of all the clubs to hit seemed like a short iron. A 195- to 200-yard shot coming down softly and rolling hardly at all is of great advantage when played to the raised and usually firm greens of a U.S. Open and Masters. And even the usually wind-swept British

Open. In fact, any type of course. The air is much safer than the ground, and with the high ball you use much less of the latter. The chance of a bad bounce is minimized. Like Michael Jordan in basketball two decades later, Nicklaus changed the way his game was played. Golf became a game played in the air. It was another of his, and America's, major influences on the old Scots game.

Nicklaus learned to play in-the-air golf, if you will, growing up on the Scioto Country Club course, in Columbus, Ohio, where his father had a membership. In terms of design Scioto is one of the best, strongest layouts in the game. Its architect was Donald Ross, whose signature design concept was the crowned green, which best accepts a high approach. Also to the point, Scioto's financially well-endowed membership demanded the course be in ideal condition. Nicklaus was a fine putter on the swiftest of greens because he was nursed on such surfaces. And, he grew up playing on impeccable fairways. One can get a two-iron well up in the air from a Scioto lie much easier than from the scruffy hardpan on which the golfers of the generations preceding Nicklaus came up.

That Nicklaus changed the way tour courses, at least, were conditioned is difficult to dispute. He played his first pro tour event, the 1962 Los Angeles Open, at the Rancho Municipal Golf Course, which annually has more rounds of golf played on it than any other public course in the nation, maybe the world. He finished well down in the field, earning a $33.33 check. He played at Rancho only two more times—1963 and 1967—and only became a regular entrant in the L.A. Open when it moved back to the Riviera Country Club in 1973. He made the point, although never publicly, that he was going to avoid as much as possible playing on Rancho-type layouts—and there were more than a few still being used. Considering his enormous celebrity and gate attractiveness, it is certain that Nicklaus prompted everyone who wanted to be somebody in big-time golf to stage their tournaments on the kind of lush courses Nicklaus cut his teeth on. He was in this respect a major influence on the quality of venues that have become standard on the PGA Tour.

But there was much more to Nicklaus's superiority than his golf technique and the impact he would have on the game. Golf has been broken down as twenty percent physical, eighty percent mental. Some would say it's ninety percent in the head. However the equation breaks down, the ability to maintain concentration, keep cool, thoroughly think through decisions, is a major determinant of success. Nicklaus had all of that and a strength of will that took him into another realm, to the highest level of golf being. A case in point. In the 1984 Memorial Tournament, an event Nicklaus founded that is played on a course he designed, Jack was in a last-round battle with Andy Bean for the victory. They were tied with one hole to play. On the par-four seventeenth, Nicklaus sprayed his drive a full fifty yards to the right and out of bounds. Bean drove in play. Nicklaus hit his second drive (third shot) in the fairway. Bean hit the green with his second shot, within comfortable two-putt range. He looked to be very much in the driver's seat what with Nicklaus having a long-iron fourth shot to play. Nicklaus hit the shot onto the front of the green, thirty-two feet from the hole. If Nicklaus and Bean both two-putted, as seemed likely, Jack would be two strokes down with a hole to play—a daunting situation even for Nicklaus. But Jack holed his putt! Bean two-putted, and took only a one-shot lead to the final hole.

At the eighteenth Nicklaus again drove poorly onto a heavily grassed island in the middle of a fairway bunker. Bean drove into the rough then missed the green with his second, but not seriously. Nicklaus's approach ended in thick grass on a steep embankment beside the green. Bean's chip stopped four feet from the hole. Nicklaus then played an excellent wedge to within five feet and made the putt! Bean missed, and on the third hole of the sudden-death play-off, Nicklaus won with a par.

It was a dazzling display of Nicklaus's championship character. Not the victory so much, or even the five-footer on the seventy-second hole— everyone was accustomed to his winning tournaments and never missing five-footers that needed to be made. It was the thirty-two-footer for a bogey five on the seventy-first hole that was so confounding. A putt of that length is far more susceptible than a five-footer of being knocked off line by the slightest unseen depression in the green, an off bit of grass, a spike mark. Gauging the speed so the ball stays on line, assuming it is on line, is more difficult; hit the ball a tad too hard or too soft and it will either speed through the break or fall short of it. Paul Runyan, the genius of the short game, once said that, starting at twelve feet the odds on making putts from that distance and farther are the same. About 30 to 1, maybe 50 to 1. For Nicklaus to make that thirty-two-foot putt when it was absolutely necessary took on a mystical quality. It was often said of Nicklaus when he did such things that the intensity of his determination to make the ball fall was so great it transcended mere earthly obstacles. So it would seem.

Although he didn't himself wax quite so poetic, Nicklaus said essentially the same thing in commenting on his play at the seventy-first hole at the conclusion of the tournament: "I just *willed* myself to get that three on the second ball. I knew I had to."

Another time, during the 1973 Ryder Cup Match, Nicklaus and Tom Weiskopf were in a tight four-ball duel with Clive Clark and Eddie Polland. Weiskopf had a twelve-footer for a par that would win the match, Nicklaus a sixteen-footer. As Nicklaus prepared to putt, he told Weiskopf to pick up his ball, he wouldn't need it. In other words, Nicklaus was going to make his putt. And he did!

Nicklaus was notorious for how long he stood over the ball when putting. It seemed hours before he drew the club back. He once explained what he was doing, that he was emptying his mind of all thoughts. He wouldn't start the stroke until the slate was clean, or the Putting God had moved into position. His self-possession, demonstrated categorically at the 1972 British Open, was eerie to mere mortals. It was the year Nicklaus had his best chance to achieve the Grand Slam. He had won the Masters, won the U.S. Open, and it was expected by one and all that if he won the British Open, he would win the PGA to complete the quadfecta. He was not a casual seeker. He remarked once that at the beginning of every year, he set the goal of winning the Grand Slam.

For the 1972 British Open he decided, apparently well in advance of his arrival in Scotland, that he would follow the same game plan he used the last time he played Muirfield. His strategy was conservative—using a two-iron from most tees to keep the ball out of the heavy rough. But in 1972 the Muirfield links was hard-baked by an unusually dry and warm Scottish summer. The fairways were like rock, the rough thinner than usual and therefore more pliable. With one round to play, Nicklaus found himself six shots behind Trevino, five behind Jacklin.

That's when he decided to take the gloves off, abandon his earlier strategy, and use his driver from the tees. On many of the early holes he nearly drove the greens of a number of par fours—the flinty fairways were giving up so much roll. A tremendous run of birdies was the result, and by the time he reached the twelfth green, he had actually taken the lead.

An extraordinary comeback. On the twelfth he had an eight-foot putt for yet another birdie. After deliberating for some time to get the line, he stood in his hunchbacked way over the ball, clearing his mind, and just when it seemed he was going to make the stroke a great roar punched through the still air. It was surely the bellow of an eagle by either Trevino or Jacklin. They were playing two holes behind, but were nearby on the tightly wound links.

Nicklaus stood up and backed away from his ball. He then went again about his pre-putt preparations as if nothing had happened. And again, while over the ball and within a moment of beginning his stroke, another roar from the tenth. It was an even bigger one. It was also an eagle, and this one we would soon find out was by the homeboy, Jacklin. Nicklaus backed off again, but this time shook his head and whispered loudly, "Whew!" Yes, the lads behind were doing some stuff. And then, the play that set Nicklaus apart from the pack.

An ordinary golfing mortal might well have been shaken to his core after those two putts he heard from behind, which twice broke up his rhythm. But Nicklaus went again into his routine, stood over the ball as long as it took, then made his achingly slow and smooth stroke and made the putt!

To the great disappointment of many, Nicklaus then backed off his uncharacteristically aggressive play except on one hole where he might have played safe, the par-five seventeenth. He hit a driver and caught the fairway bunker on the left and could only par the hole. He ended up second to Trevino, who won with an incredible, downhill chip-in from deep grass on the seventeenth. Still, Nicklaus's putt on the twelfth signaled an athlete of outsized talent and will.

That Nicklausian aura pervaded the careers of every player of his time. When Lee Trevino beat Nicklaus out of the 1971 U.S. Open in a play-off, nicked him in the 1972 British Open, and fought him off to take the 1974 PGA Championship, these accomplishments had a much richer timbre because it was Nicklaus he defeated.

Tom Watson had two memorably torrid *mano a mano* confrontations with Nicklaus, in the 1977 Masters and the 1977 British Open, and won them both. To the point, they were not considered championships that Nicklaus lost in the way Palmer's loss to Casper in the 1966 U.S. Open was characterized. Nicklaus didn't throw them away with a breakdown in his thinking or swing, he was just outplayed. Which of course made Watson's and Trevino's achievements all the more worthy.

Watson Pipes In

One wonders sometimes if there isn't some out-of-world character with a strong sense of irony writing the script of golf history. Watson is a name as common to Scotland as Jones is to America, and it was Tom Watson who would have the best record of any American in the British Open during this century—five victories, all of them on Scottish links.

Watson in fact always had a natural affinity for Scottish links and golf. Perhaps it was a legacy of his family origins. Or the windy conditions and often chilly days in the Great Plains where he grew up. Although he did not have an especially outstanding college golf career at Stanford, Watson came onto the tour in 1971 touted to be one of the new young lions of the circuit. He got off to a slow start, however, and gained a reputation as someone who couldn't handle the pressure coming down the stretch. He didn't win his first tour tournament until 1974, when he won once. He won another one in 1975, came up empty in 1976, then with his 1977 Masters victory, Watson began his excellent run of play.

Efforts were made by the media to make Watson into a Huck Finn–type character, playing off his gap-toothed smile, reddish hair and freckles, and Missouri background. Much, too, was made of the fact that he voted for George McGovern for president, a liberal political position that in the golf world was considered deviant behavior. None of it worked, however. Watson as it turned out was anything but a free-spirited, free-thinking runaway maverick. He was more in the mold of a dean of admissions at a Presbyterian seminary. He carried himself with a cramped propriety that cooled any fervor his game might have elicited. And his game was very, very good for some eight years. Then again, as would be discovered a number of years later, Watson was carrying a good bit of troublesome personal baggage. His father, who had given Watson his golf through a country club membership and a good teaching pro, Stan Thirsk, had aggressively conservative political and social views. For a number of years, he was never seen on the golf scene, even when his son was becoming one of the most accomplished players in the game. This had to do with the father's chronic alcoholism, which his golf-star son would also fight privately for many years.

As a graduate of Stanford University with a degree in psychology, Watson had an active intellect that surfaced only occasionally. He almost invariably refused to be drawn into discussions of anything other than how he was playing and how he expected to play. If anyone brought up questions about the mental side of the game (given his major at Stanford he was a natural target for such inquiries at a time when sports psychology was becoming a much explored topic), he would sometimes get visibly irritated. It was clear he had decided that, if he was to become a champion golfer, he would have to block out anything that might thin out his resolve and tunnel vision—no chat, thank you, about motivation; the will to succeed or fail; the existential solitude of the long-hitting golfer. He took the right track for him and became an outstanding champion golfer.

Ben Crenshaw came out on the tour at the same time as Watson and with far greater expectations. He won three NCAA individual championships, was named the outstanding college golfer in 1971, 1972, and 1973, and led the qualifiers for the PGA Tour by a then-record twelve strokes. Crenshaw, though, spread his attention over a wide range of golf stuff. He became an avid, well-read student of golf history, course architecture, the literature of the game. Tom Watson prepared every year for the British Open by going to Scotland and Ireland at least a week in advance to accustom himself to the wind and chill, the time change and the turf. Crenshaw on at least one occasion took a group of golf enthusiasts on a tour of Scottish links the week before the Open. He played golf with them every day, lectured on the history of the game, and schmoozed into the night. It was hardly the way to prepare for a major championship. All of which is probably why this supremely talented player almost never challenged for the British Open (or any other majors but the Masters), while Watson won eight majors and Crenshaw only two. Then again, Crenshaw is an affable, thoughtful, courteous person who seems to have no regrets about the road he has taken.

Johnny Miller, the First Presold Star

Mark McCormack and Arnold Palmer taught the golf world a lesson in how to capitalize on charisma, and perhaps, too, how to create it, and one of the first to follow up on and run with this instruction was Johnny Miller. A tall, slender northern Californian, and another blond (the hair color of champions in this period, it seemed), Miller first came to national attention at nineteen when he was low amateur in the 1966 U.S. Open on his home course, the Olympic Club in San Francisco. Being paired with Arnold Palmer added to the television coverage he got. The exposure did him well when—actually, before—he turned pro, in 1969. Miller qualified for the PGA Tour that year. But prior to taking one golf shot for money his agent, Ed Barner, had dickered for endorsement contracts worth over $150,000. That was a nice cushion to begin life on the tour. Barner, who had a background in show business agentry, knew how to get his client ready for the public. Miller had a mild skin disorder on his face, a kind of acne, and cosmeticians sanded it to smooth out the surface. He got expensive custom haircuts and was told to sign autographs as Johnny not John, as he preferred, because the diminutive had a friendlier ring. He was nicely packaged for his trip to golf's big league. But Miller was also well prepared as a player.

Miller's "American" Golf Swing

Miller did his part in the promotion of his persona by becoming a very fine golfer, and perhaps unwittingly, the exponent of the New American Golf Swing. Miller's father, a knowledgeable and good golfer himself, sent his son at the age of seven to the seasoned teacher, John Geertsen. Geertsen taught a concept he called the early set. To put it as simply as possible, the early set is breaking or hinging the wrists (the thumbs come back toward the chest) very early in the backswing, almost from the moment the club starts back. Geertsen pointed out that this eliminated what he considered the unnecessary motion of the conventional takeaway, in which the wrists are kept unhinged until at least midway in the backswing. This fosters a lateral slide of the body, a sway, or what pros call "coming off the ball." If you sway going back, you will probably sway going forward, and in all there is too much margin for error. The most efficient golf swing is one in which the body turns like a swivel, a tight winding or revolving that keeps the golfer over the ball. Geertsen's early set encourages that, and is especially effective in iron-play because it promotes a more vertical swing, which produces a crisply hit, very accurate shot with a high trajectory. When Miller was on his game he was one of the best iron-players the game has ever seen. Showing astonishing accuracy, he would hit one leaner after another, approach shots that finish very close to the pin.

Miller's swing took Nicklaus's technique one step further. It eliminated the longish dragging back of the club to start the backswing that was a holdover from earlier days. Miller's was simpler, in its nothing-fancy utilitarian way identifying itself with the American character as a whole. Just the facts, ma'am. It was also well suited to the way American courses were now being conditioned, the golf ground softer, the greens raised above the level of the fairways.

Miller's "American" golf swing has become, in modified versions, the postmodern world swing. Seve Ballesteros and Nick Faldo, to name two especially notable foreign champions who came immediately after Miller, played (and play) with the same essential action. So have the next generation of players, including Justin Leonard and Tiger Woods. The distinguishing characteristic is the club being raised up off the ground very soon in the backswing—in some cases by simply lifting it up. The wrists may not always hinge as sharply as Miller's, but by getting the club to clear the ground sooner, they are achieving the same effect.

Johnny Miller won twenty-three tournaments between 1971 and 1987, including one British and one U.S. Open. He was known best for his streaks of torrid golf. His U.S. Open victory in 1973 came off a final-round 63 at the very difficult Oakmont Country Club course, in Pennsylvania. This bested Palmer's 65 at Denver in 1960, as the lowest closing round in U.S. Open history. While Oakmont in 1973 had been softened by heavy rains, Miller's 63 was still a phenomenal score. He hit a lot of leaners.

In 1974 Miller won eight tournaments, the most wins by a tour pro in a single season since Sam Snead won eleven in 1950. Palmer won eight in 1960, but it wasn't until 1999 when Tiger Woods matched that number. For all his brilliant playing, Miller never quite got to the level of Watson or Trevino (or Nicklaus, of course). He was seen as something of a flash in the pan, and someone who did most of his winning "in the the desert," on courses in Arizona and southern California that were considered relatively easy—because of the thin air, flat, perfectly manicured fairways, and big, flat resort greens. Indeed, Miller won the Phoenix and Tucson events, and the Bob Hope Desert Classic a total of seven times. In 1974 he was 37 under par in winning those three tournaments. However, Miller also won ten times around the country and world—from Pennsylvania to Florida to South Carolina to Scotland. He had plenty of range. But in the image game that was becoming more and more a part of the sports world's culture, he suffered, one might say, from winning too much and too spectacularly on desert courses.

Then, too, Miller may not have caught the golf public's fancy entirely because it didn't seem that he was overly interested in playing the tour. Sports fans tend to turn off on athletes they perceive as not sweat-stained grinders. Miller did cut back his tournament play beginning in the late 1970s, but he had a couple of very valid reasons. One, he had helped create a large family (six children) and did not intend it to go for long periods without a father in the house. In this respect he was also something of a pioneer. The tour pros of his generation and beyond have been more inclined to play less on the road so they can be more involved with their children while they are in their developing years. The amount of money that can be earned on the tour has helped make that possible.

But Miller also had a genetic neurological problem with his knees that increasingly made walking painfully difficult. Proof that the swing he brought out in the early seventies had staying power and could overcome his physical malady, that he was no chump champ able only to win in the desert: At age forty-seven Miller came out of virtual retirement to win the 1994 AT&T Pebble Beach National Pro-Am. He then returned to the television booth, where he was beginning to become a media star.

Miller had also been taken for someone who didn't know what he was doing with a golf club, who was just one of those "naturals." In fact, in his columns for *Golf Illustrated* magazine in the late 1980s he proved to have an incisive mind when it comes to golf technique. That was quickly picked up by the television people, who found that Miller was quite articulate on his favorite subject.

The PGA Tour Goes Big Time

Joe Dey once recalled his first dealings with television rights as the new commissioner of the PGA Tour. Because he believed the tour's share of the fee for the Bing Crosby National Pro-Am was insufficient, he talked with Crosby about renegotiating the deal with NBC. He told Crosby that if they couldn't come to a satisfactory agreement, he would find another network. Crosby said he didn't care who broadcast the event, as long as the charity associated with it did not lose out. Dey then discovered that Crosby's agent had folded the telecast of the tournament in with the singer's contract with the network for his entertainment specials. The agent guaranteed NBC that it would have to pay only $350,000 for the tournament, of which the agent, by the way, got ten percent.

"Well," Dey remarked, "I discovered very quickly that this new job of mine was going to be a little different than negotiating with the members of the Country Club of Rochester to hold the USGA National Junior Girls' Championship."

Dey's successor would not be at all overwhelmed by the intricacies of negotiating with television networks, agents, tournament sponsors, or anyone else who had or sought a financial interest in the PGA Tour. In 1974, at age sixty-six, Dey retired as commissioner of the PGA Tour and was replaced by Deane Beman. Dey had given the tour the image of high-minded rectitude that it was looking for, and if not a sniffy disdain for money, a certain gentlemanly, patrician distancing from the nitty-gritty of it. Beman brought everything back to a more earthbound and very American bearing. Dey had been a vestige of nineteenth-century laissez-faire amateurism. Beman was core twentieth-century American capitalism. Professional tournament golf was about money. And so was Beman.

A writer sitting in one of Beman's daily staff meetings remembered that the commissioner was last to enter the room, and no sooner did he take his seat when he began to collect the money he won from various staff members seated around the table in a golf game the previous afternoon. Ten dollars here, five dollar there, with change made as necessary. That done, discussions began about million-dollar deals.

Beman had himself been a tour pro up to a week or so before he took the commissioner's post in March, 1974. Before turning pro he had an excellent record as a world-class amateur, winning two U.S. Amateur Championships, in 1960 and 1963; the British Amateur in 1959; and playing on four U.S. Walker Cup teams. He qualified for the PGA Tour in 1967, and in his six years on the circuit won five times. He also tied for second in the U.S. Open in 1969. A small man physically—around five feet eight inches tall and 150 pounds—Beman succeeded at golf by virtue of a brilliant short game he had honed to make up for his innate lack of power. There was also his competitive pertinacity. The latter served him and the tour very well in his new job. His experience as a tour player added a special nuance to his qualifications. No commissioner of any other sport in the United States had ever actually played in the league he was commissioning over. There was also Beman's business acumen. He was a business major at the University of Maryland, where he played on the golf team, and before turning golf pro, had been successful in insurance brokerage in the Washington, D.C., area, where he was born and grew up.

Beman reigned as commissioner for twenty years. The royal reference is not overwrought. He had the instincts of an autocrat. Beman was not entirely humorless, but laughter was something with which he was not generally associated. He was smart in the way of the business world, at times ruthless in getting his way and by all means single-minded in his work. Not long after becoming commissioner, he left his first wife and their four children, one of them retarded, to marry his secretary. He may have been driven to some extent by the small-man complex, but the main engine was good old American free enterprise. After a couple of years on the job, he flew his appointed rounds in a corporate jet. His salary and bonuses, the latter a deeply held secret, made him a millionaire. When he left the post his salary was close to $2 million a year. As much as he did for the growth of the tour, and that can't be exaggerated, Beman did not make a lot of friends in the golf community, even among the players he putatively worked for and helped make rich. Eventually, the relationship between his office and the players would be blurred until it was hard to say who worked for whom. There would be repercussions to this after Beman left the job.

Beman turned the PGA Tour once and for all into a major league professional sports enterprise. When he became the commissioner, the tour was playing for just over $8 million. In 1994, when he left the office, the total was over $56 million. By this time the tour had become too expensive for resort hotels and chambers of commerce to be the main sponsors. The tour had become a venue for corporations as title sponsors. This practice was in place when Beman took over, but he expanded it to such an extent that it was more or less reinvented.

By getting a major corporation to buy in as the title sponsor of the Los Angeles Open, say, a tournament for which the local sponsoring group— the L.A. Chamber of Commerce—could raise only $500,000, the purse could now be raised to $1 million. For its half-million dollars, the corporation gets maximum exposure of its name—the Los Angeles Open becomes the Nissan Los Angeles Open. As Nissan's clout increases, it can simply drop the Los Angeles and call it the Nissan Open, which is what happened in this case. And has happened in others. The evolution has become the stuff of satire. The original San Diego Open became, in order, the Corvair–San Diego Open, the San Diego Open Invitational, the Andy Williams–San Diego Open Invitational, the Wickes–Andy Williams–San Diego Open, the Isuzu/Andy Williams San Diego Open, the Shearson Lehman Brothers Andy Williams Open, the Shearson Lehman Hutton–Andy Williams Open, the Shearson Lehman Hutton Open, the Shearson Lehman Brothers Open, the Buick Invitational of California, and finally, at the end of the century, the Buick Invitational. The transformations mirror the history of the PGA Tour and its geographic and show business underpinnings; they are also a chronicle of corporate America.

There is an interesting bit of media and advertising history in this development. When newspapers and news services such as the Associated Press reported on sports events in the 1950s, they would not include a corporate or brand name, even if it was in the official title of the event. It was considered free advertising, or it was deemed to be pandering to advertisers past, present, or future. Thus, General Motors would put up the money for a tournament they called the Buick Open but the reporter filing the story would refer to it by the name of the city or town in which it was played. The Buick Open was played in Flint, Michigan, and was cited in the *New York Times* or in Associated Press reports as the Flint Open.

Some tour sponsors got around this by using a tournament title covering an entire industry, what might called a generic bypass. The Insurance City Open, say, was used for the tournament in Hartford, Connecticut. The Florida Citrus Open is another example. Other sponsors just went straight to the point and took their chances on getting a media mention. Most of these were breweries. There was the Labatt, Carling's, Miller High Life, and Blue Ribbon (Pabst) Opens, and the Lucky International Open.

In the early 1970s the Associated Press began to change its policy on the matter. Its rationale was described by an old AP hand this way: The Chicago Bears football team is effectively a commercial entity, just as General Motors is. So is the city, in effect. To be consistent with its nonaming policy, the Bears would have to be referred to as "the Bears Team Playing Out of Chicago." No editor was going to let that hit the news-stand.

In the end, money talked. Beer companies spent millions advertising in newspapers and on television. Eastern Airlines, the Kaiser Corporation, Avco, Monsanto Chemical Company, and so on also had hefty advertising budgets. Therefore, the golf landscape became dotted with the Doral-Eastern Open, the Kaiser International, the Kemper Open, the American Express Westchester Classic, the Motorola Western Open, the AT&T Pebble Beach National Professional-Amateur, the MONY Tournament of Champions, et cetera. We are talking American-style commercialism here. The elimination of the ban on corporate identification, as loosely applied as it was, had a lot to do with the growth of the PGA Tour. Its growth only increased the American influence on the game worldwide.

Deane Beman became the commissioner of the PGA Tour just when this "ethical" breakthrough was occurring. He didn't have all that much to do with it, but he definitely knew how to take advantage of the opportunity and expand on it now that corporations were less hesitant about investing in sports events. They wanted in as sponsors of the PGA and LPGA tours, because they were discovering the value of a connection with golf. It wasn't the number of golfers that could be reached, although that was increasing. Nor were the television ratings for golf overwhelming, strictly by the numbers. What golf offered was highly desirable demographics: people in the middle- to upper-middle-class economic rank, with considerable disposable income and an inclination to dispose of it.

Commissioner Beman got into the enviable position of having a waiting list of corporate sponsors. It was a seller's market, he had the goods, and he wasn't going to give it away cheap. Not only would sponsors have to increase their purses to get a spot on the thirty-six-event schedule (since expanded to over forty events), they would need to upgrade their venues and their production values, to use show-business terminology. Sponsors were advised that the players would be happier if they had courtesy cars available so they could get themselves around town. Also, they would very much appreciate a very good and very free lunch in the locker room while they were visiting. Those were for starters.

On a higher business plane, Beman pushed through a longer distribution of the purse money. In this he was remembering his own career on the tour as a middle-range player who had to do some scraping to make a go of it. To stretch the money farther—increase the percentage of the total purse earned by players finishing second and lower—Beman reduced the winner's share from twenty percent to eighteen percent. This didn't please those who won most often, but so be it. The money list was extended so more players who made the cut got something for their effort. For years the purse was paid down to only the top twenty-four finishers out of the seventy-two or so who qualified for the last two rounds. Those who missed the cut left town with not a penny while having spent $1,000 or more out of pocket for six or seven days of accommodations, meals, caddies, and other expenses.

Some thought the extension of the money list would dampen the competitive spirit on the tour, that a fellow who realized he was going to earn $5,000 for finishing tenth was less likely to take the chances on the course that make the game more exciting for the gallery. A romantic notion. Most golfers, and especially the tour pros, are conservative. It comes with the game. Anyway, by the 1970s the quality of the competition on the tour had gotten so deep that finishing tenth was no small achievement. Interestingly, the egalitarian spirit of Deane Beman toward the middle-of-the-pack tour pro was not apparent in the 1990s when a maverick group of players in that category sought for a minimum payout to all pros who played in an event, even if they did not make the cut. The details further on.

While Beman may have taken two percent out of the winner's share of a purse, it was more than made up for by the exponential increase in purse money during his time as commissioner. The growth had a number of interesting manifestations in terms of the quality of the competition, its depth and intensity, and the way the game would be played. To wit, young men of a large physical size, who in the past would have gone into professional football or baseball, were beginning to opt for golf. Golf is much easier on the body, there is far less chance of serious permanent injury, and therefore offers a much longer career. Now that the money was getting so good, more big guys were giving pro golf a try. It is one reason why the ball started getting "longer," and the courses "shorter."

The ideal size of a golfer had long been in the five feet eight inches, 155 to 160 pound range. Ben Hogan was a good example. A six-footer such as Byron Nelson or Cary Middlecoff was considered tall. But now the average tour pro's height was getting into the six foot range, and he was naturally heavier and more muscular. As a result, the tour pros began hitting the ball farther.

Another component of the tour's rise to major league status was that the new players were arriving on the tour with far more training and knowledge of the swing than past generations were able to get. When a colleague who was having some problems with his game asked Ben Hogan to have a look at his swing, his famous response was, "Dig it out of the dirt, the way I did." And that is largely how the old pros did learn the game, on their own, experimenting with ideas, feels, praying for divine intervention, and as Lloyd Mangrum once put it when a fan asked him how to learn this game, "Monkey-see, monkey-do." The postmodern golfer now had video cameras, precisely illustrated books by legendary teachers, including the Man himself, Mr. Hogan. What's more, there were now spacious and fully equipped practice facilities everywhere.

Finally, the new pros coming out on the tour already had extensive high-level competitive experience playing college golf. All in all, there is little wonder that European, Asian, and Australian pros began coming to the United States in increasing numbers to play their pro golf. America was where the action was.

The Aussie Invasion

There has always been a symbiotic relationship between Americans and Australians. At least between the white males with an athletic bent from these nations. The bluff, swaggery style of the Australian man-in-the-street and his American counterpart's cowboy-of-the-wild-west image ring the same bell. American sports fans will go along with a British announcer on television, even if the accent is a bit toney, but won't take warmly to British athletes. Australians, on the other hand, are accepted *en toto*. Aussies sell beer and sports vehicles on American television; British actors sell expensive jewelry and cultural programs. Perhaps, too, the bonding derives from the frontier experience of both countries—histories that are emblematic of the freelancing, take-a-chance professional tournament golfer. One way or another, Australians have always been welcome in America, and have thrived in golf, where the opportunities have always been better. The United States is a kind of extension of Australian golf. It certainly is the place where many Australians end up playing and living.

Walter Travis, Jr., aside, the American-Australian golf connection really began in the early 1930s with the Australian Joe Kirkwood. He was a fine player, who won four tournaments on the 1924 U.S. winter tour. But Kirkwood chose to make his living as a trick-shot artist. He was one of the first to take up this line of golf work, and he made many an exhibition swing with Hagen and Sarazen and on his own all over the United States, and in Australia, Asia, and Europe. Kirkwood also gave a son to American golf and the movies. Joe Kirkwood, Jr., played some golf on the American tour in the forties and early fifties, but was far more famous for his movie role as Joe Palooka, the American comic-strip heavyweight champion of the world.

The next significant early Australian import to America was Jim Ferrier, a tall, stoop-shouldered man with a gimpy leg that remained from a rugby injury as a youth. Ferrier arrived in 1940 as an amateur, but his entry to that year's U.S. Amateur Championship was rejected because he was writing on golf for an Australian newspaper. Hence, the USGA rules said, he was a professional. "I wasn't writing about *how* to play," Ferrier recalled, "just about the tournaments I played in." This rule of amateur status would also be rescinded, in due time. In any case, Ferrier gave up the journalism ghost and turned pro. When World War II started, he joined the U.S. Army and became an American citizen, and later became the first Australian to win a modern major when he took the 1947 PGA Championship.

Ferrier's journalism background shined through when he told of some of his experiences playing the U.S. tour in the 1940s:

The traveling was interesting. I remember we drove into Charlotte one night, Ky Laffoon and his wife, and me and my wife, Norma. There were no motels then, and the hotels were full so we went looking for guest homes. You could get a beautiful room in a guest home for two-fifty, three dollars a night. Well, we went into this one, a beautiful southern mansion, big pillars, beautiful rooms. The manager was showing me and Norma the two front rooms when we hear this awful racket from the other room. It's Ky chasing bloody cockroaches in the bathroom. He had a newspaper and he's swatting them. He said, "That's all right, I got them." Then he said to the manager, "I want a dollar off if we're going to have cockroaches around here."

Not all American-Australian relationships were (or are) amicable. Norman Von Nida made the occasional trip to America, but never stayed long. A short, combative man, he once got into a brawl with Henry Ransom, an equally cantankerous Texas tour pro. Australian Peter Thomson made rare appearances on the U.S. circuit, usually only in George S. May's Tam O'Shanter events, although he did win once in Texas. Thomson didn't much like American culture or lifestyle, and it showed in his body language and his verbal and written comments. Thomson was not a jock in the usual sense of that term. He ran for political office in Australia, read literature in many subjects, and went so far as to draw metaphors about golf from his reading. He was (is) a good writer with interesting views on golf and a lot of other things that most athletes tend to give short shrift. However, Thomson did come to play the U.S. Senior Tour when it first got underway and had a very good and lucrative year on that circuit. He stuck to it for another season, but the goose had laid its golden egg and didn't come up with another. Thomson returned home to stay.

Bruce Devlin began the most significant emigration of Australians to the American tour when he came over in 1962, two years after he won the Australian Open as an amateur. He has had an accomplished career in the United States, winning eight times on the PGA Tour between 1964 and 1972, then becoming a television commentator and a busy and noted golf course designer. Devlin effectively became an American. He took up permanent residence in Texas, sent his children to American schools, and one son, Kel, tried for a tour card a few times, then got into the business side of the game working with American equipment manufacturers.

Bob Charles came from New Zealand (which is sort of Australia—same accent) to play the U.S. Tour in the 1960s, and he eventually became a permanent resident. He didn't win a lot, but did defeat Californian Phil Rodgers in a play-off for the 1963 British Open. A quiet and undemonstrative man, Charles didn't make much of an impression as a personality, but he was a brilliant putter, and until Phil Mickelson came along, the best left-handed golfer to ever play the game. Charles did most of his winning on the Senior PGA Tour.

In the seventies and into the eighties, David Graham was the dominant Australian émigré to the American tour, if only because he won two majors, the 1979 PGA Championship and the 1981 U.S. Open. A crusty personality, the short and slender Graham was an especially methodical player. His performance in winning the U.S. Open at the Merion Golf Club left the impression of a French butcher working up haute cuisine cuts for a banquet. After that victory, Graham claimed his killer-calm demeanor was the result of having quit drinking coffee for three weeks prior to the championship. This may have been the first foray into more careful dieting by tour professionals. Beside the two majors, Graham won only six other tour events in his career on the PGA Tour, but he went on to become an expert club design consultant and finally an excellent golf architect. He settled in Texas.

In the 1980s Australians Greg Norman, Steve Elkington, and Wayne Grady came to the United States to make their careers. Then came Stewart Appleby, Craig Parry, and Robert Allenby. One could say, in baseball terms, Australia has been a Triple-A farm club for the U.S. PGA Tour. It will no doubt continue to be, along with such rising rivers of talent as South Africa, Zimbabwe, Sweden, and Denmark.

American Golf, Architecture Division

Golf is the only game in which the venue is intentionally made more difficult than it might otherwise be. No one would ever dream of putting a pond between first and second base, a stand of trees at the fifty-yard line, or building a basketball court with a sixty-five-degree dogleg to the right. But in golf a dead flat, treeless stretch of ground with no natural water by way of ponds, rivers, streams, or lakes is transformed into an undulating, treelined, bunker-dotted, lake-infested chamber of horrors. Even the original links in Scotland, which are revered as "natural," were laid out so the bunkers were in the way of passage to the green. The bunkers themselves were natural, formed by sheep scraping out defenses against the wind and cold, but the Scots who put golf holes down on that ground could have routed them so the bunkers were not such direct obstacles. Same for the stream or burn found occasionally on links land— Swilcan Burn, on the first hole at St. Andrews Old Course, for example. They could have put the green in front of the burn, and made it less hazardous.

In other words, all golf courses are contrived one way or another and in every instance to make it more difficult for the golfer. Not only that, whereas in baseball the distance between bases has forever been ninety feet and the basketball hoop has been at the same height for years, despite how tall the players have become, as tour golfers improve, the courses are made that much harder. But golfers want it that way. Flat, unbunkered, uncomplicated courses are denigrated as "bull rings" and "dog tracks," to be avoided unless there is absolutely no other choice. Psychobabblers insist this is an indication golfers are masochists, guilt-ridden flagellants who insist on punishing themselves. Humbug! Golfers demand courses with obstacles, hazards, stands of trees, deep grass, because otherwise the game would not be as interesting. It would be like shooting arrows into a void. Granted, the act of hitting a golf ball perfectly and with some consistency is a challenge in itself. But if there is no fight to be won with those blows, the project is pointless.

Actually, the fields on which all ball-and-stick games are played are artificially designed. Alexander Cartwright and his engineer pals who invented baseball could have made the bases seventy feet from each other and the pitching rubber farther back or closer in. What distinguishes golf courses from baseball fields is that they are more creative. A golf course seems more natural, because it's carved out of nature as it presents itself, which is another reason why the game is so endlessly fascinating. No two courses, no two *holes* are exactly alike. Each has something differentiating it from all others—elevation, placement of bunkers, type of grass, prevailing wind, background view, and so on. Even if the yardage is the same. There is nothing in the book, however, that says a hole has to be just so long or short (except as it pertains to the par of a hole), a bunker so big or shaped in a particular way. The dimensions are fluid. A tennis court is a tennis court is a tennis court. Even a baseball diamond is a baseball diamond is a baseball diamond (except for the outfield dimensions—a comparatively small matter). But every golf course is a golf course separate and distinct unto itself. All the more on the North American continent and especially in the United States.

No two Scottish links are the same in the design of the holes, but all share certain common characteristics—flattish, treeless, windswept, springy sand-based turf. In America, though, golf courses are built on parkland, in the desert, the semi-tropics, and the mountains. An incredibly diverse canvas. The diversity of the nation's geography, not to mention the size of the country and its golf population, made golf architecture another component of the game in which Americans would surpass all other golfing nations.

In the American golf architectural vanguard was Robert Trent Jones, Sr., out of Rochester, New York. There were many American-born golf architects before Jones, and some gave the art what might be considered an American touch. It was the Scottish way, perhaps out of a frugality of disposition as well as pocket, to have a few good holes per course and let the rest be ordinary. Charles Blair MacDonald, a Chicagoan, thought a course should consist of eighteen exemplary holes—no commonplace ones. After all, this was America, the land of plenty. With his National Golf Links, on Long Island, New York, built in 1911, MacDonald was the first to achieve just that. Many of the holes were fashioned after well known ones in Scotland, but it was the expansiveness of MacDonald's concept that gave it an American character.

Walter Travis, Jr., thought putting surfaces should have undulation, and if there wasn't any there in the first place, he created it. He also thought fairways should be narrower, with long grass to the sides, and that cross-bunkers, which stretch midway across fairways, should be eliminated. Travis was thinking about his own game. He was small and didn't hit the ball very far, but he was accurate with his driver, and a canny putter. Like any good New World capitalist, Travis's design ideas were neatly self-serving.

After MacDonald and Travis there was a flowering of American-born golf architects such as Albert Tillinghast, Charles Banks, Perry Maxwell, and George Thomas. Scottish-born Donald Ross and Alister MacKenzie made their careers in the United States—Ross, in particular. But all of the above were heavily influenced in their designs by the Scottish links and were proud of it. Robert Trent Jones, Sr., knew his Scottish links and a good bit of his earliest work was in that vein, but he would veer into what has been recognized as a distinctly American style. The distinction mainly had to do with dimension, the American predilection for size.

Two basic design concepts developed in golf architecture prior to Jones, who began his career in the 1930s. They were the penal and the strategic. Penal allows only one way to get to a hole, and if the correct path is not taken, there is no hope of recovery. The periphery is the dread slough of despond. "A shot lost is one never recovered," as it was put by one of penal's staunchest proponents, William Fownes, who designed the brutal Oakmont Country Club (in Pittsburgh, Pennsylvania). Strategic design is a bit more forgiving in that it offers both a penal-type route but also a safer, albeit longer, alternative one to the promised land. He who wants to try the shorter but more dangerous route is free to have a go, but should he fail he will pay a heavy price. Robert Trent Jones devised a third architectural style, which he called heroic.

A good golfer as a youth, who was educated at an Ivy League school (Cornell), Jones was an articulate man with a flair for the catchy phrase. One of his best known was "Every hole should be a hard par and an easy bogey," which defined his heroic concept. The word "heroic" has an American resonance, but on the ground is really nothing more than a little less of the penal, a little more of the strategic.

Jones was the first person to train formally for golf architecture. He devised his own curriculum at Cornell, which included horticulture, landscaping, and surveying. He also took a course in sketching at the Rochester School of Art, to learn to create a better sales tool for making presentations to clients. He was fond of drawing a golf hole on anything at hand, like a napkin in a restaurant during an interview. This wasn't entirely original. Jones began his career as an apprentice to the highly regarded Canadian golf architect, Stanley Thompson, from whom he learned much, including how to make a presentation. Thompson was noted for producing ornate artwork of his conceptions, including elaborate drawings and models in clay and papier-mâché.

Many of Jones's first projects were funded by the United States government and its depression-era WPA program, which was charged with creating jobs. As the Great Depression waned, Jones was in a good position to move ahead in the business. Tillinghast had left golf to run an antique shop in Los Angeles and Ross was slowing down with age, as were Thompson and other top designers. Jones had continued to work through the hard times so he remained current. He was also very personable and masterful at dealing with people with money. He would design courses for the Rockefellers and such major corporations as IBM and National Cash Register. But the biggest coup of his career came in 1948, when he was called in to consult on the redesign of some holes on the Augusta National Golf Club course. Being associated with Bobby Jones and a course and tournament with such immense prestige was a prize— like Einstein putting someone up for a physics scholarship.

Jones was involved in some significant changes to the famed Augusta

National course. As noted earlier, the par-three sixteenth went from a thoroughly undistinguished short hole fronted by a narrow ditch into one of the most famous and often-photographed holes in the game. Jones also altered the eleventh hole, which had been a fairly short and uncompli-cated par four, by moving the tee to its present position, left of the tenth green. This lengthened the hole by some fifty yards. Also, a large pond was created to the left of the eleventh green that became a major element in the hole, forcing the golfer to play to the right. Just how much of this revision work sprung from the brow of Robert Trent Jones the architect, and how much from Robert Tyre Jones the famous golfer, no one will ever know. But the architect made sure he was not confused with his client. He preferred to be known simply as Trent, and he was for the rest of his life.

Trent Jones and Cliff Roberts did not get along well, in part because Jones had removed some venerable old trees to build the new tee at the eleventh hole. Roberts was strongly opposed to this. But Roberts also disliked anyone taking commercial advantage of a connection with Au-gusta National, which Trent most certainly and understandably did. The upshot was that Trent was never called on again to rework any part of Augusta National. But never mind, he had gained all the prestige he needed.

After his Augusta National gig, Jones began to get work from the USGA to revamp courses that would be used for the U.S. Open. Revamping meant making them harder. The revisions that gained Jones the most notoriety were those he made on Oakland Hills, outside Detroit, for the 1951 U.S. Open. The course played very hard, and while the long rough and narrow fairways—USGA decisions—had something to do with that, the Jones's redesign was what got the notices. He didn't mind at all. Specifically, on a number of the par-four and par-five holes, he put fairway bunkers on both sides of the fairways at just the distance most golfers reached with their drivers. He "wasp-waisted" the fairways, making them so narrow the golfers had to walk single-file through them, as golfers like to say. The bunkers effectively took the driver out of the pros' hands, forcing them to use long irons and fairway woods to stay short of them. This left them with very long approaches. After Ben Hogan won the 1951 Open with an even par score, and one of only two rounds in the 60s that week, he was quoted (perhaps misquoted) as saying he was pleased to have brought "that monster" to its knees. With that, the word "monster" became part of golf's lexicon to designate long and hard courses.

Trent Jones was now a hot item in golf, his prominence enhanced even more when Herbert Warren Wind wrote a long and widely read profile of him in *The New Yorker* in 1951. Perhaps not entirely by coincidence, Jones also gained considerable exposure through Wind's connection to the *Shell's Wonderful World of Golf* television series. As noted earlier, Wind advised the producer on what courses to use for the program, and a number of them were designed by Jones. One was the Houston (Texas) Country Club, where Sam Snead and Ben Hogan played their celebrated match. What few knew at the time (and even now) is that when Jones first completed the job, he did only seventeen holes. Somehow, he forgot one. When the shortfall was discovered, Jones came back and, now having little room to work with, squeezed in a sharp double-doglegged par-five with a green almost parallel to the tee on the other side of a copse—a poor hole. When Hogan heard the story while playing a practice round he snapped (with Oakland Hills in mind?), "Anyone can put out a shingle that says golf architect."

The incident was evidence of how busy Jones had become. In order to keep up with the contracts, Jones devised an architectural concept by which courses could be stamped out without his having to be around much, if at all, to oversee the work. The tees were straight rectangles eighty to one hundred yards long, fifteen to twenty yards wide—"airplane ramps," they came to be called. The program also included huge greens that averaged eight thousand square feet; one was ten thousand square feet, the biggest anyone had ever seen save for St. Andrews's double-greens. To allay criticism that the tees were monotonous, Jones said they left room to make the hole play longer or shorter. The huge greens offered at least six pin positions, which also provided variety. Both features were also rationalized as reducing the cost of construction and making maintenance simpler and cheaper. The same riding mower used for the fairways could be used for the tees, saving money and time needed for small mowers. The huge size of the greens spread the traffic so the delicate putting surfaces held up better under heavy use. Because the fairways and bunkers were in proportion to the tees and greens, the courses were impressive not for their aesthetic appeal—they were on the whole quite uninteresting—but for their size. Jones cranked these courses out the way General Motors did its massive high-fin Cadillacs.

Jones made up for the monotony of his tees, fairways, and greens with another departure from traditional course design as it had been handed down by the Scots. He added the element of water to course design. Not that there hadn't been water holes before—Jones simply expanded on the concept. Exaggerated might be the better word. He enlarged water holes where he found them—at Augusta National's sixteenth and eleventh holes, for example—and almost all his from-scratch layouts had at least one highly visible water hazard. He did this in part to create a place for collecting runoff of rain water (and melting winter snow) for use in irrigating the course, but also because a big expanse of water makes a compelling visual statement. (Later, when environmental protection issues arose, all course builders dug water hazards on the course to keep the chemicals in the runoff contained.) Jones told the author in a late 1960s interview that he made a point to build at least one hole on each of his courses that was particularly photogenic. It need not be a sound hole in strictly golf terms, but it did need to photograph well. Holes with enormous lakes somewhere on them made the most tantalizing, eye-catching pictures. These holes were the ones used in promotional materials, advertisements, and brochures of resort courses. Jones called them signature holes, because they speak for the rest of the course even if they actually do not. This term, too, has become part of golf's glossary: The course's "signature hole." It is also used to describe entire courses built by celebrity designers, as in a "Jack Nicklaus signature course."

Jones had become so popular that anyone who wanted to bring immediate attention and customers to a new golf resort would give him a call. It was a point of good business to be able to promote your course as a "Robert Trent Jones championship course." Naturally, other architects followed the leader and gave clients what they wanted. Thus, in the sixties and seventies sprawling water-crowded layouts proliferated all over golfworld—in Europe and Asia as well as in the United States, and their style dubbed the "new American architecture." They were American only in that they reflected the American predilection for bigger being better. It was an "image thing." Water was easier to comprehend than a subtle, camouflaging Donald Ross mound.

Finally, Jones sculpted his bunkers to catch the eye from above—aerial photography of golf courses was coming into fashion. His friend Herb Wind wrote a description of a Jones bunker for the Shell television program, which was photographed from a helicopter, that said it had a "whirly-gigging Picassolike effect." The announcer wouldn't read the line.

Jones had a genius, and unbounded energy, for self-promotion. It may have been what he did most, leaving the actual work to others. Close associates of Jones remember that he had trouble reading a topographical map. One time he was seven hours late for a presentation to prospective clients and excused himself by saying he had needed more time to work up his maps and charts. When he spread out the map of the potential course—Bedens Brook, in south New Jersey—he couldn't locate the first tee. He lost the commission to Dick Wilson, a brilliant contemporary of Jones who didn't have his public relations gifts, but left a number of outstanding courses on the American landscape before he died, at age sixty-one.

From 1945 through 1963, Jones's chief assistant was Frank Duane, who had a degree in landscape architecture and, when he left Jones, did a number of new courses and revamped others on his own and with Arnold Palmer, to considerable praise. (Palmer, by the way, was well known for not getting overly involved in the design of courses built under his name.) It is entirely possible that many of the best courses credited to Jones alone were mainly Duane's creations. Roger Rulewich, who followed after Duane and worked for Jones for some thirty-five years, commented after he went out on his own that during his tenure with Jones he had been responsible for the design of just about every golf course created under his chief's name. This includes the highly regarded Robert Trent Jones Golf Club outside Washington, D.C., where the first two international President's Cup matches were played; it is a potential U.S. Open venue. It took the insistence of his friends to get Rulewich to come out of the closet, as it were. A soft-spoken, almost painfully shy man, for years he refused to say anything about his relationship with his boss. No one from the Jones family, Trent himself or his two sons, Robert Trent, Jr., and Rees, also successful golf architects, have ever denied Rulewich's claim.

Robert Trent Jones, Sr., may have had some charlatan in him as a golf architect, but he unquestionably brought a level of recognition to his profession that had never before been reached. Every golf architect who has followed after owes him a thank-you for this contribution to their careers.

In the past only golf aficionados recognized golf architecture as an art and craft, and architects as artists and craftsmen. Now, even the once-a-week public-fee golfer knows that a good golf course doesn't just happen: It is the result of an individual with ideas, creativity, and talent.

The repute Trent Jones gave golf architecture stimulated the entry into the field of many more course designers, if only because hundreds of courses were being built every year, and Trent couldn't do them all. At least three designers began to gain prominence in this period: Bob Von Hagge, George Fazio, and Pete Dye. Von Hagge did rather quirky work that has not gained long-term recognition. In the late 1960s he hypothesized that one day there would be golf courses composed entirely of artificial turf that could rolled up every year or so and completely redesigned. So far, no. So far, good! Dye and Fazio reacted to Jones's penchant for oversize tees and greens by going in the opposite direction, Dye in particular. Dye had built some courses in the early 1960s, after leaving a successful career in the insurance business, and a couple of them have become classics—Harbour Town Golf Links, Crooked Stick, The Golf Club, and Casa de Campo. He achieved his first renown with the Harbour Town layout, which is on Hilton Head Island, off the coast of South Carolina. This was the course by which Dye broke the bigger-is-better syndrome. He built very small greens that were about as flat as the Outer Banks terrain he had to work with. Just get the ball on the green and you had a decent chance to make the putt, none of which were going to be over fifty feet.

What's more, Dye didn't try to change the character of the property, which had a smallish parcel of land that contained a small forest of moss-draped live oak trees. He cut away just enough trees to fit in fairways of moderate width, kept the course nicely under 7,000 yards at its longest, and everyone appreciated it immensely. It is a wonderful walk through a charming, even somewhat eerie, moss bedecked corridor. Dye got big notices for going small, and the trend in golf architecture began to move away from the large courses popularized by Trent Jones.

George Fazio brought back the Scottish look, but without the edges. His courses had (and have) a smoother, harmonic look and feel. Fazio liked to say his work reflected his Italian heritage, and there is something to say for that. The best Fazio courses do indeed have a musical quality—Puccini, Verdi, with some Rossini on the side for a bit of fun.

What Fazio and Dye brought back to golf architecture was the designer who could play really good golf. Jones was a decent enough player as a young man, but Dye had won an Indiana State Amateur Championship and contended in other high-level amateur competitions. He had the stuff of a tour pro. His wife Alice, too. One of the better woman golfers in the country, Alice Dye has had a lot of input on her husband's design work. Pete makes a point of that. George Fazio might have been one of the best tour pros of his time had he taken more interest in it. As it was he won a Canadian Open and was in a play-off with Lloyd Mangrum and Ben Hogan for the 1950 U.S. Open. Dye and Fazio brought to their designs a player's eye for contour, size, and strategic placement of hazards.

Dye would in years to come move away from the good but comfortable, instead developing a reputation as a builder of killer courses. He even made an American Express commercial highlighting that theme. In this Dye was for the most part fulfilling the demands of his clients, many of whom wanted to boast of offering the "toughest golf course in the world."

George Fazio gave golf some fine courses—not all that many, because he started late and died in his sixties—but he also left behind his nephew Tom Fazio, who learned the business working for his uncle from the time he was fourteen years old. By the end of the twentieth century, Tom Fazio amassed a copious collection of outstanding layouts, and can be cited as one of the finest golf architects the game has ever had.

Blacks Break Through, at Last

As the campaign for racial equality in American society heated up in the 1960s, criticism of the Masters tournament for having never invited an African-American to play was beginning to be heard. Cliff Roberts's standard response was that when a black player qualified according to the system in place, he would be welcomed. The one instance when Bobby Jones was asked to comment on the subject, he reiterated what Roberts had said.

The system Roberts referred to had changed little over the years, and then only in the number of players invited. Through the 1960s it was as follows: champions of past and present Masters, U.S. and British Opens, and PGA Championship, plus current U.S. and British Amateur champions; current Ryder and Walker Cup team members from both sides; the top twenty-four finishers in the previous year's Masters; the top sixteen finishers in the previous year's U.S. Open; the two professionals not otherwise qualified who established the best scoring record during the current winter tour; and one pro not otherwise qualified selected by ballot of former U.S. Open and Masters champions. There was also a point system, whereby the winner of a tour event earned 30 Masters points, the second-place finisher received 24 points, the third place finisher 23, and so on down until the points were exhausted.

The first black man who might have gotten an invitation to the Masters, based on his playing performance, was Charlie Sifford, especially after he won the 1969 Los Angeles Open. Sifford had already won on the tour, the 1967 Hartford Open, but it was in 1969 when he was most eligible. Besides winning in Los Angeles, he had played well in other events that winter. The invitation never went to Sifford, however, because according to the Masters he did not accumulate enough Masters points. The number was never published, so no one was clear just how many points were required. In 1969 Bob Murphy, who did not win on the tour that year, got the invitation. It came under the best scoring average on the just concluded winter tour or via the ballot of past Masters and U.S. Open champions. Just how many votes of the latter were required was never revealed. It was probably a majority, because Art Wall, Jr., went out of his way to tell the author that he voted for Sifford.

For the record, in the PGA Tour's ranking of players in the 1960 to 1969 period, Sifford stood forty-sixth, Murphy ninety-fifth. The ranking was based on total performance—victories, second and third place finishes, and top ten and top twenty-five finishes. In short, Sifford deserved, indeed had *earned*, an invitation to the Masters.

Cliff Roberts and Bobby Jones swore by their invitational system, but one or the other or both could have broken the mold if they had wanted to. It was their tournament, and they were well known for doing whatever they wanted with it, including rules calls, known at Augusta National as "interpretations." Gary Player received his first invitation after his father wrote a letter to Roberts asking if he would send one to his son. Player had yet to make his international reputation. Given the Masters' enormous prestige, it is safe to say that if Roberts and Jones had extended an invitation to Sifford, they would have helped assuage racial discrimination in the United States. It didn't happen, because they did not want to.

That is not surprising, given their personal backgrounds. Jones was a white son of the Old South, born and raised in a segregated society that he accepted as a matter of course. It was all he knew during his most formative years. Roberts was not a Southerner in the classic sense. He was a Prairie American who grew up in a world not very populated by Negroes. However, as David Owen reported in his 1999 hagiography of Roberts and the Masters—*The Making of the Masters*, the copyright for which is owned by the Augusta National Golf Club—when Roberts was ten years old, his father wrote a letter to his wife telling about selling his business *and a family of Negroes*. Cliff Roberts had learned about black and white racial inequality firsthand and at a most impressionable age. He saw there was a division of peoples, a high and low, and that he was on the high side. Like any hustler who came from difficult financial straits, he was going to stay there. It was the better place to be.

The rationale offered by Owens and others for the failure of Jones and Roberts to invite any African-American to play in the Masters is that they were simply men of their time, with attitudes no different from millions of others. True enough. But somehow, one expected more of Jones, at least. His gentle mien as it came through at the televised presentation ceremony following each Masters, the graceful writing style in which he offered his insights on golf, the magnitude of his golfing achievements, seemed to suggest that he was more than just another post-Reconstruction southerner. Roberts might also be expected to have a more progressive view of the world and race, if he were true to the image of the tournament he had worked so hard to project—that of a gracious worldliness. But of course, the ambiance of the Masters was more illusion than reality, a flight of fancy as dated and unreal as Scarlett O'Hara's Tara.

Abraham Lincoln, who was from Kentucky, was a man of his times until he finally decided slavery was wrong. So was President Truman of Missouri, when he pointedly integrated the United States military. So was Branch Rickey from Ohio, when he went out of his way to bring Jackie Robinson into major league baseball. They were special people, who had a vision or a sense of what was right and the fortitude to act on it. Jones and Roberts were indeed just men of their moment, who were not willing to rise above the mores of their times and milieu. They were not men of forward vision. If anything, they had rearview vision. So be it.

Eventually, Roberts gave in when the rising tide of criticism threatened the sanctity of his godchild, the Masters. In 1972 the qualification system was altered. The past Masters and U.S. Open champions ballot was dropped, perhaps at the players' request when the issue got hot. And, it was decreed that anyone winning a PGA Tour event in the year between one Masters and the next automatically received an invitation. In 1974 Lee Elder, an African-American, won the Monsanto Open and played in the 1975 Masters. In the run-up to this moment, which received considerable media attention, Roberts, who was also tone-deaf to the whole race issue, remarked in phrases freighted with Freudian slips of tongue, "It's been very trying. You don't know how much we are praying down here that a black boy will somehow qualify. We want to get this monkey off our back." Finally, it was off.

The LPGA Gets a Hotshot Commissioner and Nancy with the Golden Smile

Women's golf got on a better track in the 1970s, after a stumble or two. The feminist movement in the country was in full swing, and there were serious attempts to connect with it. In sports this was largely via the aforementioned Title IX federal regulation requiring that college women sports get equal funding from any government money the institution receives.

Carol Mann was in the vanguard of the struggle for women athletes. She was president of the LPGA during this period and not in any way as a figurehead. An imposing woman at well over six feet tall and an LPGA Hall of Fame player (twenty-eight career victories on the LPGA tour, including a U.S. Women's Open), Mann had (and has) strong, not always conventional, but always well thought out and articulated views on issues of moment. Mann was a trustee of the Women's Sports Foundation and its president for five years (1985 to 1990). She brought various issues concerning women athletes before three sitting United States presidents—Jimmy Carter, Ronald Reagan, and George Bush. These included, in particular, efforts by the NCAA and Notre Dame University president, Fr. Theodore Hesburgh, to kill Title IX on grounds that it would hurt their men's football programs. Mann was typically not shy in addressing these efforts and taking direct action when required. Notre Dame and the NCAA lost.

In 1972 the LPGA faced a crisis that was uncomfortable, although it would have been so for the men's tour as well. One of its top players, Jane Blaylock, was accused of cheating in tournament play. It was believed she marked and replaced her ball on greens in an illegal way to avoid spike marks or indentations in the greens. Blaylock adamantly denied the charges and filed a $5 million antitrust suit against the LPGA, which had suspended her. Not only did the LPGA not have anywhere near that kind of money in its treasury, the publicity accruing from the incident, no matter who was right, was hurtful to the image of the association. The LPGA attorney handling the suit advised Carol Mann to fight the battle to the death in the courts. Mann wasn't sure that was the right way to go, and through PGA Tour commissioner Deane Beman found another lawyer, William Rogers, who served as Secretary of State under President Reagan, to handle the case. Rogers said the LPGA didn't have a chance against Blaylock and should settle with her out of court, to kill the matter. Blaylock only wanted her legal fees, around $100,000, and treble the first-prize money she might have won had she not been barred from playing in an LPGA event in Baltimore. Case settled.

"The settlement money was a lot for us," Mann recalled, "we were living from hand-to-mouth. But it was the best way out of a bad situation that could have ruined us."

In 1974 Mann was faced with having to fire the LPGA's executive director, Bud Erickson. A private company had been hired to assess Erickson's work, and the review was very critical—basically, he didn't tell the members much of what was going on in their behalf. Mann bit the bullet, and while they took a New York City taxi to a function she told Erickson he was out. An executive search firm was hired to determine what type of person the LPGA needed for the executive job. The answer was a good marketing type, and after an extensive search Mann and others on the board decided on Ray Volpe, who had been a marketing man with the National Hockey League. It was a fortunate choice. Mann changed his title to commissioner, and Volpe took off.

A lively personality with talent for his work, in his five years on the job Volpe increased the LPGA's total purse money from $1.7 to $4.4 million. In 1979 he left the job because he felt he had done all he could. The break was entirely amicable, although there had been the usual rumblings of discontent. The LPGA felt it now needed someone more golf oriented in the job. Volpe wasn't a golf junkie, just a marketing man, albeit a very good one.

Volpe was helped along in his good works by the formidable presence of David Foster, CEO of the Colgate-Palmolive Company. Foster, in effect, became the LPGA's angel for much of the seventies. It was a unique situation, but one not uncommon to golf. Foster professed a love of the game itself, and great admiration for women golfers. No one questioned that. But he also had business in mind. Women bought a lot of Colgate-Palmolive products, and the association with the LPGA was a way to reach that market in the United States. Even more important, it would help Colgate-Palmolive get into overseas markets, especially in the Far East, where it was having trouble getting shelfspace. Foster used LPGA players in a series of Colgate-Palmolive television commercials, paying the participants "scale," as Mann recalled. Mann also said that at one point near the end of the relationship with Colgate, Foster told her with no little pride that Colgate-Palmolive had become a $2 billion company. Getting into those Far East markets had helped.

The LPGA didn't feel it was being used, and it certainly wasn't abused. On one Far East junket an LPGA player checked through twenty-seven pieces of luggage, and Colgate covered the $10,000 excess-baggage charge. Colgate didn't put money into purses, but bought a lot of advertising minutes on LPGA telecasts. This made Volpe's job of selling the tour to television a lot easier. The LPGA was not a network favorite, because the ratings were so poor. Even golf's vaunted demographics didn't always help.

If network television was finding the LPGA Tour a hard sell, the LPGA was also having a hard time trying to recruit new young players to join the circuit. Mann recalled that promising young women playing golf in college were reticent to go pro with the LPGA because "they saw us being too serious about our golf. We were, after all, professionals, but there wasn't a lot of money in it. The LPGA didn't seem a good career choice for them."

With the recruiting dilemma in mind, Mann and her compatriots saw a fine chance to improve the situation in a young woman named Nancy Lopez, who was playing for Tulsa University at the time. As an amateur Lopez compiled an excellent record. She twice won the USGA Junior

Girls' Championship and won the Western Golf Association Junior Girls three times. She also tied for second in the 1975 U.S. Women's Open. After her college career ended and she joined the LPGA circuit, Mann referred to Lopez as, "Our second Title IX baby. Pat Bradley [Florida International University] was the first." Lopez held to her potential when, in her first U.S. Women's Open as a professional, she finished sole second.

Lopez was the best thing to happen to the LPGA since Mickey Wright. Better, actually, because along with her ability to play championship golf, she had a beautiful white-toothed smile that gleamed out of a fine olive complexion. Lopez exuded authentic charm and was unquestionably feminine. "We didn't realize she would be so good under pressure," said Mann. In her first two years on the LPGA circuit—1978 to 1979—Lopez won seventeen tournaments. The highlight of her emergence was a five-tournament winning streak in 1978. Winning streaks in sports are particularly appealing to sports fans and the players for the consistency they reflect, and with hers Lopez gave the LPGA tour wide recognition in sportsworld. Her personality was an important bonus, a corrective to the many stone-faced women who were so prevalent on the tour. So was her marriage to Ray Knight, the major league ballplayer, and that she began to have a family soon after.

Lopez's success did exactly what Mann and her associates thought it would—attract new young blood to the LPGA circuit. Her domestic life helped dispel the tiresome but persistent assumption that all the women on the LPGA circuit were lesbians. This was also helped along, to some extent, by two young women coming onto the circuit who were definitely pin-up types. One was Jan Stephenson, an Australian with a shapely slim figure and a fine bosom she did not hide behind an athletic bra. Stephenson had some show-off in her character. She posed for Dunlop ads (she was on the company's golf staff) lying in a bathtub, hence in the nude (at least it appeared that way) amid a "sea" of golf balls. In another ad she simulated the famous Marilyn Monroe sidewalk-grate shot. Stephenson was not quite as revealing, but her flouncy white skirt did get up around her thighs, showing a bit of panty. Her sex siren bits were not appreciated by some of her LPGA mates, who thought these appearances a bit sleazy and denigrating. However, she brought attention to the tour and women's golf, and she may have quieted the sexual orientation stereotypes a little.

Of course, if Stephenson hadn't been a good player her cheesecake antics would have been the stuff of parody. But she could definitely play. She won only twice in the seventies but contended often, and in the 1980s won fourteen times. Those victories included a U.S. Women's Open and an LPGA Championship—two majors.

The other sexpot to join the LPGA in the seventies was Laura Baugh, also slender, also blonde, and very attractive in an all-American-girl way. Baugh, however, was not the player that Stephenson was. She qualified for the tour in 1973, and won the rookie-of-the-year honor, but without winning a tournament. Although she did have ten second-place finishes during her career, Baugh won only once, in 1988. It is possible the sexy siren thing and the attendant publicity she received did Baugh more personal harm than good. She had six children from an otherwise troubled marriage with tour pro Bobby Coles that eventually ended in divorce and she suffered a very serious mid-life crisis during which she was revealed as a suicidal alcoholic.

Even with the good luck of Colgate-Palmolive, Nancy Lopez, and the good work of Ray Volpe, the LPGA was still not considered out of the woods and a secure professional sports enterprise. It would go through another commissioner who did not come through as hoped, and when Colgate-Palmolive dropped its involvement when Foster retired, the usual financial and sponsor problems recurred. Then came the Senior PGA Tour to cut into its market. But the circuit was gaining in the battle for recognition and permanence. In the 1990s there was another injection of outstanding playing talent and corporate support that kept the LPGA afloat.

Ping! Another Equipment Evolution

It came as no surprise to anyone that by the 1960s, golf equipment manufacturers would increasingly draw ideas from the flourishing field of aerospace technology. It is not too far a fetch to use a spacecraft launch as metaphor for the flight of a golf ball. Both start from a standstill and soar with great speed upward on a majestic parabola. And of course, elemental aerodynamic principles apply, the dimple being a good example. At first, and for many years after, all golf balls had the same number of dimples—336—all the same size and depth. But as studies in aerodynamics became more sophisticated, so did the dimple, until there is a variety now in numbers per ball, their shape, and their depth, all of which affect flight characteristics.

Golf club makers somehow didn't get as involved in the dynamics of air flow ballistics, physics, and other such sciences until the 1960s. There had been some nods toward this. Ben Hogan put what came to be called a "speed slot" on the back of his drivers, which was meant to cut down air resistance, and get the club moving faster at impact. Some experts thought the slot was in the wrong place and began slotting the outer or toe end of the head. Even in the book *The Search for the Perfect Swing*, published in 1968 and still the most thorough scientific study ever made on golf equipment and the golf swing, there was not all that much information on clubs—only a few pages compared to many on the ball. But the time was ripe, and a man named Karsten Solheim, a Norwegian-born engineer, worked nights in the garage of his California home and came up with a putter based on the moment of inertia.

Moment of inertia sounds highly technical, but simply put it is this: The more force it takes to move an object, the higher its moment of inertia. Solheim knew that most golfers do not hit the ball on the "sweet-spot," generally the point directly in the middle of the club face, at least not regularly. When the ball is hit either to the right or left of center on a conventionally weighted clubhead—with the weight evenly distributed throughout its length and width—the angle of the face will change at impact. With a putter, a ball hit to the right of center, toward the toe, will go to the right of the target. If hit to left of center, on the heel, it will go to the left. With this in mind, Solheim reasoned that if more weight were put on the toe and heel of a putter head, when the ball is struck off-center it will be less likely to change its angle. The ball will still go toward the target because of the higher moment of inertia at those points. The result, introduced in 1961, was the Ping putter, with heel-and-toe weighting, also called perimeter weighting. It was a huge success, and put Solheim on the golf map.

It followed that Solheim should adapt the same weighting concept to irons, and he did. Just as with his putter, he took weight from the center of the club head and redistributed it on the toe and heel. The total weight of the club head would be the same within established weight parameters—not too heavy, not too light. Because of the weight displacement, the middle of the back of the club head had a cavity. Solheim began experimenting with heel-and-toe weighting in irons in 1961, but didn't bring out his first commercial model, the Ping K-1, until 1969. It, too, was an almost immediate and astounding success.

The effect of the heel-and-toe weighting concept was far more apparent with irons, because of the greater force at impact than with a putter. Golfers catching the ball off center with their Ping irons were still getting accuracy and not losing much if any distance. A dream come true. It had always been thought that more weight directly behind the center of the club face on irons was preferable, that it would add more punch to shots. That is where manufacturers would add a dollop of weight. Clubs with this feature were called "muscle-backs." But Solheim realized, as did the scientists who researched and wrote *The Search for the Perfect Swing*, that if you hit the ball dead-center on the club face you are using the full weight of the entire head and do not really need anything extra behind the ball to get maximum power. Even if that spot became a cavity, the same concept applied.

There was another aspect to Solheim's innovative club that was just as influential in the industry. His irons were produced by what is called investment casting or the lost-wax process. We will forgo the science of this, and say only that the clubs were made by pouring the steel into molds. When the steel hardened, they needed virtually no hand work—no grinding of the heads to refine their shape, no buffing necessary, no coating process, all of which was the norm with the forged steel irons that had been used since forever. The investment casting method cut the cost of manufacture significantly, and every head was exactly like all the others. No waste.

With the combination of perimeter weighting and investment casting, Solheim and his Karsten Manufacturing Company set golfworld on its head. In only a year or so he captured some forty percent of the iron market, and every equipment maker in the business retooled to keep up with Solheim.

Karsten Solheim's is another classic American folk story—an anthem to the promised land. He came to this country as a two-year-old from Norway. The family settled in Seattle, Washington, and young Karsten showed an early affinity for mechanics and working with his hands. He learned the shoemaking trade, which was in the family, supplemented his income selling shoes, and also took courses in engineering at the University of Washington. When he ran out of money he dropped out of school, but he became a beneficiary of a program cosponsored by the federal government and General Electric to train electrical engineers. After the training period, he went to work at GE for $45 a week. Then the company sent him to Cornell University for additional electronics training. Karsten had no experience in golf, but at Cornell he got interested in the game not so much as a player, but from an engineering point of view. He was especially intrigued by the huge variety of putter shapes and how much trouble golfers seemed to have with this part of the game.

When he went back home to northern California and his job with GE, Solheim got to work in his garage in Redwood City, outside San Francisco. After he formed his company, Solheim moved it to Phoenix, Arizona, and became a world leader in golf equipment manufacture. When he died, in 2000, he was rightfully honored by golfdom as a brilliant innovator who forwarded the pleasure people got out of golf. No one went on much about his having realized the classic American dream, but he did, and in the process also added to the repertoire of America, the Monarch of Golf.

The 1980s: Marketing, Marketing, Marketing

The Mulligan to End All Mulligans; LPGA Gets Pinched; Ryder Cup Gets Hot;
A Star Is Burned; "Gurus" and "Shrinks"; Another Equipment Debacle

The Mulligan to End All Mulligans

At the 1963 Masters Gene Sarazen was lunching with Fred Raphael, producer of *Shell's Wonderful World of Golf*, the popular television program of which Sarazen was the host. It was before Sarazen became an honorary starter and noncompetitor in the tournament, and when Raphael asked him who he was playing with in the first round the next day, Sarazen said: "At 10:52 tomorrow an old legend tees off with a new legend, Arnold Palmer." It was a casual remark with a touch of Sarazen's sardonic humor. He had no idea where it would lead, or how far.

Fred Raphael was taken by the word "legend," and tucked it away in the back of his mind. It reemerged some thirteen years later and set the stage for one of the most extraordinary new sports enterprises in this century, the Senior PGA Tour.

Raphael continued to produce the Shell show for the next seven years, took a rest, then in 1977, conceived the idea for a new golf television program he called *The Legends of Golf*. It would be a fifty-four-hole two-man-team best-ball competition, at stroke-play. The competitors had to be at least fifty years old and the winner of a major championship, or a Ryder Cup golfer or a leading money winner in any given year on the tour.

Raphael was catching the mood of a substantial segment of the nation. Everyone forty years old and older was feeling nostalgic. A sign of this sentiment in sports was the growing number of Old-Timers Days at major league baseball games. Retired ballplayers were donning the old uniform, doffing their caps to the crowd, playing a couple of innings, and slipping back into the dugout to much warm applause. Raphael thought, wouldn't it be something if older golf fans could see the glorious stars of their generation in action again? It might also be a treat for the current, younger age group, which had only heard about Snead and Demaret, Hogan, Boros, Bolt, Burke, and others.

Raphael received considerable advice on how to put the show together from Jimmy Demaret, who had emceed the Shell show for its last seven years. Demaret helped devise the competitive format and convince his old tour pro pals, including himself, to play. When NBC, the network Raphael sold on the project, decided it wanted a live broadcast, not the prefilmed, canned show Raphael had in mind, Demaret said he was afraid he and his fellow pros would look bad after so many years away from competition. In a filmed show the poor shots could be dropped on the cutting room floor. On a live broadcast these rightfully proud men might be seen hitting some very poor shots. But in the end it was their pride that led them to accept the challenge. Calling the players "legends" surely helped, too. It may have been a slight stretch of the term, but those chosen to compete didn't mind the honorific. Neither did the audience. It gave everybody, players and fans, a intimate feeling of having been part of an inspiring past. It definitely inspired the old pros to get out and practice and play more than they had for years. Demaret himself, who had almost quit playing even casual golf, prepared for *The Legends of Golf* by going to Florida to play six rounds in six days.

There was another enticement for the old-timers to practice and get their games back in decent working order. It was the old reliable. Although Raphael didn't have a sponsor for the first year and had trouble raising the purse money, he fixed on a $400,000 purse. The winning team would split $100,000; the last-place finishers $20,000. When two-time PGA champion Paul Runyan heard the money news, he told Raphael that by finishing last in this new tournament he could win more than he did when he was the PGA Tour's first official leading money winner (in 1934, with $6,767 and six victories). Indeed, some of the golf legends had not done all that well financially; this tournament would prove a most welcome windfall.

"Sam Snead was one of the few who wasn't worried about his game,"

Raphael recalled. "He was sure he would play well." Snead did just that, and in doing so, he made the show an immediate hit.

The first *Legends of Golf* tournament was held in April, 1978, at the Onion Creek Country Club, in Austin, Texas. Demaret had designed the course for a real estate developer, and the exposure the show would give it was expected to sell more than a few plots of land and club memberships. It did. Fittingly, the first player to tee off on the first day of play was Gene Sarazen. There was no television coverage of Friday's opening round. The telecast began with Saturday's second round and almost didn't make it. The show was scheduled to go on air at 4:00 p.m. Eastern Standard Time, but a close baseball game between the Cincinnati Reds and New York Mets caused a delay, and the golf didn't come on until 4:45. That was when a good piece of golf history began to be made.

Snead hit one fine shot after another, his swing as long and rhythmic as ever. He made six birdies with some excellent approach shots, and he holed a number of putts using the side-saddle stance he had adopted a few years back. He stood to the left of his ball, parallel to it, facing himself directly at the target. Snead had adopted the stance in an effort to beat the "yips," a peculiar malady of the nerves that sometimes strikes older golfers' putting; it takes the form of a spasmodic twitch of the hands during the stroke, or the body rises up or jerks to one side, or all three. The ball then skirts to one side or the other of the hole, comes up short, or goes too far past. In his first version Snead straddled the ball as he faced the target, then he putted it from between his legs. When the USGA ruled this illegal, he altered it. Demaret needled Snead about the stance, belittling it as not looking professional, but Sam didn't mind at all; it put ten more years on his career. The stance alone caught everyone's attention, especially because Snead was making a lot of shorter putts, which had always been the one weak spot in his magnificent game.

As a way of further twanging the nostalgic heartstrings, the gallery was allowed to go onto the fairway and right up next to the players. That had been the way until the 1950s, when the ropes went up to keep the crowds to the sides of the fairway. Snead was mobbed. He and his partner, Gardner Dickinson, scored a 62 (10 under par) on Saturday and took the lead into Sunday's final round.

On Sunday Snead had another superb day. He and Dickinson scored a

66, and their 17-under par total of 193 won the fifty-four-hole competition by a stroke over Peter Thomson and Kel Nagle. Over the three days of play, the sixty-six-year-old Snead made fourteen of his team's eighteen birdies; the team bogeyed only one hole.

Snead wasn't the only senior to prove that the oldies still had some gold-value golf in them. In the third round, Julius Boros and Roberto DeVicenzo combined for a round of 61. Thomson and Nagle were obviously excellent, and seventy-six-year-old Sarazen with his seventy-year-old partner Runyan were tied for fourth after the first round of play. It was all quite impressive. The show got excellent reviews and NBC renewed its option.

The next year was even better. It was the keynote speech, so to speak, in the development of big-league senior golf. At the end of the scheduled fifty-four holes, the team of Boros and DeVicenzo was tied with Tommy Bolt and Art Wall, Jr. In the sudden-death play-off Boros and Wall played well, but it was DeVicenzo and Bolt who made the show. They traded fine approach shots, showing the kind of shot-making that defined their era—drawing the ball, putting a bit of a cut on it, knocking it down low— and both made crucial longish putts. There was plenty of hard-nosed competitor in the both of them, but they went at it with a clearly amiable camaraderie.

The play-off turned into a minor classic in the developing history of senior golf. On the fifth and penultimate extra hole, Bolt holed a clutch putt of about eighteen feet, and after the ball fell, he pointed a finger at Roberto as if to say, "Take that, partner." DeVicenzo then holed his slightly shorter putt right on top of Bolt's and returned the gesture. Everyone could see it was in good spirits, two older guys reliving their past in golf, not all that far from where it was when they were young and enjoying it more. It was warmly sentimental, but with just enough fire beneath. The baseball old-timers who did their inning or two at Yankee Stadium lumbered rigidly for fly balls, chugged down the first base line, strained to throw a decent pitch, played old. Not these young old-time golfers.

Boros and DeVicenzo won the play-off against Bolt and Wall, but it didn't make any difference who came away with the trophy. It was very good golf that spoke volumes for the idea of the seniors displaying their game in public again. They all had recognized credentials as superb players—they were champions—and proved they hadn't forgotten their art.

Boros, with his swing-easy style, was still a genius out of the bunkers. Bolt still had his jaw-jutting irascible edge to go with his classic shot-making ability. Sarazen could still whack the ball with force. DeVicenzo still had his simple and powerful swing, and he hadn't lost the Continental charm he exhibited at the 1968 Masters, when he signed an incorrect scorecard and lost a chance for a play-off against Bob Goalby. Snead was simply astonishing. While people were disappointed that Ben Hogan never deigned to play in the *Legends of Golf* tournament—and he was pleaded with regularly to do so—it was probably just as well. He wouldn't have changed his demeanor, and *The Legends of Golf* didn't need his austerity.

The Nielsen rating recorded that approximately six million households were tuned in to the Bolt-DeVicenzo duel. With an average of 1.5 viewers per household, plus an estimated two million watching in locker rooms, bars, et cetera, some eleven million people saw the legends at play. Television was going to do it again for golf.

After the 1979 tournament Raphael had no trouble finding a title sponsor. The Liberty Mutual Insurance Company picked it up as the permanent sponsor. But the consequences of the tournament's success went well beyond Raphael's personal good fortune and the Legends tournament. In late 1979 Gardner Dickinson and Dan Sikes, a one-time tour pro who had a degree in law, decided there was potential for a lot more than one golden oldies show a year. They got together with Julius Boros, Bob Goalby, Don January, and Sam Snead to discuss the formation of a tournament circuit for senior pros. They founded the Professional Golfers Association of Seniors.

The PGA of Seniors's first move was to ask commissioner Deane Beman to take the circuit under the wing of the PGA Tour. However, according to Leonard DeCof, a Rhode Island lawyer who represented Dickinson, Sikes, and others, and would end up battling the commissioner in court in the square-grooves debacle, initially Beman was not interested. He felt there was no demand for such a circuit, it couldn't get on television, and it would take attention and gallery from his PGA Tour. This last item was surely the one uppermost in Beman's decision. Dickinson and Sikes, two crusty and smart old pros, decided to do the tour on their own. They contacted sports television producer Don Ohlmeyer, who expressed interest in putting the events on the air. With that Beman changed his tune and added the senior circuit to his charge; it became the Senior PGA Tour.

The first Senior PGA Tour event was held in June of 1980. It was called the Atlantic City International and was played at the Atlantic City Country Club, where more than a little golf history had already been written. The term "birdie," meaning one under par, was coined at the Atlantic City CC, and this was the club where Johnny MacDermott had been head pro before the grievous misfortunes that ended his career. The total purse in the Atlantic City International was $250,000. Don January won and claimed the $35,000 first prize. There was only one other tournament on that first year's schedule, held in November in Melbourne, Florida—the Suntree Classic, which was won by Charlie Sifford. However, in case any doubt lingered concerning the viability of a senior circuit, late in 1980 in the long-running PGA Senior Championship (a PGA of America event begun in 1937), Arnold Palmer won. It was his first event as a senior (he was born in September, 1929), and it naturally reaped considerable notice. Palmer became a regular on the senior circuit and its biggest draw.

Even the USGA didn't wait long to pick up on this new idea. It had been staging the U.S. Senior Amateur Championships for men and women since 1960 and 1962, respectively, but now saw the need for an open version for men. The inaugural U.S. Senior Open, which took place in June, 1980, was won by Roberto DeVicenzo on the famed Winged Foot Country Club's East Course, in Mamaroneck, New York, where four U.S. Opens had been held. While the seniors didn't play The Foot from the tips, and there was not the usual U.S. Open heavy rough and narrow fairways, it was still a rugged test. That DeVicenzo went seventy-two holes in only one over par was yet another indication of how much game was still left in the over-fifty gang.

In 1981 the Senior PGA Tour had a five-event schedule, plus the *Legends* tournament, which rather ironically, given its contribution to the senior tour, was deemed an unofficial event. That was (and is) mainly because the PGA Tour does not control it. In 1982 there were eleven tournaments on the circuit and a total purse of $1.3 million. It was a stunning spurt that became a cataract. In 1983 the total for the year went to $3.3 million; in 1999 it was up to $49 million. No sporting enterprise has ever seen such huge growth in so short a time.

How to account for it? The nostalgia trip was one thing, Arnold Palmer another. He increased the live gate manyfold on the senior circuit and kept the television people happy. Apparently Arnold's contribution wasn't entirely an altruistic donation of his time and fame. He allegedly commanded a $25,000 appearance fee for every senior tour event he entered. If so, it was worth it. This writer recalls playing at Onion Creek on a Tuesday during an early *Legends* tournament week. It was late afternoon and very quiet on the course. Suddenly people began appearing from all directions, coming out of the woods, backyards, and seemingly up from the ground—all headed in one direction. What was happening? Word had gotten out that Arnie had just arrived and was going to play a practice round. It was an amazing, eerie encounter with the power of Palmer's appeal.

In the 1990s so many more players wanted in on the PGA Senior Tour that some lesser senior players complained the fields were too small. The response from headquarters was that bigger fields would require a cut after thirty-six holes, which would probably eliminate Palmer from the weekend; his game had deteriorated badly as he closed in on his seventieth birthday. That was not a good option. Palmer's pull was still quite tangible.

There was something else, a bit more subtle perhaps, that made the senior pro tour so engaging in its formative years. Compared to the bronzed, tight-skinned faces and taut-muscled bodies of the junior pros, you could see that the seniors had been around the horn a few times. A life spent in the sun has left their faces and napes and arms and hands brown and onion-skinned, spotted, veiny, dotted with wens and warts. You knew, too, that not all the crowfeet were sun made. They were evidence of marriages good and not-so-good, and extra-maritals and children and deaths in the family and business failures and too many drinks and cigarettes and food and serious illness and threats of serious illness. Of joys and disappointments, parents and close relatives passed, and friends who died too early. Of putts missed, swing rhythms lost. The thickened faces and bodies limned lives fully lived. Somehow, despite a popular culture that detests growing old and spends billions on cosmetics and cosmetic surgery, this visual testimony of experience appealed to the players' contemporaries outside the ropes. Maybe it did even more so because the pros were still athletes, able to hit the ball with good power, play fine shots from bunkers, hit hundreds of balls on the range, and shoot in the 60s. Like the old-time Hollywood-handsome movie stars—Robert Taylor,

Clark Gable—who were more interesting looking in the character parts of their last pictures, so it was with the senior golf pros.

When the senior tour first got off the ground and was clearly destined for success, it came to be referred to as "golf's greatest mulligan ever." A mulligan, of course, is the second chance one gets to hit a good drive off the first tee. Indeed. Bob Murphy was a middle-range PGA Tour player from 1968 through 1986, winning five tournaments, none of them majors, and $1.6 million. But from 1993 through 1998 on the senior circuit, while suffering the effects of a severe variety of arthritis, Murphy won eleven tournaments and just over $5 million. Lee Trevino had a permanent steel plate installed in his back to counter a bulging disk, the result of all those years of beating golf balls on the range, and soldiered on to win over $12 million. Jim Colbert fought off cancer to lead the tour in money winning two straight years. Arnold Palmer and Jim Ferree fought off prostate cancer. Jack Nicklaus has an artificial hip.

But never mind. Americans are a motley crew. They can appreciate old age, and they can also ignore the passage of time and shoot for eternal youth. The senior tour hits both ends of the spectrum. The pros take their daily dose of Advil, which is known amongst them as "tour candy," and carry on making a new life and a very good living as golf's senior citizens. What a country!

Women Feel the Pinch

The success of the Senior PGA Tour caused pain for the LPGA. Once the men seniors got going, the women's circuit found it more difficult than ever to acquire new sponsors. It also began losing some sponsors, who jumped to the seniors. On the surface it was hard to define the problems the LPGA was having, even without the intervention of the new circuit. The women were playing excellent golf and the quality was improving with the arrival of more young players from the college ranks, and from Europe and Asia. Amy Alcott, a Californian who won the U.S. Women's Open in 1980 at age twenty-four, had a fine swing and was an expressive and entertaining interview. Tall, reed-thin Beth Daniel was an excellent new player with a classic swing. Sexy Jan Stephenson and the more wholesomely attractive Nancy Lopez were continuing to give the women's tour a feminine character, along with superb golf. And yet, there seemed to be a certain malaise in the golf community when it came to the LPGA. It failed to become a fully accepted and well-fixed sporting enterprise in the business sense.

Numbers can be interpreted in many ways, but there is no manipulation of straight-out Nielsen ratings. The LPGA just didn't get good ratings; in fact, the numbers were discouragingly low. The major networks didn't much care about televising an LPGA event and only broadcast the U.S. Women's Open so it could get the U.S. Men's Open. (Take the women or no men was the deal, and the same stipulation held for the U.S. Men's Amateur telecast.) In some instances the LPGA had to pay a network such as ESPN or, in the nineties, the Golf Channel to get a tournament telecast.

Perhaps because it seemed the LPGA had a new commissioner every other year, the public didn't have confidence in the organization. In 1982 Ray Volpe left the commissioner's post. He had done a very good job of marketing the women, but apparently had gathered some resentment for being too macho. Also, Volpe was not a "golf guy"; he didn't have much background in the game. John Laupheimer, who had been part of the golf establishment for many years, replaced Volpe and brought in a softer, understated style. Also, he had been part of the golf establishment for many years. He was at one time an executive on the USGA's salaried administrative staff. Laupheimer stayed on for a few years with the LPGA and did a commendable job. But it turned out he was too reserved—there was no hustle in him. Which is why he was replaced by Bill Blue, a zippy young man with a big smile and sharp suits. But Blue had poor-to-no knowledge of golf and not much in the way of marketing skills either. It wasn't quite clear why he got the job. He was gone within a year.

The impression left behind by all this change of leadership evoked a hackneyed image of women—that they were flighty and could never make up their minds. In other words, gender stereotyping. And the old bugaboo, sexual orientation, was still an issue. Betty Hicks, an astute woman who was one of the influential pioneers of women's golf in America, addressed catch-22 bluntly when she was quoted in Liz Kahn's history of the LPGA: "If there aren't any men around you, you're a lesbian, and if there are too many, you're a whore."

The women pros do indeed face a double-edged sword. If a woman comes along who can really hit the ball powerfully and for distance, jokes are made about her true gender being male. But the woman who is not long off the tee, no matter how well she scores, is considered a "typical" woman—a powder puff—and a dull show.

The women pros as a whole didn't help their public relations situation, however. The majority of journalists covering golf are men, and because they are not allowed into the locker room, they have a hard time reaching the women players for interviews and getting to know them casually, the way they can get to know the men. Most of the women were disinclined to go out of their way to help the media people, making themselves available only in formal press conferences. At night they disappeared altogether, which kept akindle the "in the closet" innuendos and the rumors of "sexual deviance" among the LPGA players.

For all that, the power of golf as a way to reach a specific audience kept the LPGA alive. Enough sponsors were found who wanted to reach a specific audience, and where in 1980 the women pros played for $5 million, in 1989 there was a $14 million kitty.

The Ryder Revival

By the mid-1970s the Ryder Cup was on the verge of being discontinued. It was simply not competitive. The United States had dominated the event from the onset up through the early 1970s—the U.S. won eighteen, tied one, and lost three in the first twenty-two matches. But in an increasingly crowded sports-entertainment market, less and less attention was being paid it, including that of the American pros. To help expand its player base, in 1973 native-born Irish pros were allowed onto what became the Great Britain/Ireland Ryder Cup team. It didn't help. The U.S. won the next three times out. Then, at the suggestion of Jack Nicklaus, another expansion of the British player pool was effected. Golfers native to all countries on the European continent could now compete for what became the European team. This change made a big difference.

Coincident to this expansion of eligibility, there happened to be an influx of outstanding continental players into the game. These included Seve Ballesteros, Bernhard Langer, Jose Maria Canizares, and eventually Jose Maria Olazabal. Furthermore, the British themselves had produced three world-class players—Nick Faldo, Sandy Lyle, and Ian Woosnam.

In the first United States versus Europe Ryder Cup Match, in 1979, the effect of the new eligibility rule was not immediately apparent. The U.S. team, which included its first-ever black Ryder Cupper, Lee Elder, won 17 to 11. The U.S. won again in 1981, in England, but there was a sense that the Europeans were not going to be patsies much longer. Spain's Ballesteros had made a big impression on world golf in 1979 when he won a PGA Tour event—the Greater Greensboro Open—and his first Masters and British Open titles. An intense, arousing personality, as well as a brilliant golfer, Ballesteros was never shy about expressing a fervent desire to defeat the Americans in the Ryder Cup. He was the rallying force among the players, and his energy began to be felt.

In 1983 the transformation of the competition began in earnest. Significantly, Tony Jacklin, the fellow who gave Britain a jumpstart back to prominence in world golf, was now the captain of the European team. The European captain was then fairly permanent, whereas the American system had evolved into a new captain every time out. This continuity in leadership may have had something to do with the success the European team would begin to have. Jacklin brought a lively and brightminded personality, and a high level of enthusiasm, to the European side.

Past British Ryder Cup captains were traditionally staid Englishmen who, by American standards, carried themselves as losers. Jacklin was quite the opposite in all respects. He had impressive playing credentials as winner of a British and a U.S. open. To heighten or instill an upbeat attitude among his players, Jacklin did some small things that can have a large impact on attitude. He ordered a fine line of smart clothing for his players to wear in the competition, and he had them transported around in a more stylish (read, expensive) way. Jacklin's verve and Ballesteros's fanaticism became a stalwart combination.

In the 1983 Ryder Cup Match in West Palm Beach, Florida, the U.S. team just squeaked by with a one-point victory. It came down to a couple of brilliant clutch shots at the end, one for each side. On the final hole of his Singles match, Ballesteros hit a brilliant three-wood shot from a fairway bunker—a difficult play rarely seen. The 240-yard shot reached the front fringe of the green. With a chip and a putt Ballesteros earned a desperately needed half point that kept the Match alive. But Lanny Wadkins, also a fierce competitor and especially in one-on-one play, performed his own heroics to save the American side. One down with one hole to go against Jose Maria Canizares, Wadkins hit a sixty-yard wedge third shot to within a foot of the hole for a birdie, which halved his match and clinched the American victory. There had been more than a few of such gallant individual matches in the history of Ryder Cup golf, but somehow these two had a sharper accent because the Europeans were now very clearly putting up a *total* battle.

The next time out, 1985, it was total victory for the Europeans, who won at home by a score of 16 ½ to 11 ½. But in 1989 the American loss was especially embarrassing. The 1987 Ryder Cup was played at the Muirfield Village Golf Course, the course Jack Nicklaus built in his own hometown (actually in Dublin, a suburb of Columbus, Ohio), and Nicklaus himself was captain of the American side. In the face of all this, the Europeans defeated the Americans by two points. As Jimmy Durante, the old vaudeville and cabaret performer would have put it, "What a revoltin' development."

It would get even more revolting for the Americans. Despite the loss in Ohio, U.S. captain Raymond Floyd, who was never above an arrogant demeanor when it came to his own game, introduced his 1989 team at a pre-match dinner as "the twelve greatest players in the world." He was echoing a line delivered by Ben Hogan when he captained the 1967 U.S. team. At the time Hogan was right. Presumably, Floyd was trying to instill confidence in his charges. But of course, it only charged the opponent's batteries even more. After two days of play, Floyd's twelve greatest were two points down.

The highlight of the European's play was the partnership of Ballesteros and Olazabal, who with the brio of bullfighters beat Tom Watson and Mark O'Meara in the Four-Ball, then defeated Curtis Strange and Tom Kite in the Foursomes. In the Singles that always conclude the Match, Christy O'Connor, Jr., a solid player but with only a middling record, surprised everyone by defeating the glamorous Fred Couples, one-up. It was a clutch match coming at the end of the day, and O'Connor did his deed with a splendid approach into the wind on the tough par-four eighteenth at the Belfry, in Sutton Coldfield, England. The Europeans kept the cup, and actually brought Couples to tears.

No one expected such an outburst of emotion from Couples, a fellow noted for a cool demeanor that was sometimes taken for indifference. That last was clearly a misperception, at least when it came to Ryder Cup play. Couples's sobs revealed just how weighty the Ryder Cup competition was becoming for the Americans now that their hegemony was slipping away. It slipped a good deal farther the next time out, to a point that provoked traumatic hysteria, as we will see in the next chapter.

How Green Is My Golf Course . . . and How Hard It Is To Play

Sometime in the 1970s the powers-that-be operating the Old Course at St. Andrews, Scotland, installed an underground irrigation system. That is like Ella Fitzgerald scat singing the Koran or an Orthodox rabbi ordering ham hocks and a glass of milk on the first day of Passover.

For hundreds of years sheep grazed St. Andrews's turf and kept it short for the *gowf*. The furze and whins and gorse grew where the sheep grazed less, and all went untouched by human hands, let alone mechanical devices. When the rains came, the good earth accepted it and gave back lovely green turf. When it was warm for a spell and dry, the good earth became firm, even hard, and tan. So be it. The hallowed ground of the Old Course was tended to by nature—God, if you will—and the Scots let the chips falls where they may.

In time the Scots adopted more modern ways of tending their golfing grounds—fairways and greens were mowed by machine mower—but otherwise the conditions were left to a higher will. No one can recall those sprinklers at St. Andrews ever being turned on, and it has been noted they are rusting in the ground, but that they were put in at all was a final concession by the Scots that their game had been usurped by the Americans.

American golfers were the biggest source of golf tourist income to Scotland; everyone came over to pay reverence to the birthplace of the ancient game. Aye, but the Yanks insisted on playing on green grass, no matter what. The American requirement of lush green golf courses began in the late 1950s and early 1960s, and is considered a legacy of the Masters tournament once it was televised in color. Every April golfworld saw Augusta National's spotlessly clean and deep green from end to end. Being so cherished in golf's collective heart, Augusta National's conditions became the standard everyone else sought to attain.

Golf will always have a rich man's connotation, and rich men want everything around them to reflect their well-being. Lush green grass does that, brown does not. That the color of American money is green may only be incidental, but worth a mention. Such is the infatuation with green-grass golf that when the producer of *Shell's Wonderful World of Golf* arrived at a course in the Caribbean and found it as brown as a deer's coat, he had the place painted before the match was filmed. A crop duster sprayed the entire course, and in a matter of hours redid the dun-colored acreage into a landscape verdant as the Garden of Eden. And let it be known that, although the masters of Augusta National have never to anyone's knowledge painted their golf course in this way, they have for many years dyed the ponds so that they are a rich shade of aqua.

All of which is but another expression of conspicuous consumption, which Americans didn't invent but in the twentieth century ripened to a fare-thee-well. It is also part of the image machine, at which America has become so proficient an operator. However, the green compulsion has taken an intrinsic element out of golf. A golf course's natural cycles of condition are not allowed to prevail. If left to nature, in wet periods courses get soft and green. In dry periods they become firm, sometimes hard, and tan. Each condition requires a different type of golf. Soft turf wants high shots for carry, because the ground will give up little roll. Firm turf wants low shots, because high shots are less apt to stay near to where they land. One gets more roll on firm ground, but the bounce and roll must be accounted for when playing shots. The differences make for an interesting diversity. The same course is not quite the same from day to day, week to week, from one solstice to another. The golfer is challenged to adapt to nature.

But brown doesn't sell. It doesn't sell resort golf or residential communities with a golf course as the backyard. Marketing mavens and real estate agents dictate how most golf in the United States is played today. If the backyard is brown, you can't show or sell the house. So it's kept green all year long, no matter the cost of the chemicals or the environmental dangers. Playability of the course is not even understood, let alone considered. If the course superintendent doesn't keep the course green, he must look for another job.

The all-green-all-the-time golf course began to evolve in earnest with the coming of television and high-quality color photography. The actual design of courses was influenced by the same forces. Golf architects following the lead of Robert Trent Jones began including at least one signature hole in their layouts. But then their clients, especially those building resort courses, wanted more; they wanted signature golf courses. This usually translated into more difficult courses to play—"monsters." The Doral Hotel in Miami, Florida, was built in the 1960s and called its premier course the Blue Monster. It got its first national exposure as a site for a match on *Shell's Wonderful World of Golf*, then became the home of a long-running PGA Tour event. The Concord Hotel, in the Catskill Mountains of New York State, built its own "Monster," which is more monstrous than Doral's.

Monsters proliferated everywhere, if not always in name certainly in layout. It became the mantra of every resort and real estate developer to have "the toughest golf course in the world." It was a way of getting a major tournament played on it, hopefully, and thereby obtaining highly valuable exposure. If such a tournament doesn't come their way, and few do, a course with spectacular stretches of water and white sand looks terrific in brochures and magazine articles. It makes for striking photography, and it also plays on the intrinsic difficulty of the game. As previously noted, golfers have more than a little of the masochist in their makeup.

The architects had no choice but to comply with their clients' wishes. It was their living. The result has been hundreds and hundreds of courses all over the world (for American golf led the way in this area, too) that are playable only by the best players in the game. The best of the best rarely if ever play them, however. Which leaves them to average golfers, who pay hefty green fees for the privilege of getting beat up physically and psychologically. Not every hole on these monsters is beyond the capacity of the average golfer, but at least four or five require such a high degree of accuracy and length, and punish poor shots so terribly, that the average golfer often can't finish them. Unable to play a complete round, he misses the point of the game—shoot the lowest score possible.

By the end of the twentieth century enough complaints were coming in from golfers themselves to convince golf course developers and architects to back off from such difficult layouts. In some instances, new private clubs were formed on the strength of a signature golf course (by Nicklaus, Dye, Jones, Fazio, and others) that turned out to be so hard to play, a less severe one was built beside it to keep the members on board and paying dues. A balancing act has been in effect whereby courses are at the same time photogenic without being unplayable for the average golfer. Sometimes even, the photogenic part is yielded for the sake of just good golf. Green, however, is still de rigeur.

Jack's Last Hurrah

In the 1980s Jack Nicklaus was concentrating more and more on his golf architecture business. He was becoming very busy with it and getting paid quite handsomely—a $1 million basic fee per course, an unheard of figure until then. Pete Dye and the other architects didn't resent Jack's price tag, because, as Dye put it, "Jack upped the ante for all of us. We all could ask for more money."

Nicklaus put down forty new courses in the eighties and did approximately twelve renovations. This reduced his playing schedule even more than usual. And yet, he won three more major championships—the 1980 U.S. Open and PGA Championship and the 1986 Masters. In the Open he set a new seventy-two-hole scoring record of 272, eight under par, which included a first-round 63 on the grueling Lower Course of the Baltusrol Golf Club in New Jersey. He won the PGA on another storied championship layout, Oak Hill, in Rochester, New York, by a record seven strokes (over Andy Bean). He also won on the tour: the 1982 Colonial National Invitational and the 1984 Memorial, his own tournament.

But it was in 1986 that Nicklaus captivated everyone. At the age of forty-six he put together one of his rare come-from-behind charges to win his sixth Masters. Sixth! Starting the final round four strokes behind the leader, Greg Norman, Nicklaus turned in one-under 35, then came back with a mind-numbing 30 that included an eagle and two birdies on the fifteenth through seventeenth holes. The birdie two on the sixteenth came on a twisting forty-five-foot putt across the roller-coaster green. When it went in, Nicklaus and his caddie gave gestures of joy that will forever be recorded in the photo annals of the game—Nicklaus bent low, putter stretched out in front of him, a sly smile on his face; his caddie leaping in the air with his arms raised straight up and high. It was sensational theater and another instance of Nicklaus's extraordinary talent.

It would also be his last victory at that level. He would win two U.S. Senior Opens and the PGA Seniors Championships, majors in the senior category, but his 1986 Masters victory closed out his main playing career, and in the way a great champion should finish. What a career he had: eighteen professional major titles (four U.S. Opens, two British Opens, five PGA Championships, and the six Masters). What's more, he finished second seventeen times in the four majors. He set the standard for everyone to shoot after in the next millennium.

Although he played often and won many tournaments outside the United States, South Africa's Gary Player was the first foreign-born golfer to establish his credentials as a world-class champion through his achievements on the American professional tournament circuit. Player is one of only four golfers—the others being Americans Gene Sarazen, Ben Hogan, and Jack Nicklaus—to win all four of golf's major titles.

After an unremarkable amateur and college golf career, Tom Watson of Kansas City, Missouri, found his game in the pros, and he proved especially adept at Scottish links golf. He won *five* British Opens--an ultimate expression of American dominance in world golf that took a firm hold beginning in 1960.

Although he won quite a lot of tournaments around the world, Greg Norman did not produce a winning record in major championships anywhere near the superstar standing he was afforded. What he mastered above all was the art of modern-day, American-style marketing of athletic celebrity, by which he became a wealthy businessman/golfer.

The outstanding competitive record of Nancy Lopez, combined with her authentically warm and magnetic smile which was a tonic, lifted the image of women's professional golf to new heights.

From 1956 through 1966, Mickey Wright was the world's nonpareil woman golfer. She won 80 tournaments in that time frame, including four U.S. Women's Opens. Her golf swing was a paradigm of perfection and her demeanor was a reflection of the understated style of the 1950s and '60s in sports.

This is a Billy Casper the golf public rarely, if ever, saw. Had the fans and media seen more of this high-spirited Casper, his outstanding competitive record might be that much more acknowledged.

Lee Trevino personified the American Story—a dirt-poor minority-group kid who rose as high as one can go in sports on the strength of nerve, will, hard work, and talent.

A self-possessed Ben Hogan (*top*) cast a mesmerizing but austere light on American golf, which made the arrival of the exuberant Arnold Palmer (*bottom*) a breath of fresh and festive air. The transition from the Hogan to the Palmer Era was not only a changing of the competitive guard, but of temperament as well.

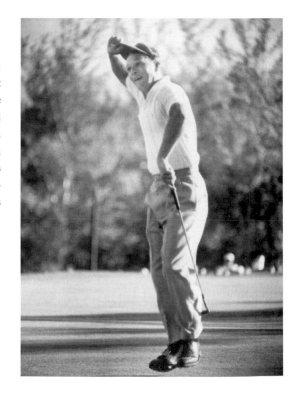

When Sam Snead arrived on the national golf scene, he played out the role of a barefoot country boy (*top*) and got the looked-for attention. But in the end it was his marvelously fluid swing (*bottom*) and sheer talent for the game that made him a star for the ages.

Byron Nelson set a standard of excellence that may never be surpassed—11 straight victories, and 18 total in 1945. So stunning was the accuracy of his shotmaking that when a testing machine was designed to simulate a golf swing it was called the Iron Byron.

Cary Middlecoff (*center*), after winning the 1949 U.S. Open, poses with O'Neal "Buck" White (*left*) and Clayton Heafner (*right*) who were close contenders. Middlecoff was one of American golf's most brilliant players ever (winner of two U.S. Opens, a Masters, and 39 tournaments in all), but was obscured by the large shadow cast by Ben Hogan and Sam Snead.

Jackie Burke, Jr. put together one of the longest winning streaks after Byron Nelson's with four in a row in 1952. He won a PGA Championship and a Masters in his fine career, then founded one of the best golf clubs in America (Champions, in Houston), and in his later years became the golf sage of sages.

Johnny Miller flashed across the golfing firmament with a relatively short but rather spectacular career. He won a U.S. and British Open, the latter with a phenomenal final-round 63, and deeply influenced the way golfers would begin to swing the club.

Bill Spiller, who had a college degree in education, was the first African-American to directly confront the exclusion of his race from mainstream American golf. He threatened to bring lawsuits, faced down the highest officer of the PGA of America, and made an effective appeal to the California Attorney General. While he did not personally gain from his efforts, they paved the way for others—including Tiger Woods—to participate fully in the American Dream, Golf Department. *Photo courtesy of Bill Spiller, Jr.*

Jack Nicklaus was not usually this animated in success, but this picture is an explicit evocation of his mastery of the game and the competition—he was smarter, more controlled, and more determined to win than any golfer of his time, and he had all the talent necessary, and then some.

Tiger Woods is the preeminent manifestation of the American domination of world golf–ethnically, in his consummate articulation of the rainbow coalition, athletically, in his height, strength, intelligence, and innate talent–as complete a delineation of the genre as has ever come into the sport.

Norman's Invasion

In each era throughout most of its history, the PGA Tour had two or three players who gave the circuit marquee value. There was Hagen and Sarazen; Nelson, Hogan and Snead; Palmer, Nicklaus, and Player; Nicklaus and Trevino and Watson. In all these cases the overriding index of their place as icons was competitive achievement. All were big winners of the biggest championships and more than once. They each also had a certain bearing that signified someone special, but it was their records as players that were foremost. By the 1980s there was a gap developing in this pattern of evolving superstars, and the equation by which they were anointed.

Palmer was well past his winning days; Nicklaus had an excellent first half of the eighties, with victories in the U.S. Open and PGA, then the 1986 Masters, but he was not playing as much and seeming to be winding down. Trevino was closing in on the senior circuit. Tom Watson was at the top of his game early in the decade, but for all his great ability, dedication, work ethic, and all that good stuff, he was not someone who projected the kind of personality that adds up to charisma. Perhaps because he didn't want to.

Thus, the search was on for a new superstar. Some thought the PGA Tour didn't need one anymore, because the depth of talent out there was so great fans could just take their pick. This assumed that the average golf fan was a purist who appreciated great shot-making for its own sake, no matter what sort of personality the golfer projected. Those kind are always in the minority. Most sports fans like a little extra glitter with their stars. Besides, there were so many professional sports vying for attention in the United States—each offering high-powered, quick-moving action and many attractive athletes—that golf could get lost in the wilds of the hand-held remote. The week-to-week tour events were becoming difficult to separate one from another. All of the courses were Augusta green. The players, most of them young and blond and well grounded in the fundamentals of classic technique, seemed all to be wearing the same clothes and making the same type of swing.

The media was getting antsy, too. There was heavy competition between newspapers and magazines and television—as intense as on the playing fields they were covering. Every journalist and television director was looking for an athlete that had what salesmen call "sizzle." When all the steaks are sirloin, the one that has the best sauce, or sizzle, is going to get sold before the others. There were quite a few outstanding golfers playing the PGA Tour, but most languished on the media's equivalent of the cutting-room floor because they didn't have the accoutrements of celebrity—that certain something that went beyond talent. The next marquee player had to be a very good player, but marketing techniques had taken over popular culture and were cleverly, insidiously deconstructing the value system that stood on real achievement. You didn't have to be *that* good. What the superstar definitely needed was a certain look, style, something—sizzle—that could be quickly perceived. Quickly was the operative word. The story had to be told quickly or the audience would start surfing.

The answer in golf during the eighties was Australia's Greg Norman, who came to play full time on the American pro tour in 1983. Norman had all the famous-person material, sports department. Sun-blond hair, worn fashionably long; handsomeness (although not necessarily in profile), with a bright-toothed smile and an athletic physique—broad shoulders, trim waist. He came with a catchy nickname, too—the Shark—derived from his youthful days swimming off the Great Barrier Reef. It was sometimes stretched to the Great White Shark when his game was going well. When not, the Australian golf press, especially Rupert Murdoch's "tabs," would reduce their countryman to the Minnow and the Great White Sheep. The American press was much easier on him, and in fact welcomed Norman with relish. He hit the ball hard and far and shot some really low scores every now and then. He had looks and the shark thing and he drove very expensive cars very fast and flew fast airplanes and jumped out of them. Good copy and easy to write.

Norman began his pro career in 1976 in Australia, and from that year through 1983 he won twenty-three tournaments, half on the European tour and half in Australia, Fiji, and Japan. It was an impressive record, but made in the equivalent of the high minor leagues. On the United States PGA Tour his first wins came in 1984 at the Kemper Open and Canadian Open. He didn't win again in the U.S. until 1986, when he took the Panasonic–Las Vegas Invitational by a stunning seventeen strokes, and his second Kemper Open. He also won his first major in 1986, the British Open, but he had shown ominous signs of being unable to deal with maximum pressure in major championships.

In the 1984 U.S. Open, at Winged Foot, Norman needed a par four on the seventy-second hole to maintain a tie with Fuzzy Zoeller, who was playing a group behind him. Norman had a six-iron approach to the green from a good lie in the fairway. Golf teachers will tell you that because of the length of the club, the six-iron is the one club all golfers, even the worst chops, tend to play best. Norman's six-iron at Winged Foot's eighteenth was a power shank. The ball shot off the hosel of his club and flew some forty yards to the right of the green, up against the grandstand. After getting a free drop, he pitched onto the far left side of the green about forty-five feet from the hole. It was a very difficult putt that twisted in a couple of directions, but Norman knocked it in. Astounding, especially after so poor a second shot. What sort of fellow do we have here? The easygoing Zoeller, watching Norman hole the putt from back in the fairway, waved a white towel as if in surrender—a nice gesture. Zoeller then made his four, routinely.

In the play-off the next day, both players birdied the first hole, Norman holing a putt on top of Zoeller's. But on the second hole, Zoeller rolled in a sixty-eight-foot putt for a birdie. Norman then tried to force an eighteen-footer for par, ended up three-putting for a double-bogey, and was never in it after that. Zoeller defeated Norman, 67 to 75.

It was in 1986 that Norman's closure problem was ultimately exposed. He led all four majors going into the final round and won one, which was a walkover. In the Masters, which would become the most incredible of his flopsites, Norman needed a par four on the last hole to tie Jack Nicklaus, who had already finished with his wondrous 65. From a slightly uphill lie in the middle of the fairway, a lie that normally brings a hooked shot, Norman pushed his four-iron some thirty yards to the right of the green. Shades of Winged Foot in 1984. He bogeyed and finished tied for second.

In the 1986 U.S. Open at Shinnecock Hills, Norman led by a shot after fifty-four holes on rounds of 71-68-71. He opened the final round with a birdie putt on the first hole that he left three-feet short, and when he missed a four-footer for par on the sixth hole he "went flat," as he later put it. When he bogeyed four holes between the ninth and thirteenth, he was done. He shot 75, and tied for twelfth. In the middle of the third round at Shinnecock there also was an unusual incident when Norman came to the ropes to challenge a drunken young man in the gallery who was calling him a "choke artist." In the middle of a round in the U.S.

Open when he was in or near the lead, he challenged a spectator to a John Wayne–style dustup. Very peculiar. And yet, he went on to shoot his best round of the tournament. We leave that to the psychologists.

To win the 1986 British Open, Norman began the final round at Turnberry with a two-shot lead over Tommy Nakajima, a run-of-the-mill tournament player. Nicklaus, Ballesteros, Langer, Zoeller, Watson, Floyd, and a few other more legitimate contenders had shot themselves out of it by this time. On the very first hole Nakajima nervously left his second shot from a greenside bunker in the sand, then three-putted for a double-bogey. He was done for the day, and with no one else giving him chase, Norman coasted home to win by five shots over Gordon Brand.

In the 1986 PGA Championship at the Inverness Club, in Toledo, Ohio, Norman led Bob Tway by four shots after three rounds. He maintained that margin after ten holes of the final round, but by the fourteenth hole Norman had hit some wayward shots and was now in a tie with Tway. That's how they stood on the eighteenth tee, from which Tway drove into heavy rough. Norman drove well. Tway hit a nine-iron approach into the right greenside bunker. Norman's wedge second shot from the fairway hit the front of the green and spun back into thickish fringe. Tway then holed out a twenty-five-foot shot from the bunker for a birdie! Needing to hole his chip, Norman hit it too hard and it was over.

Although no one had ever before holed out from a bunker on the last hole to win a major championship, which suggests something of a fluke, Tway did shoot a fine 34 on the back nine to Norman's 40. (Let's give him a 38; after his chip on the seventy-second he understandably didn't pay much attention to the putting and took three swipes for a double-bogey.) But it was Norman who got most of the press, which was almost unanimously sympathetic. Like Arnie when Casper beat him at Olympic in 1966. Tway didn't really win with his hole-out; Norman just lost to a lucky punch. But all he had to do was shoot even par on the back nine, or even one-over, a reasonable expectation for someone of his reputation, and Tway's bunker shot would have meant nothing. In fact, it probably wouldn't have happened. Norman let Tway in the game, and Tway took advantage. Furthermore, Tway shot a 64 the day before, when challengers usually play themselves into position to win. It was the low round of the tournament, by one over Norman's first-round 65. Under final-round pressure Tway hung in very well and won with fine play for the *entire* tournament.

To be fair, in the 1987 Masters Norman did seem to be snake-bit. He led by a stroke going into the final round and returned a par 72 that consisted of six birdies and six bogeys. An okay round on greens that were exceptionally difficult—harder and faster than usual. The low score for seventy-two holes was three-over par—one of the highest ever.

There was a three-way tie, with Seve Ballesteros, Larry Mize, and Norman going extra holes on Sunday late afternoon. Ballesteros three-putted the first extra hole for a bogey, Norman and Mize parred, and it was now just the two of them. At the eleventh both drove well, then Mize pushed his five-iron second shot far right of the green. Norman wisely played his approach to the right side and finished just in the fringe, about fifty feet from the hole.

Then, lightning struck. Mize played a sandwedge pitch-and-run from thirty-five yards. The ball landed just short of the green and ran dead into the hole for a birdie. Norman was stunned, as well he might be. His try for a tie failed and he walked away disconsolate. He said it was the worst feeling he'd ever had on a golf course. It was a sucker punch, more or less. But subsequently, Norman would demonstrate an incredible aptitude—aptitude?—for self-destruction.

Rises and Falls

In the meantime, there were a number of players making their way through the 1980s and writing some interesting golf history. They got a bit lost in the Norman wake, which is the way of the world. People wanted that sizzle. Tom Watson won his third, fourth, and fifth British Opens (1980, 1982, 1983), his second Masters (1981), and his one U.S. Open, in 1982. This last came at Pebble Beach, and was especially emphatic because of one shot he hit to clinch, and because it was Nicklaus he beat with it.

On one of golf's most visually attractive golf courses (and when the wind blows an excellent examination of the golfing art), Watson and Bill Rogers began the final round of the 1982 Open in the lead, with Nicklaus three strokes off the pace in third place. Nicklaus played a few groups ahead of Watson and Rogers and fired a fine 69. Rogers had shot himself out of contention, as had David Graham, Calvin Peete, Bruce Devlin, and Scott Simpson, and Watson seemed to be faltering as he came to the seventeenth hole. It appeared that the forty-two-year-old Nicklaus might have a chance to take an unprecedented fifth U.S. Open, especially after Watson's tee-shot on the par-three seventeenth ended up pin-high in thick grass just off the left edge of the green. It was a better lie than it appeared from a distance, but there was not a lot of room between his ball, the fringe, and the cup. The green was fast, and it was the U.S. Open at hand. But Watson had always shown a good touch for these shots, and using a sandwedge, he played a perfect short pitch. The ball had a little more pace on it than he might have wanted, but it hit the pin dead on and fell into the hole. A birdie two! Watson did an ecstatic run up to and around the hole with arms upraised, a level of animation unusual for him. It was fun to watch. He went on to par the eighteenth with a solid five to win by two strokes.

The television coverage of that moment at the seventeenth highlighted the growing value of the medium as the technology got better and better. After Watson holed out, Nicklaus was shown in the scorer's tent, behind the eighteenth green watching Watson on television. When Watson's chip fell, Nicklaus clearly blanched. He was stung, as well he might be, and his very human reaction was seen by millions where in the past only a very few would have noticed it.

Watson won two more British Opens after his Pebble Beach dramatics and four tour events through 1989. Then his game fell off sharply. Actually, it was just his putting. He became a better ball striker as the years went on, especially with the driver, with which he was surprisingly long. His average height and physique were misleading. With big hands, thick wrists, and milk-bottle forearms, he hit the ball with considerable power.

Watson was always a bold putter from a distance, and when he didn't make the fifteen- and twenty- and forty-foot putts, the ball usually ran two and three feet past the hole. His career was largely defined by his ability to make most of them coming back. However, the strain of those comeback putts had begun to take its toll, as they always do, and by the end of 1987 Watson went on a long and torturous no-win streak.

Bill Rogers, a lanky Texan with a pleasingly diffident personality, was the decade's best example of a young player allowing himself to be run into the ground by his managers. After winning the 1981 British Open (and a few PGA Tour events), he took too many long trips overseas to play tournaments offering exceptional appearance fees and wore himself out. He played a few more years of spotty golf on tour, then he left for other work in golf.

Calvin Peete produced the best record ever by an African-American golfer, yet seemed to make little of the impact expected for his accomplishments. In the 1980s Peete won eleven tournaments of the total of twelve he would win on the PGA Tour. They included the Tournament Players Championship, the game's unofficial fifth major. He played on two Ryder Cup teams, won a Vardon Trophy for low-stroke average on the year, for ten straight years he was statistically the most accurate driver on the tour, and he won over $2 million. For someone with his background, that was quite an amazing run.

One of the nineteen children of migrant farmworkers in Florida, Peete dropped out of school as a teenager to pick fruit and vegetables, then branched out to make his living selling trinkets and clothing to migrant workers from the back of his station wagon. He didn't learn to play golf until he was twenty-three, and had to deal with a permanently crooked left arm, the result of an improperly treated broken elbow. Like Ed Furgol before him (who also suffered a mistreated broken elbow as a youth and won a U.S. Open), Peete disproved the hoary notion that golfers must keep their left arms straight in the swing.

Peete seemed to emerge from out of nowhere, and in effect he did, given the track upon which most tour pros were traveling now—high-level, well-subsidized junior and college golf. He was thirty-two when he came out, did all that good playing, then more or less disappeared back into the woodwork. He left only a slight impression. It wasn't entirely for lack of trying. As a young peddler-entrepreneur he had two small diamonds placed in his upper front teeth to impress his customers. He removed them when he got on the PGA Tour, wanting to be known for his golf, not some bizarre fashion oddity. But it didn't make much difference. Smallish, thin, with a quiet manner, Peete just didn't light up the world. No sizzle.

Lee Trevino concluded his regular tour career with five victories in the eighties, one major, one semi—the 1980 Tournament Players Championship. The 1984 PGA Championship that Trevino won was one of the best in the event's long history. It was a fitting last-hurrah at this level of the game, not only for forty-four-year-old Trevino, but for forty-eight-year-old Gary Player, as well. In typically steamy Alabama summer weather, the wonderfully conditioned Player shot a 9 under par 63 in the second round. But Trevino was on one of his unbeatable rolls. Always a good closer when on the lead, he finished with 67-69 to win by four shots over Player and Lanny Wadkins. He took his show business shtick to television for a couple of years as a color commentator, then got back to hitting shots, his real métier.

Tom Kite had more victories than anyone else in the 1980s—twelve, one more than Calvin Peete. Kite earned billing as "the best golfer to never win a major." He did win a Players Championship, however, in 1989, and at one point was the biggest money winner in the history of the game. He finally won a major, the 1992 U.S. Open at Pebble Beach, with a brave final round in a very strong, blustery wind.

Kite and Ben Crenshaw grew up at the same time in Austin, Texas, and played golf for the University of Texas. Although Crenshaw was a natural golfer, with an uncomplicated swing action and the touch of a yegg on the putting green, Kite had to do hard labor for what he got out of the game. It looked it. The gift of poetry in motion was not his. It followed that he was an inveterate tinkerer, always looking for some new piece of swing technique or a whole system with which to play. As a result, he would have long dry spells as a competitor. One way or the other, he never could lose the awkward look of his action, and the jut-jawed expression that echoed his persistence added up to a stiff public presence.

Fred Couples didn't win nearly as much as Kite but was far more of a crowd pleaser. When he won his only major, the 1984 Masters, the victory was greeted with much delight by golfworld. A darkishly handsome fellow (his Italian-American grandfather anglicized their surname—Coppola became Couples), with a sweet butter swing and mellow mien, he built up a warm following. However, Couples's swing features a lot of upperbody torque that may have induced the severe arthritis he suffers in his back, which curtails his tournament schedule. He never seems to mind the shorter schedule, though, and he has said at times, in one of the rare moments when he speaks of himself, that he didn't really like playing golf all that much. Neither has he enjoyed, or even liked, the celebrity part of his work. Couples had modified sizzle, modified by his lack of interest in making it to or being at the top rung.

Raymond Floyd strutted through the eighties to win two majors—the 1982 PGA and the riveting 1986 U.S. Open. An oddly built fellow—short arms, heavy through the chest—Floyd made a chicken-wing swing into *poulet au jus*. When hitting a golf ball he looked like an arthritic lumberjack. But he did the same thing time after time, year after year, and combined it with a superb short game and exceptional competitive drive. Over a long twenty-five-year stretch on the tour, Floyd compiled one of the better records. He added to it on the senior circuit.

Curtis Strange made his mark in the eighties by winning sixteen of his seventeen career tournaments. They included back-to-back U.S. Opens (1988 and 1989), which was special. No one had done it since Hogan, in 1950 and 1951. Strange could be a hard case when going well. He took on a very stern demeanor, and at times he was uncontrollably profane when the gallery became obstreperous. One time, during a Western Open in which he was in the lead, he hit a shot that was disturbed by a camera click from the gallery. Strange looked over toward the criminal and called him/her/it with very articulate enunciation "a sonofabitch." It came over loud and clear on television, and it may have led to his after-tour career as a television golf commentator.

Larry Nelson came to the front in the 1980s with a remarkable record, given that he didn't take up golf until he was twenty-three, upon returning from military duty in Vietnam. Obviously a quick study, after turning professional in 1971 and joining the PGA Tour in 1974, Nelson won two tournaments in 1979 and eight in the 1980s that included three majors—two PGA Championships (1981 and 1987) and a U.S. Open (1983). Three majors in a decade, and yet Nelson effectively went unnoticed. At least by the standards of the day. He was much too quiet, modest, understated, plain.

While Greg Norman was the Australian getting all the coverage, another countryman quietly showed everyone how to close the deal in a major championship. David Graham started on the American tour in 1971, won four tournaments in that decade, and four more in the eighties. That's not a lot in numbers, but two were majors. He won the 1979 PGA Championship with a final-round 65 that got him into a play-off with Ben Crenshaw. This was at the monster Oakland Hills Country Club course where Ben Hogan won the 1951 U.S. Open.

It is interesting that in Graham's tour de force, the 1981 U.S. Open, he once again won where Hogan had, at the Merion Golf Club. Graham carved up the old layout with the tee-to-green precision of a jeweler—68, 68, 70, 67—for a total of 273 to win by three over Bill Rogers and George Burns. On a course that had changed very little in thirty-one years, and under very similar dry and warm weather conditions, Graham beat Hogan's (and Fazio's and Mangrum's) 1950 seventy-two-hole score by fourteen strokes. Which begs the question, was Graham that much better a golfer than Hogan and the others? Or had the equipment and knowledge of swing mechanics come so much further in that time period?

One way or another, Graham was, like Hogan, physically small and slender and with a not dissimilar disposition. A testy fellow and almost never demonstrative, Graham came from a dysfunctional family. His father had been adamantly opposed to his son's golf, refused any support of it, and was disowned by his son. In a sense, Graham had a suicidal father just as Hogan did.

After his more than adequate playing career on the junior tour, Graham became an equipment consultant, but has particularly distinguished himself as a golf course architect. He has designed a number of well-reviewed courses, and he has served as a consultant to Augusta National Golf Club on any changes made to the course for the Masters tournament. This is a consultancy that can enhance a career, as we know from the career paths of Robert Trent Jones and Tom Fazio.

Frank Urban Zoeller—"Fuzzy," from the first initial of his given and surnames—provided entertaining golf in this decade, whistling softly while he worked and making an oddly shaped swing that didn't help a chronic back problem, the result of a high school football injury. His leisurely tempo got him through, and when Zoeller was feeling especially well and got on his game he could win big ones. He won the 1979 Masters and the 1984 U.S. Open. A nice fellow to have around, except when he tries to be funny. A couple of his ill-thought-out cracks had racial overtones that made him sound intolerant, which is not at all the case. One in particular was a remark having to do with Tiger Woods serving up a stereotypical African-American dinner at the Masters champions dinner. Zoeller is not a racist, but got burned for the comment because of the way Woods's father, Earl, handled it. Zoeller apologized publicly, but he got no response from the Woods's camp, which was being run by Earl

Woods at the time. It was an unfortunate episode, and one edgy sponsor canceled Zoeller's lucrative endorsement contract as a result.

The Nonexempt Tour, a Security Blanket . . . for Awhile

Fuzzy Zoeller's nonchalance was a bit unusual for a touring pro, and while it reflected his personality, it could be read as emblematic of a change in the structure of the PGA Tour. Some of the insecurity was out of it. In the earliest days of the tour there was no qualifying round to get into a tournament. You showed up at the first tee, paid your entry fee, and went out and played. You could also turn pro that casually, as Byron Nelson did. Hand over your entry fee and declare you are playing for the money. Poof, you're a pro.

After World War II, though, when more players got back into the game after military service, a qualifying round was required. It was usually on the Monday of the tournament week and on the course where the event was being played. It was still fairly casual, with a lot of places available. But by the end of the 1950s the Monday qualifying round was becoming reflective of the tour's growth, both in number of players and quality of talent. The purse money had gotten to a level where one could play the tour full time, and that especially appealed to the entrepreneurial American spirit. However, with so many players trying to make a career out there on the lone prairie and only so much daylight in which to play a tournament, the field was necessarily restricted to about 144 starters prior to the thirty-six-hole cut. Hence, the qualifying round became a vale of tears.

The tour had become more structured, and a qualification system was developed whereby every week places in the field were automatically given to top money winners of the year, and in recent years, and winners of the majors—i.e., established players—as well as those who finished in the money in the previous week's tournaments. The number of spots open to Monday qualifiers gradually got smaller and more hellish, not only in terms of number of entrants but the scores required to get in. The quality of golf was going way up, as college golf programs proliferated, quality instruction became more readily available, and more athletes became interested in golf. So torturous were the Monday rabbit races that something had to be done. That is, they had to stop.

Gary McCord and Joe Porter had a lot to do with eliminating the Monday qualifying system. (There would continue to be a Monday qualifying, but it is for two or three slots open to local pros in the vicinity of the tournament site—a kind of public relations sop, and essentially negligible.) Both were middle-field grinders driven by their own desperation. McCord recalled that on the Florida swing in 1980 he shot 70 in each of three Monday qualifying rounds and didn't make it into any of the tournaments. Joe Porter remembered; "At the Kaiser tournament in the Napa Valley, Hal Underwood had three holes to go on Monday and went ace, birdie, eagle—that's five under par for three holes—*to get in a play-off for the last spot!* He got in, and finished third in the tournament."

"When I first went on tour," Porter continued, "you could get into tournaments shooting 74 on Monday. I knew it was time for me to quit when I played a Monday qualifier for the 1979 L.A. Open at the Los Angeles Country Club, North course—a hundred and thirty-five players for twenty-five spots. I shot 72 and was in a nine-man play-off for the last place. It goes nine more holes, and I make it. I was one-under par for the twenty-seven holes on one of the best golf courses in the world, and I just get into the tournament. I made the cut, but four months later quit the tour."

In 1982 McCord and Porter got busy doing something about this situation. They approached many pros, including those who were not "rabbits"—Phil Rodgers, Hale Irwin, and of course Jack Nicklaus—on the idea of an all-exempt tour. That is, a player qualifies for the entire circuit at the start of the new season via a seventy-two-hole tournament. A certain number of tour cards are the purse, so to speak. If he gets the card he doesn't have to qualify for any PGA Tour-sponsored events for one year. He can count on playing in the tournament proper, simply by entering. He has to make the thirty-six-hole cut, of course, but he gets the chance every week.

"Irwin and Nicklaus were not in favor," McCord recalled. "Why should they be, it was not a problem for them." But McCord kept at it. He would become known for his off-beat humor and quippy tongue as a commentator on CBS telecasts of golf tournaments in the 1990s, but in this case he revealed a deeper and more meaningful sensitivity. Contemporaries of his in southern California said McCord was enormously talented as a teenage golfer but because of his wide-ranging interests—he read books on

everything from sociology to Scientology—didn't have the discipline necessary for playing successful tour golf.

In the case of the all-exempt tour, though, he stuck it out and helped
create a major change in the structure of the PGA Tour. "I talked with
sociologists," said McCord, "and they said the Monday qualifying system
was very stressful, which we all knew. But they made the point that the
'rabbits' became very conservative once they got in a tournament. The
ones who learned how to qualify on Monday, and there were some who
got the knack for it, hardly ever made the cut in the tournament because
they played too cautiously. They were afraid they would have to do Monday again, and for that very reason they usually did. They developed a
good qualifying mentality, but it didn't prove anything beyond that. All
they could do was qualify."

The all-exempt system was put in effect in 1983. There were those
who droned the mantra of American individualism hitting the rocks, of
socialism making another corrupting inroad into the institutions that made
the country great. An all-exempt tour would diminish incentive, make the
tour less competitive. It was like the welfare system. There would be a
line of players who would play just hard enough to finish tenth or fifteenth
every week, taking no chances that might blow their exemption. But of
course, it didn't work that way. The all-exempt system has improved the
quality of play on the tour. Today, making the cut in a tournament has
become an accomplishment, and finishing tenth is equivalent to winning
in the 1930s. An exempt player can work on his game while out there,
do some experimenting under the gun without worrying that if it doesn't
work he'll lose his chance to play the next week. If there had been a
Monday qualifying system in the years when Ben Hogan was struggling
to find his game, and went broke three or four times in the process, there
probably would have never been a *Ben Hogan*. The tour in those days was
essentially a nonexempt circuit, which allowed Hogan to keep putting
himself under the gun of competition as long as he had a few bucks in
his kick.

The qualifying tournament for all-exempt status, known as the Q-
School, has become one of the toughest, most stressful, and competitive
tournaments in all of golf. Some players have tried and failed seven and
eight times before finally coming through, or giving it up. It has grown
from a 72-hole tournament to a 144-hole event with a substantial purse,

and you don't get into that without making it through a regional Q-School tournament.

However, the tour has become so competitive that getting the card is not an absolute guarantee you will play every event you want to enter. There are levels of qualifiers: The lowest on the list from the Q-School have fewer opportunities because of those already exempt as leading money winners or winners of major championships who may have filled up most of the field. And if after a year you are not one of the 125 leading money winners on the PGA Tour, you lose your card and have to go back to the Q-School. More than a few pros have ridden this see-saw more than once. This makes the whole program as nerve-wracking as the old Monday rabbit race. Doesn't sound like socialism from here. Sounds more like the Lone Ranger rides again.

The "Gurus"

After Ben Hogan became a successful player he would often respond, when asked if anyone had helped him find his game, that he did it all by himself. As previously noted, in one of his more ungracious moods he once told a fellow touring pro who asked him for some swing advice, to "Dig it out of the dirt, the way I did."

What Hogan meant by both those remarks was that everyone has to figure out their swing on their own, by hitting lots and lots of balls—practice, practice, practice. Quite right. But Hogan, like everyone else who has tried to fathom the unfathomable that is golf, studied a lot of different swings, asked many questions of people he thought might know something and got specific information from Henry Picard. Picard was a Masters and PGA champion in the 1930s, and for many years afterward, was one of the most respected teachers in the game. Hogan dedicated his first instruction book to Picard, thanking him for his "golfing hints." Hints, indeed. Picard gave Hogan very detailed and personalized instruction, foremost of which was the revised grip—shortened left thumb, weaker left hand position—that was the key to his breakthrough.

Hogan's attitude about getting outside help was not unusual for the pros of his time. It was a matter of pride, of ego; to say you did it all yourself was a way of bolstering self-confidence. "I did it my way," sang Frank Sinatra, and everyone believed him. Or wanted to. To the point is a story about Sam Snead and Hogan when they played as a team in the

1956 World Cup Match in Great Britain. Snead was not playing too well in the early going; Hogan was on his game. On the next to last day of play, while driving to the course, Snead complained to Hogan that he just couldn't get his game going. Hogan said he could help him. Snead asked how, but Hogan said he would tell him later. Later was when he felt sure he had the individual championship locked up, in which was Snead his main competition. The team segment was a cinch.

The next day, with an insurmountable lead on Snead, Hogan gave Snead the advice. It was a simple fundamental, a slight adjustment in his stance. Snead then went out and shot a fine round of 68. The press learned that Hogan had given Snead a tip—Fred Corcoran passed it on, it was a good story—and when asked if it had helped him shoot the 68, Snead said in a huff, "Hell, man, *I* shot the 68."

Sometime in the late 1970s a new attitude toward acknowledging swing help developed. It's hard to imagine the hippie culture of the 1960s penetrating the conservative milieu of professional golf, but perhaps the newest generation of tour pros had somehow been moved by the generous spirit of the have-a-nice-day balladeers. Then, too, it may have been that most of the new young pros were coming out of college golf; after playing on teams, they were accustomed to acknowledging the influence of others.

Whatever the case, teachers were being named. It more or less began with Nicklaus, as so much did. He made it clear that Jack Grout had taught him to play as a young boy and continued to coach him through the peak years of his career. But it was those who followed after Nicklaus—Tom Watson, Ben Crenshaw, and Curtis Strange, among others—who gave the credit-is-due movement its first large-scale thrust. Watson noted that his first teacher was Stan Thirsk, the pro at the club in Kansas City where he grew up. Later Watson went to Bryon Nelson and credited him with a lot of his success. Crenshaw and Tom Kite hailed Harvey Penick, the gentle genius of Austin, Texas, as their coach. When Penick was "discovered" it was also learned he was influential in the careers of Mickey Wright, Betsy Rawls, Kathy Whitworth, and many others. Curtis Strange, Hal Sutton and Sandy Lyle credited Jimmy Ballard with their success.

More such revelations followed, and somewhere in this time-frame the word "guru" emerged, perhaps from the popular Zen Buddhist-oriented cult novel by Michael Murphy, *Golf in the Kingdom*. The term carries a satiric connotation, suggesting it may have been coined by someone with an old school, dig-it-out-of-the-dirt-like-I-did mentality. Grout and Penick and Nelson were gurus, but the reference was really aimed at a group of young pros who more or less came out of nowhere and gained celebrity on the bag strap of a top-drawer tour player.

The first to gain prominence was Ballard. An Alabaman who learned his golf at the knee of Sam Byrd, the former New York Yankee outfielder who became a winner on the PGA Tour in the 1940s, Ballard had labored at small clubs and driving ranges until he made news as the coach of Strange, Sutton, and Lyle. When this intense man gets his steam up talking about his system, Ballard brings to mind a Sunday morning television evangelical faith healer.

Hank Haney came to gurudom because of a connection with Mark O'Meara, a budding tour star at the time and eventually a Masters and British Open champion. Jim McLean was on the golf team at the University of Houston and began his career as a guru by instructing a few players from the school who went on tour. His most notable connection was with Tom Kite, who won the U.S. Open after an intense period of instruction with McLean. John Redman brought Paul Azinger's game to major league status. Mac O'Grady was a guru to the gurus, as well as to active tour players. He was the first to work with Seve Ballesteros when the Spaniard's game began to deteriorate. Some would say O'Grady hastened the deterioration. Phil Rodgers gained wider recognition as a teacher when Jack Nicklaus went to him for help on his short game.

There were a few gurus in the women's game. Ed Oldfield and Derek Hardy gained good reputations. Strangely, no women teachers emerged as nationally known gurus. There are quite a few excellent women teachers, however.

Many others would come along, including Claude "Butch" Harmon in the 1990s, who refined Tiger Woods's swing. But the guru of gurus in terms of numbers of star players in his resume, and his own personal celebrity, has been David Leadbetter. From Rhodesia (now Zimbabwe), Leadbetter came to fame teaching Nick Faldo, the Briton who for a decade—1980 to 1990—was one of the world's best players. Nick Price, a fellow Zimbabwean who grew up with Leadbetter and was actually his first "name" pupil, was the matchmaker.

As the guru movement developed, and previous unknowns like Ballard,

Haney, and Leadbetter were seen to be making a valuable national reputation, a certain little fraud began to take place. If word got out that you were "working with" Crenshaw or Kite or another celebrity player, it could lead to full-time lesson bookings for higher-than-before rates, perhaps a job as director of instruction at a resort, plus magazine articles, books, even golf schools. Thus, every practice tee on tour became a bazaar crowded with young teaching pros hovering on the make. They would casually stop by a pro they thought or heard was approachable—Lyle, Chip Beck, Tom Purtzer—and engage him in light conversation about the grip or address position or angle of attack. Some might be bold enough to lay a hand on the pro's left arm to illustrate a point. Every now and again the guru-hopeful would glance back at the gallery or catch the eye of a roving golf journalist or another tour pro to see if he was being noticed. Later he would say to the journalist or anyone else within hearing distance that he was just "working with" Lyle/Beck/Purtzer.

There was some common ground among the gurus who rose up in the 1970s. Most were in their mid-twenties or early thirties, about the same age as the players they worked with, or only a few years older. Almost all were unknown even to the game's cognoscenti, let alone the masses. Except for Rodgers, who was a near-great player and a multi-winner on the tour, and O'Grady, who won once on the tour and was a wonderful (and ambidextrous) ball striker, none came with reputations as quality players. All of which prompted Lee Trevino to say, when asked once if he had a guru, "When I find someone who can beat me, I'll sign him up."

Except for John Redman, who took on Azinger as a raw junior college golfer, all the new gurus connected with players who were already quite good—they had outstanding records in college and were holding their own in the pros. This followed the age-old formula for success as a teacher—get students with talent in the first place and leave the duds to others.

All the new gurus had boned up on the classic teachers of the twenties and thirties—Ernest Jones, Percy Boomer, Tommy Armour—and they brought new exposure to some of the best and original teaching of the past one hundred years. We heard again Boomer's assertion that your body should turn in a barrel, and Ernest Jones's "paralysis by analysis" and "swing the club head" got renewed exposure. All the young gurus declared they were teaching Hogan in some way or another. Reference was made regularly to Hogan's book *The Five Fundamentals*. None had ever spoken with the great man and only had seen his swing on film, but they knew his book and claimed to be explaining and expanding, and surely extrapolating a little from it.

One instructional text that gathered a legion of disciples was *The Golfing Machine*, by Homer Kelly, who was an engineer by profession and couldn't break 80 on his best day. Kelly-ites swore by him, literally. Any proponent who wanted to be a Golf Machine teacher and bill himself as such was required to have a signed certificate from the leader. Kelly's book is presented in the form of an engineer's treatise or manual. The language is opaque if you're not an engineer, and the illustrations are draftsman's renditions of the various angles of the golf swing. For the average golfer Kelly's book is a barely comprehensible volume. O'Grady teaches from it and claims he is clarifying the concepts. He does so in language equally impenetrable. O'Grady once announced plans to write a five-volume series broadening, widening, and augmenting Homer Kelly's sacred scriptures. Heaven help us!

Have the young gurus of the seventies been effective? Nick Faldo was a very good tour pro on the European circuit, but wanted to become world class and Leadbetter helped him completely restructure his swing. That is unusual, and risky for a player in his prime who is doing pretty well. But it worked, for some eight years. In Leadbetter's custody Faldo won three British Opens (1987, 1990, and 1992), three Masters (1989, 1990, and 1996), and lost a play-off for the U.S. Open to Curtis Strange, in 1988. At one point Faldo was being touted as one of the best players ever, and he made no bones about Leadbetter being the man behind the gun. But when he began to play poorly in the late 1990s, Leadbetter could not get him righted. Faldo broke off the relationship. Leadbetter was effective, then he wasn't.

Or were other forces playing on Faldo at this time? He had broken up his marriage and his family (two children) through a much-publicized affair with a young American woman. Some thought he had become too analytical—gotten paralyzed by analysis.

Leadbetter critics, many of them rival gurus, remarked that he had as many "dead bodies" out there as live ones. That is, he may have hurt the games of as many players as he helped. *May have* is the operative phrase. Bob Tway and Ian Baker-Finch were cited as examples. In both of these

high-profile cases Tway and Baker-Finch went counter to the time-
honored adage, "If it ain't broke, don't fix it." Tway had just won the
1986 PGA Championship and three other tournaments the same year, but
wanted to get even better. After Baker-Finch won the 1991 British Open,
where he displayed a beautiful swing and fine tempo, he decided he
wasn't long enough off the tee. Both went to Leadbetter. Tway's game
gradually deteriorated to where, in 1992, he won a mere $47,632. In 1995
he went back to the swing that brought him to the party in the first place,
won for the first time in five years, and earned $787,000 to rank twentieth
on the money list. Baker-Finch became one of the saddest cases of a
player losing his game that has ever come along. From 1995 through 1997
he played a full schedule of tournaments and made only one cut. In 1998
he quit tournament golf altogether.

When Bobby Clampett joined the PGA Tour in 1980, he was hailed as
a star on the near horizon. In his second and third years on tour it appeared
to have arisen. He won a tournament and over $184,00 in each of those
years. But in 1982 he also had a clear chance to win the British Open and
collapsed miserably in the final round. It might only have been nerves,
but Clampett determined it was his swing and vowed to find a method
that would never allow such a collapse to happen. He took up Homer
Kelly's *Golfing Machine* and became one its strongest champions. He never
again played near his potential.

Leadbetter's fault or Homer Kelly's? Tway, Baker-Finch, and Clampett
knew the system of the teachers they were taking up with. Couldn't
Baker-Finch have told himself he was overreaching, that if he could win
a major with the length he already had why go for more? Should someone
have snatched Kelly's book from Clampett and forbade him to ever read
it again? Should Leadbetter have quit Tway and Baker-Finch when he
saw that his advice didn't seem to be taking? Or maybe it was just a matter
of time. Golf instruction is a two-way street with no certain destination.
Leadbetter, an amiable fellow with an interesting intelligence, admitted
that he didn't help everybody who came to him and maybe hurt a few
golfers. But with a Solomonic shrug he said, "You can't win 'em all." An
honest response.

How to account for the rise of the guru on the pro tours? Nick Price
thought it was because "The game has become so competitive, the money

so big, that when we get off we need to get it back as quickly as possible or get passed by. A good coach knows the player's swing, and his personal nuances, and can give a fast fix when necessary."

Gary Player thought the prize money that became available on the tours allowed pros the luxury of a guru. "They can pay the expenses to bring those fellows to big tournaments or small ones, can afford long-distance phone calls to ask for advice. We couldn't do that when I was coming up." McLean explained, "We are confidence builders. The body changes from week to week and the player has a problem with self-criticism. We give them objectivity."

And how has the rise of the guru on the pro tour affected the average golfer? The notoriety has added even more emphasis on what may be the most overtaught game going. Leadbetter remarked that the widespread use of the instant-playback video camera that every modern teacher uses has expanded the "scientific" research and is good, but only up to a point. He remarked that golfers can become too dependent on it. "Because they can check out their swing on video seconds after they make it, they get too far from the feel or instinct that should also be part of the action. Furthermore, what you see is not always what you feel, and this confusion can heighten the dilemma." Nick Price put it another way. "Leadbetter [or any other big-name guru] is not going to turn a chop into a *player*."

Still, such is the lure of the game and power of marketing that McLean, Haney, and Ballard have established successful golf schools—or academies, as they are sometimes described. These gurus personally get upwards of $500 an hour, if you can get them to stand across from you. Leadbetter was charging $1,500 a hour for his time at last count, and sees only first-rate players. He has become a millionaire from a combination of his schools, instruction books, contracts with golf periodicals, endorsements of grips, sunglasses, and teaching devices, and may be the only or at least the first golf teacher in the history of the game to have a business agent. It is, not surprisingly, International Management Group.

The "Shrinks"

The first more or less formal and concentrated study of how the mind works at golf was *The Mystery of Golf* by Arnold Haultain, a book published in 1908. Haultain was not a psychologist by training, only a Canadian writer who wrote on a wide range of topics—from religion to love to the old Scots game. How well Haultain played golf is not known, but whether he was good or bad, he certainly wasn't indifferent about it. He had exceptional insight into this most enigmatic of games, and although his book is slim in size, it is the seminal work on the mental side of golf.

Haultain's book languished in neglect for some sixty years, to be found only in the libraries of the most profound golf litterateurs. It was out of print for years. The revival of *The Mystery of Golf* coincided with a new interest in golf's cerebral machinations, which germinated in the seventies and flowered in the eighties. Michael Murphy's *Golf in the Kingdom* probably had something to do with it. About a dozen books on the mental side of golf had been published between 1908 and 1972, including Haultain's, when Murphy's book appeared in 1972. Most were by university professors who were too academic in their approach, or light humorists whose attempts weighed in accordingly. Murphy's book was in fact a serious dissertation on the metaphysics of Zen Buddhism, but done in a cleverly accessible style. It tells of a golfer (Murphy, really; he is a golf nut of the first order) profoundly enchanted by the game and seeks its holy grail in the land of its birth. He meets a mysterious, mystical man named Shivas (from the Hindu god figure Shiva) Irons, who makes magical golf shots on a midnight-dark links using a shillelagh and hits his target dead on. It was fun to read, the first time.

Around the same time, Timothy Gallway's book *The Inner Game of Tennis*, another Zen-oriented exploration into the mind at games playing, was published and became a best-seller. This led to his *The Inner Game of Golf*, published in 1982, a sequel to the first book with only the name of the game and equipment nomenclature changed. Gallway was a friend of Murphy and associated with his Esalen Institute, a think tank on a sheer cliff high above the Pacific Ocean on the Monterey Peninsula. Esalen's intellectual foundation is in Eastern philosophy, especially Zen Buddhism, a calming contemplative ideology or Way of Being well-suited to the internally oriented game of golf.

One way or another, the mental side of playing all games was in the zeitgeist, and golf became a sizable part of the movement. Dr. Richard Coop, an educational psychologist at the University of North Carolina, was on the ground floor of this movement. He believes golf pros on tour became interested because the extensive and exhaustive study of swing mechanics over the past ten years or so had tightened the competition so much—there was so little difference between how well the number one player hit the ball compared to the fiftieth—that "everyone began looking for another edge, another way to get a leg up on the competition."

Pro golfers began to delve into why they had that weak, hollow feeling in their stomach when crouched over a three-foot putt to win a tournament. Or why, when they should be concentrating entirely on what club to use for a crucial shot at the eighteenth hole, their mind wandered off to where they were going to eat dinner that night. They wanted to know why, and what to do about such scatterings of the brain.

Dr. Coop's first golfer (he prefers to call them players, not clients and definitely not patients) was Nina Faust, who in the late 1970s was having trouble qualifying to play the LPGA tour. Their sessions led to Faust earning her first tour card. Coop also took on Sally Austin, another LPGA player. His first male player was Jim Simons, who had a brief spurt in the spotlight. Ben Crenshaw went to Coop in 1985. Crenshaw was going through serious hyperthyroid problems related to stress, and he had lost around fifteen pounds off an already slim physique. He worked with Coop for four years and benefited greatly. So did Coop, after Crenshaw made it known that the psychologist had helped him.

Most of the men pros, though, weren't leafing through the Yellow Pages to find a psychologist. Nonetheless, enough of the new generation, anxious about their chances on the circuit, were ready to let someone play with their mind. They found Dr. Coop; Dr. Bob Rotella, a brightly loquacious man who had a degree in sports psychology; and Chuck Hogan, a former golf pro not trained in psychology but who had worked up a program based on some of its fundamental principles. It is interesting to note, however, that except for Crenshaw, in the early days of the movement, the men tour players who went to sports psychologists would not acknowledge it and didn't want anyone to know. Payne Stewart, Coop's most prominent player after Crenshaw, insisted on this. So did Raymond Floyd. This attitude toward psychology was typical of most male Americans and especially athletes. Seeing a "shrink" is unmanly, a sign of weakness of character. Tell me I'm swinging on the wrong plane because my posture at address is poor, but don't tell me I can't release the club at impact on important approach shots because I have this fear of winning, or losing, or had a problem with toilet training as a young child.

Rotella, Coop, Hogan, and most of the others who came after them in what has become a crowded field, didn't do much, if any, Freudian on-the-couch psychoanalysis. At least as far as doctor-patient confidentiality would let anyone say. It was mostly educational rather than clinical psychology, although sometime after Payne Stewart won his first U.S. Open in 1991, Coop noticed he had symptoms of attention deficit syndrome. He had Stewart take some tests that proved his suspicions, then sent him off for more qualified help. Stewart came to understand his lapses into rude indifference to others and the periods of distraction on the golf course that hurt his game, and was able to make important changes in his attitude and behavior in the year or two before his tragic death in a plane accident.

Sports psychologists have concentrated on fairly standard principles of the mental process. How to stay focused—a mantra in the field, also jargonized as "staying in the present tense." Your only thought when playing a shot is that shot, not the last one, and you don't think of what that is going to mean in the competition at hand, or your relationship with your wife and children. How to create a positive mental image of the shot at hand is another fundamental of sports psychology—don't see the water in front of the green, only the pin and the trajectory of the shot you want to hit to it. Develop a positive self-image, by all means—don't ever think poorly of yourself, no matter how badly you missed your last shot.

Techniques to realize these goals are prescribed. Develop a set routine for playing every shot. If there is an interruption, go back to the beginning and start over again. A routine offers a kind of comfort that helps a player get through tense situations. Avoid tension by emptying your mind of long-term goals. Take deep breaths when under pressure and before starting your swing.

The teachings of the sports psychologists is something any reasonably sentient human being can work out for himself. Millions have, and a few golfers, too. Ben Hogan not only played as often as he could with golfers with a slower swing tempo so he might capture some of it and slow his own swing, he also drove to the golf course under the speed limit to the same end. He also understood the idea of narrow focus—staying in the present tense, tunnel vision—well before any trained psychologist aired the concept. In the 1959 U.S. Open, at the Winged Foot Golf Club, Hogan was paired one day with Claude Harmon, Sr., the head professional at the club. While walking past the clubhouse from the ninth green to the tenth tee, Harmon quite naturally recognized and had brief conversations with some of the members of the club. Hogan berated Harmon (whom he admired very much as a player), for the fraternizing. Harmon said those people were his bosses, he couldn't just brush by them. Hogan said he could, and should, that not to was to break his concentration on golf.

Billy Casper knew about a consistent playing routine before Dr. Coop was a pup. Whenever he was disturbed while getting set to play a shot—even after pulling a club from his bag—Casper would put the club back and begin his routine from the beginning. When the pressure was mounting in a match, Sam Snead would watch an opponent carefully to see if he changed his routine for playing shots. If the opponent did, Snead knew he was feeling the tension and that he, Snead, had a better chance of winning. To wit, Snead's recall of his match against Jim Turnesa for the 1942 PGA Championship: "Well, I had won the ninth hole to get even and at the tenth I threw a fade around the dogleg and he changed his mannerism and hooked into the trap. That just shot me right up. I said, 'Uh-huh, that's it.' You see, he got to taking two more waggles than he usually did. I knew he was getting tight, and now I have more confidence in myself. I beat him two and one."

Isn't that a more charming description of the situation than any academic wording might have for it? But to the main point, the modern-day sports psychologists aren't really plumbing new ground in their work. And the pros they counsel could surely come up with solutions for better focus or whatever on their own. So is the rise of the sports psychologist in golf (and in some other sports, including major league baseball) merely another sign of American conspicuous consumption? Not really. It is a measure of the success of the PGA Tour, in terms of the money that can be earned out there. It helps buy convenience. Just as the players can afford to have a swing guru, they can also pay for a psychologist. So why not? By offering a quick and easy, and well-informed avenue of self-examination, Coop, Rotella and the many others practicing in the field help players reduce the time and energy it takes to investigate what makes them tick mentally as golfers—just as Leadbetter and Harmon help them with their swing plane, pivot, footwork, et cetera.

There has been no evidence that sports psychology has hurt anyone, and more than a few players have claimed it has helped. It has become a rather large cottage industry. By 1999 Bob Rotella had left his academic position at the University of West Virginia to become a full-time consultant in sports psychology. Who could blame him? He was commanding as much as $15,000 a day for his lectures and consulting gigs with individual professional athletes and teams, including men's and women's college golf teams.

As Dr. Freud might have also said, sometimes a cigar is only a golf club—gold plated.

The Square-Groove (False) Issue

In the 1980s the top governors of American golf were growing more and more concerned that the game was getting too easy for the best players, and that it was the equipment, not their talent, at the heart of the matter. The USGA insisted it wasn't the ball being too lively, that it was going maybe five yards farther than it had ten years earlier. No big deal. Nothing could be done about shafts as long as they were straight and round. Nor could anything be done about the improved physical condition, overall size, and knowledge of the swing that the modern player brought to the scorer's table. Certainly there could be no restrictions on the intelligence and insights sports psychologists were offering golfers. And so, the titular American defenders of golf's integrity went after the square groove.

When irons began to be produced by the investment-cast system it was discovered that the internal shape of the groove did not come out V-shaped. The groove was a kind of three-sided box, and square at the bottom, hence a square groove. Grooves on forged irons, the standard in the industry, had always been V-shaped and that became the official configuration according to USGA rules. In one of its rare concessions to golf industry needs, the USGA took into account that making the square grooves V-shaped would require an expensive extra step. Besides, it could not definitively measure or assess one from the other, and in 1984 it changed the rule to allow for square grooves.

Karsten Solheim, who introduced investment casting to the golf industry, thought the square groove might give players a bit of an advantage, but not enough to advertise the feature. However, a lot of players on the men's and women's tours had gone over to Ping irons, either as paid representatives or because they just believed they were the best clubs out there. A perception grew among those who weren't playing the club that square grooves produced more holding spin than V-shaped ones—in fact, too much spin. Murmurs of discontent rumbled through the community of non-Ping-playing tour golfers that eventually became a clamor to have the square groove banned. The episode opened a window on administrative power, on who in fact controlled or tried to control the game—it was a classic American boardroom battle—and on the tour pros' proclivity for uninformed opinions based entirely on self-interest. The debate consumed a lot of time, money, and intellectual energy far beyond its true value. A burp in a windstorm.

Tests were made to compare the effect of square grooves with V-shaped ones. It turned out that the square groove produced some twenty percent more spin, *but only when the ball was played out of wet grass*, especially *long* wet grass. Reason being, moisture that gets down in the groove is more apt to remain down there. That leaves less on the club face. Water on the club face retards the amount of spin that can be put on the ball, which then rolls more after landing. A dry club face is especially helpful on shots from ninety yards and in. The tests also indicated that the percentage of spin with square grooves decreases as the loft on the club lessens—i.e., there is hardly any effect with a five- or three-iron, *and there is no discernible effect with any club when playing from short (or long) dry grass.*

Despite that clear-cut evidence, those who were not playing Ping clubs remained unconvinced, including stars such as Tom Watson and Jack Nicklaus, who insisted that square grooves put too much spin on the ball from any kind of lie. More than once when they were commenting on television and someone hit a wedge shot that spun back toward the hole or stopped dead after landing right beside the cup, Nicklaus and Watson would lament, "Oh, those square grooves!"

Because Watson and Nicklaus were champion players, and therefore not only high-profile personalities but presumptive experts in everything golf-related, the USGA reevaluated its position on square grooves. Deane Beman, who was against the groove, stated that the PGA Tour would go along with whatever the USGA decided. But when the decision was one he didn't like, he didn't. The issue began to get jumbled.

After six or so months of being in play, another element in the controversy emerged. It was discovered that the Ping irons were scuffing and shaving the balls, especially the softer balata-covered ones the pros used. Solheim investigated and found that the stamping process left the grooves with very sharp edges on the surface of the club face. So he filed the edges a bit—rounded or softened them. After inspection the USGA said the grooves were too close together now, and therefore illegal. According to the rules, a groove cannot be wider than 0.9 millimeters, and the distance between them not less than three times the width of the groove, or not less than 1.9 millimeters, whichever comes first. Solheim said that by his way of measuring the distance between grooves, his clubs conformed. The USGA said its way of measuring was correct, and they threatened to ban all Ping irons that did not conform to its measurement system. Solheim said he would bring suit for $300 million.

The USGA was prepared to fight it out. A situation arose in which men would try their souls, fret and worry, go to court and spend millions in legal fees for what was finally determined to be two-thousandths of an inch difference between grooves. "That's half the width of a human hair," said Leonard DeCof, Karsten's attorney in the case.

In taking its position the USGA stood to lose only legal fees. Solheim had a far more serious problem. He didn't want to take $300 million out of the USGA treasury—he didn't want any money at all—he only wanted to protect the nearly two million sets of irons already out in the world from being declared illegal. Most golfers couldn't care less, because they don't play in USGA-sanctioned tournaments or in any tournaments at all, but for Solheim such a ruling would have an onerous ring. Solheim's company would suffer the blot of producing illegal clubs. On the ground, a recall of all the clubs not in conformance with the rule would come at a huge cost and probably put Solheim out of business and a lot of people out of work. That was reality.

Eventually, the two parties came to an out-of-court settlement. The USGA grandfathered for all time all Ping irons already in play; they could be used in all its championships. In return, Solheim retooled so his new irons conformed to the USGA's method of measuring the distance between grooves.

However, Deane Beman was not pleased with the outcome. He quietly tried to persuade the USGA to ban even those Ping irons already out there. DeCof suggested this was because Beman had cut a deal with the Ben Hogan Company that, in return for its sponsorship of the new high minor league Ben Hogan Tour, the company would have exclusive access to the practice tee at the events. It is on the practice tees at pro tour stops where club manufacturers can mostly readily get pros to try out their equipment and hopefully get them to use it in competition. The tee would also not be littered by the logos of rivals.

When the USGA would not change its position, Beman hired Dave Pelz, a golf pro who had been a club manufacturer and later a short-game guru, to run what was billed as an objective performance test of clubs for their spin-making capacity. Ping clubs were found to produce excessive spin. The USGA didn't buy the results, saying the outcome had been predetermined.

Beman went to court, claiming the Ping clubs gave its players an unfair advantage over those that didn't use them. Also, he believed his organization could dictate equipment usage in events under its jurisdiction. Attorney DeCof countered that the PGA Tour could not dictate equipment used by its members (the players) because they are free agents. In the process, DeCof took depositions from Nicklaus and Watson. He forced Nicklaus to admit he was not a trained engineer, had no expertise in aerodynamics, and couldn't really make a learned judgment on the effect of square grooves. Watson was made to admit that while he was the co-author, with Frank Hannigan, of a book on *The Rules of Golf*, he didn't know the rules all that well. Under oath, Watson testified that the book was written entirely by Hannigan, a former USGA executive secretary, and that he had just put his name on the cover. End of their witness credibility. Also, Tom Kite sided with the PGA Tour on the square-groove matter, saying at one point that everyone should play the same equipment in order to level the playing field for all. On the witness stand DeCof asked Kite if he knew anything about Andy North's clubs. North, a two-time U.S. Open champion, is a tall, broad-shouldered man, whereas Kite is quite a bit smaller. Kite said North's clubs were extra long, had built-up grips, and were shafted in such a way as to make them much stiffer than normal. Could Kite play with those clubs? DeCof asked. "No way," said Kite. End of Kite's argument that everyone should play with the same equipment.

The case against the PGA Tour was heard in San Francisco by a golfing judge whom the tour thought would favor its view. He didn't. Beman and the PGA Tour lost. Whether it was related to this loss, which might be construed as a loss of face, is not clear, but about a year after the decision in the San Francisco court, Beman resigned his post as commissioner.

Every club manufacturer in the golf industry now turns out square-grooved irons with the correct USGA specified spacing. There has been no indication that the integrity of the game has been weakened by this or that scores have been lower on days when courses are wet from heavy rains.

Neither has there been any noticeable change in scoring with another major advance in equipment that took hold in the 1980s, the graphite shaft. The graphite shaft was first introduced in the 1970s, but the manufacturing process was not yet sound and it proved too inconsistent in performance. By the 1980s, though, many improvements were made and the graphite shaft has become the shaft of choice for many average golfers because they are lighter and easier to swing. The manufacturers prefer them because the profit margin is higher. Even the tour pros are using graphite, although mainly the seniors, and then only in the driver because the lighter weight helps generate more swing speed. In irons they are still considered too inconsistent. Graphite also absorbs more shock, making them easier on the hands.

Despite all these technological advances, if they can be so considered, the average handicap for the common golfer nationwide has not dropped. It's still around a 16. Even the tour pro's average score per round on the year has remained fairly steady. In 1950 Sam Snead won the Vardon Trophy for low-stroke average per round of the year with 69.23. That was over ninety-six rounds of golf. In 1999 Tiger Woods had the lowest stroke average on the tour with 68.43, based on eighty-four rounds. That's less than one stroke better in fifty-five years, with Woods playing twelve fewer rounds on courses that in terms of the condition of the grass, by comparison, are what a baby's skin is to a Brillo pad.

The real difference is that today's average golfer enjoys his mishits more. The clubs are lighter to swing, get the ball airborne more readily and a little farther down the road. The game is no easier than it has ever been, it just *seems* like it. It's the image thing.

7 | The 1990s: New Young Lions, and a Tiger

One More Black Issue Addressed; PGA Tour Gets a Farm System; The Ryder Cup Goes Berserk; Norman's Last Act; Sons of Champions, Arise; Julie, Julie, Julie; The "Spring-Like Effect"?; Where's the Money?; Hold That Tiger!

The race issue didn't disappear, never to be heard from again, after Lee Elder played in the 1975 Masters. In a 1979 interview with a *New York Times* sportswriter, on the eve of his defense of the Westchester Classic, Elder said blacks were still struggling for equality in a "sport that continues to feel uncomfortable about black players. . . . It still hasn't changed enough. I overlook a lot of racial things I should be more forward about." His wife, Rose, no wallflower, expanded on her husband's remark: "The prejudice thing is still very real. You'll find some bigots in nearly every gallery. Their favorite expression is, 'Hit it, nigger.' Or somebody will yell, 'What are you doing in a white man's game?' "

Elder estimated that in the Washington, D.C., area, where he made his home and managed three city-owned public courses, "only about four or five private clubs out of fifty in the area accept black members." In this observation Elder was presaging the not-too-distant future.

The 1990 PGA Championship was played at the Shoal Creek Country Club in Birmingham, Alabama. It had been held there in 1984, too, but without controversy, because the man who founded the club, Hall Thompson, said nothing about it not having any black members. He wasn't asked. Six years later, he was. In the June 21, 1990, issue of the *Birmingham Post-Herald*, Thompson was quoted as saying, "The country club [Shoal Creek] is our home and we pick and choose who we want as members. I think we've said that we don't discriminate in any area except the blacks." Thompson uttered the unutterable. Actually, he was speaking for almost every private club in the country, but he was going to take the full brunt of his comment.

After Thompson let the door get ajar, the Southern Christian Leadership Conference and the NAACP called for picketing Shoal Creek during the PGA Championship. This was followed by something that always gets everybody's undivided attention and moves all mountains. Nearly all of the companies scheduled to advertise on the ABC telecast of the championship threatened to drop out. Thompson's remark was the reason. Immediately afterward, the PGA of America, the PGA Tour, and the USGA announced that they would not hold future tournaments at clubs that practice racial discrimination, either in policy or practice. Which meant that it would not do for a club to simply say it was willing to admit black members, it would actually have to admit one. One, for a start.

Although the event faced potential sit-ins and picketing, the PGA of America did not consider moving its 1990 championship. But the demonstrations were averted when, two weeks before the tournament was to begin, Shoal Creek took in a local African-American businessman named Louis Willie as an *honorary* member. Willie himself, according to Birmingham journalists close to the situation, could not afford the membership, which was in the $25,000 range. It was taken care of by others, and his access to the club and its services were described, privately, as minimal. The advertisers, however, were mollified and came back on board.

In the next few months after the 1990 PGA Championship, a rather dull affair played in unbearable heat and won by Australian Wayne Grady, a number of private country clubs withdrew as PGA Tour or USGA championship sites (or potential ones) because they would not comply with the new prerequisite and bring in at least a token black member. Among the most prestigious were the Butler National in Chicago, Cypress Point, and Merion golf clubs, and the Aronimink Country Club, which hosted the 1962 PGA Championship after Stanley Mosk and Bill Spiller forced it out of California that year. Augusta National was a club one might expect to not comply, if only because its Masters tournament is outside all jurisdiction but its own. But it did bring in one black member.

There were the expected doubting Thomases who conjectured that the compliance by formerly all-white clubs was mere tokenism—they would take in the one black person, and no more. Skeptics also presumed that those who did accede might be up to a deceitful economic expedient.

A PGA tour event or a U.S. Open can be worth over $2 million to the club in rental fees and the sale of corporate entertainment facilities and merchandise with logos.

Just as predictably, these reservations were decried as crass cynicism. However, in the first ten years after the guideline was decreed, there was very little evidence that the complying clubs had added any more blacks to their membership. Nor was there any indication that private clubs with no tournament interests had done so.

Things change and things remain the same. Charlie Sifford smoked cigars on the golf course for years, yet he was never offered a cigar-endorsement contract. But when the cigar-chomping Larry Laoretti, a white career club pro who retired to play the senior circuit, won the 1992 U.S. Senior Open, he was signed up to endorse a cigar brand. By the turn of the century Tiger Woods was the only African-American on the PGA Tour, there were none on the LPGA circuit, and none appeared to be waiting in the wings, including the minor-league circuits and college teams. A number of African-Americans were on the Senior PGA Tour, of course, having played on the PGA Tour in the sixties and seventies, the most fecund period in black participation. These included Jim Dent, Jim Thorpe, Calvin Peete, Lee Elder, Bobby Stroble, and Walter Morgan. Charlie Sifford, at seventy-eight, was retired. There also wasn't any sign that African-Americans were becoming members of the PGA of America and getting jobs as professionals at private clubs with an almost entirely white membership (which meant all clubs, since there are no known all-black private golf clubs). Only a handful of African-Americans hold such positions at public courses, and almost invariably those courses cater to a black clientele. This is not the PGA of America's doing; it is now open to black membership. African-Americans just haven't been trying to get into mainstream golf because they don't see much opportunity.

And yet, the player who became the most dominant in golf worldwide at the end of the twentieth century was (is) Eldrick "Tiger" Woods. Strictly speaking, Woods is a mix of various racial strains. His mother is half Thai, a quarter Chinese, a quarter white. His father has a touch of white, a good bit of Native American and Chinese, and half black African blood. Which brings to mind an opinion once expressed by Cliff Roberts, the cofounder of the Masters tournament, who said, "Marriage between members of different races was a mistake," and that "mixed breeds were

the most worthless of all in every respect." Against such wrongminded-
ness, Tiger Woods stands tall and straight, lithe and strong. He is articulate, intelligent, and apparently the next great golf champion.

When Woods first joined the PGA Tour, at the age of twenty-one, he
was reluctant to inject himself into the race issue, often making the point
that he is multi-ethnic. Nonetheless, to most Americans, even though
Woods is only one-fourth black African, he is black. He understands that,
and after his first year on the PGA Tour, when he became one of highest
profile athletes in sport, he began to get more involved in programs to
bring inner-city kids, in particular African-Americans, into golf. Some of
his first efforts, however, were ill-advised, especially two television
commercials made by Woods's most visible and richest corporate re-
tainer, Nike. In one advertisement Woods said on camera that he still
had trouble getting on certain golf courses because of his color. This was
sharply criticized and very soon withdrawn, because no one believed it
for a minute. The second commercial was set in a tenement-lined neighborhood showing mainly black children standing on rooftops with sets
of golf clubs at their side or walking through a busy Harlem street with
a bag of clubs over their shoulder on the way to a golf course. It was
pie-in-the-sky, a case of a corporation attempting to declare a social reality that didn't exist, or certainly didn't yet, while trying to locate a new
market for its footwear.

Soon after, the Tiger Woods Foundation was established to promote
realistic efforts to get minority youngsters into golf. This added on to, and
began to help, already existing smaller organizations led by dedicated
individuals who work in the trenches toward the same end. These are
usually run by African-American men, but not exclusively. For instance,
Gregory Hunt, an African-American in Virginia Beach, Virginia, and Chuck
Cohen, a Jew in Toledo, Ohio, provide practice facilities and instruction
on golf fundamentals for minority kids, put on tournaments, teach the
kids how to caddie, and find places for them to do it. They depend on
donations from wherever they can get them. Hunt made a contact with
David Duval, who donated $5,000 to his program. The American Golf
Corporation, which operates hundreds of municipally owned public
courses around the country on a lease basis, many of them inner-city sites,
makes its facilities available for as little as $1 and sometimes free. Amer-
ican Golf also solicits golf equipment manufacturers to donate clubs and

balls for the youngsters in these programs. Tiger Woods and American Golf contracted for five years to produce at least five clinics at various American Golf facilities around the country. Woods has shown sincere interest in these clinics, which he will not do at private clubs, only at inner-city facilities. He is relaxed, doesn't rush, and thoughtfully puts each youngster's hands correctly on the grip, checks out the stance, and all the rest. He has received high marks for his work in this area.

Golf's institutional entities began making contributions in the wake of Woods's much-publicized participation in efforts to bring golf to poor and minority youths. The USGA's donations to organizations such as those run by Hunt and Cohen, in increments from $10,000 to $25,000, came to 4.5 million in 1999. The First Tee Foundation is an ambitious project origi-nated by the PGA of America and joined in by the LPGA, USGA, PGA Tour, and Augusta National Golf Club. Its aim is to create at least one hundred facilities for juniors, mainly inner-city minorities, to be intro-duced to golf. Five major equipment manufacturers—Callaway, Titleist/ Cobra, Taylor Made, Wilson, and Spalding—have committed to providing a First Tee line of clubs. And in 2000, Joe Louis Barrow, son of the great heavyweight champion, Joe Louis, who helped break the color barrier on the PGA Tour, became head of the First Tee project.

A lot of good things were put in the works in the 1990s to stimulate the involvement of young people with golf as a result of Tiger Woods's star burst onto the scene. Some smaller-scale projects, such as those run by Hunt and Cohen, among others, have been in existence for some years, but with Woods's ascendance the game's establishment has finally become more active. It was recognized well before Woods came along that the diminishing use of caddies, the game's traditional entry point for recruits, and the rising cost of playing made it important to find ways to sustain growth in the game. Whether the First Tee Program and the other projects will succeed on a long-term basis is not certain. Will the new generation of youth, inner- or outer-city, growing up in a computerized, remote-controlled, instant-gratification world have the patience for a game that gratifies in dribs and drabs, when at all? But even if the results are not as grand as everyone hopes they will be, something of value will emerge. A few kids will surely spring from the pot and write another chapter in the classic American success saga—young boy or girl from austere circumstances is inspired to play this ball-and-stick game and becomes a rich and famous champion of the world . . . or at least, as Marlon Brando put it, "a contenduh."

A Farm System for the Tour

Professional tournament golf had become a bazaar. The PGA Tour's growth since the early 1970s, under the leadership of commissioner Deane Beman, was steady and impressively upward. The total purse money in 1980 was $13.3 million, and in ten years rose to $46.2 million. By 1999 the pros were playing for $100 million. With that kind of money on offer, literally thousands of young men were trying to find a game that would give them a chance to get at all that cash. Many small circuits, called mini-tours, began sprouting up all over the country, where these hopefuls could find out if they had enough stuff to try for the main arena. One of the first and most successful was the Space Coast Tour, in Florida, which was started by a one-time middle-range tour player named J. C. Goosie.

By the mid-1990s hundreds of such tours were available, offering a series of events, usually at thirty-six holes, one a week, in which the golfers played for the combined entry fees, plus a share of whatever the tour operator could raise from local sponsors. Not all the tour operators were on the level. There were disappearing acts, tour operators cooking the books then eating them, writing checks with a high rubber content. Most, though, were run honestly. The courses weren't first-rate in design or conditioning, but they were places to play and compete.

Inevitably, the PGA Tour got involved. In 1990 the Ben Hogan Tour was inaugurated. It was more extensive than the local or regional mini-tours, and it has become the PGA Tour's triple-A minor league. The Ben Hogan Company sponsored the original tour and set a kind of precedent in the history of tournament golf in America. There had been individual tour events sponsored by club manufacturers—True Temper was the first, in the 1940s—but except for Wilson's heavy but not well-publicized support of the LPGA in its first years, none had ever backed an entire circuit. The Hogan Company, which was trying to get back as a major player in the equipment industry, decide to use this outlet to promote that goal and guaranteed the whole circuit to the tune of some $3 million. Purses ranged between $225,000 and $400,000 per event. The tour was meant mainly for young players who had their eye on making it to the PGA Tour for the first time, and for those who had lost their playing privileges on the big circuit, a chance to regain their sharps and take another stab at it.

Commissioner Beman expected the Hogan tour to function as the pro tour did in the old days, with the sites in smaller cities and towns and the players having to drive their cars to get to them. (In an interview Ben Hogan gave to help promote the tour, he was asked what advice he would give to the pros who would be driving the circuit as he did. He replied, "Don't get hit by a bus.") Also, Beman set the purse money at a level that would never be quite enough for someone to make a real living unless they won every week. The average winner's share in the first year or two was $20,000.

When the Ben Hogan Company began to have serious financial problems two years after the circuit kicked off, it dropped its sponsorship. The tour was picked up by the Nike Company, which sponsored the circuit until 1999. Then it was taken over by Buy.com, an Internet retailer. This tour was certainly moving with the times.

One way or another, in 1999 the average winner's share of the purse had risen to around $40,000 and in some cases $60,000. The 1999 schedule had thirty seventy-two hole tournaments, with a total purse of over $7 million. By the middle of the year there were seven players who had earned over $100,000. In other words, it is now a circuit on which one can make a decent living. Still, that is never the aim of its players. It is a stepping-stone to the major league, and it has an impressive roster of alumni who have gone off to bigger and better things.

Among the more luminous graduates are Tom Lehman, a British Open winner; Ernie Els, a two-time U.S. Open winner; David Duval and Jim Furyk, both of whom have achieved star status, with Duval's a bit higher. And John Daly, who has become one of the game's most fascinating, and so far, semi-tragic figures.

Daly played on the inaugural Hogan tour, won a tournament—the Utah Classic—and finished ninth on its money list that year. The following year, Daly became a fairy tale figure in golf. Nick Price dropped out of the 1991 PGA Championship, which was being played at the Crooked Stick Golf Club in Carmel, Indiana, because his wife was giving birth to their first child. His spot was taken by Daly, who was the ninth and last alternate. When he got the call that he was in the tournament, Daly drove through the night from his home in Arkansas to make the date. Without a practice round he shot an opening round of 69, followed that with rounds of 67, 69, and 71, and won by three strokes over Bruce Lietzke. Winning a major championship on such short notice is an amazing achievement by itself, and the fact that Daly had virtually no previous experience playing at that level was even more incredible. The tale was capped by Daly's extraordinary power. With a driver he was up to one hundred yards farther than anyone else in the field. What's more, he generated this power with a fantastically long backswing—at its completion the club was almost vertical and pointing at the ground. The swing was obviously under control, it just looked wild, and the average golfer-fan fell for Daly in a minute. Just as all the Joe Hackers had identified with Arnold Palmer's whirlwind swing, so did they identify with Daly's 1990s version.

Daly was one of them, and besides his swing, looked it. His appeal to the so-called blue collar golf crowd—basically public fee golfers, who make up the majority of those who play the game—was augmented by his appearance and manner. A little overweight, shirt creeping out of his pants, a cigarette going regularly, he drank a lot of beer (and whiskey, as was soon discovered), and he gave no sign that he felt he was anyone special. He clearly enjoyed hitting the ball as hard and far as he did, responding delightedly to the raucous pleasure his big hitting gave the gallery. When asked about his power-hitting technique, he said, "I just grip it and rip it." The phrase may not have originated with him, but he gave it great currency and became identified with it. And vice versa. Thanks to the even longer reach of television in the 1990s, Daly became a folk hero even faster than did Arnold Palmer.

However, Daly's rise to fame and fortune—rich endorsement contracts came quickly—soon turned into an ongoing soap opera that, unfortunately, didn't end after the credits were run. Daly came from a troubled background. There was parental alcoholism and angry, destructive tempers, and physical abuse. When he drank or was otherwise distraught, Daly regurgitated his personal history. He broke up hotel rooms and physically abused his wives, of which he had three within an eight-year-period of time (and two children). During the times when he quit drinking, he would compensate or replace that addiction with others.

He ate great quantities of fast food, candy, soda pop. And he gambled heavily, making single bets of as much $400,000 and losing millions in various casinos.

Amazingly, in the midst all the turmoil of his personal life, after his PGA victory Daly still was able to win a couple of tournaments—the 1992 B.C. Open, the 1994 Bell South Classic, and most impressively another major title, the 1995 British Open. He is an extremely talented golfer with a wonderfully soft touch for chipping and putting, something not usually expected of sluggers. When on his game and when he has his personal demons under some control, he is a formidable force on the course.

Unfortunately, after winning the British Open, Daly's behavior became increasingly eccentric and his contract with his original equipment sponsor, Wilson, was canceled. He also lost other lucrative endorsement contracts. Daly was rescued by Ely Callaway, the founder and chairman of his eponymous golf equipment company. Callaway knew something about alcoholism from personal experience and otherwise showed a fine streak of benevolence when he signed Daly to use his equipment. He also paid off a large share of Daly's huge gambling debt. The only stipulation was, Daly had to attend Alcoholics Anonymous meetings and otherwise control his comportment. The relationship lasted less than two years, when Daly finally gave it up saying he could not deal with the restrictions, that he planned to drink and smoke and eat and let the chips falls where they may. A quiet, pleasant fellow when at ease, it would be a blessing if he can survive his private-life problems and give more of his ability to the golf world. The jury is still out on that.

Daly is reminiscent of the old days of the tour, when the players came out of working-class homes, didn't get anywhere near a college degree, drank and smoked, and for exercise hit practice balls and played golf. As the tour grew up, especially in the last third of the century, the profile of tournament pros became very different. They now for the most part come from financially comfortable middle-class homes and grow up with professional instruction and more than adequate practice and playing facilities. They go to college, some even graduate, and they play college and upscale amateur golf before going pro. This evolution reflects how golf as a whole has developed in the United States—from rough-hewn improvisation to the clean-cut predictability of the mall. It is not likely that we'll ever see another Gene Sarazen come along, a hard-up kid from the caddie ranks who has to fight against ethnic prejudice, find his own money, learn the game by the monkey-see-monkey-do method, and depend precariously on the favors of influential people to move up. We are still seeing that sort of thing among some players, in particular those coming from so-called Third World countries—Paraguay's Carlos Franco has been a recent example—but for the most part the postmodern pro golfer comes up via a smooth escalator compared to the freight elevator of the past. Either way, there is still the Game to deal with, and it knows no economic (or ethnic) differences.

Bonkers at the Ryder Cup

The 1991 Ryder Cup Match was held at the Ocean Course on Kiawah Island, one of the outerbank islands off the coast of South Carolina. It is a Pete Dye–designed course, and extremely difficult even under calm conditions, which almost never occur. After two consecutive matches in which the Europeans maintained possession of the cup—they won in 1987 and tied in 1989—the 1991 contest was being hustled in the American press as the "War by the Shore." This was another indication of the proportion to which the competition had been blown up. What had always been billed as a hands-across-the-sea manifestation of golfing espirit de corps was being unveiled for its real self, an out-and-out case of impassioned nationalism. In fact, the Ryder Cup had always been a partisan rivalry. When the match is in Europe, the European galleries do not hold back their glee when an American shot goes awry—cheers abound. When the game is in the United States, American fans return the favor. Nothing wrong with this, it's all perfectly normal, except it was not supposed to be that way according to the propaganda. The us-versus-them disposition was getting all the more transparent now that the playing field had been leveled—leveled, it should be remembered, by an American initiative.

Nationalism is not quite the right term for the European team's attitude which includes representatives from a number of nations, but in the sense that all its players are out to beat the all-mighty Americans, they are unified as a nation of nations. With the establishment of the European Union in the mid-1990s, that identification is even more valid. Anyway, American pros and others criticized the war-by-the-shore rhetoric, and the language was toned down a bit. But that didn't hide the fact that the Americans were hell-bent to defend the honor of their flag and country.

The nationalist ardor was clearly getting the better of the American players, and an episode at Kiawah in 1991 laid it bare. In the singles on the last day of play, Mark Calcavecchia was four up on Colin Montgomerie with four holes to play. It looked like a sure point for the U.S. and an important one in a competition that was coming down to yet another close decision. However, on the fifteenth hole Calcavecchia sprayed a drive into the ocean and lost the hole. He lost the sixteenth when his approach flew over the green and ended up in a poor lie. Then, at the seventeenth hole, he had a truly traumatic time. Truly.

The seventeenth hole is an extremely difficult par three of 197 yards, playing over a goodly stretch of water, and into or against or with or across a whimsical wind. A hard hole. Montgomerie had the honor and hit his tee-shot in the water. Calcavecchia now appeared to have a lock of locks on the match. A good long-iron player, and having grown up in Florida an experienced wind player, he had also proven himself to be a tough-skinned competitor. But at the seventeenth at Kiawah he made as poorly timed a swing with his two-iron as anyone had ever seen him make. The ball traveled about one hundred yards, then dove into the water like a loopy teenager leaping feet first from the high board into the pool. For a tie that would end the match in Calcavecchia's favor, he needed a twenty-inch putt for a double-bogey. He missed it; the ball never touched any part of the hole.

On the eighteenth Calcavecchia drove well but this time he hit too good a long-iron. His approach overshot the green. Montgomerie made the fringe in two on the par-four. Calcavecchia had a difficult lie and pitched to within twelve feet of the hole. Montgomerie got down in two for a par, and Calcavecchia needed to make his putt to halve the hole and win the match. He missed again. The match ended in a tie, a half-point for each side.

Calcavecchia was so distraught that he reeled off the green and made his way to the nearby beach, where he was discovered by his wife and Peter Kostis, his swing coach, on his knees in grief and despair. He was crying hard and hyperventilating and seemed to be on the brink of a nervous breakdown. Calcavecchia got over it, but not right away. He carried the experience with him for a couple of years, and at one point early in his recuperation remarked that he was through with Ryder Cup golf. Too much pressure.

Calcavecchia was not an untried novice in pressure-packed championship golf. Well before the Kiawah debacle he had made a lot of money on the tour with a rather makeshift full swing, but a fine short game and an obstinate competitive drive. When he won the 1989 British Open in a play-off, he closed the deal on the fourth extra hole with a brave five-iron from deep rough far to the right of the fairway. That was for a major championship, a title that gives a player a career leg-up on thousands of aspirants. And yet in the Ryder Cup, a contest that doesn't come close to such a level of importance as a measure of professional substance, Calcavecchia crumbled like soft stone and became sick with shame.

Even Hale Irwin, a hard-nosed veteran and winner of three U.S. Opens, showed Ryder Cup tremors at Kiawah. All even with Bernhard Langer in the final singles match, and his half-point needed for the United States to take back the cup for the first time since 1985, Irwin hit a very loose approach far right of the green, pitched poorly, and two-putted for a bogey. Langer had hit the green in regulation, but hit his first putt, from forty-five feet, six feet past the hole. If he made the putt, the match would be tied and the cup would go back to Europe. Langer hit a good putt, but it didn't take the break. The Americans roared with joy. Or relief?

The Calcavecchia episode, especially, and Irwin's shaky closing suggested, that when it came to the Ryder Cup the Americans had become like the frenzied victims of a raging apostolic preacher. They began shaking in fear of retribution for their sins, for lack of faith, for failing their godhead. It also seemed that the more patriotic fervor injected into the proceedings by the Americans, the worse they played.

And yet, despite the criticism raised by the rifle-rattling, bomb-dropping analogies the Americans put out at Kiawah, at the opening ceremony for the 1995 Ryder Cup Match at the Oak Hill Country Club in Rochester, New York, the PGA of America had a squadron of U.S. Air Force jet fighters roar overhead in conjunction with the playing of the national anthem by a big brass band. Another allusion to armed conflict. And the Europeans won by a point.

In the 1997 Ryder Cup the U.S. team got snookered, or allowed itself to be. The Match was played at the Valderrama Golf Club in Sotogrande, Spain. Seve Ballesteros, the European captain, had lobbied hard for the site. Valderrama is a tricky little layout with some quirky doglegs that take a lot of local knowledge. The American players didn't travel over to play many or any practice rounds, and the Europeans took advantage of their experience with the course's peculiar nooks and crannies—it has staged a European Tour event—to win by a point.

It was surprising that the American side, given all their professions of how honored they were to represent their flag and country, did so little to prepare for Valderrama. Perhaps this laissez-faire attitude reflected a new, less hyperbolic attitude among the new breed of young Americans who were now Ryder Cuppers—Tiger Woods, Phil Mickelson, and David Duval. Indeed, a kind of cool nineties sensibility was in the air prior to the 1999 Ryder Cup Match that found its outlet in an argument over money. Of all things.

When the Ryder Cup became a true competition, it also became a financial bonanza for the PGA of America, which owns, so to say, the American end of the contest. The cost of television rights jumped munificently, and the same marketing and money-generating schemes that were now part of every major championship—the sale of logoed merchandise, corporate hospitality tents and tables, and the like—and much larger live gates, made each Ryder Cup Match a multimillion-dollar business. In the September, 1999, issue of *Golf Digest* magazine, the details of all this were revealed for the first time. It was noted that the 1999 Match would gross some $63 million, out of which the PGA of America was expected to net close to $17.5 million. The Country Club, where the Match was being played, was going to make an estimated $6 million for *hosting* the event. Meanwhile, the players were being given a mere $5,000 for their week—which amounted to a $60,000 blip out of the total. That was not only for playing emotionally charged competitive golf, but included being carted around to a number of dinners and cocktail parties to do public relations work.

When the *Golf Digest* financial report came out—the numbers not denied by the PGA of America or The Country Club—Woods, Duval, Mickelson, and Mark O'Meara, known for his careful attitude about money bringing up the elderly statesman rear, became very outspoken about how the money was being distributed. Woods had the strongest voice, although Duval was most quoted because he referred to the match as "not that big a deal," and claimed that it was only "an exhibition." An exhibition? Sacrilege! The four renegades took the position that the players should be getting a much larger share of the money. They also said they didn't want the money for themselves, but for charities of their own choice. This last was ignored in the first storm of angry criticism sent their way. The atmosphere that grew up around the issue brought to mind a convening of the House Un-American Activities Committee.

Many of the older Ryder Cup players and captain Ben Crenshaw were seriously peeved at the Duval-Woods clique. Some retorted that they would play for nothing for the honor of representing their country. Tom Lehman went so far as to say he would pay out of his own pocket for the privilege. Right! In fact, there had been hints of dissatisfaction with the financial arrangements at least two years before. O'Meara said in 1995 that the players should be getting more money for their efforts. And in 1995 Payne Stewart was quoted in *Golf Illustrated* magazine as saying that with all the money being made "maybe the Ryder Cup players ought to start getting a cut of the action." In the 1999 hubbub team member Stewart, adamantly against Duval and Woods, apparently forgot his 1995 remark, which may have been motivated by the fact that he didn't make the team that year.

The PGA of America responded by saying the money raised from the Ryder Cup went to further junior golf via the First Tee Program, a National Minority College Golf Championship, the PGA Learning Center, and educational programs for its members. However, there was no accounting issued of those outlays, only word-of-mouth. The players were also reminded that its own organization, the PGA Tour, received $2.5 million of the Ryder Cup swag as a kind of fee for services—i.e., the players. It was explained that the players would get access to this money because it was part of the $5 million purse for the World Golf Championship. However, the field for this event includes not only Ryder Cup players but members of the President's Cup teams. Which is to say, the Ryder Cuppers are sharing the Ryder Cup money with players who haven't given service to the Ryder Cup. Even then, they have to play another week's worth of golf to get in on that cash.

Aside from being accused of flag-burning, the attitude of the Duval-Woods group was viewed by some observers as yet another eruption of the selfish, self-absorbed "Me Generation" of the 1990s. Closer to the truth, they were acting out the cynicism of their generation, that came out of knowing, for example, that while the PGA of America's chief operating officer, Jim Awtry, was pledging allegiance to the flag of his nation and the purity of the Ryder Cup competition, he was earning an annual salary of $850,000. A healthy living for someone running a nonprofit association. And then there are the bonuses and perks. Surely such an income was aided by the Ryder Cup's revenue flow. The hypocrisy reached a zenith when, at the closing ceremony of the 1990 match, the PGA of America's president, Will Mann, said, with Orwellian incredulity, that the competition just concluded was "devoid of commercialism and resplendent in its honor." Everyone, even Tom Lehman, snickered at that one. Mann's remark was what could be called stuffing two pounds of prepared image into a one-pound sack of reality.

The real solution to this matter would be to take the money out of the event. Do not sell corporate tents and tables and logoed merchandise. Put host back in its correct context and pay the club where the match is being played a token fee for the honor, and something extra for the cost of preparations and cleanup. The PGA of America could use the live gate and television fee for its pension fund and for programs promoting golf among youth. And, as a show of belief in their flag, all the golf journalists who chided Duval and the others for their crass and craven disrespect should take a week's unpaid vacation in order to cover the contest. Then just let the game begin.

Not a chance. To salve the dissident players's complaints, at the end of 1999 the PGA of America announced a plan to "share the $20 million windfall from Brookline." (Apparently, that was the after-costs net.) Each member of the 1999 team (and presumably those of subsequent teams) would receive $200,000, half going to a charity of the player's choice, the other half earmarked for "a university in support of a PGA of America growth-of-the-game initiative." All the players on the 1999 Ryder Cup team gave half the money to the university where they played their golf. The other $100,000 per man was distributed in ways that showed a fine sensibility for what is really important to them. For example, Ben Crenshaw gave to the West Austin (Texas) Youth Association and Helping Hands Home for Children Foundation and Hospice Austin; Mark O'Meara to the Winnie Palmer Fund/Orlando Regional Health Care Foundation; Phil Mickelson spread his share out among such groups as the Wellness Community-Central Arizona, the Crisis Nursery, the Children's Cancer Center and the Alzheimer's Association. Many gave to churches. In all, the money was well spent, and distributed in places that larger and less subjective corporation-type organizations would not reach. Protest can produce some real value.

Feeling the sting of the criticism about its rental fee, the good and wealthy members of The Country Club also announced it was giving $500,000 to the Brookline (Massachusetts) Community Fund to establish programs aimed at helping children of low-income families. Isn't it interesting that they had to be embarrassed first, or found out, before they made such a donation?

For all that fine giving, however, the PGA of America said nothing about the possibility of raising ticket prices or the cost of corporate hospitality tents or an increased television fee, by which it could easily make up the $2.4 million being given to the players. And nothing was put on paper that the next host of the Ryder Cup will automatically contribute a portion of its take to good works.

Money will remain the axis on which the Ryder Cup spins, and the chances of the television fees going up and the other sources of income escalating are very good based on the exceptionally exhilarating, albeit controversial and revealing, competition that decided the 1999 match.

At least thirty-five thousand tickets were sold for each day's play, far too many for the venue to comfortably hold—The Country Club is a relic of golf's past, built on a relatively small plot of ground made narrower by many stands of old trees. The quarters were cramped.

The guests of the various corporations had access to an open bar all week, and the many public bars scattered around the course did a rousing business among the hoi polloi. There were more than a few drunks roaming the property, and this, combined with a Boston sporting public long known for its rudeness to visiting players and even their own if they do poorly, made for a boisterous atmosphere featuring many crude, profane remarks hurled from the ropes at the European players, in particular at Colin Montgomerie, who is well-known for a thin skin. On the final day, Montgomerie's father was so put off by the barbs aimed at his son that he left his gallery for the presumed sanctity of the clubhouse. On top of all that, the American players, including the normally laconic David Duval, were encouraging the fans with fist-pumping and arm waves signaling them to root more—louder, harder—for the Yanks.

That was the ambiance in the late afternoon of the third and final day of the 1999 Ryder Cup Match, which effectively came down to the seventeenth green in the match between Justin Leonard and Jose Maria Olazabal. Leonard had a putt of about forty-five feet from the front edge of the green for a birdie three. Olazabal had a twenty-five-footer on approximately the same line, also for a birdie. Leonard had pulled even with Olazabal by making a terrific comeback from four down after ten holes. It was a mirror of the entire U.S. team's comeback that day. The United States was four points down going into the singles, and in the history of the competition no team had ever come from that far behind to win or tie. All of which heightened the already volatile situation. Leonard needed only to tie Olazabal to clinch the victory for the United States, which had lost the previous two matches.

Leonard hit his putt perfectly, at exactly the correct speed and on exactly the right line. It curved a tad to the right at the end of its journey above ground, then found the bottom of the cup. Leonard leaped in the air, arms upraised, and almost the entire U.S. team and their wives and caddies, all of whom were greenside watching the action, also leaped high and dashed onto the green toward Leonard. They were yelling, screaming with joy, hugging each other and of course Leonard. Ben Crenshaw got to his knees and kissed the earth. Never mind the tumult and shouting that rose from the huge, jam-packed gallery, which was well into its beer cups by this time of day. The gallery response was natural. The uncontrolled behavior of the American players, their wives and girlfriends, and caddies was one of the worst displays of unprofessional and unsportsmanlike behavior ever seen in golf or any other sport. That it happened in golf, with its long tradition of tasteful decorum, was astonishing.

The American reaction was based on the assumption that Leonard's putt clinched the contest. But it didn't. Olazabal still had a chance. If he made his putt to halve the hole, he could still win the match on the eighteenth, which would give the Europeans an overall tie and allow them to keep the cup. Europe's captain, Mark James, who like all his mates and, it must be said, many Americans was appalled by the demonstration on the seventeenth green, remarked that the American celebrants had stepped in Olazabal's line of putt during their hijinks, "I'd say about thirty times." (By the way, has anyone ever noticed the wives of the players in the dugout of a World Series team or on the bench at the Super Bowl?) It didn't appear that was the case even once; everyone ran along the left side of the green and Olazabal's ball was pretty much in the middle. The real distraction was that the Spaniard had to wait as much as four or five minutes for the celebration by the Americans to end before he could even begin to consider his putt. It was not an unmakeable putt by any stretch of the imagination, especially in that Olazabal is one of the best putters in the game and outstanding under pressure. He won his first Masters, in 1994, without three-putting a green, an astounding feat on the marble-top Alpine slopes of Augusta National.

In this case, Olazabal couldn't cover Leonard's putt. He made a worthy effort, he didn't leave it short, and when it missed his match and the Match were indeed over. Leonard conceded the last hole to Olazabal, so their match ended up a tie, but only for the record. The U.S. team won the match by a point, 14½ to 13½.

The consensus of the American celebrants on their behavior at the seventeenth green was that it was unfortunate, it shouldn't have happened, but it was an honest outburst of emotion that was "understandable and forgivable," as Tom Lehman put it. As in "kids will be kids." But they weren't kids, they were grown men and professionals. The celebration and their reaction to criticism of it afterward showed how desperate the American players were to prove their superiority. It also reflected how certain they were that they were the best, win or lose. Not even thinking to give Olazabal a proper chance to respond to Leonard's putt was an act of supreme and overbearing arrogance.

Quite a transformation in American golf's attitude—or at least that of its elite players—in the eighty-six years since Francis Ouimet holed a crucial putt on that very same seventeenth green at The Country Club. It vaulted him into the play-off for the U.S. Open that he won over Harry Vardon and Ted Ray. After proudly but modestly accepting congratulations all around, Ouimet walked across the street from the club to have supper at home with his mother and father.

Sons of Champions

Speaking of having advantages, in trying to succeed in modern-day professional golf one would think the children of champion golfers would have a leg-up on other players. That was not the case at all until the last decade of the twentieth century, when we began to see a few sons of champions have a better time following in their famous fathers' footsteps.

All of history is littered with sad stories of children of famous parents who could not handle the burden. Golf has not had such doleful episodes as those of Winston Churchill's or Franklin D. Roosevelt's offspring, for instance, but it was not easy being Jack Nicklaus's first son, or Julius Boros's, or Walter Hagen's. Hagen, Jr., had a pat response to the many people who told him, when he was a young man playing national-level amateur golf and for the Notre Dame University team, that he wasn't anywhere near the golfer his father was: "That's right, and neither was anyone else."

Hagen the Younger was dealing with a standard reaction to the son of a champion—the expectation that he should be as good as, if not better than, his dad. It is of course totally unfair, even more so in golf because the father plays to a very high standard much longer than a baseball or basketball player, which makes direct comparison easier. We have seen many children of long-retired major league baseball and football players become extremely successful in the same sport because they didn't have to go up against their fathers. By comparison, when Jack Nicklaus had his wonderful victory in the 1986 Masters, at age forty-six, his eldest son, Jack, Jr., was a prime twenty-five-year-old with aspirations to play in the pros. When Jackie, Jr., played in tournaments he would draw big galleries, sometimes because people wanted to see if he had the same stuff as Pop, other times because Pop was in the gallery and everyone wanted to see him. A tough situation for the son.

Also, a lot of fathers didn't (or don't) comprehend how uncomfortable the situation can be for their children. More than a few compounded the problem by giving them the same first name. Finally, with their high standards in mind plus their own ego and pride, fathers have made too great demands on their sons. Sometimes not subtly. Ed Sneed, a former tour player, recalled once playing golf with Jack Nicklaus and his son, Jackie; when the boy hit a wildly bad drive his father berated him sharply in front of the rest of the group.

The behavior of tour pro fathers, especially the winners of major championships, went through some welcome changes as the twentieth century wound to a close. Gary Nicklaus, the second youngest son of the famous man, struggled for a number of years to make it to the PGA Tour. He failed to get through the Q-School eight times in a row, played a number of small tours around the world and on U.S. mini-tours. Through it all he was encouraged by his father (and given some financial support, too, it must be said). In 1999 it all paid off when, at age thirty-one, Gary made the grade with a smashing final-round 63 in the Q-School qualifying tournament to earn an exemption onto the 2000 PGA Tour. Later that year, Gary lost in a play-off to Phil Mickelson for the Bell South Classic, in Atlanta, Georgia.

Had Gary Nicklaus won the Bell South event he would have been only the third son of an American major championship winner to be victorious on the PGA Tour. The first was the youngest son of Julius Boros, Guy, who won the 1996 Greater Vancouver (Canada) Open. Then came Brent Geiberger, adopted son of 1966 PGA champion, Al, who won the 1999 Canon Greater Hartford (Connecticut) Open. Dave Stockton, twice a PGA champion, has a son by the same name who has not yet won but has had some very good showings on the PGA Tour, and one expects there will be more such success stories as times goes on and the attitudes of fathers toward their athletic sons (and daughters) continue to change.

Another Incredible Equipment Fuss

Yet another equipment technology argument developed during this decade. In early 1998 F. Morgan "Buzz" Taylor, newly named president of the USGA, came out aggressively against metal drivers made from titanium, the miracle metal of the moment. USGA research found that the face of these clubs produced a "springlike effect" which, according to Rule 4-1d in Appendix II is the *Rules of Golf*, was illegal. Briefly, the USGA said the club face, which is quite thin, depresses when contacting the ball, then springs back in time to cast the ball forward and produce distances disproportionate to the club head speed the golfer has generated.

The equipment makers sharply questioned the USGA's testing methods, pointing out that the club face on the old persimmon drivers also compressed at impact and then returned to its original plane. They also noted independent tester's reports that the golf ball doesn't stay on the club face long enough for any springlike effect to help propel the ball forward any farther than normal. If at all. The manufacturers threatened to sue the USGA, and the USGA said it was prepared to fight the suit; it was doing well in the stockmarket and had ample funds to cover the legal fees. Taylor then did a bulldog number, saying, "Our [the USGA] franchise is to preserve and protect the game's ancient and honorable traditions. I intend to do that, and there's not one lawyer in the world who is going to get in our way of doing that."

In one of those exquisite little ironies, a few years earlier Taylor was a partner in a company producing the Polara golf ball, which the USGA outlawed because it was self-correcting in flight. Polara sued, and got an out-of-court settlement for around $1 million.

The spring-effect issue was met head-on at a special open meeting the day before play began in the 1998 U.S. Open at the Olympic Club, in San Francisco. The USGA said it would explain its position. There was a prefight atmosphere in the room, as many chief executives of major equipment companies were on hand. But there was no fight. President Taylor was on the dais, but kept (or was kept) a silent partner. David Fay, executive secretary of the USGA, opened with a long, somewhat tortured statement in which he averred that the USGA believed in its testing procedure and would go forward with it. But, he added, most pertinently, all titanium drivers currently in the marketplace would never be declared illegal. They were grandfathered in perpetuity, like the Ping irons with nonconforming grooves.

The USGA backed off on that one, but said it had developed a new way to test golf balls for their liveliness and trajectory control. More trouble. The USGA's test for initial velocity—how fast the ball is going immediately after it leaves the club face—would involve shooting the ball from a gunlike device against a metal plate. Here again, the manufacturers were upset and threatened a legal confrontation. They said the new method was unrealistic and just the opposite of what actually happens. A golf ball is hit by a moving object, it does not fly into an inert one. The manufacturers complained that by changing the testing method, many if not all of their products could be nonconforming, and would cost millions for recalling, redesigning, and retooling. On this and the club face issues, little more was heard for some months. A sense was growing that some cooler heads were beginning to prevail at the USGA. Then again, the association had built a massive new addition to its headquarters meant exclusively for equipment research and testing. Perhaps to justify the expense, in early 2000 the USGA banned a new Callaway driver for having too springy a face. At that, the club proved to increase distance by only five or six yards, but also proved to be less accurate and those pros who had tried it quickly retired it from their bags. It might behoove the USGA to fully test new equipment, in the field, before making its determinations.

One conclusive disclosure came out of the meeting at the Olympic Club. The USGA admitted that distance was its only real concern, and that the ball was going too far *only for tournament professionals.* The USGA didn't seem to mind how far the average golfer hit the ball, but was prepared to spend millions in legal fees to prevent 250 to 300 golfers, out of the millions who play, from hitting the ball too far.

One wonders, first of all, if the USGA is not being delinquent in risking money in the stock market that it takes in from dues, the U.S. Open, and all other sources in the name of servicing the Game. What if the market crashed? Would the American golfer be indemnified and continue to get the services the association is obliged to provide? To the point, in early 2000 the United States Tennis Association announced that it had lost considerable money in the stock market and would have to cut back on or eliminate a number of its various regional programs.

Second of all, in the 1998 U.S. Open, at least two-thirds of the field were using titanium drivers with "springy" faces, including the two longest hitters in the game, Tiger Woods and John Daly, but the winner was the relatively short-hitting Lee Janzen. That would hardly indicate that the club face and the ball are destroying the integrity of the game, and that distance is the be-all, end-all of the game. In early 2000, Tiger Woods won six tournaments in a row, and during that time he dropped to sixth place in the driving statistics gathered by the PGA Tour. In other words, like all super-long hitters of the ball, once they get into the big-time competition they learn that accuracy is more vital than distance and they throttle back their swings for more ball-flight control. It has been ever thus. One would think the USGA, as golf's "guiding light," would recognize that and legislate accordingly.

It is interesting that the concern over the club face and the ball had been exclusively an American one. The R&A has pointedly stayed out of the controversy and has shown some irritation with the USGA for its pestering. Either the R&A doesn't think there is a concern, or it has not done well on the stock exchange.

For Women Everywhere, the Game Is Over Here

Until 1979 the only place where a woman who wanted to play professional tournament golf could do so was in the United States. In that year, the European women's pro tour was formed. But it has never matched the LPGA circuit in the amount of prize money offered or the level of competition. As a result, the foreign presence on the LPGA circuit has been so strong that it could be seen as more of an international than an American arena. On the other hand, a good many of the top foreign women on the LPGA circuit have honed their games via scholarships at American universities and competition in American college golf. What's more, the great majority of women on the best circuit in the game are Americans, and they give the British and Australian and Asian golfers exactly what they come for, a good game.

Patriotic salutations aside, the foreign presence on the LPGA circuit offers a window on how women's golf has developed around the world. In the 1980s the Swedish government began the same type of national program for training young golfers that it did to develop tennis stars such as Bjorn Borg. The payoff began in the 1990s, among men and women. On the men's side, Jesper Parnevik has made the biggest impression to date, almost winning the British Open in 1998 and well over $4 million on the PGA Tour and four victories. But Swedish women have been the most prolific graduates of their country's program. The first to make good on the LPGA circuit was Liselotte Neumann, who won the 1988 U.S. Open and captured twelve LPGA events through 1999. Then came Helen Alfredsson and Annika Sorenstam. Alfredsson, contrary to stereotypical Swedish character, is a rather high-strung, chatty young woman. This may account for her winning only four times on the LPGA Tour from 1992 through 1999 (if one accepts the hypothesis that to play golf well you need a muted, even dull personality). However, one of those victories was a major—the 1993 Dinah Shore.

Sorenstam has been the most successful of the Swedish women pros, a superstar to the extent that she can be headlined by her first name only. Of course, there aren't that many Annikas around. Sorenstam completed her golf training with a scholarship at the University of Arizona, where she won seven individual titles and the NCAA national individual championship. Tall and slender, and moderately outgoing, she hits the ball quite far with a classic swing. She turned pro in 1994 and won the U.S. Open in 1995 and 1996. She has won over seventeen tournaments in the U.S. and in 1997 earned a single-year record for a woman—$1.2 million in prize money.

Japan and Korea have sent a number of outstanding women to the

American tour. Japan's Ayako Okamoto was a consistent contender in the eighties and won seventeen LPGA Tour events between 1982 and 1992. South Korea's Se Ri Pak came to the LPGA in the late nineties and was an immediate sensation. In 1998 her first year on the circuit, she won the U.S. Open and LPGA Championships. However, Asian golfers get tremendous pressure from their governments, commercial sponsors, and even parents to succeed or continue their success, and their national media hounds them incessantly. Pak suffered all that in spades after her tremendous 1998 season, for which she was hailed as the Pride of Korea. But when her game went off in early 1999, everyone at home, from Samsun to her father, was on her case to play better or else. No one specified what the *else* would be, but the twenty-two-year-old golfer finally told everybody to ease off. When they didn't she took up permanent residence in the United States. Not long after, she won two tournaments and regained her sanity. An inscrutable turn. One would expect the ever upbeat, even frenetic American world of sports to be more unnerving than the presumably placid bosom of the Orient.

In 1996 Karrie Webb became the next outstanding Australian woman after Jan Stephenson to make good in America. In her first year on the LPGA circuit Webb won just over $1 million and was such a quick success story that she too soon was burdened with the "honor" of being called one of the best players to never win a major. It didn't take her all that long. She won the 1999 du Maurier Classic for her first. Webb is an attractive athlete with a fine swing, good power, and considerable determination. She could become the next Mickey Wright. The trouble is (or was?), she seems to be of the same personality type as the great Wright—a demeanor on the golf course, which she termed her "office"—of a CPA. Early in 2000, however, after winning her first four tournaments, Webb apparently had a mild metamorphosis, learning to smile a bit and otherwise become more personable. Public relations is no small matter in the promotion and growth of women's golf, not to mention in other areas in life—and Webb is learning the lesson.

In 1987 Britain's Laura Davies won the U.S. Women's Open and the next year joined the LPGA circuit. Quite large physically, she hits the ball farther than any other woman golfer ever has. Like John Daly, Davies is also a power hitter with a fine feel for the short game. Since coming on the LPGA circuit she has won sixteen tournaments and four majors titles.

Also like Daly, Davies has a gambler's tooth, so to say. Horses, mainly. But she has considerable control over the off-course aspects of her life. She is a very pleasant woman, maybe even too sweet-tempered to become the superstar winner her ability would suggest for her.

Even with the Senior PGA Tour cutting into their action, the LPGA was doing all right. It was given a big boost when Karsten Solheim gave something back to the game after all his success as an equipment manufacturer. He sponsored the Solheim Cup, a woman's version of the Ryder Cup Match. As it happens, much of the European team has been composed of women who regularly play the LPGA circuit, so there is something a bit repetitive about the competition. It doesn't really distinguish which "nation" has the best players, if that is important to anyone. Nonetheless, the Solheim Cup is a worthy addition to the game's calendar of events.

The Futures Tour, which began as a privately run women's mini-tour out of Tampa, Florida, in 1981, became the official development tour of the LPGA in 1999. Like the Buy.com, nee Hogan, Tour, the Futures has been true to its title. It has been a training ground for such star players as Laura Davies, Donna Andrews, Meg Mallon, Michelle McGann, and Karrie Webb. In 1999 the Futures Tour consisted of some eighteen tournaments, with $1 million in total prize money. Players from all over the world ride the circuit and stop in towns and cities such as Lima, Ohio, and Morgantown, West Virginia. It is expected to turn out many more outstanding women players over the years.

On the administrative side, the LPGA had another round of musical chairs in its commissioner's office when Bill Black didn't turn out well. However, he was replaced by Charlie Mecham in 1990, who was just the ticket. An older man with an avuncular style, he had been for many years the chairman of the board of Taft Broadcasting, which had been involved in sponsoring LPGA events. Mecham had good contacts and relationships with many important people in the game. Also, as the father of two enterprising daughters, he had a good understanding of and appreciation for the situation of women trying to participate in professional golf.

The LPGA Tour aside for the moment, there was a large influx of new women golfers in the late eighties, part of the game's big spurt in general interest. The development was trumpeted by the National Golf Foundation, the game's national chamber of commerce. What wasn't mentioned, though, was that not long after they got into golf many of these women got out of it. For one thing, they found that the game was harder than they expected. It didn't come nearly as quickly as tennis or racquetball, if at all. But women were also turning away from golf because of the continuing difficulty they had breaking down male chauvinist attitudes in a male-dominated game. For all the efforts to correct this situation, including lawsuits won, women still have a difficult time getting equal treatment in terms of tee times and other conventional privileges at private clubs. Old attitudes persist about women playing too slowly, which is not a general rule, and old-fashioned machos even point out that their presence on the course intrudes on such male freedoms as telling dirty jokes, cursing, and relieving themselves beside a tree. One arrogant male member of a club in the East responded to women's complaints about the latter by telling them they were free to do the same. The battle of the sexes pip-squeaks on. Charles Mecham said he would take the LPGA commissioner's job for only a five-year term, and in 1996 he was replaced by Jim Ritts, another young marketing and communications type. Ritts was entirely satisfactory in his work, but in an unexplained surprise move he abruptly resigned in 1999. His replacement was another youngish man, Ty Votaw, a lawyer who also has a degree in journalism. He came up through the LPGA organization, having been hired by Mecham as general counsel. Votaw also served as liaison between the players, sponsors, and the media, and eventually rose to develop and manage such programs as the Solheim Cup.

If timing means anything, Votaw's is very good. He was in place when Julie Inkster delighted golfworld with a great 1999 season. Also, Nancy Lopez remained a gallery favorite through the end of the 1990s, her third decade on the circuit. She was still winning tournaments in the nineties—seven, including an LPGA Championship. But she is in her forties and has three daughters to raise; her time at the top is drawing nigh. She will probably go down as the Sam Snead of women's golf, in that she has never been able to win the U.S. Open. Every time she tries she is rooted on enthusiastically and sympathetically, but as the years go by her chances grow less likely. She may not make that goal but, as with Snead, it won't diminish her contributions to the game and the long-term excellence of her play. She gave everyone a good long show, and although an intense competitor, she always found a moment to flash her wonderful smile and the occasional tear.

Beth Daniel won seven tournaments in 1990 alone (fourteen, all told, in the decade), but here again a splendid golfer has so far been unable to win the U.S. Women's Open, which remains a bellwether of success in golf.

Patty Sheehan had a big decade in the nineties, winning fifteen times, including four majors, and finally the U.S. Open after a number of disappointing almosts. In fact, just to make sure, she won two U.S. Opens. Sheehan is a feisty, emotional player reminiscent of Billie Jean King, the tennis champion. She is fun to watch for the quality of her game, but also for her emotional expression.

Betsy King is a bit dry and programmed in her approach to the game. Her career was winding down by the end of the century, but she was a big winner for over a decade, with thirty-one victories on the LPGA tour from 1984 through 1999, including six majors. She is still the tour's all-time leading money winner, at over $6 million.

Dottie Pepper, one of the best of the Furman University scholarship golfers (Daniels and King were others), is a woman with a rather biting personality that matches the quality of her golf. She won thirteen tournaments and over $5 million in the nineties.

But the woman who captured everyone's heart as the century closed was Julie Inkster. From the San Francisco Bay area, she was a four-time collegiate All-American at San Jose State University (another shining example of Title IX at work), and she won three consecutive U.S. Women's Amateur Championships. She won her first professional tournament five starts into her career, which began in 1983. She won thirteen times in the eighties including three majors, and she continued to play well even when she became the mother of two.

Married to Brian Inkster, a golf professional who was influential in the early development of her game, the couple had their first child in 1990 and another in 1994. Julie's tournament schedule was cut back for the sake of motherhood, but she kept her game up enough to win four times between 1991 and 1998. In 1999, though, she extended herself. She won her second U.S. Open with a splendid finish. Then, less than a month later, she won the LPGA Championship in a closely fought battle that she concluded with a stunning run of golf—eagle, birdie, birdie—for a final-round 65. She won by four strokes over Liselotte Neumann.

Nothing could have better suited the image the LPGA was trying so hard to develop or solidify, and the one it wanted so badly to submerge, than Inkster's superb play to close out the century. Here was a woman all the way, an athletic thirty-nine-year-old raising two preteen daughters and responding to championship pressure with fine golf swings, firmly hit shots, clutch putts, and a worldly perspective on life. As she strode the last fairway in the LPGA Championship, she sent winks of pleasure and joy to her family on the sidelines.

Stirring and Straining Seniors

Throughout the bulk of his career, Jack Nicklaus had been a colossus in the game: his style of golf and manner of being were so overwhelming that he was never a very sympathetic figure. Which is what made his performance in the 1998 Masters so poignant. At fifty-eight, Nicklaus was showing his age. He was a bit gaunt, the skin looser around his neck and jowls. The sun had done its usual job on a blond. He was showing the strains of business problems, of raising a big family, all those thousands of hours on practice tees and putting greens, and of dealing with the brutal reality of a great athlete on the downward slide of the slope. There was also a serious problem with his hip, which would be replaced within the year. You could see him struggling to walk the steep hills of Augusta, a slight give with every step that would have been more pronounced if he weren't so proud. After the tournament he would say, of course, that he was fine. But he wasn't.

Yet, through three rounds of the 1998 Masters he was very much in contention. He was only five shots off the lead, going into the last round along with Tiger Woods, who wasn't born until ten years after Jack had won his first Masters, and Colin Montgomerie, who was a mere twelve-year-old at the time. Nicklaus began his fourth round with a par, and when he made a fine birdie from a greenside bunker at the par-five second hole, his name moved up a notch closer on the leader board. A familiar buzz hummed through the gallery. On the third hole, he took the place by storm. His approach to the par-four spun back off the green some five yards, from where he hit a soft pitch-and-run that curled into the hole for another birdie. The roar from the huge gallery surrounding the green was, excuse the hyperbole, on the order of Beethoven's choral movement. It brought tears to some eyes.

Nicklaus went on to shoot a 68, two shots better than Woods and Montgomerie, and he tied for sixth. He didn't have to win. He had long before validated his place at the pinnacle of the game. This was a curtain call, one rich in emotion.

About a year into his career on the Senior PGA Tour, someone asked Lee Trevino how it was out there. He said, "Man, it's like picking gold bricks up off the ground." It wasn't quite that easy, but he did very well right from the start. In his first full year on the circuit, 1990, Trevino won seven tournaments, including the U.S. Senior Open (defeating Nicklaus by one stroke), and just over $1 million.

In between his last victory on the PGA Tour, the 1984 PGA Championship, at age forty-five, and his start on the senior circuit, Trevino did television commercials for cars and golf equipment and was an analyst on network golf telecasts. A lot of his money had been lost through poor management, but he was getting well again on that score, largely because of his new young wife, half his age, who handled the finances. They began a new family with a daughter, born in 1989, and a son, in 1992.

Trevino had always been a ball beater, a range rat, but after forty years it finally got to him. In 1994 he needed an operation to correct a bulging disk in his neck. He came out of the surgery with a piece of metal permanently positioned near his right shoulder. He laughed as he said he'd never be able to brush his teeth normally again. "Gotta bend more at the waist," he said, but he was not about to quit playing. He revamped his swing a bit to accommodate the new neckwear and won four tournaments from 1995 through 1998. Still, there was more gray hair peeking out from under his cap, on hilly courses on hot days he was sometimes slumping to the finish line, and he wasn't the competitive threat he had been. He had been at the top for a long time, and would always reflect an archetypal American success story: minority kid born without a pot, never knew his father, weathered the slurs of discrimination, but had talent and nerve and was willing to work very hard to make something more of himself than his birthright promised.

Arnold Palmer thickened through the chest, and his old hammer-swing had gotten much shorter; it was more labored than vehement. He had surgery for prostrate cancer, one of his daughters had earlier dealt with cancer, and in 1999 his wife, Winnie, died of the disease. The late nineties were not a good time for Palmer, and they were made worse by the scores he was shooting. Arnold's golf is very important to him. Some scores were terribly embarrassing to him, especially the 89, 87 at his beloved Augusta National in 1997. Whenever it was suggested that he might be diminishing the memory of his vigor, his power, and his charisma and that he might do well to retire from competition, Palmer became irritated. But in 1998 he did begin to discuss it. Like a great actor on a farewell tour, Palmer made his last appearances at the U.S. Open, at Oakmont, and the British Open, at St. Andrews, all heavy laden with teary emotion. The ovations for him were long and deeply felt. It had been a very long run, and he was still much revered.

With those giants of the game on the wane, the senior tour began to feel the strain. Television ratings were never all that high in the first place, but now they were dipping down where the LPGA was living. All of this, paradoxically, as the quality of play got even better than it had been. The new old blood coming on had prepared by continuing to play the junior tour. Hale Irwin won his fourth U.S. Open in 1990, at the age of forty-five, continued to play the PGA Tour for the next five years, and when he got to the senior circuit looked as trim and hard as the defensive back he had been at the University of Colorado. He was almost in a world of his own. In his first five years on the senior circuit he won twenty-five tournaments.

Hale Irwin, Tom Watson, Tom Kite, and Lanny Wadkins, among others who just slid right over to the seniors circuit in excellent physical condition, with no sabbatical from competition, dissipated the nostalgia factor on which the tour originally thrived. The newcomers to the senior tour hadn't been away, and so they weren't missed. What's more, they were so physically vigorous one thought a check of birth certificates might be in order. There wasn't any sense of the human vulnerability among them that had been part of the original appeal of the circuit.

For a couple of years Irwin's main opposition was Gil Morgan, a very quiet, undemonstrative Oklahoman who had a high-mediocre career on the junior tour. Oddly, although a trained optician he didn't discover a serious problem with his eyesight until he was near the end of his junior tour career. After getting it corrected, close to when he joined the seniors, he began holing every putt within view. He won fifteen tournaments in his first four years on the senior circuit (1996 to 1999).

Before Irwin and Morgan muscled in on the action, Chi-Chi Rodriguez, Jim Colbert, and Dave Stockton had fine runs. Chi-Chi was very popular, a box-office attraction for his hat-over-the-hole and sword-brandishing gestures and little-guy-as-winner personality. He won the last nine of his total of twenty-two senior tournament victories in the early 1990s, though, and finally wore himself out from an incredibly heavy schedule of exhibitions and tournaments. In 1998 he had a minor heart attack. Through his Chi-Chi Rodriguez Foundation, which is not necessarily for golfers, Rodriguez had long been active in helping young people from difficult backgrounds get a leg-up on the world.

Colbert and Stockton won nineteen and fourteen tournaments each in the nineties. They put on a good show of golf, and Colbert in particular exhibited some personality, with his bucket hat pulled low on his head and a misleading swagger step—he is not an arrogant man. The problem was, except for Chi-Chi, the Irwins and Morgans and Colberts and others didn't have any electricity, or candle power. They were nice guys, very good players, but lacked that certain je ne sais quoi.

It was hoped that Watson, Kite, and Wadkins might perk up the party when they came aboard in 1999 and 2000, especially Watson. But after winning the third tournament for which he was eligible, the 1999 Bank One Championship, Watson strangely disappeared from view. That he will be the catalyst for a revival of interest in the senior tour is probably wishful thinking. The gallery never really warmed to Watson, and when he became a self-appointed moral guardian in the Gary McCord–Masters debacle, he probably turned golf fans off entirely.

McCord had become a great favorite of television golf viewers for his faintly irreverent wisecracking style of reportage. However, it was not much appreciated by the masters of Augusta National, who had for a couple of years been trying to get him removed from the telecast of their tournament. They got their chance during the CBS telecast of the 1991 Masters. McCord grew satirical on the excessive speed of the greens, always a sensitive subject at Augusta National, at one point suggesting the greens had been given a coat of bikini wax. He also said so many guys were three-putting that the body bags were beginning to stack up in the locker room. Something like that. The cloistered members of Augusta National probably didn't know what bikini wax was, but the body bags reference was clear and definitely in bad taste—enough for the members to command McCord's dismissal from the booth.

But just to make sure, Tom Watson took it upon himself to write a letter to CBS that also went public, saying, in effect, that the sacrilegious McCord was desecrating the sacred font of golf, was tearing at the fabric of common decency, and that he should never again set foot on the grounds, let alone report on play from one of the club's exalted towers. Something like that. In other words, he wanted McCord fired from his job. Many golf fans do indeed love the Masters and the Augusta National Golf Club with a passion, but a sanctimonious prig (who, it might be added, was caught in a dalliance that ended his long first marriage) can take a walk.

Still, for all the lack of a charismatic superstar and the rise of a vital group of new young stars reviving an intense interest in the junior tour, the senior circuit is not likely to go away. It reaches a much-prized de-mographic market and gives corporations who can't get a place on the main stem a billboard for exposing their logo and entertaining clients. That is how American professional tournament golf got started in the first place, as a venue for selling something else, and the concept still works.

The Norman Inquest

In the 1990s Greg Norman made the case for a reversal of the dictum that form follows function. In the parabola of his competitive career, as it wound down at the end of the twentieth century, he proved that function follows form, that you only have to look like a winner to be perceived as one. The proof, if you will, was in the pudding of Norman's collapses in the face of conquest. Two, in particular.

In the 1990 British Open Norman started the third round tied for the lead with Nick Faldo, with whom he was paired. Everyone was looking forward to a smashing duel in the Nicklaus-Watson class. Faldo was at the top of his game and being touted as the equivalent of Ben Hogan for his resolute control of his golf ball and his emotions. Norman was the long-ball-hitting Australian with flash, always threatening to become a great winner but not quite there, yet. Maybe this time?

The Faldo-Norman duel turned into a dud. It was all Faldo, no Nor-man. On a beautifully sunny and calm day, when St. Andrews Old Course was a patsy, Norman shot a 75 to Faldo's solid 68. Faldo won his third British Open; Norman finished back in the pack.

Then there was the colossal blow up at the 1996 Masters, when Nor-man took a six-shot lead over Faldo into the last round, but shot a 78 to

Faldo's 67. Faldo won by five over Norman. Blowup may not be quite the right way to describe Norman's performance. It suggests one disastrous shot or hole that upended his equilibrium or one fantastic shot by his opponent at the proper moment that changed the momentum. No, it was a slow shot-by-shot, hole-by-hole disintegration, the Chinese water torture dripped out on the magnificent greensward of Augusta National. He just hit a lot of ordinary shots, missed greens and couldn't get up and down for his pars, misaligned a lot of putts—kind of sleepwalked through the day. There was not a hint of the swashbuckling fighter of sharks, flyer of fast jets, and driver of fast cars. The only zip he showed was in his practice swings before each shot, hard swipes, as though he were trying to unglue his ligature.

In the press room afterward, Norman's remarks about what happened were measured. He felt no anger or remorse, only disappointment as he gave a fatalistic shrug and uttered the game's most enduring proverb, "That's golf." He said that the loss was not the end of the world, he would get up the next morning and have breakfast and go about his life, which was a good one. His children and their children's children would never have to worry about having a roof over their heads. He felt fortunate he could still contend in major championships and that maybe next year it would be his turn to come through. Norman had been reading a book on Zen and the martial arts. It seemed the Zen part made the deepest impression on him. He was as calm as Buddha. Well and good. It is only a game, there are more important things in the world, starting with your family. Yet, there was a sense that Norman was indulging in a kind of coverup, that he was in deep denial about his inability to handle ultimate competitive pressure. Some in the pressroom would have liked to see him throw a chair, beat his head against a wall, *show* what he *really felt*. He must have been peeved, at least. Maybe when he writes his autobiography.

Norman obviously did some excellent playing during his prime years. His victory in the 1994 Players Championship was outstanding. He set a scoring record of 264, twenty-four under par, on an exceptionally strong layout. With a 267 Norman set another winning-score record in taking his second British Open victory, in 1993. Of his two victories in official majors, this was his most convincing. Faldo gave him a go for it, and he stayed the course. Norman won the Doral Ryder Open three times on another of the best tests in the game, in two of those victories overpowering the course and field—twenty-four under par (1993) and twenty under (1996). Four times between 1988 and 1995 Norman had the lowest stroke average on the PGA Tour, and in 1986, 1990, and 1995, he was the leading money winner on the circuit.

There was so much good playing in that record that Norman's collapses in majors are perplexing. It is generally called choking, but that term suggests a fear of winning (or losing) so great you can't take a breath. It didn't seem Norman was afraid to win, he just kind of seized up, froze mentally and then physically, when it came to closing the deal. Norman was often criticized as a one-dimensional player. That is, when in a tight spot he invariably hit the ball as hard as he could when a bit of finesse might have served him and the situation better. It was as if he felt the force generated from a hard swing would unfreeze him. So many misses to the right suggest he could not get the necessary meltdown.

The major championships are generally accepted as conclusive measure of a player's greatness. Norman did not come up to that, in the end. Nonetheless, on the strength of coming close to it, he became one of the richest of professional athletes through endorsements, the creation of his own line of products (clothing, perfume, wine, restaurants), course architecture, huge fees for exhibitions and tournament appearances, and prize money ($12.5 million through 1999 on the U.S. tour). Should he give the money back? Not on your life. More power to him for making out so well on a record scant in comparison to a Nicklaus, Palmer, Hogan, Snead— only eighteen wins on the US PGA Tour and two majors. He marketed his image to a tee.

On the (PGA Tour) Waterfront

In 1993 PGA Tour, Inc. had gross receipts from all its revenue sources of $236 million and a $71 million reserve fund. Quite a growth curve from the days when the wives of the pros were hustling sponsors to add $500 or a $1,000 to a tournament purse. The modern PGA Tour's income derives from numerous marketing and operational undertakings, aside from its main function. The circuit itself brought in the biggest share of the total, but a lot was derived from such things as the Tournament Players

Club (TPC) courses. These public and semi-private clubs were designed and constructed by an arm of the PGA Tour and in most cases operated by another arm of the organization. There are also TPC golf schools, a television production division and a publishing division, and retail golf shops in airports. There is also income from the sale of television rights to its tournaments and corporate affiliations, as in "Delta, the Official Airline of the PGA Tour."

The administrative organization that created and oversees all that business has grown apace. The headquarters offices in Ponte Vedra, Florida, are well staffed in numbers. The salaries of the highest executive that are known are commensurate to the wealth that has been created. No one knows about the bonuses. When Deane Beman left the job only a very, very few knew the extent of his retirement package. Rumors abounded that it was very, very substantial, and perhaps ongoing.

A lot of hard, detailed information about the tour's finances were not well known, or known at all by the players. However, the purse money kept going up and everyone seemed satisfied with the way things were. Besides, the players had enough to do keeping their game sharp enough to stay out there. To get involved in any in-depth scrutiny of their organization would surely have had a negative impact on their golf game.

There was one exception among the players, one who was not too reticent to ask some pertinent questions. In 1998 Danny Edwards, a five-time winner on the tour, began to make waves. Edwards had more or less quit the tour for a time to found a golf grip company, Royal, that became a nice success. It eventually merged with the Precision Company, a maker of shafts. After the merger and the new company was up and running, Edwards, the president and chief operating officer, began to play the tour again. He also began to vociferously and passionately question the workings of the tour's administration, in particular where the money went. He wondered why the players weren't playing for even bigger purses, given all the money the tour was generating. He put together figures showing that on a ratio basis, the PGA pros were among the lowest earners in major league sports. He noted that the PGA Tour returns only fifteen percent of its revenues to the players, while football, basketball, baseball, and hockey players get approximately sixty percent. Edwards also noted that every major-league baseball player who gets into at least one game in a season receives a check at the end of that season for some $70,000 as his share of the baseball card revenues the league brings in. He asked why the PGA Tour players didn't have the same arrangement for its cards. A lot of the pros didn't even know that program existed. Edwards also wondered aloud why the tour pros did not have a voice, an actual vote, on the hiring and firing of the commissioner and how much he was paid, and for who sat on the tour's important policy board.

Edwards had a lot more questions, and to give them some sort of official basis, in 1998 he formed the Tournament Players Association (TPA). He was joined by Larry Rinker, an eighteen-year tour member, and Mark Brooks, another tour veteran and the 1996 PGA champion, who served as officers. A few other tour players joined the TPA at the outset, but not enough to make it seem like much of a threat to the status quo. No marquee players joined who could give the group higher visibility. It appeared as if the TPA was just a small band of no-name bottomfeeders, middle-of-the-pack or lower grinders who didn't make much difference to the popularity or fortunes of the PGA Tour but wanted to be paid like stars. The group was given short shrift as whiners.

But Edwards was determined, and using his business expertise and experience as a tour player, he forged ahead. He began writing letters to commissioner Tim Finchem pointing out areas of contention. At the Hartford tournament in the summer of 1998, Edwards confronted the commissioner face-to-face on the practice putting green and asked him if he thought every player in a tournament should get some compensation even if he doesn't make the thirty-six-hole cut. It was an idea proposed a few years earlier by Tom Lehman and Rick Fehr. Finchem hadn't responded then, and in 1998 in Hartford, told Edwards that he did not think the players were for the idea. Edwards took a poll of players later that day and found that ninety percent of them were in favor of some compensation. A battle was underway.

The TPA was mainly interested in getting a full disclosure of the PGA Tour's finances—exactly how much money was coming in from what sources and exactly how much was going out in costs, salaries, and benefits to everyone in the administration. Why, the TPA asked, had there not been an *independent* audit of the tour's books in twenty-five years? There was so much secrecy. For example, the dissident group discovered and made known that commissioner Berman's salary had always been determined by a "specialist" at the tour's official accounting firm, Ernst and

Young. It was as if the tour players were working for the commissioner and his people, when the whole point of founding the PGA Tour back in 1969 was just the opposite.

Another incident that suggested the tour administration saw itself as outside the control of its constituency: in early 2000 it was learned that commissioner Finchem, who in a prior life was a deputy advisor on economic affairs in President Jimmy Carter's administration, approved in 1999 a $20,000 contribution to the Democratic Congressional Campaign Committee. This in the name, presumably, of a membership—the players— that is easily ninety percent Republican. But of course, it wasn't the political aspect of the donation that was the point of the players complaints, it was that it was made without their knowledge.

The TPA's idea of every player in a tournament getting some compensation, even when missing the cut, was what first caught everyone's attention. It touched and threatened to sully an endearing image of the tour pro as an Ayn Randian superman who shrugs off with disdain any hint of a welfare state handout. Edwards's argument for the compensation is that every pro who comes into a tournament does public relations work for the tour when he plays in the pro-am and otherwise comports himself in a friendly manner with the folks on-site. He thereby earns the compensation. Furthermore, he puts a thousand or more dollars into the local economy in the form of hotel rooms, meals, et cetera. Even if he only plays thirty-six holes and misses the cut, he should get something for his effort. Not a bad argument.

In reply to all of the above commissioner Finchem did make some financial data available. But it was essentially the same that had been offered all along—generalized pie charts delineating percentages of income from various sources, percentages of outgo, but no real details. Also, there was an incident at a players meeting in which Edwards was to get a half hour to explain to the players what the TPA was trying to do. As soon as he began, the proceeding was interrupted by some players throwing out questions and talking loudly among themselves, and after five minutes the commissioner told Edwards that the meeting was adjourned.

There were a lot of signs that the commissioner was doing some Nixonian stonewalling. That was how the media began to see it, after some of its members with influential outlets had, at first, derided the TPA as a gang of sourgrapes losers. Perhaps on reflection they remembered that when they don't get a paycheck at the end of the week, they are not about to write more deathless prose. What's more, some high marquee players such as Tiger Woods, Greg Norman, Lee Janzen, and Tom Lehman began to speak up for an objective look at the books. Lehman in fact joined the TPA, becoming its first "marquee" member. Everyone was wondering if in fact there was something fishy in Florida? If Finchem didn't want to give out the real numbers, then he must have something to hide.

However this matter comes out, the episode brings to mind the celebrated American movie *On the Waterfront*, which revolves around a labor union leader who becomes a despotic all-powerful master over the workers who elected him and pay him to be their representative. The difference seems to be, the majority of the tour pros, at this point, are against bringing any kind of action against the commissioner's office demanding financial disclosure. Only about seventy-five players had joined the TPA by early 2000, and although a Maryland statute (the PGA Tour is incorporated in that state) says that a nonprofit organization must make its financial books available to the membership, Edwards was holding off taking legal action because he didn't think he had enough support among the players.

It seems rather curious that these touring pros, who take such a large personal financial risk to play the circuit, wouldn't want to know all about the money that they, by their talent, create. If there were no players, there would be nothing for the administration to administer. It doesn't jibe with the image of the tour pro that has always been projected, the hard-eyed opportunists who protected their rights with vigor, even anger, and never let a loose coin lay about. Perhaps the postmodern tour pros, coming as most do from the comfy middle-class suburbs, don't fight city hall because they never had to.

Tiger Raises the Competitive Bar

Some of the magic went out of the senior tour in the 1990s because the junior circuit became much more interesting than it had been for awhile. Within a four-year period a new group of young players led by Phil Mickelson, Justin Leonard, David Duval, and especially Tiger Woods arrived with exceptional ability and a fresh perspective. They took the game seriously, to be sure, but without the particular anxieties that shaped the character of those who came through the Great Depression and World War II. They had a more collegial relationship with their opponents, many having played with or against each other since their junior golf days. It wasn't necessarily nicey-nicey out there, but the tour didn't retain the hard-bitten, secretive feel of the past.

Old hands might complain it is too sweet out there, that there should be more rivalry between players. Hell, everybody knew Arnie the club pro's kid didn't much like Jack the member's son, and Hogan and Snead never spoke off course. The tour needs some of that, right? Not necessarily, anymore. For the new generation of Young Lions there is plenty of money to go around—a couple of good years and you could be financially secure for life—and they are not touched by any compelling social issues. They have only their private compulsions and personal histories to manage as they mold their game. That is never easy, but the anxiety quotient is reduced by one. The overall effect has been golf at a very high level.

Phil Mickelson came first, a solidly built six-footer with a fine touch around the greens, a vivid imagination for unusual trouble shots and the talent to pull them off. He began hitting golf balls at eighteen months, and its the only thing he does left handed. The reason is presumed to be that he watched his father as if in a mirror demonstrating how to hold the club and swing it. His airline pilot father raised his family in San Diego, and Phil was a product of the city's long-running and exceptionally successful youth golf program (to which he gave a portion of his 1999 Ryder Cup money).

Mickelson went to Arizona State University on a scholarship, and he is one of only three golfers to win the NCAA individual title and the U.S. Amateur Championship in the same year. The other two are Jack Nicklaus and Tiger Woods. In 1991 Mickelson became the first amateur since 1985 (and one of but four or five ever) to win a PGA Tour event, the Northern Telecom (Tucson) Open. He turned pro the next year, at twenty-two.

When Mickelson first came out on the PGA Tour, he brought with him a public relations handbook and acted out all the fundamental techniques. He had a big smile for everyone, amiable nods to the gallery, a free hand with autographs. It was patently programmed, and if a correlation can be made, the effort it took him to play the diplomat role may well have slowed his climb up the ladder. By about a year and a half. That's when he dropped the charade. He is a naturally charming person, and when he let his personality play out naturally, he became a winner. However, Mickelson revealed a nervous tension in the major championships that didn't show during regular tour events. His velvet putting touch got woolly, his eyes widened like a deer's in headlights, and he looked like he was fighting a migraine. He was expected to win majors right off the bat, but still hadn't by the end of the twentieth century. He did seem less strained in the 1999 U.S. Open, though, perhaps because of a recent marriage and a first child about to be born. He got second place, but might have won if not for Payne Stewart's heroic finish.

When David Duval appeared on the national golf scene he gave the impression he had just been unstrapped from Dr. Frankenstein's worktable. He was totally expressionless below the dark wraparound sunglasses he wore on the course. To further obfuscate, he grew a modified Fu-Manchu goatee, didn't always speak when spoken to, and when he did could be condescendingly abrupt. Just another one of those smug, self-absorbed, selfish and spoiled modern athletes? Not really. Duval is a good example of why we should not make judgments of athletes by their public persona alone.

When Duval first came on tour, very few people knew of the deep psychological pain he had borne as a young boy. An excellent profile of Duval by Gary Smith, in an April, 1999 issue of *Sports Illustrated* magazine was most revealing. His older brother was stricken with aplastic anemia at age twelve. The best chance of survival was a bone marrow transplant, using David's marrow. It doesn't always take, and Brent Duval died. David felt he had killed his beloved brother. He didn't, of course, but he was only nine. He lost faith in everything. It didn't help when his mother and father split up and finally divorced after the trauma of their eldest son's death. David went into a shell and got *very* serious about golf. The game for loners was his sanctuary from an unfair, unkind world. He sharpened his natural gifts for the game—his father had always been a tour-quality player, but didn't pursue it until he became a senior—with hundreds and hundreds of hours of unaccompanied practice.

Duval won the USGA Junior Championship, and for three years he played number one for the Georgia Tech golf team. Strangely, he never won an individual college tournament. And he failed in his first two tries at the PGA Tour Q-School. He played on the Nike Tour for two years and hated every minute of it, feeling he was too good for that level. He said as much, for public consumption. He proved he was right when he did earn a tour card. In his first three PGA Tour events he finished fourteenth, sixth, and second, and was 37 under par for his first twelve rounds. But again, he was unable to win. He came close often enough on tour and in the majors, but kept failing in the stretch. This prompted the usual assessment. He was a choker. He dealt with the criticism with a combination of phlegmy no-comments or sardonic wit—he reads seriously and has a sharp, clever tongue when it is unwound.

In 1997 Duval broke through at last, and with a vengeance. He won the Michelob Classic in a play-off, then won the following week, then again the week after that, this last the prestigious Tour Championship. Arrivée! He then began to loosen up a bit in public, removing his sunglasses after rounds and otherwise acknowledging the crowd. He showed more animation than had ever been seen from him after holing the putt on the last hole of the 1999 Bob Hope Desert Classic, for a round of 59 and one of his four victories of the year.

Duval stuck by his position vis-à-vis the Ryder Cup funds after the contest ended, but had already begun to be less aloof—at least in public. Indeed, he even gesticulated, albeit in an oddly cramped, ungainly way, to stir the already frenzied crowd in Boston into more supportive tumult. The effort to change his image into a more amiable one continued into the new century, perhaps encouraged by his new managers, the International Management Group. The agency sold their new client to various up-scale corporations as a spokesman in television advertisements in which Duval was portrayed as a (relatively) socially involved and outgoing personality. And, Duval came out on the tour to start the 2000 season much trimmer physically than he had been. He said that over the winter he had undergone an exercise program to build his strength, but to many observers it appeared he had overdone it; he looked like he had been on a hunger strike.

The interesting thing about all the above is that as the 2000 season progressed into mid-year, Duval—even while winning a considerable amount of prize money in tournament play—did not win a tournament. He collapsed under intense pressure in the last round of the Masters, when he was heavily contending, by hitting a very poor iron shot and didn't seem at all the killer player he had been before what might be termed his makeover. Ken Venturi once remarked that when you are going well, when your game is on a high note, don't make any drastic changes in your habits; and especially your body—alter the workings, the metabolism, the weight distribution, whatever, and you are upsetting a fine-tuned machine. Perhaps that is behind Duval's erratic play in early 2000. That, and his effort to go down the p.r. (for public relations) chute, a phrase old journalists used for those who abandoned the high ground to make big money. An American kind of thing to do.

Justin Leonard brought with him out of Texas as deft a wedge game as has ever been seen and excellent putting skills. That he is a relatively short hitter off the tee but has still been able to win a major—the 1997 British Open—and the 1998 Players Championship, is another example of how the concern over the distance of the golf ball and the "springy" driver face is overwrought. While he didn't win in 1999, he had the fourth best scoring average of the season—69.59.

Leonard augments his ball-control skills with androidal game management and emotional controls that are extensions of his personal habits. He is self-consciously stylish, adopting a baseball-style cap with a lower crown in order to look different and wearing fashionable clothes that fit perfectly and are always neatly pressed and color coordinated.

Until Tiger Woods strode onto center stage. Mickelson and Leonard were the putative leaders of the New Wave, with Duval on the verge. At the same time, there was a very talented and pleasing group of what might be called the Slightly Used Wave. They all had (have) distinguishable styles of play and other characteristics that set them apart, along with an ability to win, or contend, regularly. All together, the American tour in the nineties was a kind of gourmet stew. There was Fred Couples, the Casual; Payne Stewart in his colorful knickered costumes with his buttery swing (the latter, in particular, will always be missed); Paul Azinger's eighty-five-shooter grip that his teacher, John Redman, wisely did not try to change, and his courageous return from serious lymphoma cancer; Mark O'Meara's Ellingtonian swing tempo; Lee Janzen's clunky style but sturdy determination to hang tough and win on hard courses (two U.S. Opens and a Players Championship); Davis Love III, whose tall and slender physique gives his beautiful swing a swanlike grace; Tom Lehman's working-class aspect, his hairy stories of life on the Asian Tour, and his fortuitous de-

cision to stick it out on the PGA Tour one more year rather than take a
deadend club job; Nick Price, so accommodating he took questions from
shopping-news weekly reporters in the middle of a backswing, and when
he slowed his swing down just a tad became a big winner; Ernie Els, the
strapping South African whose nicely balanced swing matches his "Big
Easy" manner; Jasper Parnevik, son of Sweden's most famous comedian,
himself a character with his Dead-End Kid turned-up hat brim (on which
a product logo is lucratively situated), and his pencil-thin pants and vol-
canic ash breakfasts.

An interesting mix that has been topped off, literally and figuratively,
by Tiger Woods. Woods is in a number of ways the synthesis of all that
has happened in American golf over the past one hundred years. There
is, first off, his ethnic background. Woods personifies America's immigrant
history—he is an Ellis Island in golf shoes—and by all means Jesse Jackson's Rainbow Coalition.

Leaving aside his natural gifts for golf, Woods has profited from the
wealth of information about swing mechanics that over the last half century has been uncovered or rediscovered and so widely disseminated, and
which is exhibited in his symmetrically sound swing. There is in Woods's
swing action nothing unusual, such as Hogan's pronated flat plane or Nicklaus's flying right elbow. If anything, he did have an uncommonly vigorous
hip turn in the downswing. He has had a sports psychologist since his late
teens to act as an objective sounding board for any doubts he may harbor.
He has become a model of what modern weight training and flexibility
exercises can do.

To serve the physical and psychological growth and change that Woods
represents in American golf, he is playing with the best golf ball the game
has ever had; the strongest and most consistent steel shafts; new golf
grasses and innovations in golf course conditioning and maintenance producing impeccable turf that gives very good lies and allows infinitely more
predictable results. All of this synergized in a young man with what ap-
pears to be an intrinsic genius for physical timing, intelligence, and an
unmistakable urge to be a champion among champions in his game.

Woods followed up on a superlative amateur golf career—featuring an
NCAA individual championship while he was at Stanford University and
an unprecedented three consecutive U.S. Amateur championship victo-

ries—with a swift start in professional golf. He won two of his first six tournaments, and in 1997 swept the Masters as no one ever had before—winning by twelve strokes, at 18 under par. All of which naturally generated an exceptionally high level of future expectations. But things being the way they are in the instant-everything postmodern world, the future expectations didn't come fast enough. When Woods didn't win another major title until the 1999 PGA Championship, questions arose about the potential assigned him. Perhaps he didn't have it, after all. Never mind that during the hiatus between majors victories, he won six tournaments on the PGA Tour, had six top ten finishes in majors, and won over $6 million.

Not too bad by ordinary standards, but of course Woods's standards are not common. However, he himself thought he was not living up to his notices. He did a kind of Faldo-to-Leadbetter thing, with Claude "Butch" Harmon going about making important changes in his swing. What needed improving? He could be wild with a driver, especially when the situation really needed accuracy and length—such as in the U.S. Open. A glaring problem was his tendency to overhit the greens with short-iron approaches. From 100 to 140 yards he didn't seem able to translate the distance properly to his swing and touch, which nullified his distance advantage with the driver. It is an especially serious problem on fast U.S. Open and Masters greens. Greens tend to slope down from the back to the front. The accuracy and distance problems were thought to be in part because of the tremendously fast and unbridled hip turn Woods was making in the hitting zone. His putting was erratic in the crucial six- to sixteen-foot range. He was either very good or just mediocre, and mediocre doesn't cut it at his level.

With Harmon at his side, Woods shortened his backswing to gain better control of both accuracy and distance. If he lost a few yards, he could easily afford it. He also changed the angle of his wrists in the backswing, cupping them more. He slowed his hip turn. It all took a little over a year, and as improved ball striking often does, his putting became steady with bursts of brilliance. The payoff was a huge 1999 season that carried into 2000—nine victories in the United States, five of them in a row. At the start of 2000, he came out some twenty pounds heavier but not fatter; he had bulked up with a program of weight training and flexibility exercises.

The spindly kid with the superfast swing was gone, replaced by a big, broad-chested 180-pounder, with enormous power and excellent control not only of his golf shots, but his life. To have made these adjustments when already doing so well is the mark of Woods's dedication to his craft and the extent of his self-confidence. He felt he could make changes and not get hurt in the process.

At the same time he was taking care of his game, Woods apparently decided that if he improved his off-course situations, that might also feed into better on-course and off-course performances. He released his long-time caddie, Fluff Cowan, who had himself become a minor celebrity (which is probably the main reason he was let go). He also sacked the IMG agent who had wheeled his first very lucrative endorsement deals. And he may well have put in a gag order on his overbearing and some-times outlandish father.

Earl Woods was without question the main force in getting his son to the point he is at in his career. He planned Tiger's career from the mo-ment he was born. A good athlete himself, Woods played baseball at Kan-sas State University, took golf up in middle age, and in due time became a low-handicap player. He started Tiger in golf by hitting balls into a mattress in their garage while his ten-month-old son watched from a high chair. Six months later the infant was swinging a club himself and with excellent form. His father saw the gift and made sure it was not frittered away. He said he didn't have to force his boy to play, Tiger went for it immediately and unequivocally. At three Tiger appeared on the Mike Douglas television show with Bob Hope, hitting wiffle balls into the au-dience. He was a sensation and was invited to appear on other shows. He got used to playing before a big audience very early on, and he clearly enjoyed it.

Earl Woods retired as a lieutenant colonel from the Green Berets after doing two tours of combat duty in Vietnam, and settled in the Los Angeles area. Tiger played most of his first golf on military golf courses where his father had inexpensive access. The day after he turned four Tiger shot a nine-hole score of 48, playing from the red tees on a full-size golf course. When Tiger was seven, his father began training his mind for golf. While the boy was preparing to hit a shot, Earl would suddenly rattle pocket change, rip open a Velcro tab, put a negative thought in his head, and make other disturbances. It was meant to toughen Tiger's mind and his ability to concentrate. One of Tiger's early professional teachers likened the prodigy to Mozart, a born golf genius. Earl Woods was the equivalent of Wolfgang's father, pushing him, putting him on show, and eventually cashing in.

Was the father grinding the son down and for his own ends? Earl Woods resents any mention of the former notion, and although Tiger has not weighed in definitively on the question, he has said the time of the mind-training drills was the worse two months of his life. He doesn't seem the worse for it, though. He is far from the lobotomized drone the early training might lead one to expect. He is an intelligent, sensitive young man with a healthy, albeit rather determined, outlook on his work and life. Indeed, he may have outgrown his father.

Earl Woods knew racial prejudice. When he was at Kansas State University he was the first man of color to play ball in the Big Seven Conference, but did not eat in the same restaurants as his teammates when on the road. He said he wanted his son to play golf, in no small part because it was the white man's game. Tiger would show them a thing or two, and Earl Woods would get even for his hurts. Tiger experienced a few racial incidents growing up in a mixed (but mainly white) neighborhood. In grade school once, some older whites boys tied him to a tree. There were some racial slurs. But overall he had a relatively uneventful journey through that minefield as a youth. He doesn't seem to be carrying a chip on his shoulder. His father does, and in at least one incident, he made that clear. When Tiger won his third straight U.S. Amateur Championship, at the Newport Golf Club on Rhode Island, after the presentation ceremony Tiger, Earl, the club's head pro, Billy Harmon, and a few others were standing around with champagne, having some chat. At one point, Earl Woods, who had already said for public consumption that his son was the Messiah, God's gift to the world, boasted that his son would someday win more major titles than Jack Nicklaus. He also speculated aloud that Bobby Jones must be turning in his grave knowing a black boy won three amateurs in a row, something even Jones didn't do. The room went quiet, and Tiger was embarrassed.

Cut Earl Woods some slack on all that; he had been given "the treatment" as a black in mid-century America. Give the effects of champagne its due, too. But another incident could hardly be excused, let alone condoned. At a dinner in early 1999 Earl Woods was introduced by Mark

McCormack and asked what was the biggest influence on his life. Woods responded, *"Mein Kampf."* When asked how it had influenced him, Woods said he was just kidding. Too late. Hitler's book is no more a kidding matter than gags about blacks being lynched in Mississippi. It wasn't long after that remark that Earl Woods seemed to slip back into the wings, perhaps put on a back burner, quieted. It is entirely possible his son had something to do with it.

In his first four years as a pro—1996 to 2000—Tiger Woods has had a truly phenomenal passage through time and has continued his pace into the new century. He made comprehensive changes in his swing technique, traveled thousands of miles overseas to play tournaments and give exhibitions, did hands-on clinics with young inner-city kids, and repeatedly defeated the cream of the game's professionals in high-powered competition. In the 2000 U.S. Open he broke every record on the books in winning by a phenomenal 15 strokes. All by the age of twenty-four. Quite a saga going with a young man who stands as the ultimate expression of the golden age of American golf.

Afterword

One of the warmest acts of fraternity between competitors this writer has ever seen in sports was on the last green at the conclusion of the 1996 Masters. Nick Faldo, the winner, didn't merely shake hands with Greg Norman, the loser, he put his arms around him and gave him a deep and meaningful hug. Asked afterward if he had rehearsed that gesture in his mind, if it was premeditated, Faldo said, "No, you don't make that sort of thing up. It just happened. I felt he needed a hug."

Indeed. Among the major championships Norman lost by falling on his own sword, this one was the most spectacular. As noted earlier, he slowly, inexorably dissipated the six-stroke lead he had had over Faldo going into the last round. After a terrific first-round 64, then steady follow-up rounds of 69 and 71, it looked like he at last would win the tournament he said he prized above all others. He failed miserably, and it was painful for everyone watching him go down, including Faldo. Hence, the hug.

What gave the gesture even more poignancy was Faldo's reputation as a smug, cold, insensitive person with a crabby wit. Which is to say once again that you can't always judge a person by his public cover.

Faldo's act wasn't an isolated one. At the 1999 U.S. Open Payne Stewart, after holing an eighteen-footer on the seventy-second hole for a par to win the championship by a stroke over Phil Mickelson, clasped the loser's cheeks between his hands and wished him well with his first child, which was to be born any minute. And, after Sergio Garcia gave exuberant and exciting chase to Tiger Woods in the 1999 PGA Championship, the two young men embraced when it was over like a groom and the best man after the wedding ceremony, a display of mutual admiration and appreciation for each other and the excitement of the moment.

It is unimaginable that Ben Hogan would have ever clamped onto Sam Snead or Byron Nelson in such a way, or that Arnold Palmer would have wrapped his arms around Jack Nicklaus after they fought it out for a championship. Or vice versa. As postmodern golf moves into the twenty-first century, there are signs of a more worldly, compassionate attitude among its players. Maybe it's because they are all so well-off financially compared to the previous generations that they can indulge in more humane behavior toward their fellow competitors. If so, then the colossal growth of the pro tour has done more than fill to bursting a lot of bank accounts. But even then, it is also encouraging to see when considering how hypnotized our society has become by the cool, impersonal technology, the digital this and modem that which consumes and shapes our daily lives. Golfers are especially attracted to or prone to this kind of world order because the game is such an internalizing exercise. To be played well, golf demands the solitary distancing from social intercourse that describes our increasingly computerized world.

But at the same time, beneath the phlegmatic surface of golfers, at least those who can contain themselves in the face of its constant frustrations, there boils all the feral emotions that have driven humans since the Stone Age—pride, ego, restless passion, the hunger that drives you to be better and smarter than the other guy. That, in this writer's opinion, has been the overriding force in the development of golf in the United States, and in the world, over the past one hundred years, and the central thrust of this history. The supposedly detached, objective decisions of the game's administrators have always been shaped by fundamental human drives, just as has the performance of the players and their behavior in the heat of competition, and elsewhere. For good and not so good.

Inevitably, in the striving for achievement, for power, there is considerable deception and hypocrisy. That has been pointed out more than once in this chronicle of American golf. But there has also been a deep vein of unalloyed honesty running through the story. This last has emanated for the most part from the players side of the ledger, rather than the administrative and business side. This is not necessarily because the players are all forthright and unfailingly honorable and virtuous persons, but because they deal head-on with the game itself. Those who slug it out day after day on the practice tee and in competition are in constant touch with real reality. Playing golf is facing the naked truth. You either make the shot or you don't; you either shoot the best score or you don't. And that is that. No boardroom wheeling and dealing can change the numbers that declare the winner.

Which is to say, the game itself overrides all the scheming for money and power of the businessmen, as well as the airy and often misguided cerebrations of the so-called watchdogs of the game, who believe they are upholding its grand traditions and integrity and protecting it and us poor saps against incursions by the evil forces of technology. I wonder sometimes if the people who administer the game act out at times the resentment or envy of those who can't play as well as those who can. For example, when Payne Stewart was fighting down the stretch with a chance to win the 1998 U.S. Open at the Olympic Club, he hit a perfect drive on the par-four twelfth only to find his ball in a divot—actually atop the sandy fill that covered the divot. A bad break, for one thing, especially as his game was beginning to unravel a bit at this point. But also a mark of the carelessness with which the USGA sometimes upholds the integrity of the game. Such fill in a divot should either be packed tightly down or not filled at all. Stewart would have preferred playing his ball out of the hole, because he had a better chance of getting his club on it and a good idea of how the ball would come out. That aside, he took a good bit of time to contemplate the lie, and what to do about it. Being in the last twosome on the course, he was not holding up play, and after all he was trying to win the U.S. Open. But after he hit a poor nine-iron shot from the divot fill that eventually cost him a bogey, USGA official Tom Meeks had the unconscionable bad manners to approach Stewart and tell him he was playing too slowly and was being timed.

What prompted the USGA, in the same 1998 U.S. Open, to cut the hole in the middle of the steep slope on the slick-fast eighteenth green so that it was unputtable from the sides or above the hole? The officials knew it when they did it, but did it anyway. The apology made afterward was pointless, irrelevant. The damage had been done. Perfectly hit putts from twelve feet to the side of the hole that just missed going in ended up thirty-five to forty feet away, at the bottom of the green.

Why would the USGA misrepresent Donald Ross's great Pinehurst

No. 2 course for the 1999 U.S. Open with exaggerated slopes running off the sides of the greens, turning them into something akin to a miniature-golf course without the windmills?

What could have been in the minds of the officers of the Royal and Ancient Golf Club of St. Andrews, watchdogs over the oldest and most revered championship in golf, to allow the Carnoustie green superintendent, a man whose expertise is in agronomy, to set up the course in terms of fairway width and depth of the rough? Given his head, the superintendent acted out one of the oldest emotions in golf—course pride. He was not going to let those hot shot pros shoot up *his* golf course. And so the keepers of the flame let their championship become a cartoon.

Was all of this in the name of protecting the integrity of the game, or was it, somewhere in the deep subconscious—and perhaps not all that deep—getting back at how good the modern players have become? Or some sort of spite in light of the equipment that couldn't be banned?

Why won't the commissioner of the PGA Tour reveal to the players the complete financial details of the organization that is, putatively, owned by the players? Does he think they're too dense to appreciate the niceties of his business deals, because all they do is beat golf balls all day, every day?

What can one imagine the International Management Group had in mind when it hired Tiger Woods's father, Earl, as a well-paid consultant to consult on no one was sure what, while his son was completing his brilliant amateur career? Is it possible the super-agency was subsidizing an amateur's expenses before signing him to a contract worth many millions when he turned professional? More than a few people-in-the-street thought so, with a skeptical nudge-nudge. How come the USGA didn't look into this arrangement? Or did it, and decide not to do anything about it because Woods was (is) a star of stars and a person of color?

But then you see Tiger Woods, at the Players Championship, hit a 202-yard five-iron from a soft lie in a fairway bunker that gets a mile up in the air then lands softly and stops five feet from the hole on the narrow, water-and-bunker-guarded green of a par-five hole, and you say to yourself, to hell with all the agents and rules mavens and other operators around the periphery of the game, a shot like Woods just hit is so beautiful, so pure, so replete with skill, it absorbs and nullifies all the conniving, the posturing, the platitudinous palaver of the manipulators. The

Game wins out, in the end, and those who play it at any and all levels. We refer to, or use the top players as examples, only because they test themselves at the game in its ultimate situation. The play of raw human nature is by definition more vivid when major championships are at stake.

Consider the 1999 Masters, which had a Darwinian complexion. With eight holes to play it came down to a face-off between Jose Maria Olazabal and Greg Norman. Olazabal was coming back from a crippling foot ailment that threatened to end his career at the age of thirty. He was saved when a doctor diagnosed a back problem, not something wrong with his feet. The Masters was a definitive test of his recovery, if only because hilly Augusta National is a hard walk. Norman, too, was making a physical comeback from shoulder surgery. And of course, he was fighting as always the psychological demons that kept snagging his search for true greatness as a player.

Olazabal had a three-stroke lead going into the final round, but on the front nine gave it all back and at the turn was tied with Norman, Steve Pate, and Davis Love III. Pate dropped out of the running soon after. Love remained a presence to the end, actually finishing ahead of Norman, but oddly not a factor in the drama.

Olazabal birdied the tenth hole to take a one-stroke lead over Norman, who then birdied the eleventh to pull even with Ollie. At the par-three twelfth Olazabal saved his par from the back bunker, and Norman bogeyed from the front bunker to fall a stroke behind. Then came the moment of truth or the one that led to others. On the par-five thirteenth Norman hit an excellent second shot onto the green some twenty-five feet from the hole—a reasonable eagle chance. The shorter hitting Olazabal laid up short of the creek with his second shot, and he pitched his third on the green about eighteen feet above the hole. Norman then holed his putt for a three! An exhilarating result, and the gallery responded thunderously. It was a Norman crowd, as Olazabal knew all along, and perhaps that was part of what spurred him to do what he did a few moments later.

Olazabal needed his eighteen-footer to remain in a tie with Norman. There is such a thing as momentum in sports, and Norman's putt could easily set him off on more heroics. Olazabal could just as readily fall into a funk. His putt was not from a good place, going downhill at Augusta on Sunday. But the Spaniard proved why he is rated one of the best putters in golf and a resolute competitor. He hit his putt at just the right speed and on just the right line. It slid gently into the center of the hole. He matched Norman's grand play, not in actual score but in competitive response.

Norman showed no emotion after Olazabal's hole-out, but actions speak louder than words and the cliché held. Norman repeated his history when given hard chase by a proven star. He drove off the fairway to the right on the fourteenth, and on a hole that normally calls for a pitching wedge approach, he had to punch a low shot under the trees. His ball ran over the green, he chipped poorly, and bogeyed the hole. Olzabal made a routine par to take a one-shot lead.

On the par-five fifteenth, Norman again drove to the right into the stand of trees newly installed to put a greater premium on driving accuracy on this hole. He gave up his advantage in length and had to lay up his second shot short of the pond. He was alongside Olazabal, who also laid up, about ninety-five yards from the hole in the middle of the fairway. Both had slightly downhill lies. Norman went first and hushed all hopeful admirers when he sloughed his wedge shot into the right front corner bunker. The *New York Times* golf writer wrote afterward that Norman "was denied" another Masters title, suggesting someone took it away from him. But when one of the best golfers in the world is unable to put a ninety-five-yard wedge shot somewhere on the green in a shoot-out for the Masters, isn't he denying himself?

Olazabal, the working-class kid who doesn't own a yacht or a garage full of expensive cars, who doesn't have a clothing line on the market or a chain of restaurants, was now given his chance to put Norman away. And of course, he did. He hit his ninety-four-and-a-half yard wedge shot some twelve feet from the hole. Norman bogeyed from the bunker, Olazabal got down in two, and it was effectively over. Olazabal's fine tee-shot on the par-three sixteenth and the snaky-fast short putt for a birdie were icing. Olazabal won by two over Love, by three over Norman.

It was a survival-of-the-fittest story that Olazabal and Norman played out, which of course included not only who had the biggest biceps.

Luckily, it rained the first two days of the 1999 U.S. Open and the course was softened enough to be playable. When it dried out, the last two days the greens played like a Coney Island roller-coaster ride. Even as tactful and pleasant a fellow as Nick Price said, afterward, that the next time they hold the open at Pinehurst, he won't be there.

The week was saved by Payne Stewarts's invigorating competitive spirit and talent. He found a way to make a very difficult putt for a birdie on the seventeenth (seventy-first) hole, and on the eighteenth he rammed in a saving par from twenty-one feet to win the title. Sheer guts took the day.

The preparation of the Carnoustie golf course for the 1999 British Open has been sufficiently commented upon, but the finale of the championship spoke of a dimension of human nature far more interesting than the foibles of a misguided (unguided) course superintendent. Beginning the last hole of regulation play, Frenchman Jean Van de Velde had a three-stroke lead and was in the last pairing. How could he lose, even this fellow who had won only once in eleven years on the European Tour and had never come close to contending in this one and only major title for which he had ever been eligible? He could make a double-bogey on the last hole and still win by a stroke. He did worse.

Instead of playing safely with a long iron from the eighteenth tee and simply putting the ball a couple of hundred yards ahead in the fairway, he used his driver and hit the ball far, far to the right in the heather and gorse and hay. Luckily, he came up with a decent lie some 185 yards from the green, which was a few yards beyond the Barry Burn, a creek. He tried for the green with a two-iron and hit the ball well, but again to the right. Then he got unlucky. His ball easily carried the creek but ricocheted off the grandstand railing and caromed back across the burn into very deep and tangled rough. From here he tried for the green, some thirty yards ahead, but the grass was so deep and thick he could move the ball only a few yards. It went in the burn.

Van de Velde thought he could play the ball from the water because part of it was above the water surface. He removed his shoes and socks, rolled up his pant legs and stepped in. But before he could get to it the entire ball sank. Van de Velde gave up the idea. He dropped back in the wicked deep rough to play his fifth shot. Now he needed to get down in two to win, three to tie Justin Leonard and Paul Lawrie. He took a Herculean hack at the ball, and this time carried the water. But it landed in the front right bunker. Incredibly, and to his great credit after all that transpired in the past fifteen minutes, Van de Velde had the composure to play a fine bunker shot to within six feet of the hole and enough nerves left to hole the putt and get into a play-off. He should be forever congratulated on the bunker shot and putt, no matter what.

Van de Velde did not win the play-off. He was never a factor in it, which was predictable after what he'd been through. It was also better for the sake of the saga. Historians can be selfish that way. If he had won, his seventy-second hole would have been only a weird but ultimately minor incident. Most golf aficionados in the media came down hard on Van de Velde, saying he was flat-out stupid, and/or terribly misled by his caddie, who was blamed for letting Van de Velde use the driver on the tee and the two-iron for his second, and so on.

To the golfing public, though, Van de Velde came out a sympathetic figure, a kind of hero manqué. Part of this reaction had to do with how he handled the disaster in the aftermath. He was as French as any stereotypist could have portrayed him—the existential *c'est la vie* Gallic shrug and self-deprecating humor. "So, you still love me," he said to two young girls while giving them his autograph afterward. Van de Velde's wife added to the tone when she said, "Usually he makes more stupid mistakes on the golf course. This was the only one he made all week."

That one mistake was using his driver from the tee at the eighteenth. Laying up his second shot was not that easy, for one thing, because the fairway was so narrow and firm he would have had to hit one hell of a shot to hit it and hold it. He was terrifically unlucky with the two-iron. How many shots will hit the knob of a railing and come back thirty yards as his did? About one in every 10,000? If it just stays up in the grandstand, or bounces out (or off) into the rough across the burn, as it would 9,999 times out of . . . he's home free.

In his first and most revealing response to his strategy at the seventy-second hole, Van de Velde said, "I had been using my driver all week, and hitting it well. I didn't see any point in changing that. And I didn't feel comfortable hitting a wedge [after his wayward drive]. To me it was against the spirit of the game. I'm going to hit a two- or three-iron, then a wedge, then another wedge maybe, then three putts from thirty feet to win by one shot? Okay, I win by one, but what a way to finish!"

With a victory in the British Open, Van de Velde would have earned a right tidy sum of money in endorsements and lifetime security in his homeland as a hero among heroes for having defeated the damned British at their own game (and become only the second Frenchman ever to win the British Open—Arnaud Massy, in 1907, was the other one). He gave that up, or took a chance on giving it up and did, because he reverted to one of man's most primal instincts, hubris. With a little art for art's sake thrown in, for good measure. *C'est la vie.*

In the 1999 PGA Championship, at the storied Medinah Country Club outside Chicago, Tiger Woods gave every indication that he was ready to assume, if he hadn't quite already, the role he had been cast to play since he was ten months old—golf's next great champion. As noted earlier, he had made important changes in his swing mechanics and reorganized his business and personal affairs. He still overshot greens at times with short-irons, but less and less often. As a very public figure—the comparisons with Michael Jordan were beginning—who draws huge and boisterous galleries wherever he goes, he was beginning to be less severe in his reactions to the boiling crowd. On the golf course he was showing fewer bursts of explosive temper and impatience—he was going to more Buddhist church services with his mother, which may explain the greater calm. Medinah was Tiger Woods's melding pot.

He began the championship with a solid 70 and was four off the pace set by the even younger Spanish sensation, Sergio Garcia. Woods's second-round 67 moved him to within two of Garcia, and then he put his game in high gear—a third-round 68. He was tied for the lead with Mike Weir, a young Canadian left-hander with no previous credentials but having the week of his life. They were two shots up on Garcia and Stewart Cink.

From the beginning of the final round it was clear that Weir was not going to hold up under the pressure (he shot an 80), while Woods hummed along at three to four under par. It looked like it was going to be a cakewalk in, but the nineteen-year-old Garcia, playing a group ahead of Woods, was not having any of that. He was having a solid round and staying within range of Woods—he was five behind going to the par-three thirteenth when he went into his attack mode. He rolled in a slick eighteen-foot downhill putt for a birdie two, and as he strode to the cup to retrieve his ball he looked back at Woods standing on the tee. It was a conscious glance, he later admitted, meant to communicate, "I'm still around, you'll have to keep playing."

And don't you know, Woods overshot the thirteenth green, drew a terrible lie in long grass, hacked the ball off the front of the green, made an ordinary chip, missed the putt, and with a double-bogey was now only a stroke ahead of Garcia. A three-shot swing on one hole. The game was on!

Both parred the fourteenth and Garcia gave a shot back at the fifteenth when he drove into the right rough. On the next hole, Garcia again drove into the rough, this time hitting the ball too straight and far—it ran through the dogleg left and up against the trunk of a tree. He wasn't behind the tree, but to the side of it, so he could make a full swing. If he could get his club face on the ball and put a big left-to-right cut on it, he had a chance. The issue revolved around what was under his ball, which was between two roots of the tree. Was it sitting on another root? If so, and Garcia tried a full-swing shot, the club was likely to come to a jolting stop at impact and cause a potentially career-ending wrist or hand injury. He carefully checked around his ball, determined there was no root directly under it, and with a six-iron had a full go at the green. He caught the ball solidly, but instinctively closed his eyes at impact and immediately jumped to the side in case the ball hit the tree and came back at him. It most certainly didn't. It was an amazingly wondrous shot, the ball flying high and strong and turning to the right. It ran up onto the green.

The extra added attraction was Garcia's reaction. Once he realized the ball was well away he sprinted out into the fairway and leapt up two or three times to see over the brow of a small rise in the fairway for the results of his shot. It was the enthusiasm of a high school kid trying to pull off a miracle against his buddies in a friendly match, except this was for the PGA Championship. As he began walking briskly to the green he repeatedly tapped his heart as if to indicate it was beating very hard from both the exertion of the leaps and bounds and the frightening nature of the lie he had just played from.

Garcia two-putted for his par. Coming up from behind, well aware of Garcia's dramatics a moment before, Woods hit a two-iron from the tee into the fairway. A safe play. He had 185 yards uphill to the green. He took an eight-iron. We will not get into how anyone can possibly hit an eight-iron 185 yards uphill. In fact, Woods couldn't. Perhaps subconsciously thinking of his tendency to overshoot greens with short-irons, this time he under-clubbed. He needed a seven-iron, which is still mind-boggling to older golfers. His shot finished in a bunker short of the green, and he bogeyed. His lead was cut to one shot.

Garcia parred the par-three seventeenth, and it was here where Woods showed the stuff of which he is made. With a six-iron this time he did overshoot the green. Adrenaline. And pressure. His swing had speeded up over the last two or three holes. His ball ended up in long grass on a down slope. A tough shot. He did a fine job of it, though, with a controlled hack getting the ball to within six feet. This was the championship-defining putt. If he missed he would lose a comfortable lead and be tied. Anything could have happened then. But with a display of calm worthy of Buddha himself, he got his read—slightly left-to-right—stood immutably still and hit an absolutely solid putt into the center of the hole. It was the stuff of Jack Nicklaus. Woods may miss some clutch putts over the years, but that one will stand out as the one that confirmed his eminence.

Garcia concluded his pyrotechnics with a par four at the eighteenth, and Woods played the hole perfectly with a short wedge to the middle of the green and a routine two-putt par. The second putt was from a foot-and-a-half, and when it fell he didn't go into his usual fist-pumping routine. He slumped for a moment, head on his chest, and breathed a sigh of relief that it was over.

Tiger Woods hits the ball farther than 99.9 percent of the world's golfers, which is considered a huge advantage. Equipment manufacturers sell distance before anything else, like a drug dealer feeding an addict's obsession. The USGA battles it constantly, with Calvinist zeal. And yet, in the 1999 PGA Championship, the issue came down to a super-long hitter using a fast ball and a thin-faced driver who claimed victory by playing two shots (at the seventeenth green) covering some twenty-five feet. Woods had to extricate his ball from a tangled mass of grass in a way that required anything but power, that wanted quality carpentry. Then he had to roll a ball over a six-foot swatch of grass, which again asks for no force. All it wants is minimal but sound technique, and much steadiness of hand and mind, the same skills that served hunters in the Stone Age.

It is such courage under fire, honed talent, the touch of an artist and the skill of an artisan on which golf has always drawn its support, its interest. It was true at the beginning of the twentieth century, when Harry Vardon made his monumental exhibition tour of the United States and stirred the golfing blood of the country with his graceful and powerful game. It was true of Walter Hagen, who played with a flair for the special occasion. It was true of Hagen's compatriot, the feisty Gene Sarazen, then Bobby Jones, and then the first great American triumvirate of Nelson, Snead, and Hogan. Palmer, Nicklaus, and Player, then Trevino. And so many others. In the words of the neo-evolutionist, Robert Wright, all were "non-zero-sum" gamers. Through their gift for their game, they gave pleasure for the moment and left a fertile future for those to come. Sam Snead was asked many times in his later years if he resented the great sums of money the modern tour pros play for, a Fort Knoxian lode compared to the Five-and-Dime store receipts of his day. He said he didn't mind at all. There was in his response just the hint of self-satisfaction, a pride that said he helped make it happen with his talent. It was his legacy, his and the Game's, and the only kind that really counts.

Index